Between Page and Screen

VERBAL ARTS :: STUDIES IN POETICS
· ·
SERIES EDITORS :: Lazar Fleishman and Haun Saussy

Between Page and Screen

REMAKING LITERATURE THROUGH
CINEMA AND CYBERSPACE

Edited by
Kiene Brillenburg Wurth

FORDHAM UNIVERSITY PRESS *New York* 2012

Fordham University Press has no responsibility for the
persistence or accuracy of URLs for external or third-
party Internet websites referred to in this publication
and does not guarantee that any content on such
websites is, or will remain, accurate or appropriate.

Fordham University Press also publishes its books in a
variety of electronic formats. Some content that appears
in print may not be available in electronic books.

Library of Congress Cataloging-in-Publication Data
is available from the publisher.

Printed in the United States of America
14 13 12   5 4 3 2 1
First edition

To Titus

CONTENTS

ACKNOWLEDGMENTS

This book could never have been realized without the financial support of Program Committee Transformations in Art and Culture of NWO, the Netherlands Organization for Scientific Research. I particularly thank Ben Peperkamp for his dedicated help and Franz Ruiter for his informed advice. Coming out of the conference Re-mediating Literature, held at Utrecht University in 2007, this volume has grown out of an inspiring and productive cooperation with Ann Rigney. I thank her for her continued involvement in this project. Finally, I thank Thomas Lay, Eric Newman, and Helen Tartar at Fordham University Press and the outside readers for their wonderful work.

Chapter 4, Kiene Brillenburg Wurth's "Posthuman Selves, Assembled Textualities," was originally published in a slightly different version as "Posthumanities and Post-textualities: Reading *The Raw Shark Texts* and *Woman's World*," *Comparative Literature* 63, no. 2 (2011): 119–141; copyright 2011 *Comparative Literature*, University of Oregon; reprinted with permission of Duke University Press. Chapter 5, Katherine Hayles's "Intermediation: The Pursuit of a Vision," was originally published in *New Literary History* 38, no. 1 (2007): 99–125; copyright 2007 *New Literary History*, University of Virginia; reprinted with permission of the Johns Hopkins University Press. I thank Canongate and Atlantic Books as well for granting permission to reprint illustrated pages from *The Raw Shark Texts* and *Woman's World*.

Between Page and Screen

Introduction

KIENE BRILLENBURG WURTH

This book advocates an integrative approach to literature and screen-based media—not only literature and digital media, but also film and television. This comprehensive approach allows us to reassess current remediations of literature in relation to its earlier transformations on screen. Since the early twentieth century, literary genres have been traveling across magnetic, wireless, and electronic planes. These travels have changed "the literary" as a heterogeneous field. Literature may be anything from acoustic poetry and oral performance to verbal-visual constellations in print and on screen, cinematic narratives, and hyperfiction and cell phone novels. New technologies have left their imprint on literature as a paper-based medium, and vice versa. Literature no longer has a single material location, and one may wonder if it ever had one.

What, indeed, is the location of literature? In her design for a new comparative literature, Emily Apter has argued for a comparative practice without location, without "national predicate."[1] Such a practice would rather center on the space and interactions between languages. This volume adds to that project the dimension of intermediality, focusing on a literature that has no single material predicate—or at least, a literature that has different material locations, rather than the book and the paper page alone. Our contribution to such a more multidimensional comparative literature is to map the "literary" as a mode in between page and screen technologies: books, film, television, and digital media. Our aim is to analyze the interactions between pages and screens during the last three decades, and to thus come to an understanding of the ways in which pages have operated *as* screens, and screens in turn have adapted to or resisted the "tyranny" of the page.[2]

Typically, digital screens have been placed in opposition to the book and paper page in the last two decades: either to defend the latter as the last trace of a material humanist tradition against the incursions of a network of digital distraction, or to promote digitization as liberation from the material constraints of paper and print (from an allegedly "fixed" to a dynamic page, from "static" to moving, dancing, illuminated letters). This animosity, so to speak, between page and screen has only been invigorated by the introduction of e-readers, which have been promoted (or, conversely, vilified) as the replacement of books. Apparently, either electronic or paper books can survive, rather than both serving different functions alongside each other.[3] This book, instead of contributing to a fruitless debate on the end of this or the dawn of that medium, aims to reconsider literature—as an "experimental" practice—*already* as a rematerialization of and challenge to the alleged constraints of the paper page. In this, we differ from Peter Stoicheff and Andrew Taylor's excellent *The Future of the Page*. Their book focuses on the materiality of the page as such, rather than on *literature* as a practice of (or against) the page and the different, moving, luminous, electronic "pages" it has come to interact with in the twentieth and twenty-first centuries.[4] As a body of literature, is the page not already a screen, or a "screenic" mode? Screens are things to hide things with, or project things onto. Screens are frames, or rather, they frame, and framing is crucial to literature as it is a condition of possibility for fiction—a demarcation of the imaginary. In the last century, "the screen" (cinema, TV, computer) has transformed the ways in which we design and approach narratives in literature. Thus, like the page, the screen should be a topical concept in literary studies.

Between Page and Screen wants to reconsider the recent digital transformation of literature and "the literary"—modes of (novelistic) narration, of poetic practice, or of self-writing, on paper or other surfaces and fields of inscription—in the context of the interactions between paper page and the cinematic screen in the twentieth century. This wider perspective is warranted not only because digital literature nowadays is also a literature to watch, now that flash has become a common mode of literary presentation on screen and online, but also because, as Lev Manovich has argued, the modern digital computer is born from cinema.[5] Interactions between literature and digital screens, on the one hand, and cinematic screens, on the other, may therefore deepen our insight into the issue of adaptation or intermedial "translation" in comparative literature. How do stories and how does writing travel from one medium to another? How do cinematic and digital screen technologies incorporate paper-based modes and genres of literary writing, and how, in turn, do these technologies affect this writing? Why does cinema remain a dominant cultural metaphor in digital times in the most recent of paper literatures[6]—and how has cinema helped to forge experimental "currents" in paper-based literature that have, in turn, been formative for "new," digital modes of literature? These questions need to be addressed to assess in full the significance of "e-" and "p-" literature today—especially, perhaps, now that the "storage" medium of film has given way to "display" media online.[7]

Thus, this volume aims to bring together debates in e-literature and intermediation (the complex interaction between code, speech, and writing), on the one hand, and adaptation (relations between literature and cinema, cinema and literature), on the other. With respect to the first, we build on groundbreaking research of the last decade, notably the work of Katherine Hayles, Brian Kim Stefans's *Fashionable Noise: On Digital Poetics* (2003), Jerome McGann's *Radiant Textuality* (2004), Adalaide Morris and Thomas Swiss's *New Media Poetics* (2005), Peter Stoicheff's *The Future of the Page*, Bruce Clarke's *Posthuman Metamorphosis: Narrative and Systems* (2008), Matthew Kirschbaum's *Mechanisms: New Media and the Forensic Imagination* (2008), and Stephanie Harris's *Mediating Modernity* (2009). These texts have redefined paper-based literary writing as being constantly informed and refashioned by new media technologies, and vice versa. Such research has opened up a prominent space for media and computer theory within comparative literature, leading to the—justified—claim that it should start focusing on new modes of reading and writing: code reading, the writing of software programs—or the emergence of new dialects on the Internet.[8] Hayles, for that matter, has coined the term "cyborg reading" to refer to a "new" mode of reading that is no longer attuned to a flat, two-dimensional text. Instead, reading becomes an orienting activity in a topographical space: the text has become a virtual, often three-dimensional space with depths and corners and openings to explore, "with layered strata, hidden openings, crosscutting pathways, links between different world levels, and other spatial and temporal unfoldings."[9] It is necessary to reflect on this cartographic mode of reading in this introduction, since it will make clear how screens have informed the literary, and vice versa, as an immersive space of reading.

Aya Karpinska's *The Arrival of the Beebox* (2003) shows how e-literature has reshaped this immersive space. Karpinska's beebox is a three-dimensional configuration of moving words that makes possible a layered reading experience that is at once interactive and immersive. It is interactive because the reader uses the mouse to make the poem happen. When you open the page, you see three vertical planes on a horizontal axis, with words clotted on the sides. You can click on these words, and they start moving. You can zoom in on these words, and then they come closer and closer, allowing you to immerse yourself visually in them. You can see from the inside out—an affective and *spatial* experience of readerly self-loss. As a reader, you can plunge yourself into a geographical space of words, and see them as objects with different sides and dimensions rather than as flat figures. You can end up making a complete mess of the entire poem, viewing and creating it whichever way you want. This is, perhaps, only fitting. *The Arrival of the Beebox* is a remediation of Sylvia Plath's poem with the same title.[10] In Plath's poem, the "clean wood box" that the speaker has ordered appears as a coffin containing a hostile force: the bees, "Minute and shrunk for export,/black on black, angrily chambering," could never be held in check.[11] In Karpinska's redesign, the clustered bees have become clustered words, and the reader opens the boxes, releasing the volatile force, yet as a force of *words*, which stretch and flutter out and take their "temporary" positions—words that can be controlled in a game.

How to read? From front to back, left to right, or both in reverse? Interestingly, in the mere attempts to discover directions, the reader/ user is already experiencing ways of reading that are more explicitly spatially informed. Karpinska herself, in this context, refers to old cube poems and word squares such as *The Enigma of Sator* (second century CE) that can be read horizontally, vertically, and backwards. The beebox likewise ushers in an explorative kind of reading that resists the sense of an ending. There are hints of the evanescence of the momentary ("this is a collection of moments gone by"; "each moment shows a different face"), scattered allusions to crowds and loneliness, to dancing, to speed and velocity—but then you discover that you can discard linear reading strategies and simply pick a phrase to go with another: "this is a collection of moments gone by/to protect me from loneliness," or: "this is a collection of moments gone by/when our blinking memories/in the stuttered flow of uneven rhythm/sharpen one mind against another." This is a random-creative reading that is, however, not entirely new: it is, almost literally, a readerly version of William Burroughs's cut-up and fold-in method, likewise arranged along rules of association.

If Karpinska's poem (like so much other digitally born poetry) recasts immersive reading as a spatial experience, critics such as Jessica Pressman have mapped new modes of critical, close cyborg reading that the cinematic e-poetry of Young Hae Chang Heavy Industries has provoked. Their *Dakota* (2002)—a reworking of Ezra Pound's reworking of book 11 of the *Odyssey* in his *Cantos I* and *II*—is about text: bare, black text set in Monaco font, hugely augmented letters and words that move against a bare, white background. Set to a rousing jazzy drumbeat performed by Art Blakey, the words already perform the idea of movement, of travel, they "recount" as they flash by on screen. (It should be noted that conventional references as to what words do on the paper page become problematic in the context of *Dakota*: words here are above all things that move, appear, disappear—according to the rhythm of the music, mimicking the beats of the drum visually.) Now, on the one hand, *Dakota* invites the kind of passive consumptive reading that has come to be negatively associated with screen culture: as a reader, all you can do is sit back, enjoy the beat, and try to follow the lead of the words that move by quite quickly onscreen. There is no opening to intervene, to reset, or to interact with the text; the text is closed, set, gone.[12]

Thus, the speeding text of *Dakota* is at once, and almost literally, highly accessible and completely inaccessible: highly accessible insofar as the text and its programmed rhythm "do" the reading for the reader. However, and as Pressman emphasizes, since YHCHI openly frames *Dakota* as a remake of the *Cantos*, urging us to read for a plot, the text becomes highly inaccessible—just as inaccessible as the *Cantos*—because of this lack of control. The sheer speed of the text resists close reading: one cannot leaf through the text, stop here, reread there, or replay and isolate parts of it. And yet it is precisely because of the *Cantos* clue provided by YHCHI that readers are triggered to read more actively, more closely, and more critically. According to Pressman, this inaccessibility is part and parcel of a strategy of "digital modernism" that *Dakota* appears to practice: electronic works that "use central aspects of modernism to highlight their literariness, authorize their experiments, and situate electronic literature at the center of a contemporary digital culture that privileges images, navigation, and interactivity over narrative, reading, and textuality."[13] This requires a special kind of "close reading." To read *Dakota* closely, as a mode of critical cyborg reading, is to read it rapidly, visually, to wrestle with its rhythm, its electronic inaccessibility and to unravel its cinematic "feel."

For Pressman, the cinematic feel of *Dakota* is not of decisive importance: "YHCHI's authorial claim asserts a connection between *Dakota* and high modernism rather than cinema."[14] As we will see, however, high literary modernism is, precisely, cinematographically informed—one only has to think of James Joyce or John Dos Passos. The return of cinema in much recent electronic literary work, but also in popular paper-based literature such as Mark Danielewski's *House of Leaves*, suggests that "new" modes of e-writing and e-reading are still thoroughly mediated by cinematographic techniques and metaphors. To understand cyborg reading, one must take cinema into consideration.

This topicality of cinema in screen literature gives a fresh urgency to concepts such as "adaptation" in current debates on literature and the new media. Traditionally, adaptation has been framed in a hierarchical conception of a source as a narrative in stable print. Here, however, we follow the trends set in Linda Hutcheon's *Adaptation* (2002), Robert Stam's groundbreaking *Literature Through Film* (2003), and Robert Palmer's *Twentieth Century American Fiction on Film* (2007),[15] which have suspended the limited focus on comparative case studies often hampered by the dominance of the fidelity issue, and often lacking rigorous theoretical reflection. Thus, Stam has moved beyond the fidelity issue (how does the film compare to the novel?) in adaptation studies—if ever it was a coherent field[16]—by centering on the ways in which literature has premeditated cinema (see Gustave Flaubert's *Madame Bovary*), or on the postmodernist archaeologies of literature and film. For Stam, cinema is palimpsestic, since it always bears the imprint of other media: we like to propose it is so for any medium. Likewise, Hutcheon's approach to adaptation is interdisciplinary. It seeks to analyze crossings between different media by employing concepts (such as "interactivity") that can be made operative in different media environments. Hutcheon thus explores these environments in terms of what Hayles would call "feedback loops"—the mutual interaction between a mediating system and its milieu—and this is precisely what we will do here.[17]

What this book adds to these innovative studies in adaptation is not only an integrative approach to film and literature studies, on the one hand, and electronic literature studies, on the other, but also the reuse of the concept of adaptation as a revision, so to speak, of paper- and screen-mediated *subjectivities*. Literary writing has been conventionally identified as a space of subject formation or identification (Jonathan Culler, Nancy Armstrong). In the last decades, scholars such as Laura Mulvey, Kaja Silverman, and bell hooks have shown to great critical acclaim how the screen of cinema is centrally involved in such formation, both as a psychological and a cultural process. More recently, scholars in cyberculture, Donna Haraway prominently among them, have argued that our very idea of a human subjectivity needs to be reconsidered. What if we are all machines to start with, or, as Bernard Stiegler has argued, always already technologically mediated?[18] Adaptation, in this context, returns to its biological setting (evolution theory) as it comes to denote processes of interaction between humans and machines, humans and screens, and the ways in which both affect each other, merging into something that cannot be reduced to either.

As we show, interactions between paper-based and electronic textualities, as well as between literature and film, incorporate and project emerging visions of "humanity" and "posthumanity": The first connotes an allegedly natural, bodily materiality, the latter a materiality that is always already mediated and extended towards an (electronic) machine culture. "Paper" and "screen," then, do not merely refer to a technology, but also to a network of contrived subjectivities of "humanness" and "posthumanness," or even "inhumanness," whereby the latter is evoked as a machine extension. Significantly, even today ideas of "humanness," rooted in eighteenth- and nineteenth-century conceptions of solitary selfhood, are still closely aligned with book pages and book covers.[19] The association between paper culture and the ideology of a stable self is persistent to say the least. It may be no accident that Derrida has linked the commonsense view of paper as a body-substance, an "immobile and impassable surface underlying the traces that may come along and affect it from the outside," to the naïve and essentialist views on substance or the subject.[20] There still is a myth of interiority—to extend Judith Butler's claim—where the paper surface is concerned. By contrast, this immobile surface can, in a Derridean view, already be viewed as an infolded exterior, just as new media are never entirely new, themselves, but the infolded effect of older medial regimes: always already remediations.

There is thus an interesting parallel between new modes of thinking about subjectivity as being technologically constituted—or more generally: constituted through the "decision" of another, be it cultural, sociological, technological, or historical—and about (new) media as being never entirely pure, never entirely selfsame. As Derrida observes with respect to paper in new media:

> The page remains a screen. . . . It is primarily a figure of paper (of the book or codex), but the page nowadays continues . . . to govern a large number of surfaces of inscription, even where the body of paper is no longer there in person, so to speak, thus continuing to haunt the computer screen and all internet navigations in voyages of all kinds.[21]

The extension of paper even extends beyond this, as we still familiarly write on computers "*with a view* to the final printing on paper"; hence, all "norms and figures of paper" are virtually present in the computer screen. Thus, Derrida concludes, the "order of the page, even as a bare survival, will prolong the afterlife of paper—far beyond its disappearance of withdrawal."[22] There is an uncanniness to computer screens, as there will always be the beckoning call or ghostly presence of the substance that once was. Significantly, however, paper is, or was, or has been, for Derrida always already a multimedium insofar as it contains traces of diverse practices and imprints (as well as values): "Paper is utilized in an experience involving the body, beginning with hands, eyes, voice, ears, so it mobilizes both time and space"—thus projecting its own "retrospective" resources.[23] We could say that the past of paper as multimedium has really reached us only now, in the electronic age. As such, however, and despite the increasing significance of screens to self-presentation, paper continues to maintain a "certain legitimating authority": apart from electronic fingerprints and iris scans, we still sign paper documents for legitimization.[24]

In other words, we still have to contend with paper, just as we still have to contend with the book in the present and the immediate future. Both cinema and digital media have, in their very own ways, rivaled the book as a dominant cultural medium and now that the latter threaten— according to some—to absorb not only the book but also cinema and other media, the book and the many metaphors it embodies continues to haunt digital screens. For Derrida, at least, it is obvious that the World Wide Web materializes the *end* of the book less in the sense of death than in the sense of achievement: the web revives an old desire, of a "book to come," an absolute book, encompassing the world; it is "the ubiquitous book reconstituted, the book of God, the great book of Nature, or the World book finally achieved." Thus, digitization, and the emergence of the web, has made for a "constant reinvestment in the book project," even if that reinvestment has led to other writing regimens contesting the book project and properties and rights associated with that project—such as copyrights.[25]

For at the same time, the web is "beyond the closure of the book, the disruption, the dislocation, the dissemination with no possible gathering, the irreversible dispersion of this total codex."[26] It is both at once: totalizing and, in Pierre Levy's concepts, universalizing without being totalizing—that is to say, without being bound by an "all-encompassing mastery of signification," to which writing may have tended in Levy's model.[27] Cyberspace, according to Levy, has disengaged universality and totalization: "the real-time interconnection and dynamism of online memory once again create a shared context, the same immense living hypertext for the participants in a communication. . . . Any text can become the fragment that passes unnoticed through the moving hypertext that surrounds it."[28] This would mean that writing, the book (conceived of in terms of totalization, that is), is in effect undone by cyberspace—or at least the universality to which writing would have given rise. Whether one agrees or disagrees with these generalizing observations, a study of the movements between paper and screen will remain incomplete without taking into account the specifically "new" dimensions of screenic writing in the present. This is why the present volume also prominently centers on issues relative to networked writing, new literacies on the net, accessibility, and, in relation to it, changing conceptions of authorship.

The makeup of this volume will thus be as follows. Part I centers on the concepts of media and mediation in relation to "new" digital textualities and "new" posthuman subjectivities. Part II focuses on the specific dynamics of such digital textualities as paper-based literary writing becomes electronic writing. Part III analyzes crisscrossings between paper-based fictions and film, critically reassessing the concept of adaptation through readings of the inverse directions from film to literature. Part IV reassembles the first three parts by offering a more general outlook on media, subjects, (new) literacies and learning, and cultural change. Which, as William Uricchio puts it in this volume, are the competencies required in today's screen culture? In what ways do these competencies reflect an ongoing entanglement of paper-based writing, electronic writing, and visual mediations rather than one replacing the other? What is the value of print-based writing for our ability to read present-day visual and digital mediations of subjectivity? What, in short, is the cultural literacy legacy of the "old" medium of

print-based literature and, by extension, comparative literature, in a
culture no longer dominated by paper-based modes of inscription and
data storage? In the digital age, such literacy is increasingly bound up
with the question of accessibility. This volume therefore fittingly concludes with a retrospect of and a proposal for open access on the net.

OVERVIEW

Part I: Mediality, Digitality, Subjectivity

This first part of *Between Page and Screen* focuses on the question of
how mediality is constituted through an internal movement or self-
animation; how language performs an instance of this self-animation as
self-reflection, and how paper-based writing alters as a practice of writing the self in the digital age. Samuel Weber's "Medium, Reflexivity,
and the Economy of the Self" opens this part and deepens Bolter's and
Grusin's concept of remediation in a critical way. It offers a new, philosophical way of thinking about "medium" and "mediality" (which,
unlike mediation, for Weber does not function to relate to an outside)
on the basis of Walter Benjamin's dissertation, "The Concept of Criticism in German Romanticism."[29] As Weber points out, Benjamin uses
"medium" in a very distinctive sense, namely, "as a process that does
not communicate anything external—a meaning, for instance."
For Benjamin there is thus no conventional or instrumental semantic
aspect to "medium," and this is how he posits language: it is self-
presentational and to that extent "imparts" itself immediately.

   Language and self-reflection, the constant return of self to self, therefore go hand in hand here, each informing the other, so that the one
cannot be thought without the other. As a medium, language thus
embodies a kind of enigmatic self-movement or *Selbstbewegung*: it
impels itself. Yet this movement is never identical. As Weber quotes
Benjamin: "Under the term 'reflection' is understood the transformative
(*umformende*)—and nothing but the transformative." Reflection equals
transformation equals alterity: the self in the process of self-reflection is
always already other to itself. Or, differently said: insofar as a medium
(like language) is self-presentational and apparently self-imparted, this
imparting always already involves a partition that keeps going the
movement of reflection-as-transformation (or: self-reflection with a
difference). Thus we have continuous movement, on the one hand,

and disruptions, on the other. Weber uses this duplicity to approach "medium" as follows:

> "Medium" here names a process that never stays the same: all that is continual is its transformations and changes, and these are discontinuous: continual discontinuity. It is this discontinuous movement that constitutes the very "liveliness" of the medium: it is "alive" to the extent that it does not stay the same.

There is no definite beginning or endpoint from or to which this process tends; its ruling principle, if you will, is constant and perhaps also unpredictable unfolding. In connection with this unfolding, Weber brings forward the idea of "media event" in a very specific, unstable sense, namely, as "a happening that cannot be identically repeated, like an 'installation' or a 'happening,' although this does not mean that it cannot be repeated at all." Repetition and singularity go hand in hand since, as we have seen, the movement of reflection is one of "transformative recurrence." Relating this conception of media event to romantic, Schlegelian ideas of the artwork, Weber ultimately criticizes the ways in which mass media nowadays tend to hide the differential constitution of mediality from view, and focus on Presence. Presence (whose presence?) is a problematic issue because it is always already about self-presence—and presuppositions of the Self as Presence. This Self, Weber argues, "continues to dominate the media" and this might well affect the very moving principle of mediality: its transformative potential.

Relating to Weber's analysis, Anthony Curtis Adler's "Analog in the Age of Digital Reproduction: Audiophilia, Semi-Aura, and the Cultural Memory of the Phonograph" analyses the spectral presence of the phonograph within a digital omnipresence: its afterlife as a material echo of the past. Though Adler's contribution is not about screens, and thus falls outside the immediate range of this project, it adds something vital to our understanding of old and new media. Analyzing audiophilia—basically a desire for material presence—in the apparently disembodied age of the digital, Adler shows how the former is as it were animated as aura by the effects of the latter (infinite simulation). New media do not merely refashion or repurpose but in fact *produce* old media (photocopied texts as a stamp of authenticity in personal zines—an instance of paperphilia—are a case in point).[30] As Adler argues, analog mediation (vinyl) becomes auratic in the Benjaminian sense of the term due to its dysfunctionality: its very limitations and imperfections that render it *sens(i)bly material*. This dysfunctionality only comes to the fore as a trace of a materiality in relation to the allegedly disembodied digital recordings and archivings on the net.

It is, in this respect, interesting to point to an older digital poem by Jason Nelson, "Another Emotion."[31] The poem's design is reminiscent of those magic lanterns that we used long ago to view Disney slides fixed in strips—moving the strips from left to right, the images appeared on screen. It is no accident that "Another Emotion" strongly evokes a sense of things past: this was one of the first times Nelson used the organic crackle and filmlike spreading lines that not just remediate old, fading filmic images within a digital setting, but in this way also render the interface a distinctly temporal dimension.[32] Specifically, "Another Emotion" evokes the sense of a time past by foregrounding and refurbishing in its interface the defects, withering, and intrusive accidentals (the spreading lines) of an older medium. (This is reinforced by the nostalgic piano music—it could be a romanticized fragment of a J. S. Bach prelude, or just a Bach-like invention—which repeats itself without interruption). Thus, as Adler describes, the digital renders itself imperfect to mimic the "real presence" of analog media: even media have cultural memories that are typically not the effect of the past itself but of its mediation in the present.

So, here too, presence becomes aftereffect rather than self-presence. How would this facilitate insights into the conditions of possibility of self-presence in the digital sphere? In her "What if Foucault Had Had a Blog?" Joanna Zylinska offers an answer to this question by reinterpreting bioethics (which Zylinska interprets as a performative ethics of life) in terms of blogging. As a form of self-writing, blogs materialize selves and thus participate in a Foucauldian ethos understood as a practice, embodiment, and style of life: know thyself, care for thyself in a free relation of the self to itself. Starting from this, Zylinska seeks to assess to what extent social networking portals such as LiveJournal, MySpace, and Flickr, as well as blogs, could be read as facilitating the care of the self Foucault analyses in Greco-Roman culture, and perhaps even enacting a new ethical way of being in the world. She performs this analysis by means of the concept of Narcissism in a Derridean reading of the term: as a positive basis of becoming. Thus, Zylinska proposes that we "read blogging as being as much about experiencing and enacting the simultaneous difficulty and necessity of relationality as a condition of being in the world." Within the frames of the digital, Zylinska situates the writing and technology of the self as an originary technology—the acceptance of the self as a becoming self is also the acceptance of the technicity at the heart of that self.

Pursuing this technicity of the self in relation to practices of writing, I relate so-called posthuman subjectivities to contemporary paper-based fictions affected by the digital in "Assembled Textualities, Posthuman Selves: Remediated Print in the Digital Age." Focusing on two print novels, Steven Hall's *The Raw Shark Texts* (2007) and Graham Rawle's *Woman's World* (2005), I show how paper-based literary writings affected by digital modes of inscription come to perform anxieties of self-fragmentation relative to the posthuman.[33] Thus, I analyze the parallels and interactions between paper substance and self-substance, showing how these alleged substances are presented in both *The Raw Shark Texts* and *Woman's World* in terms of process rather than essence. I approach both *The Raw Shark Texts* and *Woman's World* as display texts: texts rehearsing the Barthean/Foucauldean idea of text as a node in a network of other texts, yet exploding the signifying potential of the space in between texts by totalizing that space as a norm. Such texts are screens insofar as they function as portals to assembled fragments of existing texts and games, magazines, TV series, and films. How can we thus postulate a "posthuman" textuality, a textuality at once digressing from and feeding on humanist textualities; thoroughly prosthetic yet at the same time still prominently, creatively, paper-based? How do such textualities *materially* perform a posthuman figuration of identity; an identity that is always already other at its core through an originary act of mediation?

Part II: Digital Reflexivities: Fiction, Poetry, Code Writing

Part II centers on electronic reconfigurations of literary writing: its reconfigurations as moveable type, its animation or becoming mobile. Focusing on the form and materiality of language, words, and letters as objects, electronic literature (literature that is digitally born) brings to mind early twentieth-century formalist practices of literary writing: a literature foregrounding its material *as* writing, *as* inscription, and often privileging such foregrounding over the referential uses of language. These practices extended well into the twentieth century (think of concrete poetry) and together make up a significant prehistory of digital poetry. However, they are not its *only* source. As Loss Glazier has shown, paper-based concrete poetry is a vital source for digital poetry, but video, film titling, and holography are equally crucial premeditations.[34] This renders the concept of remediation of central importance to electronic literatures—and to the papers in this volume.

Elaborating on an already-existent field of criticism, Part II merges perspectives on hyperfiction, e-poetry, and code writing within comparative literature studies and media studies. It opens with one of Katherine Hayles's foundational texts on electronic literature: "Intermediation: The Pursuit of a Vision."[35] Intermediation here functions as a concept to analyze the computational nature of twenty-first-century literature, whether digitally born, scanned, or printed by digital presses. As already indicated above, intermediation—as a critical reworking of Bolter and Grusin's "remediation"—refers to the ways in which the accumulated knowledge of old media are transformatively incorporated and animated in new media. Thus, the "poetic conventions, narrative structures, and figurative tropes"—as well as typographic experiments—of modern and postmodern print literature have been replicated but also rematerialized within electronic literature. Screens are no longer imagined as pages of a book, as they were in the early years of electronic literature, but are now conceptualized differently (even though the page, and scroll, still haunt even the most recent, innovative instances of electronic literature on the web). Hayles traces this development by analyzing Michael Joyce's "Afternoon, a Story" (1987) and his *Twelve Blue* (1991) as embodiments of hypertextuality in its infancy and in its electronic adolescence. The difference between the two is a tendency toward conventional reader-decoding or mystery solving and playing, the one haunted by print, the other web-born.

In Hayles's paper, however, intermediation is not just about print and electronic textuality, but also about the feedback loops between "humans, animals, and networked and programmable machines": intermediations are exchanges between "different kinds of cognizers." This is why intermediation is not just about medialities but also—as Hayles shows with respect to the work of Maria Mencia—about changing literacies (a term that will figure prominently in Part IV). Literacies are about cultural frameworks of cognition and mediation, and Hayles shows how present-day digital hypertexts change such frameworks as they project and indeed perform the "inmixing" of humans and machines. What are the consequences of such inmixing for the humanities and, on a more pragmatic level, for literary criticism and analysis? How should such criticism redirect itself as a criticism of code?

In Chapter 6, Marie-Laure Ryan practices such a new literary criticism in her analysis of dysfunctional net art foregrounding its own electronic materiality. As for Weber and Hayles, media—digital media—are here framed in terms of a reflective engagement: "For net.art, reflecting on its medium is not so much a search for identity, as it *is* identity." Medial identity is constituted out of a reflective movement. As with Hayles, remediation here figures as a feedback loop between inscription modes, but also between these modes and human intelligence. As for the latter, this concerns the feedback loop between computer and human cognition that animates both at the same time, yet also the measure of control that human intelligence is able to exert on computer technology. Thus, the net.art that Ryan analyzes foregrounds the issue of control by featuring what Ryan calls "dysfunctional uses of digital technology." Such foregrounded dysfunctionality, reminiscent of Adler's analysis of aura and the dysfunctional, triggers a critical engagement with digital technology and its modes of inscription also alluded to in Weber's contribution.

Ryan considers work by Richard Powers, John Klima, and Lisa Jevbratt, who all in different ways revisit romantic-modernist-postmodernist practices of self-reflexivity as a critical engagement with new media systems. Thus, "They Come in a Steady Stream Now" by Richard Powers frames a standard-model email application that features emails from Richard Powers—the email system, however, is soon paralyzed by spam. Echoing the more or less accidentally collaborative email fiction *Blue Company* and *Kind of Blue*, by Rob Wittig and Scott Rettberg, respectively, "They Come" shows how the digital has transformed letter-writing to frame a mediation on ageing and the eternal youth of a posthuman species—yet at the same time it highlights the accidents effectuated by these transformations: the hampering that they have themselves occasioned. In turn, "Jack & Jill" foregrounds code and codework insofar as the game story that it features is "duplicated . . . by the text of the code," which is to say that it combines a narrative with a performative presentation: The code presents what it does and does what it presents on screen. This is the kind of ingenious performativity of writing that can occur in programming. Its foregrounded dysfunctionality occurs in the humoristic simplicity of the game: it is too simple even to be played. Finally, Ryan discusses Lisa Jevbratt's *1:1*, which revolves around the issue of a perfectly self-reflexive map of cyberspace, so that it would transform itself into its other (which in a loose way might be the case for all interfaces). Such a perfect self-reflexivity would be an impossible option, and, indeed, Jevbratt's interface really gets the user nowhere in particular—its practicality is constantly in question.

As a concept, remediation here illuminates Ryan's analyses of the connection between self-reflexivity and dysfunctionality: Writing is refashioned on screen, in codework not only insofar as such writing does what it says as code, or in slipping away through its own dysfunctionalities, but also because in this way—as Ryan puts it—it "undermine[s] the kind of immersion in digital technology that limits our attention to the surface of the computer screen." Literally, writing keeps the user alive. It is presented as a "non-utilitarian activity," an event revolving around its own "doing." There is thus a trace of the Kantian esthetic here: subjective finality and purposeful purposelessness.[36]

Chapter 7, "Moving (the) Text: From Print to Digital," analyzes the kinesthetic qualities of letters and words in digital environments: their ability to move—dis/appear, dance, rotate, etc.—seemingly voluntarily in an electronic simulation. Elaborating on Glazier, Katalin Sándor shows how the "artistic practices of print visual literature might function as a . . . continually recycled and repositioned tradition for digital poetry." This tradition is at once continuous and discontinuous: it seems as if the aspect of time and interactivity provided by the digital medium can at once be seen as departures from and extensions of print visual poetry (such as concrete poetry).

As Sándor shows in her analysis, the concept of movement is crucial to digital visual poetries: These poetries have unfixed writing quite literally as letters begin to dance and move and even move away (Jim Andrews's *Seattle Drift*) to be disciplined once more. Even so, such animated texts obviously predate the digital revolution—as is evident in text-movies, holopoetry, video and television poetries, and film titling—and likewise signal a double function of writing as language and as animated image (Alex Gopher's *The Child*). Animation is at stake in a number of ways in the digital visual poetries that Sándor discusses. First, there is the reader-viewer who is animated as he or she is compelled to "do" the text: who is compelled to move and interact. Then, in the case of *Seattle Drift*, there is the digital text reflecting on itself as poetic text, and finally there is the suggestion of a "live" language in Brian Kim Stefans's *Star Wars, One Letter at a Time*: Letters here become as fleeting and elusive as in spoken language. As in the articles in Part I, Sándor emphasizes the processual nature of animated texts: These texts are about the act of letters appearing and disappearing, and they emphasize the idea of language as movement without substance or finality. *Star Wars* thus makes visible acts of remediation (a typewriter displayed on the digital screen, the mobilization of language) and also indicates that such remediation renders both media (print and the digital, paper and screen) different: the "impossible re-inscription of the typewriter exposes the differences of the digital." It is the dynamic of the in-between that thus produces new, that is, reconfigured medialities.

Chapter 8, Federica Frabetti's "Technology Made Legible," puts into practice Hayles's plea for textual criticism that takes due note of the computational dimension of literary writing. Frabetti proposes an analytical framework for the cultural understanding of software as a particular manifestation of "text" in the digital age. Building her analysis on the concept of software advanced by software engineering, she shows—on the basis of theories by Jacques Derrida and Katherine Hayles—how software creates "new" textualities and materialities. Software, for Frabetti, is "a form of writing that makes things happen in the material world." In contrast to the more pessimistic cultural theorists who fear an impending future of signifiers without a material base in an increasingly digitally mastered world, Frabetti argues that textuality and materiality are not opposed, that materiality is the condition for signification, and that thus every code is always already material.

Part III: Intermedial Reflexivities: Film, Literature, Script

After the explorations of Part II into the more recent interactions between page and screen, Part III focuses on the feedback loops between paper-based literary writing and fiction films. Revisiting the concept of adaptation, Part III analyzes the ways in which this feedback loop can be rethought in a digital age, where remediation is revealed as a constitutive force of media and mediation. To express this, we have focused prominently on "countermovements," movements from screen to page, and the circulation of "shadow-texts": novelizations and scripts. As a framing article, Peter Verstraten's "Cinema as a Digest of Literature: A 'Remedy' Against Adaptation Fever" confronts the old fidelity issue in adaptation studies—and the old prejudice in film studies that cinema can evolve into an art form only when it keeps at bay the influences of literature and film. In contrast to these fears and prejudices, and on the basis of Charlie Kaufman's film *Adaptation.* (2002), Verstraten instead shows how literary narrative and film constantly animate *and* hamper each other in a complex process of remediation. It is, in this instance, significant that *Adaptation* presents an account of the obstacles encountered in the painstaking attempt to write a script on the basis of a book called *The Orchid Thief*; once more, the emphasis is on the process and on film reflecting on its own conditions of production (including the stereotyped events and turns typical of postmodern Hollywood films), and on the protagonist reflecting on himself. As Verstraten puts it, "The film does not imitate the book as a *product*, but it reproduces the *process* of creation: the writing of the book keeps track with the making of the film"—a transformative recurrence that restyles adaptation as a reproduction of effects. Thus, the move from paper to screen is here ruled not by accurate cinematic imitation, but by functional likeness. For Verstraten this is how film and literature, as two different modes of inscription, can animate each other most fruitfully: as parallel processes without a hierarchical relation.

Such interactive processes are further explored in Chapter 10, which analyzes cinematography as a concept in modernist and postmodernist fictions. What happens when novels start to behave "cinematographically"? Yet, what is "cinematographic"? The authors argue that—in literary studies—"cinematographic" should be deployed not as a given (as montage, for instance), but as a concept in the Deleuzian sense: a multifaceted dimension of the verbal and the visual that emerges as an *effect* of paper-based writings rather than preceding them as a stable norm. Thus in Luigi Pirandello's *Shoot!* (1925) "cinematographic" materializes in paper in a paradoxical double sense, in terms of a detached mode of perception that is at once technologically ("posthumanistically") and aesthetically ("humanistically") connoted. Yet what, the question then arises, is the common ground between paper-based literature and cinema such that the latter can rematerialize itself according to something—a mediation—associated with the former?

Following Garrett Stewart and David Trotter, "Cinematography as a Literary Concept" analyzes modernist and postmodernist modes of presentation in literature and film as parallel manifestations of a shared textuality ruled by automatism. In this approach, literature and film share a discourse network, rather than acting as separate mediations affecting each other: the discourse of technologically mediated, "depersonalized" realities and subjectivities. Chapter 10 expands the perspective of Stewart and of Trotter from the modernist to the postmodernist era, showing how the shared textuality of automatism can be seen to frame both. On the basis of Pirandello's *Shoot!* and Thomas Pynchon's *Gravity's Rainbow* (1973), the authors observe that the "cinematographic" in these texts emerges within a mode of cultural criticism that—in the manner of Theodor W. Adorno's cultural criticism—is directed against the effects of the mass domination of "mainstream" film while drawing on the experimental techniques of avant-garde cinema to *materialize* that criticism in literary writing.

In a similar countermovement from screen to page, and likewise circumventing the fidelity issue, Jan Baetens in Chapter 11, "Novelizing Tati," explores the transmedial potential of novelizations: textual adaptations of films (or more precisely: scripts—an issue, Baetens emphasizes, that in turn undermines the transmedial potential of novelizations). Baetens's position is to promote a culturally framed reading of novelizations, to analyze such texts as *cultural media* rather than expressions of a technological medium alone; to read textual form always already as (to invoke Raymond Williams) a *cultural* form. Thus, Baetens suggests that we analyze novelizations as objects of productive reception: as objects regulating the reception of films and, thus, as records of such reception. Novelizations are not simply adaptations of films: sometimes they are released before the release of a film (as was the case with *King Kong* in 1932), thus co-regulating the reception of that film, and sometimes they even prepare the audience for a film to come. As Baetens shows, this is the case with Jean-Claude Carrière's novelization of Jacques Tati's *Les Vacances de M. Hulot* (1951); it premeditated and intervened in the future reception of Tati's *Mon Oncle*.

Although novelizations, as Baetens stresses, move from script to book, the screen cannot simply be erased from the trajectory. This especially holds for Carrière's novelization, for this is a novelization of a film without narrative or dialogue. One could say it is a novelization of a series of extended, cinematographic mime sketches. Baetens shows how Carrière's text renders anew the Tati film: shifting the "objective" perspective of the film to the "subjective" perspective of a narrating voice, the theatrical format of the film is translated into a diary in the novelization (echoing *Shoot!*), as well as visual into verbal humor. Most significantly, however, cinematic simultaneity is translated into textual linearity. As in *Adaptation*, such translation revolves around functional likeness—the recreation of effects, like those of simultaneity—and how this affects the ways in which media can remediate each other, or rather, force each other to change. Thus, Baetens points out, Carrière's novelization creatively tackles the clash between visual enunciated and verbal enunciation. While many novelizations avoid this clash, quite literally writing around it by copying the storyline alone, *Les Vacances de M. Hulot* confronts all major aspects of novelization as a transmedial cultural form, moving from one medium to another: it addresses the

impossibility of any literal transmedialization; it demonstrates that novelization should not be reduced to a question of storytelling, and it suggests that to novelize is always an act that both changes the source text
and influences the cultural context in which it appears.

Continuing this critical analysis of the relations between page and
screen, Martijn Engelberts in Chapter 12 considers the literary dimension of film scripts in France. Crucial to understanding this dimension is
the competition between film- and paper-based fiction in the twentieth
century, and the ambitions of the former to position itself as an art
independent of paper-based fiction. Yet what is, and has been, the fate
of the script in such ambitions? If film is displayed as an autonomously
visual medium—a display reinforced by the (critical) decision of many
Nouvelle Vague directors to work on the basis of improvisation rather
than a written scenario—what would be the position of the film script
and its own aspirations toward a status as art? As Engelberts argues,
precisely the desire to consider film as a medium on its own—rather
than a medium of adaptation—gave rise in the twentieth century to a
more or less implicit ban on considering the literary aspects of films-
cripts. Nevertheless, the extent to which printed scripts were "integrated in the literary field, as far as their production by publishers is
concerned, was rather high until the mid-seventies, but has generally
been shrinking ever since that turning point."

Part IV: New Literacies, Education, and Accessibility

This final part of the volume returns to its opening chapters: the intermediation between "new," electronic modes of writing and the reconfigured subjectivities such writing interpellates. More specifically,
engaged with users and uses of writing, this part considers electronic
writing in relation to media literacy, networked education, and issues
of open access on screen: if writing is changed into a digital-cultural—
that is, shared and formative—writing, how is such writing processed
and transferred? Which new literacies does such writing project on
screen, and which old literacies does it remediate? What is, indeed, "literacy" in an age of ongoing medial, scriptorial transformations? In view
of these very transformations, William Uricchio in "New Literacies.
Technology and Cultural Form" proposes to use the concept only in the
plural so as to include by definition, so to speak, its many different
transformations over time (and in relation to different media). Still, as
Uricchio points out, in criticism "literacy," in the sense of "the reading

and writing of words," remained a relatively stable concept until the mid- and even late twentieth century—which is remarkable, to say the least, in an age of so many new and emerging "cultural competencies."

Changing "literacy" to "literacies" for Uricchio not only affirms the heterogeneity of practices of inscription and reading in a medially complex environment, but also challenges the social dynamics and hierarchies of power implicit in the old-fashioned, static use of "literacy" (an issue comparable, of course, to debates surrounding the literary canon—literary canons). Thus offering a new "definitional strategy," rather than simply a new definition, Uricchio uses "literacies" as a concept that is "inclusive of both traditional modes of literacy and the new ones; of both word-based modes of expression and the broader array of affordances associated with text, image and sound in digital media." Such an inclusive concept befits an age, in Uricchio's view, of "exponential change," indeed a paradigm shift in the means of cultural production due to a screen-based network culture that revolves most prominently around modes of participation, rather than—as in the "old" culture industry—an allegedly passive consumption. Or, the computer network facilitates a culture of participation (though it remediates older community practices) that is of a more radical nature, on a grander scale, and with more far-reaching consequences. Indeed, Uricchio concludes, if today literacies relate to new cultural competencies on screen, such competencies no longer—as in the traditional meaning of "literacy"—bear simply on changing modes of readerships, but rather on newly invented modes of authorship: shared, individual, public, or private.

In Chapter 14, Asunción López-Varela Azcárate elaborates on this network paradigm with its emphasis on participation. Starting from the thesis that media materialities are never neutral, but always already culturally formatted, she explores the interrelation between digital media materialities, the ways humans interact with (and constitute themselves through) such materialities, and how such interaction materializes in networked educational processes (blogging, wikis) that have emerged during the last decade. Elaborating on Mark Poster's concept of the humachine, as an interface between humans and digital machines that questions the distinction between subject and object, López-Varela analyzes the materiality of digital media. On this basis, she analyzes the ways in which human subjectivities are configured within digital network systems, such as blogs (constituting an easily accessible "home identity"), that undo distinctions between public and private. How do

such systems operate as education systems, and how would they contribute to radical, dialogic pedagogical views?

In answer to both questions, López-Varela focuses on the participatory and distributed dimension of the means and practices of cultural
production in education blogs. Emphasizing the multimodal nature of
blogs, López-Varela points out how they facilitate "a construction of
subjectivity within a greater networked community consciousness."
What could this mean for blogging within educational environments?
How do blogs foster the organization of knowledge? López-Varela
shows that blogs contribute to communication and problem-solving
skills, yet though one of their prime function is interaction and
exchange, it remains to be seen to what extent blogging in the classroom
(and outside of it) displays a radical dialogicity.

Finally, in Chapter 15, Gary Hall outlines his open access program of
the present and for the future. While Uricchio and López-Varela already
analyze the *uses* of media technology in terms of networked participation, Hall's reading of the uses of digital technology and literacy focuses
on open access. Hall defines the term "open access" as follows: "Putting
peer-reviewed scientific and scholarly literature on the Internet. Making
it available free of charge and free of most copyright and licensing
restrictions. Removing the barriers to serious research." He thinks
through the implications of open access—though never in such a general sense—on the basis of his own open access archive, CSeARCH
(which stands for Cultural Studies e-Archive).

Like López-Varela—and, for that matter, Hayles, Ryan, Frabetti, and
others in this volume—Hall stresses the materiality of (digital) media,
which he in turn sees as a prerequisite for situated, specific criticism
and analysis of such media technologies. Yet Hall sees this emphasis on
materiality as a phase in media theory that could be superseded by a
next phase, a criticism—in line with Uricchio—that is concerned with
the uses of media technologies as network technologies in a heterogeneous domain where old and new media, private and networked, closed
and open modes of inscription coexist, or even converge. What is the
role of open access in such as a domain? Focusing on academic open
access, Hall invokes the way in which "open-access publishing and
archiving of academic scholarship and research constitutes a strategic
use of a specific form of digital culture within particular institutional
and sociopolitical contexts." He argues that other open-access practices
on the net might operate differently. Not all peer-to-peer systems function in the same manner, even though they are generally catalogued

under the rubric "networked participation." Such differences should, according to Hall, prevent us from invoking the idea of cultural paradigm shifts, as by their very nature such shifts imply an overall, all-inclusive movement.

Within these parameters, Hall focuses on the role of digital textualities in open access and the ways in which such textualities not only remediate old modes of inscription but also affect existing modes of knowledge. In other words, how does open access and archiving—as a remediation and transformation of disciplines of knowledge and the paper medium—affect academic research and output? Hall makes a number of suggestions, and he comes to the conclusion that open-access archives (and what to include in them) compel us to rethink literary, as well as cultural, studies, "how we are going to decide this; and with what authority and legitimacy such decisions can be made." It may even go farther than this and affect the way we think of the university and learning in general. Yet we should always do so, for Hall, in the singular (as the title of his chapter indicates: "The Singularity of New Media"). For if Hall's new media theory 3G became operational, it would "involve paying far closer attention to the affective, performative aspect of particular instances of new media in a relation of singularity to finite, 'concrete' conjunctions of the 'here' and 'now.'" This means that this new media theory is a theory of events, rather than lasting gestures.

PART ONE

Mediality, Digitality, Subjectivity

CHAPTER ONE

Medium, Reflexivity, and the Economy of the Self

SAMUEL WEBER

I

In an often-cited footnote to the first chapter of the *Critique of Pure Reason*, Immanuel Kant defends his use of the word "aesthetic" there to designate "the a priori principles of sensibility" and criticizes another use of the term, namely, the tendency, widespread among the Germans of his day, to employ the word in order "to designate what others call the critique of taste." Kant argues that if the word "aesthetic" is understood to imply a truly transcendental science of a priori principles, it could never be used in the sense aspired to by Baumgarten, namely, as the name of a rational system of principles governing judgments of beauty. For such rules, Kant insists, can never transcend their essentially empirical origins and thus can never attain the universality required of truly transcendental, scientific principles. The term aesthetics, he therefore concludes, should therefore either be abandoned entirely or, if retained, should be clearly limited to the study of sense experience. Aesthetics in this latter meaning should be divided into two branches: a genuinely scientific study of the condition of sensibility, as in his own Transcendental Aesthetics, analyzing Space and Time as forms of outer and inner intuition, and a purely empirical study of psychological experience.[1]

As is well known, only nine years later (1791), when Kant sought to complete his *Critical Philosophy Through an Analysis of the Faculty of*

Judgment, he saw himself obliged to modify this earlier evaluation of the term "aesthetic." Indeed, the *Third Critique* begins with precisely what Kant had rejected in the earlier text, namely, with his attempt to construct a transcendentally valid *Critique of Aesthetic Judgment* dealing with judgments of the beautiful and of the sublime.

The problems, however, that led Kant first to reject and then to adopt the term *aesthetics* as appropriate for designating universally valid principles of judgment, as opposed to principles of sensibility, are no less relevant today than they were for Kant. Perhaps uppermost among them is the problem of how to construe the relation of *universality* to *singularity*—a problem that lurks behind the entire Kantian project of constructing a "critical" philosophy that would not be dependent upon empirically contingent rules with relative and restricted validity.

The fact that many of those writing on "media aesthetics" today are not particularly preoccupied with such epistemological problems does not necessarily mean that those concerns have in the meanwhile been successfully resolved. Above all, the problem of "singularity" remains, in my view, one of the decisive concerns of contemporary thought, and one that has vast implications for the study of media, "aesthetic" or otherwise.

There is in the United States an expression that strikes me as both highly distinctive of widespread American attitudes, and at the same time in the process of imposing its perspective, if not its wording, on a globalized world. It is the expression "That's history," taken to mean that the past is "over and done with" (another, complementary American expression)—and that it therefore can be relegated to the dustbin of history (sound familiar?). The notion of history as a dustbin persists, I would argue, in the tendency to draw a radical opposition between "old" and "new" media—a tendency that itself is as old as the "quarrel between the ancients and the moderns" that broke out in the seventeenth century. Nothing is more characteristic of Western modernity than this attempt to set up a clear-cut opposition between the New and the Old, an opposition that also implies—as oppositions always do—a hierarchy. A relatively recent manifestation of this attitude was the use made of Canguilhem's notion of the "epistemological break," popularized by Foucault in his early writings. That the appeal of this idea continues up until today, and that it is by no means limited to academic areas such as media studies or the history of ideas, was demonstrated by the 2007 presidential elections in France, where the victor, Nicolas

Sarkozy, waged a successful campaign built around the term *la rup-ture*—the break. In contrast to the essentially linear notion of a "break" between Old and New, in which the latter is construed as being entirely unburdened and unaffected by the former, I want to suggest that, as the words themselves imply, discontinuities can only be measured in terms of continuities, and that the relationship of old and new—as in "old" and "new media"—has to be thought otherwise than according to the paradigm of a mutually exclusive opposition, which, as Nietzsche argued at the beginning of *Beyond Good and Evil*, constitutes the largely unquestioned matrix of metaphysical identity-thinking itself.

As I have already suggested, one of these continuities, which spans both old *and* new media, involves the status of the singular, of singular "events." Is the singular that which merely "breaks" with the old, free-ing itself of its history, or is it a product of that history? And if so, how does it differentiate itself from what preceded it? Such a question calls for a thinking that is emphatically concerned with relations, not with substances. And for which all knowledge is inextricably relational, and situational, in a way that problematizes not just the traditional philo-sophical aspiration to universal validity, but also the unphilosophical belief that if knowledge is to be valid, it must be universally valid, thus transcending the spatial-temporal conditions of its own emergence. In the United States today, and no doubt elsewhere as well, those who insist on the relational structure of knowledge production are often attacked as "cultural relativists," if not as outright "nihilists." (Kate Hayles can tell you something about those polemics from her own firsthand experience.) Nietzsche once wrote that the belief in the abso-lute validity of grammar was in fact the condition for the belief in God. A correlative of that statement, perhaps, would be that as long as we take nouns qua substantives for granted, we will never be able to ques-tion the logic of identity. For instance, as long as we use words such as "media" or "aesthetics" as though their meaning, if not self-evident, was at least unequivocal, that is, as long as we have no compunctions about using the definite article, to speak of "the" media—so long will we be assuming the kind of time and space transcending universality that is blind to its own situation and relationality. Or, to speak in another vocabulary that is both very old and yet also very contempo-rary, the unreflective use of the definite article to constitute an object of knowledge that is univocally defined and self-identical—this is tanta-mount to a denial of the network of relations in which every event is inevitably inscribed, and in so doing it overlooks the fact that every such relational network is inevitably an "inter-net." All thought and experience thus begins and ends with a certain "inter." But this "inter"—which is anything but simply "internal"—implies and entails a certain relation to language. All reflection on media, as on aesthetics, is conditioned first by the medium of language in which it is articulated, with its by no means universalizable syntax and grammar, which in turn entail a distinctive history and specific, nonuniversal traditions. Linguistic traditions and histories of course do not exist in a vacuum: they are also defined by distinctive cultural traditions that are almost always geopolitically specific.

If this sounds abstract—and I apologize for that—let me give an example that will hopefully make it more concrete. A speaker of American English, or indeed of any language, whose experience of "the media" is limited to or dominated by the television programming available to residents of the United States would take it for granted, as an immutable fact of nature, that it is "normal" for programs to be interrupted every five or ten minutes by commercials lasting almost as long. If he or she were more sophisticated, he or she might see a social dimension to this situation, but still construe the alternative as being a totalitarian, state-financed broadcast network, the epitome of unfreedom and oppression. Fox News, on the contrary, would appear as the best possible solution compatible not just with the technical but with the economic conditions of this "new medium"—namely, "television."

What I want to argue, by contrast, is that there is a historical dimension to the word *medium* that allows us to do what absolutist or ontological theories of "media" tend to exclude: namely, to envisage alternatives to what often presents itself as the inevitable and exclusive "reality" of "the media." But such alternative aspects can be discerned and developed only to the extent that this monolithic notion of "the media" is challenged, not in the abstract, but in terms of its own history. In what follows, I want to present one small chapter in that history—not in the history of "the media" per se, but in the use of the word at a certain place and time, and by a writer whose work has been extremely influential in shaping many of our conceptions of the new media, in their relation to the old.[2]

II

What makes the work of Walter Benjamin particularly fascinating in this respect is the way in which his thoughts on the new media emerge from a very distinctive analysis of the old media. One outstanding instance of this emergence can be found in a very early text, namely, Benjamin's doctoral dissertation, "The Concept of Criticism in German Romanticism." In German the title is slightly but suggestively different from this translation: *Der Begriff der Kunstkritik in der deutschen Romantik.* Although previously I myself have argued for translating *Kunstkritik* as "criticism," given that the latter term in English today is generally (although not always) associated with art or literature, it is also important to recall that "art" and indeed "poetry" are the privileged objects of "criticism" as Benjamin uses the word in his dissertation. As you probably know, Benjamin, who aspired to become the leading critic of twentieth-century Germany, has in recent decades become one of the most cited and criticized critics. His dissertation, however, perhaps because of its rather academic style and subject matter, has not attracted the same attention, even in literary-critical circles. And where his dissertation has been discussed, one particular aspect of his dissertation has been almost entirely ignored. It is with this dimension of his text that I will be concerned in this essay.

In order to interpret the different words employed in the title of his thesis, above all "art," "criticism," and "concept," Benjamin introduces another term that distinguishes itself from almost all the other terms he uses, which are almost all taken from the writings that he is interpreting. But in this one case, the word is not used by any of the writers he is analyzing—not Friedrich Schlegel, not Novalis, and not even the shadowy figure who appears briefly at the beginning and toward the end of the thesis, both framing and transcending the text in its entirety, namely, Friedrich Hölderlin. No, this word appears to have no history, to come from nowhere, and yet it plays a decisive role in the construction of Benjamin's overall argument. This word is—quite simply, or not so simply—"medium."

That it should have come to play such a significant part in Benjamin's dissertation is both understandable and enigmatic. Understandable, since Benjamin himself had used the term, as well as its adjectival-adverbial variations (*medial, mediality*) extensively several years earlier in an important but unpublished essay, "Language in General and the Language of Man" (1916). In that essay he elaborates a notion of language as a "medium" in a very distinct sense, namely, as a process that does not communicate anything external—a meaning, for instance. In other words, as Benjamin puts it in that essay, language is a *medium,* but not a means to any end external to itself. It is therefore not to be confused with any form of instrumentality, or of mediation. Rather, its function is that of imparting itself *immediately—unmittelbar*—that is, without the mediation of anything external to itself:

> Each language imparts itself in and of itself [*Jede Sprache teilt sich in sich selbst mit*], it is in the purest sense the "medium" of imparting. The medial, i.e., the *immedi*acy [Unmittel*barkeit*] of all spiritual imparting is the fundamental problem of all theory of language.[3]

Mediality is thus not to be confused with *mediation*, in the Hegelian (dialectical) or any other sense: it is neither a function of dialectical negativity nor of any relation to an outside. And it is precisely its immediacy that anticipates the main concern that Benjamin will identify in his discussion of Schlegel and Novalis in his dissertation, as the opening sentence of its first chapter makes unmistakably clear:

> Thinking reflecting upon itself in self-consciousness is the fundamental fact from which Friedrich Schlegel's epistemological deliberations, and most of Novalis's as well, take their point of departure. The relation of thinking to itself as it is found in reflection is considered to be the most proximate form of thinking as such, out of which all other forms [of thought] develop.

It is not surprising, therefore, that Benjamin would reintroduce the term "medium" in order to describe the Romantics' valorization of reflection, even though this concept is associated first of all with *thinking* rather than with *language*. However, Benjamin's early conception of language as essentially naming entailed a strong reflexive element. In describing language as a medium that imparts itself, and does so immediately, Benjamin was already construing language as a process of self-reflection, a word that is a pleonasm insofar as "reflection" generally implies the return of a self to itself. This, however, is precisely the question that will tacitly inform Benjamin's discussion of Schlegel and the Romantics: namely, that of the link between "reflection" and the "self." As we will see, in his discussion of Schlegel, Benjamin will seek to problematize that link and, in his strong but unelaborated allusions to Hölderlin, point to an alternative in which a certain repetition will come to replace reflection and the first person singular—the I—will replace the "self," albeit in a very different way from the Fichtean notion of a self-positing Ego.

Given his own earlier use of this word, then, it is therefore not entirely surprising that Benjamin would invoke the notion of "medium" in his dissertation to describe the process of reflection itself. But if it is therefore not entirely surprising, Benjamin's use of this word in the dissertation nevertheless displays an enigmatic aspect, or at least one that is not simply self-evident. On the one hand, Benjamin contrasts Schlegel's notion of "reflection" with that of the philosopher Fichte, who construed it as dependent on and limited by an Absolute Ego positing itself. For the Romantics, on the contrary, the positing of an Ego was only a subsidiary, not an essential dimension of reflection, because the latter was conceived of not as the result of an act of positing, but rather as a process that Benjamin—not Schlegel—designates as that of a *medium*:

> Schlegel's concept of the absolute . . . would most correctly be designated as the medium of reflection [*Reflexionsmedium*]. With this term the whole of Schlegel's theoretical philosophy may be collected and designated. . . . Reflection constitutes the absolute, and it constitutes it as a medium.

What is surprising and intriguing about Benjamin's use of this word here is, as I have already suggested, that he explicitly emphasizes that this term is not to be found in the writings of Schlegel:

> Schlegel did not use the term "medium" himself; nonetheless, he attached the greatest importance to the *constantly uniform connection* in the absolute or in the system, both of which must be interpreted as the connection of the real not in its substance (which is everywhere the same) but in the degrees of clarity with which it unfolds.[4]

Schlegel did not have the one word available to him that, according to Benjamin, more than any other designates the essential characteristics of his own system of thought—namely, of the absolute reflection with which he was primarily concerned. In a footnote, Benjamin suggests that the relation of "medium" to "reflection" is double, entailing a certain ambiguity (*Doppelsinn*), which, however, upon further examination resolves into a consistent account:

> For, on the one hand, reflection is itself a medium—by virtue of its constant connectivity, while on the other hand the medium in question is one within which reflection moves itself [*sich bewegt*]—for the latter, as the absolute, moves itself in and of itself [*bewegt sich in sich selbst*].

What, then, does the word "medium" signify for Benjamin such that it becomes indispensable to him in his account of Romantic reflexivity? First of all, as we have seen, for Benjamin "mediality" signifies a certain *immediacy*, the capacity to function without external mediation. The

German word *Un-mittel-barkeit*, which Benjamin in his earlier essay breaks up into its components, signifies for him the potential (*–barkeit*) of acting without serving as a "means," that is, without entering into a mediating or mediated relation to anything else. The medium, whether as language in the 1916 essay or as Absolute Reflection in the 1920 dissertation, entails the potentiality, indeed the power of operating without external reference (a reference that in both cases can be assimilated to a certain notion of "meaning"). Language does not serve primarily to communicate meaning any more than reflection serves to provide knowledge, at least in the traditional sense of that word.

At the same time, the German word *Unmittelbarkeit* must be understood as yet another of those *barkeiten*, those "-abilities," that characterize Benjamin's conceptualization from beginning to end.[5] This fact suggests that the mode of being of the *medium* will never be that of a self-identical or self-present reality, but rather of a kind of virtuality that in principle perhaps can never be realized as such—or rather, whose realizations are marked by a dynamics of self-transformation rather than one of self-fulfillment.

In contrast to Fichte, the Romantics do not shy away from affirming the "absolute" dimension of "reflection," and Benjamin explains this precisely through the notion of medium. But his use of the term here, far from resolving the ambiguities of the Romantic tendency to regard reflection as Absolute, actually brings them to the fore. They can be described in the following way. On the one hand, "medium" designates a process that is not simply instrumental or teleological but that seems to have a certain autonomy: It functions immediately, as indicated, and leaves nothing outside of itself. This in turn tends to construe the medium of reflection as ultimately a movement of the "self," a *Selbstbewegung*. On the other hand, this "movement" is never simply circular or self-contained: it may be "continual" or "constant"—*stetig* is the German word Benjamin uses—and it may also entail a kind of unfolding or development—*Entfaltung*—but it is also and above all a *transformation*. In the first pages of his dissertation, Benjamin emphasizes this point: "Under the term 'reflection' is understood the transformative [*umformende*]—and nothing but the transformative—reflecting on a form." Form is already a reflective category that in reflecting itself further alters and transforms itself. A certain alterity is thus essentially at work at the heart of the reflective movement.

The ambiguity or tension thus results between such alterity, on the one hand, associated with a dynamics of transformation and alteration, and, on the other, the notion of a movement of the self returning to itself, also associated with the notion of reflection. The nature of the movement itself "reflects" this constitutive ambiguity: on the one hand, it is *stetig*, continual, on the other, it moves by leaps and bounds. Benjamin quotes Friedrich Schlegel's assertion that the "transition [*Übergang*] . . . must always be a leap [*ein Sprung*]" and comments on this as follows:

> This immediacy, which is originary [*prinzipiell*] although not absolute but rather mediated [*vermittelte*], is that in which the liveliness [*Lebendigkeit*] of the connection [*Zusammenhang*] is grounded.

The medium is thus defined spatially rather than temporally—as a *Zusammenhang* rather than as a *Fortgang*—but its spatiality is not at all static. It involves not just a context—which would be the most common English rendering of the German word that plays such an important role in Benjamin's discussion of medium here, namely, *Zusammenhang*. Rather, what this word seems to imply is both a state of connectedness and a process of linkage in which connections are made and unmade through leaps and bounds rather than through continuous evolution or unfolding.

In short, "medium" here names a process that never stays the same: all that is continual is its transformations and changes, and these are discontinuous: continual discontinuity. It is this discontinuous movement that constitutes the very "liveliness" of the medium: it is "alive" to the extent that it does not stay the same. The liveliness of the medial connection involves a certain overcoming of temporal finitude, but only through disconnections (my word for discontinuous connectivity). Such disconnections thus are determined (in the German sense of *bestimmt*— that is, defined) as *discrete, singular events*. As a medium of reflection, thinking is thus distinguished from the Fichtean antithetics of Ego and Non-Ego, not in order to be dissolved into a higher continuum, but to subsist as the connectedness of discreet singularities—a connectivity that does not simply absorb the singularities into a more comprehensive synthesis.

In this context, early on his dissertation Benjamin cites a name that will return toward its end to frame his discussion of the Romantic concept of criticism and at the same time to transcend it. That name, as I have already indicated, is Hölderlin. The citation seems at first sight flat and banal:

Hölderlin, who without direct involvement with the early Romantics nevertheless spoke the final and incomparably profound word concerning certain of their ideas, writes at a point when he seeks to express an intimate, highly relevant connection [*Zusammenhang*]: "infinitely (exactly) connected" [*unendlich (genau) zusammenhängen*]. Schlegel and Novalis had the same idea when they understood the infinitude of reflection as a fulfilled infinitude of connectedness. . . . Today we would say "systematically" for what Hölderlin expresses more simply, as "exactly" connected.

Throughout this text, as with many others of the same general period, Hölderlin will emerge as the poet who has the first and last word—although precisely because of this claim, the word or words that Hölderlin is said to speak will remain quite obscure in Benjamin's text. Benjamin will never discuss just what "infinite exactitude" might mean in respect to "connectedness." But his text allows us to make connections that address the question. And ironically or not, such connections emerge as soon as we direct our attention to the way in which Benjamin "connects" his text to the texts of Hölderlin. The reference Benjamin provides in a footnote—to a text entitled "Infidelity of Wisdom"—turns out itself to be unfaithful, or, as some might say, erroneous. The quote, which is taken from Hölderlin's gloss to his Pindar translations, "where," as Benjamin puts it, "Hölderlin seeks to express an intimate, highly relevant connectedness," is not from the gloss to Pindar's poem, "Untreue der Weisheit," but rather from the gloss to another Pindar fragment, which Hölderlin translates as "The Infinite" ("Das Unendliche"). Benjamin's connects to Hölderlin's text by reinscribing "the infinite" as "infidelity of wisdom." Since, as this reinscription suggests, Hölderlin's text, including both the translation of Pindar and the commentary on it, are cited by Benjamin as being extremely pertinent to the notion of the "reflection medium," allow me to venture a rough translation of Hölderlin's Pindar translation and then translate part of its equally short commentary. First the poem:

> Although I scale the wall of Right,
> The high or crooked deception,
> And so myself
> Circumscribing, beyond
> Me live, about this
> I am of a mixed
> Mind, to say it exactly.
>
> *Ob ich des Rechtes Mauer,*
> *Die hohe, oder krummer Täuschung*
> *Ersteig und so mich selbst*

Umschreibend, hinaus
Mich lebe, darüber
Hab ich zweideutig ein
Gemüt, genau es zu sagen.

That the poet should be of "a mixed mind to say exactly" what he has written in the poem, Hölderlin then glosses as follows:

> The fact that I then discover that the connection between right and cleverness must be ascribed not to these themselves but to a third [*nicht ihnen selber, sondern einem dritten*], through which their connection is infinitely exact—that is why I am of a mixed mind.[6]

The "intimate and profound connection" to which Benjamin refers has thus to do with—is "connected" to—the way things are connected for a finite living being—an "I," although hardly the Fichtean Ego, since unlike the latter it is the result not of a process of *Setzung*—of positing—but of a "writing around and about," an *Umschreibung* through which the "I" "lives itself out," irreparably separated from its "me" (*hinaus/mich lebe*). The process of writing, which involves negotiating between the "wall" of a certain "legality" (*die Mauer des Rechts*) and the deceptiveness of "cleverness" that its generality necessarily entails for any *singular* mortal being, splits the poet's temper (*Gemüt*), revealing his dependence upon something that transcends the duality of Right and Deception, *Recht* and *Täuschung*. What that "third" is the poet cannot or will not say: he preserves its unnamable alterity by limiting himself to recording its *effects* on him: it splits his mind and heart, which, qua "mixed"—*zweideutig*—is no longer at one with itself. Reflection here does not reestablish a primordial unity but rather exacerbates an irreducible heterogeneity that can be written, but hardly said. Or rather, it can be said with "infinite exactitude" only be being circumscribed, in and as split connection between poem, translation, and commentary.

Benjamin, to be sure, avoids any discussion of the context from which his Hölderlin quote is taken—and given the difficulties of the text, both Pindar's and Hölderlin's, this is no doubt a wise decision for someone writing a thesis—and perhaps even for someone commenting it. What a reading of Hölderlin's text suggests, however, is that the "infinitely exact" connectivity that characterizes the medium of reflection also exceeds it, since the "links" it establishes only hang together by virtue of forces that are external to them. Those forces cannot be entirely contained within the medial configuration *as it is given at any single time*. The word "infinite" or "infinitely"—the German *unendlich* can mean either—does not suggest an eternity of the same but rather dependence on an excluded third that never ends—is *un-endlich*. And this third is experienced through and as a certain circuitous *writing*, which Hölderlin formulates significantly using not the present indicative but rather the present participle, which suggests an immediacy that is ongoing (*stetig*) but never fully present, indefinitely repetitive but never intrinsically determinable. It is a writing about and around: *umschreibend*, for which no end is ever in sight, but only the ever-present possibility of being interrupted, broken off. Such writing marks a limit of the visible in this medial process, since the "third" upon which its connections depend—and without connections there can be no writing—can never be brought into view, remaining irreducibly outside the field of the visible, which, however, it also delimits. There is a striking anticipation here of how practices of inscription—what Benjamin will later call techniques of reproducibility—condition the field of the visible and the audible, framing that field through interruptions, as in cinematography (a form of writing—the inscription of movement as sequence of images).

It is this perspective—if one can call it that, given its nonvisual, and indeed nonphenomenal character—that allows us to surmise why and how, for Benjamin, Hölderlin's words here both define and surpass the problems addressed by Schlegel and Novalis, and in particular the notion of "absolute reflection," or in Benjamin's transposition, the "medium of reflection." For Schlegel, as we have seen, the framework of this medium is ultimately determined by a concept of the Self as Self-Identity: reflection is construed as a movement by which thinking, through alteration and transformation, ultimately manifests itself. The Absolute is ultimately the Self. Hölderlin's insistence on the "third" as the condition of all connectivity, by contrast, points to a sphere of alterity and difference that can no longer be absorbed into an Absolute Self.

For Benjamin, something of this tendency is already latent in the Romantic conception of reflection as Absolute. Benjamin describes this as a third-order mode of reflection: it is a thinking that has as its object reflection in the traditional, here Fichtean, sense, which is to say, the thinking of thinking. There is first of all thinking as thought of an object; then there is second-order thinking, which reflects this first-order thought—this is reflection in the traditional sense (that of the Cartesian Cogito, for instance). And finally, there is a third kind of thinking, which reflects this second-order reflection itself. From this results a tension between Self and Other that the Romantics act out rather than recognize, and that Benjamin sees articulated more profoundly in Hölderlin's work. The ambiguity, to be sure, is that such a third-order reflection undercuts the process by which a "self" can be determined, which is to say limited and identified.

Thus, on the one hand, for the Romantics "everything is self," in contrast to Fichte, for whom "only the I is a Self." But in attempting to think thought as self-contained, third-order reflection reveals an infinite regress or indefinite mise en abyme, the upshot of which, in Hölderlin's translation and commentary, is the feeling of ambivalence (*zweideutiges Gemüt*) that leaves the poet of two minds.

Third-order reflection reveals the primordial "Ur-Form" of reflection according to Benjamin, not as the fulfillment of the Self but rather as its decomposition:

> On the third and every following higher level of reflection, however, in this Ur-form a process of decomposition proceeds (*geht . . . eine Zersetzung vor sich*), which announces itself in a distinctive ambiguity (*Doppeldeutigkeit*).

Benjamin's German here is difficult to translate in its precision. The process of decomposition (*Zersetzung*) "geht . . . vor sich": literally, "goes . . . before itself." It reintroduces a temporal dimension into the ostensible spatiality of the medium as a reflexive process, but it introduces a temporal process that is not going anywhere in the sense of a goal-directed, teleological movement. This process brings forth singular events that do not stay the same but rather alter themselves in connecting with others. This justifies the word "critique" in its etymological dimension, derived from the Greek *krinein*, to separate. Separation—criticism—is, however, not the act of an ultimately self-identical subject, of a self-consciousness, but rather the result of the split that emerges out of the medium of reflection as such. The decisive difference, however, between the Jena Romantics and Hölderlin, as already suggested, is that the former still try to construe this "as such" of the self-separating medium as ultimately a process of Self-fulfillment, whereas Hölderlin, as in his poetic commentary to Pindar alluded to by Benjamin, makes the "infinite exactness" of the "connection" dependent not on a Self but on a process of circumscribing in which the first person singular is not effaced but rather "lives itself out" (*hinaus mich lebe*).

In the other fragment, to which Benjamin (mistakenly) alludes, "Infidelity of Wisdom," there is a short phrase that suggests that his "error" was by no means entirely arbitrary. Hölderlin writes: "If the understanding is trained intensively / It will derive energy even from dispersion; insofar as it easily recognizes the foreign in its own honed acuity [*geschliffenen Schärfe*], it will not easily be led astray in uncertain situations" (669). In short, if the "understanding" "easily" recognizes its own acuity as in part foreign, it will not be totally lost "in uncertain situations."

The "medium of reflection" names Schlegel's and Benjamin's effort to describe this process of "easily" acknowledging the "foreign" and "alien"—*das Fremde*—as a condition of one's "own" ability to "hone" (*Schleifen*): that is, to make distinctions and connections. In Schlegel, however, such "honing" remains ultimately enclosed and encapsulated in a notion of Reflection as a function of the Self, and it is this that limits the scope and significance of the reflection-medium for Benjamin in this essay. As Benjamin puts it, Schlegel never discarded the basic axiom that "reflection does not dissolve into empty infinitude but is *in itself* [in sich selbst] substantial and fulfilled." Reflection, for Schlegel, qua Medium is ultimately and originally self-identical and self-contained, as expressed in the term *Urreflexion*: Original or Primary Reflection, and this in turn defines its limits for Benjamin, who in a long footnote toward the end of the first half of his dissertation explains why he will not pursue the question of the medium of reflection beyond what he has already done. The problem is that, for Schlegel, "criticism" as the quintessence of the medium of reflection can never be negative, can never be really critical, since it always involves a transformation that is construed as a fulfillment of the Self. It is at this point that Benjamin offers a "critical" remark that is not critical in the Schlegelian sense, for it implies a move beyond the Romantics' homogeneous notion of reflection:

> [For Schlegel and the Romantics] Reflection can be augmented but never reduced. . . . Only a breaking-off, no reduction of reflective intensification [*Reflexionssteigerung*] is thinkable. . . . On the occasion of this isolated critical remark it should be noted that the theory of the medium of reflection will not be pursued here beyond the extent to which the Romantics elaborated it, since this is all that is required to deploy the concept of criticism systematically. From a purely critical and logical standpoint it would be desirable to elaborate this theory further, beyond the obscurity in which the Romantics left it. It must be feared, however, that such an elaboration would itself lead only to further obscurity. Whereas certain individual aesthetical [*kunsttheoretischen*] propositions can be extraordinarily fruitful, the theory

as a whole leads to logically unresolvable contradictions; above all in respect to the problem of Ur-reflection.

There is no time here to explore some of those "extraordinarily fruitful propositions" at any length, although it would certainly be worthwhile. I will limit myself to just one remark of Friedrich Schlegel's that Benjamin cites, namely, "that words often understand themselves better than those by whom they are used." What might be understood by this is suggested by Schlegel's theory of "wit," as well as in his notion of "mystical terminology," in which "that conceptual medium appears in a flash" (*blitzartig in Erscheinung tritt*). Both "wit" and "mystical terminology" "understand themselves" only by abruptly and unpredictably taking leave of their senses, in all senses of the word "sense"—that is, by shedding the univocal meanings that are generally attributed to them, and instead "appearing in a flash" as singular signifying events that cannot be reduced or identified with any one self-identical meaning. Such appearance in a flash is what Benjamin later was to associate with cinema, for instance, or, in a different way, with photography—but also with Baudelaire's "Passante" in his poem dedicated to that fleeting figure. To "understand" such figures is not to immobilize them in a concept but to retrace their evanescent "meteoric"—or as I would say, their mediauric"—trajectories.

For Benjamin, however, it was not just images that flashed by, but also words. Words such as "medium," which he perhaps would have considered one of these "mystical terms" of which Schlegel wrote: one that would be all the more mystical for its not having ever appeared in Schlegel's writing. Rather, it was Benjamin who coined the term to designate the ambivalent and silent quintessence of Schlegel's thought. In so doing, he opens Schlegel to an afterlife.

For, as Benjamin writes, a certain "constancy of a medial connection, a medium reflective of concepts" must be presupposed if any event, unpredictable in its singularity, is ever to occur. Insight into the relationality and alterity of such singular events is what transforms reflection into "critique" in the Benjaminian, not Schlegelian sense. For Schlegel critique remains a function of the reflection-medium and hence ultimately of the Self; for Benjamin the mediality of critique carries it beyond the restricted economy of the self. One form this takes is the process through which "a medially constant transition (*Überführung*) of the work from one language into another" take place, namely, in and as "the infinitely enigmatic" process of "translation." Since this is a problem that Benjamin will address far more fully in a later essay, "The Task of the Translator," I will not pursue it here, except to note that it addresses what might be considered the main problem posed by the notion of medium in general, and that of medium of reflection in particular: namely, the relation of singular works or events to the ongoing process of transformative linking connecting and disconnecting in which Benjamin sees the essential dynamic of the medium.

It is in the second section of his thesis that Benjamin addresses a central aspect of this problem, namely, in his discussion of the distinctive status of the "work"—the work of art, and in particular, the work of poetry—as a moment in the process of the medium of reflection. This could be of considerable interest to contemporary discussions of media, and in particular to those concerned with media "aesthetics." For the notion of "aesthetics," in the modern sense of the word criticized by Kant, tends to be inextricably linked to that of the individual "work," whereas the notion of medium questions the traditional notion of work. For instance, in the broadcast media (radio, television) as well as on the Internet, one rarely speaks of "works," but of "programs": in French, *emissions*; in German, *Sendungen*. This shift in terminology is significant: a media "event" is defined by a dynamic relation not to a genre but to the medium as a process. The traditional work of art, by contrast, is defined as the instantiation of a more general, generic and generative "genre": tragedy, comedy, lyric, novel, and so on. This relationship is no longer applicable to media events. I would interpret the significance of this shift in terminology by suggesting that the structure of such events involves an irreducible *singularity*, which, however, must not be confused with *individuality*. I take the word "individual" here in its etymological sense of being "in-divisible." The singular by contrast I take to be highly divisible and relational, in the sense that Lacan, in his seminar on "The Purloined Letter," finds in Poe's story: the singular is the "odd," that which doesn't *fit in*. The singular is the exceptional, the extraordinary. As such, however, it is part and parcel a *relational* concept, whereas the individual can be seen as a *substantial* one. Both singular and individual can be designated by the word "one," but in the case of the individual this word is compatible with the definite article, whereas in the case of the singular only the indefinite article is fully appropriate (in languages such as French and German but not in English, "one" and "an" are condensed, in *un* or *une* and *ein* or *eine*; English, by contrast, distinguishes between "one" and "an" or "a").

The phrase "media event" can be used to designate both individual and singular. As individual it is understood, and usually disparaged, as the fully predetermined product of a general machination. But a media event could also designate a happening that cannot be identically repeated, like an "installation" or a "happening," although this does not mean that it cannot be repeated at all. In a certain sense— Benjaminian or Derridean—it can only come to be through repetition, but it is a repetition that does not aim at producing fully identical copies, but rather acknowledges alteration as its greatest resource.

In regard to the early Romantics, Benjamin emphasizes that Schlegel's attitude toward the poetical work was ambivalent. On the one hand, he sought to free the work from its domination by genre: the work was to be understood as a moment of the medium of reflection, forming part of a universal poetry, the essence of which was prose. But this also meant that the work was incomplete and required fulfillment through criticism as the continuation of its reflective essence:

> Because each singular reflection in this medium can only be isolated and contingent, the unity of the work with respect to that of art can only be a relative one; the work remains burdened with a moment of contingency.

The singular is still understood by Schlegel as a property of the work, and hence as part of a self-fulfilling universal. For Schlegel it is the task of critical reflection, which is to say, of criticism *as* reflection, to extend and complete the singular work beyond the bounds of its contingent "aesthetic" existence:

> The more closed the reflection, the more stringent the form of the work is, the more variegatedly and intensely [*vielfacher und intensiver*] criticism can fulfill its task of driving the work out of itself [*aus sich heraustreibt*], dissolving the original reflection in a higher one and continuing thus.

As the word "drive"—in German, *treiben*—suggests, this process of transformation requires a certain violence to be done to the original work, which is altered in the process of transformation, driven beyond the boundaries of its initial and inherent form. A new singular event is thus produced, which in turn becomes the object of a new transformation and alteration. What, however, remains of the singular work or event in this process of medial transformation?

And it is here that Benjamin comes upon a category that has the potential to provide a powerful critical tool for the development of medial practices that can perhaps even contribute to the transformation of the new media as well as the old. It is what he calls "formal irony," which he emphatically distinguishes from all forms of subjective or authorial irony. Benjamin's literary example is, significantly, the comedies of the German Romantic writer Ludwig Tieck, but for those more familiar with English literature, an excellent instance could be found in Sterne's *Tristram Shandy* (which Benjamin does not mention). Formal irony is distinguished from criticism, insofar as the latter, according to Benjamin, "sacrifices the work entirely for the sake of the one general connection" (*des einen Zusammenhanges*). Formal irony, by contrast, preserves the work while redefining its significance. The latter no longer consists exclusively or primarily in its mimetic, thematic representational content, understood as a self-contained referent, as what in Saussurean language would be called a "signified," but rather as itself *significant* of something that does not appear within it directly. Benjamin, following the Romantics, describes such irony as "the storm that raises [*aufhebt*] the curtain," exposing "the transcendental order of art," an order that reaches beyond the "borders of the visible work." In a footnote he offers a precious indication as to just what such "transcendence" could mean in artistic practice. It is no accident that his example is taken from theater, the sole traditional aesthetic medium that has to do not so much with works, but with "plays" (or in French, *pièces*, and in German, *Stücke*). In a footnote Benjamin describes the actual process by which formal irony functions in Tieck's comedies and perhaps, he adds, in "all literary comedies" as well: "The spectators, the author, the theater personnel" all "take part in the play" (*spielen . . . mit*). The generic framework of traditional aesthetic *forms*, based on *genre*, is thus relativized and opened to their conditions of possibility, which also function as enabling limits: audience, author, theater personnel. These factors, defining the theatrical scene, can themselves never be exhaustively predetermined or identified: they are singular in the sense of being always different, not just from others but also from themselves, just as the performance of one evening can never be fully identical to that of another.

That Benjamin uses the German word *aufhebt* here in its literal sense to describe the "raising" or "lifting" of the "curtain" of the work effected by formal irony is significant in at least two senses. First, it recalls the master term of the Hegelian dialectic, that which names the negative production of synthesis. Second, however, the word also underscores what is distinctively *non-Hegelian* in Benjamin's use of it. For the singular work is simultaneously both destroyed and preserved by formal irony, but it is never thereby elevated or absorbed into a more comprehensive, totalizing process. In related, theological terms, one can say that the work survives—Benjamin writes of its *Überleben*—but is never resurrected. Formal irony is no simple remake of the original. Schlegel himself, whom Benjamin cites, compares it to an "infinite series of propositions, an irrational number . . . incommensurable." And although Schlegel also designates this series as a "progressive" movement, Benjamin for his part emphasizes that this notion of formal irony is incompatible with the modern idea of "progress" as a goal-directed becoming. Rather, what it presupposes is more like a "chaos," which thereby emerges as the "sensual image of the absolute medium." To be sure, such "chaos" is understood by Schlegel as the anticipation and condition of the emergence of a "harmonious world," which remains, however, a function of the ostensibly chaotic transformations that constitute the "absolute medium."

For Benjamin, the attempt to articulate the medial interaction of chaos and harmony, singularity and connectivity, defines the limits of the Romantic concept of art criticism. Once again it is the figure and language of Hölderlin that is invoked, toward the end of the dissertation as in its beginning, to frame Benjamin's discussion, but only by delimiting it, which is to say, by allowing it to point beyond itself to a realm that remains largely unthematized and unexamined in Romantic writing. For while the Romantics could only gesture toward this realm, Hölderlin "surveyed and dominated" it. What characterizes this realm can be approached in terms of a different notion of "medium." Whereas for Schlegel, who, we must remember, does not use the word, "absolute reflection"—for Benjamin, the "medium" of "reflection"—is ultimately understood as homogeneous, grounded in a notion of the unitary Self, returning to itself through, above, and beyond its reflective movement. For Hölderlin, by contrast, singularity can never be absorbed into a Self but is irrevocably dispersed in a series that is ultimately heterogeneous. Instead of *reflection*, therefore, we encounter *repetition*, instead of progression, *procedure* (*Verfahrungsart*), instead of prophecy, pedagogy, instead of elation, sobriety or discretion (*Nüchternheit*). Benjamin quotes the following passage from Hölderlin to indicate the alternative his writing embodies, but, as always with his references to this prophet-poet, without commenting on or interpreting him in any detail.[7]

> In order to acquire a stable [*bürgerliche*] existence for the poets, including ours, it will be good if, subtracting the difference between times and structures, they return to the *mechané* of the ancients. . . . Modern poetry is

particularly lacking in schooling and craft [*an der Schule und am Handwerks-mässigen*], teaching and learning its way of proceeding, which once learned, can be reliably repeated and executed. Among humans *one has above all to pay attention to each thing,* above all to see how it is something, i.e., recognizable in its means [*moyen*] in which it appears, so that the way it is conditioned can be determined and taught. . . . To this pertains first of all [*einmal*] precisely that lawful calculus [*gesetzlicher Kalkül*].[8]

In Hölderlin's insistence on the need "to pay attention to each thing," repetition replaces reflection, but does not abolish it. Repetition, in the sense of transformative recurrence, is what arises when reflection is no longer governed by the homogeneity and unity of a Self, which means by a self-consciousness. Instead Hölderlin describes a calculation that seeks to count on the incalculable. From the point of view of the latter such a situation looks like "chaos," and it is this point of view that up until today dominates what we call "the media," new no less than old. This domination derives both from the long history of the West, which especially in the Christian epoch, but also before, tends to define identity in terms of a Self that stays the Same—that is, that can withstand and transcend time as medium of change and of alteration. And in the capitalist epoch that, according to Benjamin in another essay of this period, both succeeds and prolongs this Christian tradition,[9] the notion of a homogeneous and time-transcending Self continues to dominate the media, although never without contradiction. This can be seen perhaps most clearly in the unwritten rule that excludes, as much as possible, the conditions of representation from the representations themselves. In broadcast television, this is perhaps most conspicuous in what Benjamin later called the aura—and in particular, with the aura that constitutes what he called the "star" and the "dictator"; this aura, with all of its contradictions, finds its quintessential broadcast-media manifestation in the figure of the "anchor," who "anchors" the "news" by "presenting" it—that is, by making it (seem) present: to itself and therefore to its audience. In presenting the "news" as the result of relatively isolated, ostensibly independent *individuals,* all of whom announce their names, whether as anchor or as reporter, reporting to and for the "network." The images associated with the latter are thus presented as a function of single, self-identical speakers, or of single, but rarely singular, normed voices endowing those images with a meaning that is ostensibly self-evident. Such self-evidence proceeds by excluding what Schlegel, and later Marx, demanded *not* be excluded: all those involved in the production of the event (the English word "producers" being significantly today reserved for those who put together the financing of a program, show, or film). But in a tradition in which "reality" is regarded as only that which can fit meaningfully within a frame and within the compass of a short, archaeo-teleological narrative, whatever is impersonal, whatever is relational, whatever is differential, such as the financial, organizational, technical, sometimes directly political *conditions of production,* is systematically separated from the product itself and excluded from "view."

Last, it is the hypostasis of the present itself—of the present as the self, and of the self as ever-present—that is thereby maintained and perpetuated: the notion that reality consists of self-contained, meaningful, "transparent," and "intelligible" moments that can be immediately apprehended, quickly named and definitively understood. Thus, it is the Romantic heritage of an Absolute Self that continues to dominate the broadcast media, and that seeks today to extend its hold over the very different medium that is the Internet. Such promotion of the Self as presence, and of the Present as meaningful image, constitutes the audiovisual infrastructure that strives to deprive or subordinate the transformative potential of the media in the name of short-term profit maximization and appropriation that increasingly defines what is called "globalization" as a function of finance capital. But that is getting us into another story, which, although profoundly related to the one I have just told, will have to be left for another day.

CHAPTER TWO

Analog in the Age of Digital Reproduction

Audiophilia, Semi-Aura, and the Cultural Memory of the Phonograph

ANTHONY CURTIS ADLER

I

In the study of media, the oppositions between the "mass," "popular," or "exoteric" and the "elite" or "esoteric" must be treated with a certain suspicion. If they cannot be avoided and must be granted at least a provisional or heuristic function—not least of all because the terrain of culture and media continues to structure itself through these categories—they also should not be taken at face value, for indeed the divisions that they articulate are infinitely porous and endlessly shifting. But for just this reason, if we allow these concepts any purchase at all, we must pay special attention to those moments where "esoteric" signifiers, signifiers that cannot, or at least not anymore, claim "general intelligibility," are deployed within an otherwise "popular" work. Sometimes this is done with didactic intent (thus, *Project Runway* initiates the audience into an at least somewhat technical language of fashion design), and sometimes, as in the case of certain rare and expensive things, it helps create an aura of luxury around objects that in order to be possessed by a few must be desired by the many. More frequently it is done for the sake of "mystification," as in the case of TV shows about doctors, lawyers, scientists, or denizens of Manhattan, where a more or less incomprehensible vocabulary and set of references is systematically deployed in order to create the illusion that one is peering into the work and play place of an intellectual or cultural elite. But the most telling and interesting case is where the recourse to such "esoteric signifiers" issues from a certain structural necessity: where a text from "popular culture" cannot work out its own logic but through recourse to that which withdraws from its own purported popularity and "mass intelligibility."

A striking instance of this last case is the appearance in popular entertainment of the record player, a technology, which, while functionally obsolete as a "mass medium," retains (in a sense that will become more clear as I continue) a marked esoteric signification. So, for example, in an episode of the recent television series *Ghost Whisperer*, the best friend of the heroine—a small-town antique-shop owner who speaks to the dead—purchases an old record player as a birthday present for her son. Alone in his room, he plays a record. A haunting voice comes from the speakers, the record starts skipping and the platter spins out of control, and finally, as the mother bursts into the room and tries to set the needle back on track, it discharges a near-deadly shock. *Ghost Whisperer*, with even more consequence than its sister psychic drama *Medium*, conceives of psychic powers as an ability (admittedly more passive than active) to call that which is absolutely absent, existing only as the complex of all that is left unresolved at death, back into presence: an ability that doubles, and is doubled by, the capacity of the medium of television itself to collapse dreams, hallucinations, and every sort of paranormal experience, along with a more quotidian reality, together into a single homogenous plane of simulacric seeing. And indeed what becomes present is not just the dead person, who appears almost in the flesh, but the last intentions and memories that were dissolved with his or her death, and which now, having been restored, allow for the solution of the mysteries surrounding it.

Given the ideological implications of this gesture—it is as if authorial intention were itself being resurrected in full force to serve as the law of the medium—it is all the more striking that phonography plays no less vital a role in an episode from *CSI Las Vegas* (the acronym stands for "crime scene investigation"), a TV program whose worldview is almost diametrically opposed, at least within the genre of "mystery" and "detective" shows, to *Ghost Whisperer*. Here the dead also speak, but only through the trace evidence produced in the moment of violent death: the question of intentions, and traditional detective work, is shunted aside in the name of the "hard" science of forensic analysis.

The episode in question is particularly noteworthy, not only because of its explicit invocations of the Ur-mystery *Oedipus Rex*, but also because it presents with unusual clarity the fundamental conceit of the "scientific" crime show exemplified by the *CSI* franchise: the perfect mastery of a fully materialistic and empirical rationality over the irrationality of passion, crime, and madness. An apparent rape-murder at an institution for the criminally insane—the conjunction of passion, crime, and insanity is revealing—is solved only when the lead investigator realizes that it would be possible to play a piece of pottery fashioned in an art class at the asylum as if it were a phonograph record, restoring the sounds of a conversation etched into the clay during its manufacture. Thus it is revealed that one of the nurses addressed a ward as "angel": the same sobriquet used in letters sent to him by his mother, with whom he had an incestuous relation since his father's death. This in turn leads to the discovery that this nurse and the mother are one and the same, and that she, and not one of inmates, committed the murder out of jealousy.[1]

If these two examples of the ghostly and uncanny appearance of the phonograph in television are especially suggestive, it is not least of all because they literalize one of the founding myths of phonography. The "ghostly" qualities of the phonograph are, indeed, well known: its earliest promoters promised that it would allow people to hear again and again the voices of loved ones long after they had died. The dead could even speak at their own wakes.[2] But this does not yet exhaust the significance of the specific appearance of phonography. While the power of making the absent present is perhaps strongly associated with sound-reproduction, promising as it does the reproduction of voice in its living presence as pure interiority, nevertheless this phonographic tendency motivates all mass media, and not least of all television, while at the same time the phonograph itself has been largely replaced by other analog and digital sound-reproducing technologies. What is striking in these episodes, this is to say, is that this general tendency is thematized through recourse to the literal phonograph: a media that for the most part has already fallen into obsolescence. More than two decades after being pronounced dead with the advent of digital reproductive media, it is the record player itself that still seems to haunt the present, refusing to let its voice fade away. It is as if the ghostly properties of the reproductive media in general could only present themselves through the specific "haunting" of the newer media by the old.

It is tempting to ascribe the persistence of the phonograph, and especially of the phonograph as icon, to a nostalgia always at work in visual and sonic culture.[3] Yet the record player is not just one archaic object among many, but itself involves a system of memorialization and memory retrieval that is, in many ways, of great significance for the experience of memory in the late nineteenth and twentieth centuries. The nostalgia for the phonograph is not so much the desire to bring back, and bring back to life, lost experiences, but rather to hold on to a means of recovering memories that is itself threatened with obsolescence. The record player not only belongs to a past that contains most of the founding myths of popular music, but it also promises the resurrection of collections of music, and associated memories, that most people, with the advent of the CD, had put away in storage. Indeed, with the advent of phonographic technologies, the system of cultural memory became dependent in an unprecedented way on the specific technologies that allow access to the transcription of an event: the very evolution of the technologies that promise the preservation of the past obstructs access to whole strata of past recorded experience, which in turn assume a most strange half- and afterlife within a system that seemed to promise the total recall of whatever of the past could be captured as a recording.

Hence the shock of the phonograph, made literal in *Ghost Whisperer*. With the emergence both of digital technologies of reproduction and of a global system of electronic content transfer, phonographic technology seems to have fulfilled the wildest promises of its beginnings. That more or less every recorded sound and image content is now available more or less on demand and instantaneously is perhaps the least of it. With the Internet a realm of concrete collective experience has opened up which, at least on the surface, transcends the limits of space, time, and human finitude. But the persistence of the analog phonograph, in a world in which phonographic technologies seem to have fulfilled their *telos* in the digital, is the persistence, above all, of a complication to a system of memory that seems to have resolved into a purely instantaneous and omnipresent availability. The afterlife of the phonograph, in other words, involves a certain kind of depth to memory. In a world in which, it would seem, memory images and sounds are available "on tap," the phonograph works as a capacitor: it stores and releases, unexpectedly, and to a shocking effect. And indeed it is an aleatory capacitor, since what is stored is sometimes itself something accidental, like the trace evidence from a crime scene, created outside of a system of fulfilled intentions and rational control.

II

The persistence of the phonograph goes hand in hand with the development of an esoteric audiophile culture that for the most part continues
to maintain the superiority of the LP to at least the more popular digital
recording formats, and in some cases the intrinsic superiority of analog
over digital.[4]

What is interesting about the claims to vinyl's superiority, whatever
their possible validity, is that they involve a conception of what the
experience of recorded music is, and indeed of the very nature of the
media of musical reproduction, that differs radically from those of what
we might call the mainstream music-consuming public. The polemical
exchanges between the various sides quickly reveal disagreements about
the nature of judgment and aesthetics and indeed the criterion of truth
that are anything but trite, and it often appears that there can be no real
agreement regarding what constitutes the basis of judgment or the court
of appeal.[5] A simple example is the concept of signal-to-noise ratio, a
crucial measurement of acoustic fidelity. While the technical assessments of signal-to-noise ratio seem to favor the CD player, the vinyl
enthusiast would argue that, in fact, the "objective" measurement is not
the best basis of judgment, and that not all noise is the same, but that
the subjective act of listening must also be taken into account. LP noise
is more regular, more predictable, and hence either can be "tuned out"
more easily or is itself experienced not as noise but as warmth of
sound.[6] There are few places in popular culture, indeed, where the crises
of postmodernism show themselves so clearly. For the true audiophile,
the true lover of the "absolute sound," no objective criterion of technological evaluation can ever refute a certain kind of radically subjective
experience of listening that is almost mystical in its resistance to communication. Just as the mystic invents a new language to speak of the
unspeakable, the audiophile creates a new vocabulary to capture the
most mercurial and intangible aspects of acoustic experience.[7]

III

It is not just a question of the criterion of fidelity, whether subjective
experience or objective measures, but of the nature of fidelity itself, and,
by extension, of reproduction. Analog reproduction appears superior to
digital reproduction not simply because of demonstrable or even inde-
monstrable technical criterion, but because the reproduction of sound

comes to be understood as a specifically analog, rather than digital, process. What is ultimately at stake is a clash between very different conceptions of the nature of sonic reproduction, of "writing sounds," and even, ultimately, of consumer technology itself. The phonograph's persistence suggests a specifically analog, rather than digital, conception of sound recording or sound writing.

There is a tendency, even in quite subtle analyses of phonographic media, to conceive of "reproduction" principally in terms of a digital model. So, for example, Mark Katz, in his admirable study of the effect of technology on music, writes: "No longer temporally rooted, recorded music can be heard after it was originally performed and repeated more or less indefinitely."[8] This assertion is not wrong, and yet it conceals the basic difference between the analog and the digital. Whereas analog reproduction involves the transduction of a wave from one form of physical embodiment to another, digital reproduction involves the translation of a physical event into a code of information that, even if it must be contained and transmitted in some sort of material medium (such as an optical disk or the memory chip of a computer), is inherently immaterial. Every digital event, such as a musical recording or a compact disk, could be expressed as a finite, if extremely large, integer. While the dependence of digital codes on material carriers does involve the possibility of error, nevertheless the digital code itself transcends its material embodiments to the same degree as any mathematical object. The "digitalization" is this very abstraction. With analog reproduction, such a moment of "abstraction" never takes place; there is merely movement from one physical form to another, and indeed with every physical event of "reading" the inscription, the possibility of some transformation and (to use a loaded term) distortion. In the case of analog reproduction, the "more or less," in other words, takes on an entirely different meaning. Nor can we speak of a complete temporal uprooting. The temporal dimension comes to reside in the fallibility of the material itself: the symbol of which is, above all, the grooves of the LP slowly etched away by the stylus—as if the moment of inscription could never be contained just in the original recording of the sonic event, but also leaves its traces on the operation of playback.

IV

The digital is in a sense but another expression for the general form of a certain conception of writing: of writing as production of an immaterial code inherently capable of an infinite reproduction. Thus, what the phonograph's persistence suggests is a constitutively different form of writing, which is neither reducible to sound or voice (*phonē*, in other words), nor structurally opposed, but rather its haunting replication.

Jonathan Sterne, in the *Audible Past*, a study of the cultural origins of sound reproduction, suggests that his ambition, somewhat following Derrida, is to challenge the "audiovisual litany"—a list of seemingly naturalistic assumptions about the difference between hearing and vision—which is in fact rooted in a "two-thousand-year-old Christian theology of listening." By idealizing "hearing (and, by extension speech) as manifesting a kind of pure interiority," it merely restates "the long-standing spirit/letter distinction in Christian spiritualism," whose own roots can be found not only in the Gospel of John and Saint Augustine, but ultimately in the discussion of speech and writing in Plato's *Phaedrus*. Sterne goes on to discover in the earliest proponents of technologies of sound writing, such as Scott, the desire to develop a form of "natural writing," reflecting the true nature of sound, "bearing an indexical relation to speech, rather than the abstract and arbitrary relation to speech" of typography. While I am basically sympathetic with this ambition, and while certainly (as Sterne admirably demonstrates) there is much in the early history of the phonograph that suggests a rampant phonocentrism, there is also, I would argue, a different aspect of phonography, which to some extent obscures the very opposition of speech/sound/noise and writing. The "analog" moment, as it were, involves neither the preservation of sound, in its transience, through writing, nor the institution of a "perfect" writing, capable of representing the natural language of speech, but instead the replication and rewriting of a sonic event which is always already writing, but a writing which is inherently and irreducibly materially embodied. The essence of analog sound-writing, in this regard, is the inherence of noise and decay in every moment of reproduction: Analog reproduction neither negates the transience of sound, nor preserves it ad infinitum, but instead draws it out, tarries with it. It is, in other words, a certain way of experiencing finitude. This is not to say that analog is not also "theological," but it involves a theological tendency—provisionally we might refer to it as Gnostic—which to some degree stands in a contentious relation to the Western, Augustinian, spiritual tradition.

The concepts that Walter Benjamin develops in his *Das Kunstwerk im Zeitalter seiner technischen Reproduzierbarkeit* (*The Work of Art in the Age of Mechanical Reproduction*) provide a useful point of reference. For Benjamin, technical reproduction "frees (*ablöst*) what is reproduced from the realm of tradition." This realm of tradition, the auratic properties of the artwork, involve an "authenticity" and "singularity" consisting in everything that can be "handed down," from its material endurance in time to the way in which it bears witness to the circumstances in which it was made. The work of art, through its reproductive multiplication, becomes an article of mass consumption that can be actualized under whatever circumstances the consumer wishes.[9]

Benjamin's model of reproduction is, again, fundamentally digital: mechanical reproduction involves an abstraction away from the material embodiment of the original and everything that is associated with this. Insofar as tradition itself, as the "handing down" of what is materially embodied, is the medium of auratic works of art, then mechanical reproduction translates the original into an essentially different medium; a translation that could amount to nothing less than the "Erschütterung der Tradition."

V

Nowadays, in a world of MP3 players, digital cameras and video recorders, DVRs, and portable DVD players, one must wonder all the more at the prescience of Benjamin's analysis, even if his revolutionary hopes for the mechanical reproductive media have been travestied in almost every way. Analog nevertheless seems to challenge Benjamin's understanding of mechanical reproduction: it neither preserves the aura of the original artwork, nor abstracts fully away from it, but instead the aura, or indeed the distortion—the *Verkrümmerung*—of the aura, tradition as the distortion of tradition, becomes the medium. Each instance of reproduction is a handing down, not of work itself in its singularity, but of the aura as recorded trace of the singularity of the event. The aura is handed down only by being submitted to further distortion, which, however, again inscribes the moment of handing down as a singular event. One could even say that the sonic event, the wave form itself, is itself nothing else than distortion. This aspect of analog is clearest in the case of the phonograph, where the deterioration of the medium is so palpable in the mode of reproduction. Moreover, though, the mass production of the vinyl records itself involves what might be called semi-auratic aspects, of the greatest concern for audiophile collectors: Since the masters that are used in the stamping process have a limited lifespan and wear out with their repeated use, the value of what is ostensibly the "same recording" can value dramatically according to the master used in the pressing and even whether the record was produced near the beginning or the end of the life-cycle of a given master. For an audiophile, these differences in manufacturing have palpable effects: The work, far from being infinitely reproduced, is itself degrading during the process of manufacture.

For Walter Benjamin, the question of mechanical reproduction ultimately concerns the nature of the sensual perception (*Sinneswahrnehmung*) of the human collective. Sensual perception, the way in which it organizes itself and the medium in which it takes place, is, for Benjamin, historically conditioned. I would ask, in turn, whether analog, in the sense that I have discussed, also corresponds to a historically emergent mode of sensual perception. To be sure, the more recent history of mechanical reproductive techniques already suggests certain "collective effects" of the analog medium. Most striking is the nostalgia for an antiquated reproductive medium: The culture of mass production, far from abstracting the work from its historical context, seems instead to preserve the sensory "feel" of superannuated technologies, or in other words, its particular mode of distortion, as the palpable sign of bygone ages. The past, in this way, becomes not so much the object of an insatiable yearning as an object of experience. We experience the past neither as a set of atomic contents that can be preserved as a collection, nor in the unrecoverable totality of a lost world, but as the *medium* of experience. This logic of nostalgia, moreover, is inseparable from the forms of popular music that emerged following the introduction of technologies of reproduction. That mercurial "sound," the qualities of timbre that are so inseparable from the experience of music, especially rock music, is of essence a controlled distortion. The musical content comes to coincide with the medium: both rock music, and its reproductive media, amount to the same thing—the distorting reproduction of controlled reproduction.

The tendency of popular listening culture, seen in the ascendance not only of digital media but also of low-resolution formats like the MP3, seems to be to deny this elegiac dimension of music in the age of mechanical reproduction. Digital, as it were, turns the analog, and all the "sounds" of the past, back into a pure content, subject to potentially infinite reproduction. But this tendency is countered by an esoteric analog audiophile listening culture that seems to take pleasure in precisely what the more "mainstream" listening culture denies. Whereas the digitalized public regards the musical past as an immaterial collection of digital files archived *ad perpetuum* and accessible on demand, for the vinyl enthusiasts this past is embodied in material objects dispersed throughout space and time and subject to an inevitable law of decay.

VI

This other-time and other-history that the phonograph exposes reaches not only back into the past, but also into the future: Not only does the production of record players continue even at the present, but the technology of record players also does not remain static; it continues to develop. Yet this innovation follows laws that are strikingly different from those governing the development of consumer electronics meant for mass consumption, and indeed, granting that the experience of the future is, to an ever greater degree, mediated by the experience of technological innovation, it would not be wrong to say that the future itself, no less than the past, has become bifurcated into two, necessarily coexistent, paths. Whereas consumer electronics tends to become smaller, concealing an ever greater range of functions within a deceptively simple exterior—a design philosophy exemplified, above all, by the iPod—esoteric audiophile products become larger and more extravagant in their design even as the range of functions is reduced to an absolute minimum.

Granting that sensual perception is a function not just of the human body and its organs but of the media that extend these senses in time and space and develop new possibilities of communication and memory and creativity, then it seems possible that this strand of esoteric consumerism is not just an irrelevant anachronism, but that it also helps define the historical emergent logic of perception of the digital age. Perhaps sensual perception has itself become divided between analog with its continuous semi-auratic elegies and abstracted digital media. Every cultural product, and all perceptual experience, would hover, ghostlike, between these two worlds.

VII

It is indeed curious that although the audiophile seems to strive to have his or her sound-reproducing systems come as close as possible to the subtlety and rich dimensionality of "natural," nonreproduced sonic events, nevertheless no natural sound, and even those of the concert hall, could ever provide fulfillment for this quest for the perfect sound. One might call this the paradox of reproduction: The perfect sound has to be reproduced, even though no reproduced sound can ever be perfect. This may be explained in terms of the specific content to which music-reproducing technologies give access—not the random sounds of every-day life, but controlled sonic events existing only in the form of record-ings. Indeed, as many have noted, even in the world of classical music, which (Glenn Gould notwithstanding) has generally resisted the idea that the musical work could itself be created in the recording studio, nevertheless reproductive technologies have had a strong effect on the development of playing techniques and the tastes and expectations of the listening public.[10] Perhaps more significant, however, is that such technologies not only give access to contents, but allow an active con-trol over the experience that is not possible with nonreproduced sound. The "perfect" sound must be the possible object of technologies of con-trol. This element of control is an element of both exoteric and esoteric listening cultures, and yet assumes radically different forms in each. The exoteric ideal is the manipulation of contents and the "contouring" of sound to personal taste. Musical contents should not only be *on tap* to satisfy the whims of the moment, but should be recombined into an idiosyncratic collage. The esoteric ideal, in contrast, is not so much about manipulation of sound and content—almost no high-end audio products have tone controls, let alone graphic equalizers—as the abso-lute control of the system of delivery. Every link in the chain of trans-duction that leads from the source to the listener's ear must be secured against possible interference. It is not only a question of isolating the sources of distortion inherent in the devices themselves, such as the vibrations caused by the motor of a turntable or the electrical interfer-ence of an amplifier's circuitry.[11] Taken to the extreme, this control extends beyond the reproducing technology itself. Not only must the listening room be shielded from outside noises, but the turntable must also be placed on a special suspension system isolating it from all vibra-tion, and the entire system must be plugged into a special power supply, purifying the current of the public power grid of irregularities.

This control, in the case of both exoteric and esoteric listening cul-ture, seems to involve transforming sound from a public to a private event. Yet the nature of privacy is, in each case, dramatically different. Whereas exoteric privacy revolves around an ideal of individual self-expression through choice, esoteric privacy involves an environmental control that extends even into the most seemingly public of commodities. This experience, indeed, extends beyond the sense of hearing. Esoteric audio technology, with its enormous see-through acrylic plinths and visible vacuum tubes, provides a visualization of the idealized neutrality of the medium. The purity of the medium, moreover, becomes palpable as a purity of rare or valuable materials—pure acrylic, gold, diamonds, graphite—that are united in the apparatus.

These two kinds of privacy suggest different, though related, logics of sensation. The exoteric listener rejoices in the freedom to manipulate the passive experience of affect, whereas the esoteric listener seeks to free from distortion what, in the end, consists only in distortion. The one treats affect abstractly as content that can be submitted to infinite repetitions and manipulations, whereas the other inhabits the interior of affect, trying to experience in its purity that which can only be purified through its destruction.

Perhaps what is ultimately at stake in these logics of listening and sensation is the structure of cultural memory, as it is itself historically constituted. It is tempting, following a familiar motif, to think of music as originally and essentially public in character. But we should rather say that musical experience, and sonic experience more generally, has a character that is both, in a tense and even paradoxical way, private and public; that indeed, like memory, it inhabits at once the private and public, and indeed both in an extreme way. Cultural memory is perhaps this changing, almost infinitely complicated, relation between public and private—the system of folds, to use a Deleuzian figure, through which the public and private are enfolded into each other, maintaining their difference while losing the specific polarities of "inside" and "outside." The tension between the digital and analog as different ways of "privatizing" sense experience thus suggests above all a confrontation of two interrelated ways of mediating between the public and the private, or indeed constituting the public and public in such mediation. What characterizes both, and thus determines the limit of system that they establish, is that the public dimension continues to exist only as a residue that somehow has to be processed away, and yet which cannot be eliminated. It is this public dimension, in other words, that continues to haunt.

It is curious to note a striking parallel between both the "esoteric" and "exoteric" regimes of listening and memory and the dialectics of subjectivity of Fichte's early *Wissenschaftslehre*. If exoteric listening culture suggests an "I" or self that masters the content given to it

through an ironic attitude, bringing raw material into ever newly created and quickly dissolved configurations, the esoteric involves an ever
expanding program of mastery of the "not-I" by reforming it in accordance with the will. The limit of both regimes, in this way, would consist in an original positing of an opposition between "I" and "not I,"
form and content, or, as one might also say, signal and noise. This link
is significant not least of all because Fichte's attempt to ground philosophy in the self-positing of the "I" presents perhaps the most powerful
and absolute philosophical expression of the notion of radical individuality that plays such a decisive role in the ideological configurations of
capitalism. In his contribution to this collection, "Medium, Reflexivity,
and the Economy of the Self," Samuel Weber suggests the need to resist
the tendency, so common in a field such as media studies, to forget our
philosophical and conceptual past. Following the insights of Benjamin's
somewhat neglected dissertation *Der Begriff der Kunstkritik in der deutschen Romantik*, Weber suggests that the writings of Friedrich Schlegel, Novalis, and Friedrich Hölderlin provide a point of departure for a
rigorous conceptualization of media. In this vein, I would suggest that
this constellation of thinkers, each of whom (like Schelling and Hegel)
starts out from a transformative critique of Fichte's radical subjectiv-
ism, provide powerful, and even necessary resources for reconceptualiz-
ing media as cultural memory, overcoming the Fichtean moment of
radical individuality that transects the networks of media in such a way
as to preserve the illusion of a stable relation, defined by the opposi-
tional pair inside-outside, between the private and the public. The analog and the digital, both of which capture the intersection and even
convolution of the material and formal, make it possible to think, in a
way that is at once more rigorous and more concrete, what early
Romanticism tried to make comprehensible through an often baffling
array of translations of the foundational opposition synthesis and the
analysis.[12] Yet this very concreteness and conceptual articulateness
allows for the deceptive appearance that the analog and digital, and
indeed a wide range of derivative moments, could be not only isolated
in singular media practices but also regarded as systematically self-
contained units. What is necessary, as it were, is a "romanticization"
(in the strict and precise sense) of media studies: The analog and digital,
in all their various and singular versions and instantiations, must be
brought into relation to one another in the thought, in Samuel Weber's
words, of medium as continual discontinuity. If the mass media, following an impulse that might be called ideological (or ontotheological),

always seeks a compartmentalizing into a system of opposed regimes that together uphold the self-presence of pure subjectivity as their anchor and archē, media studies must insist, at every turn, on the interruptions that take place at the threshold between regimes.

This is not only possible as theory, but above all as practice—as indeed in the wake of Romanticism the opposition between theory and practice itself collapses. A striking example is the digital poem "Another Emotion" by Jason Nelson, which Kiene Brillenburg Wurth discusses in her introduction to this volume. While the text, presented through seven colored squares in a mobile horizontal arrangement, reads as a dense manifesto for a digital perspective in which everything seemingly real, sensuous, and intuitive (from the "I" to mathematics, colors, style, and even the natural world) is dissolved into a system of infinite patterns, the text, and with it the absolute digitization that it seems to propose, is interrupted at several levels by an analog residue. Not only are the words of the text divided into colored squares whose very insistence and *stylistic* coherence seems to belie the reduction of color and style into pattern, but the flickering, ever changing vertical lines, reminiscent of the crackled texture of film, cut across the screen, imposing a temporal dimension by allowing traces of an obsolete, analog medium (present only as defect and accident) to intrude onto the very site that would seem to promise, in the name of digital poetry, the perfectly accomplished self-rendering of the digital. Meanwhile, the music playing the background, a fragment that repeats endlessly without resolving, evokes at once a somewhat canned cinematic nostalgia and a characteristic mood of Bach. It is as if the *other emotion* signaled by the name of Nelson's poem stood in a certain analogy to the melancholy that Walter Benjamin, in his *Habilitationsschrift*, attributed to the German Baroque: a sadness that attends the thought of the world dissolved into mere patterns and surfaces, a feeling that seems to enter in as if through the cracks of a system that has excluded feelings in their stubborn singularity. But this is also only an analogy, written at the fissure where the digital breaks down and the analog breaks through. Perhaps the moods and emotions of the new media are also fully new, and truly *other*. Or perhaps, to use a Schlegelian motif, they are potentialized—emotions to the second or third or forth power: at the very least not just a sadness for loss, but for the loss of loss, and so on, ad infinitum.

CHAPTER THREE

What If Foucault Had Had a Blog?

JOANNA ZYLINSKA

This chapter focuses on a particular domain of contemporary media culture that blurs the boundary between the literary and the literal: blogging. I want to explore to what extent practices facilitated by blogging can be interpreted in terms of bioethics. Bioethics for me is not limited to the study of ethical issues arising from the biological and medical sciences, and involving issues of patient care. Rather, it becomes a broadly conceptualized "ethics of life," which requires judgment on what we understand by "life" in its different forms, on what we mean by "health," and on what "our" position as those who deem themselves "human" is in this bioethics. It can be argued that blogs aim at creating an experience of "total life" by building complex systems of connections between online and offline spaces, personae, and narratives. Interestingly, Foucault associates the practice of self-writing precisely with an ethos of life when he claims that "writing transforms the thing seen or heard into tissue and blood." From this perspective, diaries and blogs are not just commentaries *on* someone's life but materializations *of* it, as I will argue in this chapter.

THE ETHICS OF THE SELF

Before I get to the question included in my title—"What If Foucault Had Had a Blog?"—I would like us to take a closer look at Foucault's conceptualization of ethics, although I have to warn the reader that I will eventually part ways with Foucault in my ethical wanderings.

The subject of ethics does not feature explicitly in any of Foucault's major works. It is only in short articles and interviews, gathered in the volume *Ethics: Subjectivity and Truth* (1997) and then in the series of lectures given at the Collège de France in 1982 and published as *The Hermeneutics of the Subject* (2005) that Foucault addresses the issue of power and resistance through the ethical processes of self-fashioning and self-creation. Foucault understands ethics in terms of *ethos*, which stands for practice, embodiment, and a style of life. It is a practice of freedom derived from the game of truth.[1] Its origins lie in the twin imperatives of ancient philosophy: "know thyself" and "care for thyself," which in Christian times undergo a transformation into the principle of asceticism. The care of the self has a critical function in this relationship between self-knowledge and attention to the self, since it not only enables one to unlearn bad habits and cast away false opinions but can also play a curative role. Ethics thus becomes a vocation focused on developing a free relationship of the self to itself, and on arriving at a "subject of desire" responsible for creating new forms of pleasure. The ethics of the care of the self, especially in its Greek incarnation, is also a communal task, where subject-formation is to benefit others.

While in ancient Greece the care of the self was the consequence of a statutory situation of power exercised by individual others,[2] Foucault explains that in Roman times, particularly in Epicurean and Stoic philosophy, it is repositioned as a permanent task to be taken up by every individual throughout his life—although there of course remain both political and individual limitations to this universalism. Significantly, ethics arising from the "care of the self" principle does not rest on any prior rules of conduct, but rather on the sense of obligation and duty that imposes itself, in a direct and often uncomfortable way, on us. Foucault writes: "The care of oneself is a sort of thorn which must be struck in men's flesh, driven into their existence, and which is a principle of restlessness and movement, of continuous concern throughout life."[3] He also points out that in Hellenistic and Greco-Roman culture, the principle of taking care of oneself was a very powerful word, which entailed constant working on oneself, and was thus very different from "the Californian cult of the self," where you are supposed to discover your true self.[4] The notion of truth is vital for Foucault, but he speaks about "particular truth" to be created by each self as a relationship to what is not in it, not a preexistent general truth already in place, waiting to be discovered.

This idea of a particular truth to be arrived at and a particular way of life to be created foregrounds one of the most significant aspects of the ethics of the self: the absence from it of any prior codification or instructions on how to live. It is the ethical activity itself, "vigilant, continuous, applied, [and] regular,"[5] that is important, rather than the fulfillment of any particular commandments. The "transformation of one's self by one's own knowledge" and the elaboration of new, beautiful ways of life are of primary importance in this ethical project.[6] Foucault's ethics thus has a strong aesthetic dimension. In his discussion of nonnormative sexualities, he goes so far as to compare an imperative "to create a gay life. To become"[7] with the creation of works of art. This process does not occur in vacuum; we cannot just become who we want to be as our very self-knowledge about our wishes and the direction of our transformation need to remain subject to a critical scrutiny. We are also bound by the power of institutions and social relations, and by their disciplinary and constraining effects. But it is the *resistance* element of power relations, and the possibility of introducing change into them by rearranging the multiplicity of forces passing through the body. Power for Foucault is a strategic rather than just an oppressive relation; thus, power can also be productive, creating the possibility of agency for the subject on the way to its desire and truth.

In this project the self is established as a subject through "techniques of the self" (also translated into English as "technologies of the self"), "which permit individuals to effect by their own means, or with the help of others, a certain number of operations on their bodies and souls, thoughts, conduct, and way of being, so as to transform themselves in order to attain a certain state of happiness, purity, wisdom, perfection, or immortality."[8] Among these technologies Foucault lists dream interpretation, "taking notes on oneself to be reread, writing treatises and letters to friends to help them, and keeping notebooks in order to reactivate for oneself the truths one needed."[9] It is his focus on letter writing and diary keeping that is particularly relevant for my attempt to assess to what extent social networking portals such as LiveJournal, MySpace, and Flickr as well as blogs could be read as facilitating the very care of the self Foucault analyzes in Greco-Roman culture, and perhaps even enacting a new ethical way of being in the world.

Foucault is keen to emphasize the long-term scope of the care-of-the-self project.[10] He argues that "the general Greek problem was not the *tekhnē* of the self, it was the *tekhnē* of life, the *tekhnē tou biou*, how to live."[11] Getting to the heart of his own biological and medical rhetoric, Foucault goes so far as to insist that "permanent medical care is one of the central features of the care of the self. One must become the doctor of oneself."[12] I would like to suggest that his ethics of the self can be interpreted as a different form of *bio*ethics. By bioethics I mean a performative ethics of life that both enacts new practices of living and looks after the life of its agents who are always on the way to their selfhood/health. The ethics of the self must not be understood as an attempt on Foucault's part to promote a selfish, or worse, delusional, individualism under the guise of his "how to live" techniques. The Stoic-inspired withdrawal from the affairs of the world is to be interpreted instead as a better, more prudent preparation for being in the world, and for relating to people, things, and events. As well as becoming an art of (whole) life, the care-of-the-self principle makes life better: It is said to have a curative and therapeutic function and thus, as indicated earlier, remains in "kinship with medicine."[13] While in Plato the art of the body is clearly distinguished from the art of the soul, in the Epicureans and Stoics "the body reemerges very clearly as an object of concern so that caring for the self involves taking care of both one's soul and one's body."[14]

This "Foucauldian bioethics" presents a very different model of bioethics from the dominant one, in which the self is most often positioned as an object of medical procedures and political interventions. It provides us with a new way of thinking about what it means to live an ethical life, a healthy life, and how to care about one's life, without relying on predefined values or legal frameworks.

LIFE ON THE WEB

Blogs and social networking portals such as LiveJournal and MySpace, where millions of users are drawing on a daily basis on what Foucault described as technologies of the self, are an important domain in contemporary media culture. The aptly titled LiveJournal (LJ) was once one of the most popular sites, where users keep their blogs, predating such popular networking websites as MySpace (which in April 2007 had 185 million accounts) and Flickr (a photo sharing site). The ambition and scope of these online portals should not be underestimated; they aim at creating the experience of "total life" by building intricate systems of connections between online and offline spaces, personae, and narratives, all of which Facebook, which has supplanted most of them, has particularly succeeded in doing. According to Adam Reed, "The updating quality of weblogs is what for [bloggers] makes this text feel 'alive.'"[15]

It seems that one way of managing the novelty and rapidity of development of these social networking sites, is commenting on them in terms of old, already known technologies. Blogs then are seen, on the one hand, as a megaphone for already-existing but silenced or little-heard voices; they amplify thoughts and passions already in place and help build communities of like-minded people, be it cat-lovers or anti-globalists. They are also seen as a way of "empowering the little guy."[16] On the other hand, blogs and social networking function as "a full consensus-creating machine," where the work of the digital proletariat can be exploited. The argument goes that if we do not get on MySpace soon, we will all become obsolete, unnecessary, and disposable.

This narrative of the exploitation of the individual by the (techno)-system has been accompanied by another offshoot of the Marxist and, more broadly, modernist critique of popular culture: that concerning the alleged banality of its practices and the narcissism of its participants. As Kris R. Cohen explains, "Bloggers are said to be narcissists because they persist in publicizing their boring lives." Cohen identifies an interesting contradiction in the public perception of bloggers: They are seen as occupying a position that is simultaneously too public (that is, they are too easily noticed by peevish critics, or too easily thought of as pretentious by other bloggers) and not public enough (with the blogger just speaking to himself or herself, or worrying about losing the audience when their hit count drops). "The absence of a 'real' audience leaves the blogger seeming to stare at herself while thinking she is staring at others—pathetically deluded like Narcissus."[17]

How can we get out of this dialectical impasse in thinking about blogging and social networking online? How, in other words, can we think about these new media practices without immediately valorizing them as good or bad, productive or useless, resistant or oppressive? To do this, I want to develop what might initially seem like a negative thread that I have picked up from Cohen, and entertain for a moment the idea that blogging and "hanging out" on MySpace are perhaps indeed intrinsically linked with narcissism. Indeed, I do see these practices as a reinforcement of the ego-ideal users construct of and for themselves, and then painstakingly attempt to achieve. Even the recognition of personal failures—from "Why did he dump me?" to "Why did my paper get rejected by an academic journal?"—seems to provide the way of reinforcing the ego on its way to self-fulfillment and closure. For example, many academic and professional blogs function as veritable "brag-spaces," in which one just lists one's achievements—the notable invitations one has received, the publications one has had accepted this year. And yet there is a generous side to both academic and nonacademic blogging, where blogs and other social sites function as spaces through which one "gives" and "shares" interesting notices or funny comments with others The del.icio.us website—originally independent but then acquired by Yahoo!—is one example of such "sharing sites" on which users can store, exchange, and discover one another's web bookmarks.[18] Both types of activities—the crafting of the self according to the ego ideal and the sharing of the (data) gifts one has amassed—are narcissistic. The former—as a manifestation of one's exaggerated investment in one's image (as a lover, music fan, or professional), the latter—as an attempt to gather the whole world in one's image and then give it to others. Blogging can thus perhaps be jokingly described as a delirious activity in which the self attempts to be with others while also recoiling from the wounds that the other (blogger) inflicts on me.

THE MEDIA CULTURE OF NARCISSISM

You may now perhaps wonder whether I have not just come up with another dismissive account of blogging and social networking which inscribes itself in the negative strand of narratives about new media in general and blogging in particular. It is only if we take narcissism as a negative phenomenon, a cultural or personal pathology that has to be overcome for social relations to be established. However, I want to suggest that narcissism is inevitable, or even necessary for sociality. And, indeed, to use Derrida's words, that "There is not narcissism and non-narcissism; there are narcissisms that are more or less comprehensive, generous, open, extended."[19] Derrida goes on to argue that what is referred to as non-narcissism is only a more welcoming, hospitable narcissism, one that is much more open to the experience of the other as other. He explains:

> I believe that without a movement of narcissistic reappropriation, the relation to the other would be absolutely destroyed, it would be destroyed in advance. The relation to the other—even if it remains asymmetrical, open,

without possible reappropriation—must trace a movement of reappropriation in the image of oneself for love to be possible, for example.[20]

It is in this sense that an act of reaching to the other (through an online posting, a link to someone else's site, or a fantasy of, and desire for, multiple readers) is narcissistic, but also that narcissism is revealed as necessary to establishing this relationship.

Drawing on Derrida's playful account of the ambivalences of our psychic economy, let me thus suggest that this desire for (the death of) the other manifested by bloggers and other online social networkers is actually a condition—even if not a guarantee—of an ethical way of being with others. If we define ethics after Levinas and Derrida as openness to the infinite alterity of the other (leaving aside for a moment the Foucauldian thread developed so far in this chapter),[21] narcissism is revealed as an inextricable part of ethics. There can therefore perhaps be "good" and "bad" narcissism, where good and bad do not stand here for moral categories sanctioned by predefined philosophical or religious positions but rather for conditions of our subjectivity, our psychic health. The blogger's delirium, manifesting itself in the constant checking of the site's counter, in comparing herself with other bloggers or in instantiating flame wars in comment boxes, can be read as an attempt to construct a self. This is a much more serious and difficult project than one focused on merely expressing oneself or even on performing one's identity, whereby one either attempts to convey to oneself and others what one is "truly" like, or draws on the set of available props and identitarian positions (a white middle-class boy, a suburbanite housewife from Dallas, a dog) to enact a self or play a role. The narcissist's "delirium" is rather like the Nietzschean rapture, a positive condition of the ethos of becoming that we can also find in the work of Deleuze and Foucault.

What is so interesting and promising about Nietzsche's state of rapture is precisely its reaching to the outside—to what or whom it desires—which "draws the subject out of itself."[22] This "attraction of the outside" can also be located at the heart of the Foucauldian ethos, a suggestion that offers a possibility of rapprochement between Foucault and Levinas. Foucault himself is less concerned with the ontological conditions of this outside (which ultimately imposes a limitation on his ethics) than with the self's breaking out of the congealed, fixed forms of being in an attempt to imagine and create some new ways of life.[23] But this drive toward an outside already establishes a relation to what is not in the self (even if Foucault's own concern will remain with the self's process of becoming rather than with the forms of alterity that make the emergence of this self possible). This rapture or delirium in which the self cannot be contained within its own boundaries can thus perhaps be interpreted as the blogger's enactment of what I term "good narcissism," a reaching toward the other (blogger, reader, hacker), the material effects of whose online presence are constantly calling the blogging self into being. This is also a way of countering what Craig Saper describes as *b-logocentrism*, "a neologism in which the extra b stands for *banal narcissism*, suggest[ing] how blogs can intensify the appearance of a self-present speaker instead [of] a de-centered subject in hypertextual webs."[24]

Returning to the dialectical new media narratives sketched out earlier through which blogging and social networking are usually analyzed (good/bad, resistant/oppressive), I suggest that to read these practices in terms of the Foucauldian ethics of becoming is not to negate the possibility of interpreting them as political practices, in which citizenship is recognized at the micro-level and in which "little guys" are given the voice. But neither is it to subsume these practices under the recognizable framework of democracy, political participation, or even friendship, because doing so would mean reducing the ethical possibility of both the self and the technology with which it remains in a dynamic relationship. Nor is it to deny that banality, boredom, and self-obsession constitute part of the experience of blogging or hanging out on MySpace. It is precisely in this tension between many users' sense that these portals are merely mirroring the banality of their own and others' lives, and the possibility that they may contribute to the reworking of life forces and establish a new relation to one's life (online and off) that the ethical potential of Live Web lies. Interestingly, Foucault associates the practice of self-writing precisely with an ethos of life, as the keeping of individual notebooks and memory books focused on the recollection of the past, or capturing the already-said, or what one has managed to hear or read, is for him "a matter of constituting a *logos bioēthikos* for oneself . . . an ethics quite explicitly oriented by concern for the self toward objectives defined as: withdrawing into oneself, getting in touch with oneself, relying on oneself, benefiting from and enjoying oneself."[25] The phrase *logos bioēthikos* provides a key for my rereading of bioethics as a practice of good life, always on the way to becoming-a-good-life. But Foucault has in mind something much more material and direct than just a story *about* one's life and how it should be lived: this practice of self-writing is said to produce "a body." Drawing on Seneca, Foucault claims that "writing transforms the thing seen or heard into tissue and blood." From this perspective, diaries, blogs and online profiles are not just commentaries *on* someone's life, already lived to this point but also somehow more "real" outside its narrative, but rather materializations *of* it. Digital writing and linking is therefore not only a form of *cultural* production but also of *corporeal* one; it literally produces the body by temporarily stabilizing it as a node in the network of forces and relations: between multiple serves and computers, flows of data, users' eyes, fingers and sensations, particles of electricity, and so on.

There is of course no guarantee that such "delicate ethical work" will be undertaken, or that the work on the self—be it in the form of blog postings, MySpace links or Flickr community activities—will be ethical rather than banal or solipsistic. Even though the care of the self becomes coextensive with life (which means that, say, john23's blog is always already john23's life, not just an account of, or a secondary reflection *on*, his life, while his offline activities are somehow more real), Foucault recognizes that this practice of the self, which is "theoretically" open to everyone, will be realized by only a few. He lists the lack of courage, strength or endurance, the inability to grasp the importance of the task and see it through, and the unwillingness to listen as limitations to the universality of this ethics of the care of self. It is perhaps not surprising that a great number of blogs and individual profiles on social networking portals present themselves to many media and cultural critics as boring, replicating the most fixed ideas and values (although we cannot of course rule out critics' own intellectual and cultural preferences and values reflected in these judgments). However, to say that the care of the self is indeed a "universal practice which can only be heard by a few" and that what we can call "the event of ethics" will therefore be very rare is to assert something other than just that "every site will find its fans" or to argue that only popular sites with most hits have managed to embrace this ethical potential of the medium.[26] Popularity (or its lack) has nothing to do with the care of the self, online or offline. I therefore suggest something that perhaps goes against the grain of more typical media and cultural studies interpretations of blogging and its users. Rather than seeing LiveJournal or Flickr as being primarily about exchange, with bloggers expecting to be read, responded to, or at least tagged and thus acknowledged in one way or another, I propose to read blogging as being as much about experiencing and enacting the simultaneous difficulty and necessity of relationality as a condition of being in the world. This interpretation seems more plausible in the light of the fact that most blogs and online profiles have very few readers: in most cases, the blogger herself.[27] "Social networking" sites are thus a testing ground for enacting the dramas and (inevitable) failures of sociality.

But even if the event of ethics in blogosphere is indeed very rare, the enactment of the technology of the self through the techniques of writing and linking makes blogosphere a privileged space for analyzing the emergence of the practice of the care of the self. Naturally, we could explore the enactment of this ethics through the technologies of the self in such cultural practices as dieting, bodybuilding, or reading self-help manuals. And yet there is something very particular about how this ethics of the self takes place through writing, especially the writing that involves new media, because of the kind of self and the kind of life that are performed in this process. It could be argued that in blogging and online networking, an enactment of a more embodied, aware, and "lively" relationship of the self with technology takes place, and that "life" is thus revealed as always already technological. Foucault himself, when commenting on the coming into vogue of notebooks to be used for personal and administrative purposes in Plato's time, foregrounds the technological aspect of all writing that needs to be taken account of. Providing an interesting gloss to the current debates on the novelty of technology and "new media," he argues that in ancient Greece, "This new technology was as disrupting as the introduction of the computer into private life today. It seems to me the question of writing and the self must be posed in terms of the technical and material framework in which it arose."[28]

Social networking sites thus provide an experiential space for actively taking on, rather than merely acting out, the trace of technology in the human self. Recognizing that media users' attention is usually focused on the content of the technology rather than its machinic or formal qualities, Mark Poster states that "whenever individuals deploy media, they are in the midst of a system of power relations that remains out of phase with their conscious mind."[29] This leads to a reconfiguration of the subject-object distinction into what he calls "the humachine." Even if it is the intuitive and unconscious embracing of technology (since this process itself is simplified through the use of templates, and so on) that precedes the self's attempt to connect with others, blogging and social networking return agency to this process of being in the technoworld, of living-with-technology. This goes some way towards interpreting media culture as a productive apparatus of power, a network of nodes and temporary stabilizations of forces, where the self is neither entirely free and singular nor entirely and permanently subjugated. Rather, it emerges from this network as technological, or humachinic, and does so not just through its writing and linking activities but also through the construction of its life—past, memories, dreams, and desires—as technological traces. For Bernard Stiegler, any technical instrument registers and transmits the memory of its use. For example, a carved stone used as a knife carries a record of an act of cutting and therefore acts as a form of memory. Technology becomes for Stiegler a condition of our relationship to the past, but it also works as a kind of compass, positioning the self in the temporal network from which the linear sequence of events can be distinguished—precisely by the identi-fication of technological traces (cuts on the knife's blade, rearrange-ments of the online template).[30]

And it is precisely as the leaving of traces that Stiegler interprets human existence, an existence that is for him always already technologi-cal. He argues that what Heidegger calls *Besorgen*, more recently trans-lated as "taking care" (rather than the earlier "concern") is also "beyond the mere activity that survival requires, the will to *be*, that is to say to exist, to be in the sense of ex-isting, and therefore of *marking, leaving a trace*."[31] Existence, or life, for humans means the use of lan-guage, or writing, which in *Of Grammatology* Derrida interprets as precisely the leaving of traces, or marks. The "delete" function on one's keyboard or screen also lets users remove, or at least obscure, their traces, and to experiment with ways of narrativizing their life—and death. The MyDeathSpace.com site, which provides an archive of deaths of selected MySpace members (but is not officially affiliated to MySpace) allows for dead members' profiles to be kept "alive" by com-ments and mementoes posted by one's "friends." Of course, this can all be a hoax: to paraphrase an old adage, on the Internet, no one knows you're a ghost.

THE NODES OF POWER IN THE WEB OF LIFE

Blogging and social networking enable the self to establish an active relation to its own life and the processes of its management. It is the taking up of this challenge that I describe as *bio*ethics, that is, an ethics of life whereby the (always emergent) self takes responsibility not just for its own health, but also for life as such. Bioethics can thus be under-stood as an ethics of becoming and self-creation. The impetus for this

process, I would argue—contra Foucault—always comes from the alterity "before me," both in a temporal and spatial sense. Foucault positions his ethics as response and resistance to the organized forms of
power and its historical structuration. Situating it in the context of the
relationship with, and pleasure of and for, the Other, he defines ethics
as "*an experiment* with the possibility of going beyond" the limits
imposed upon us.[32] Ewa Ziarek argues that Foucauldian ethics limits
otherness to the endless variations on the plane of immanence, as a
result of which it cannot accommodate an obligation to the Other or
respond to an external claim. It is in Levinas's ethical call as coming
from the always already anarchic and primordial alterity of the Other
that, I believe, we can locate a more convincing ethical framework. The
Levinasian supplement to the ethics of becoming should not, however,
be seen as a one way shift from immanence to transcendence, but rather
as a different, pragmatic resolution of the question of ethical injunction,
that is, this drive that pushes the self to self-create, to forge life, to
become. It is also a way of ensuring that alterity or difference does not
get reduced to a mere *resource for* the self.

This ethics of life I am outlining is therefore situated in, or even arises
out of, the tension between bad and good narcissism, between the Foucauldian relationship to the self and the Levinasian response to the
alterity of the Other, and, last but not least, between self-creation as
neoliberal imperative for individualized productivity and an ethical
injunction for continuous restlessness and movement. This tension is
not a permanent suspension between two sets of equally valid options;
it entails a need for a decision, to be taken, always anew, in a singular
way, in an undecidable terrain. The possibility of the imperative of the
care of the self turning into bad narcissism, b-logocentrism, or moral
dandyism, and of self-creation becoming a neoliberal project in which
the self is seen as the ultimate value that needs protecting, has to be
kept in place precisely as a guarantee of the ethicality of this project.
Were we to eliminate this possibility (or even danger) in advance, we
would be turning our bioethics into a technicized schema for the
improvement of the world, predefined and carefully designed by "ethics
experts." Technology does serve an important role in this ethics of life—
not as a threatening other that needs to be overcome for the protection
of life or as a set of calculation procedures worked out in advance, but
as a container for the tensions between bad and good narcissism,
between self-creation and reaching out to alterity. The bioethics I am
proposing is thus always already technological, in the sense that it is

predicated upon the acceptance of the technicity of life as its condition of being.

To answer the question that frames my chapter—what if Foucault had had a blog?—I think he would have been a narcissist, but what I have described here a good, or ethical narcissist. As mentioned before, "good" does not stand here for an a priori universal valorization but rather for the recognition of narcissism as an inevitable condition of an ethics of the self, and of the self's being with others. So, are bloggers narcissistic? Absolutely, but also, inevitably. Are they ethical? Possibly, but also, perhaps, rarely.

CHAPTER FOUR

Posthuman Selves, Assembled Textualities

Remediated Print in the Digital Age

KIENE BRILLENBURG WURTH

There is no subject, only collective assemblages of enunciation. Subjectification is only one such assemblage.

—GILES DELEUZE AND FELIX GUATTARI, *A Thousand Plateaus*

All writing is in fact cut-ups. A collage of words read heard overhead.

—WILLIAM BURROUGHS, "The Cut-Up Method"

In recent years, media theorists and historians have extensively researched the transformative impact of modern communication and recording technologies on the human body and human embodiment: the body as it is normatively projected from the outside in a specific culture and the body as it is lived from the inside. Especially under the influence of Friedrich Kittler, but also due to the growing dominance of information technologies in Western culture, many scholars in the humanities are rethinking what it is to be human. Such scholars no longer conceive of a human essence or soul tucked away inside the body; rather, they explore provisional modes of embodiment framed, prepared, and configured by media technologies. In the work of Bernard Stiegler and others, these provisional modes of embodiment have come to be associated with the idea of an artificially extended humanity typically called *posthuman.*

This critical notion of the posthuman differs from a scientific posthumanism devoted to prolonging life in the pursuit of immortality. Although the concept "posthuman" may refer to certain fairly recent fantasies and developments in science and science fiction concerning the human and its mental as well as bodily extension over time, it also involves rethinking the basis of subjectivity as radically heterogeneous. That is, the posthuman both fulfils scientific visions of the endless extension of a liberal or autonomous humanist self subjecting the world to its free will *and*, as a critical concept, presents a means to dismantle that liberal self by exposing the very fluidity, multiplicity, and difference on which it is based.[1] In this latter sense, and as Katherine Hayles has proposed in *How We Became Human*, posthumanism signals not a technologically mediated afterstage of the human, but rather the end of a dominant conception of the human that privileges sameness, identity, and mastery. This does not mean, however, that critical posthumanism has no concern with (cyber)technology. While it has primarily focused on animality in/and humanity, critical posthumanism has also typically tried to redefine ideas of the human by reflecting on the space in between humans and machines. Such reflections have led to the idea that the self is not given, is not contained, and has no exclusive interiority from which to start: Rather, the self is an exteriority (what Stiegler calls "technics") that acts as an original incursion of that selfhood. It is this critical posthumanism that I will be concerned with here.

Recent analyses of posthuman subjectivities in film and literature have usually focused on cyberpunk and science fiction, where such subjectivities are configured digitally or in another high-tech fashion. In this chapter I examine how in some contemporary fiction the "old" medium of paper has come to function as the matter of "new" posthuman subjectivities that are the product of an "external" inscription: enactors operating on the basis of codes—not digital codes, but handwritten, printed, paper-based instructions. This is an especially interesting development, since paper has long been implicated in the construction of humanness and subjectivity in Western culture. Indeed, as Allison Muri has shown in her article "Virtually Human," the book has functioned as the locus of human consciousness in our culture since the Renaissance, while the human body has been familiarly framed as a book of nature.

Accordingly, literature—and the novel in particular—has been a mediator of human identity and consciousness, and the construction of an individual, humanistic subjectivity in Western culture has often been associated with the reading of books. Thus, for those critics warning against the growing dominance of the electronic page, the codex book captures the spiritual values of humanism and is the privileged locus of a secular consciousness: "in our secular world, the 'cathedral' of human consciousness or identity has for centuries been represented by the . . . codex or paper page."[2] For example, Sven Birkerts apocalyptically connects the waning of the private self, together with the erosion of language and the loss of historical perception, to the rise of the electronic page: once, there was the possibility of an isolated self between the covers of a book, but that possibility has now been exchanged for an open site of transition and traversal connected to innumerable nodes in an electronic network circuit. Conversely, enthusiastic advocates of new textualities argue that, since the 1990s, the electronic page has begun to dethrone the "linear and propositional structures" of the printed page as a privileged "form of reason" or mediator of consciousness. Hypertext and hypermedia, they argue, constitute a more faithful "model of the mind's typical activities," because electronic links, hypermedially informed, effectively simulate the mind's associative connections and mnemonic networks.

In short, what it means to be human and posthuman these days is an issue played out in debates about paper-based and electronic writing practices. Fears and fantasies of virtual, electronically mediated modes of inscription as "new" bodies of text invoke (sideways or head-on) visions of emerging, electronically mediated modes of embodiment and subjectivity. It is this double implication of text and subjectivity (as post/human configurations) that I want to pursue here. My argument is organized around two recent British novels that rematerialize the literary as a print-based medium in the era of the digital and so foreground a (typically humanist) connection between subjectivity and paper-based textuality.[3] The first, Steven Hall's *The Raw Shark Texts*, is a quasi-cyberpunk novel that samples existing texts and films on sharks, trauma, and amnesia (most notably Jonathan Nolan's "Memento Mori" and Chris Nolan's *Memento*) in order to create a strange, paper-cast road story about identity loss. The second, Graham Rawle's *Woman's World*, is a graphic novel that aligns gender identity with performativity by means of its cut-and-paste figuration of found magazine fragments. Yet, while both texts foreground the intimate connection between the novel, new textualities, and new or sampled subjectivities, *The Raw Shark Texts* continues to harbor within this new subjectivity traces of a humanist self and the metaphors of depth and privacy associated with it.

ASSEMBLED TEXTUALITIES: *THE RAW SHARK TEXTS* AND *WOMAN'S WORLD*

Ingeniously constructed from samples of found material, *The Raw Shark Texts* offers a resonant reading experience that immediately foregrounds an enormous number of other texts and images: Pythagoras's writings on metempsychosis, John Locke's and David Hume's theories of personal identity (and current theories on the same subject), Gothic fictions featuring doubles, memory lapses, and monsters, the Orpheus myths, Alfred Hitchcock's *Vertigo*, Robert Ludlum's *The Bourne Identity*, Steven Spielberg's *Jaws*, Haruki Murakami's *Hard-Boiled Wonderland and the End of the World*, Paul Auster's *The New York Trilogy*, Andy and Larry Wachowski's *The Matrix*, Mark Danielewski's *House of Leaves*, Hari Kunzru's *The Impressionist*, Michel Condry's *Eternal Sunshine of the Spotless Mind*, and Tom McCarthy's *Remainder*— among many others. It is not coincidental that *The Raw Shark Texts* sounds like "Rorschach Tests," since it allows readers to project ever-different meanings, genres, sources, and combinations onto its pages.

The Raw Shark Texts presents the quest (or is it a game?) of what is not quite a protagonist in the mainstream tradition of the Western realist novel, but rather, as in Kunzru's *The Impressionist*, Nolan's "Memento Mori" and McCarthy's *Remainder*, an Enactor: one (or, rather, several written and personified versions of) Eric Sanderson, who has lost for the eleventh time his long-term memory after the death by drowning of his beloved Clio. This time, however, the letters and notebooks that Eric, in a past phase of self-awareness, has left for his anticipated future self (re)direct this "future" Eric into the mediated memories of the "past" one by instructing him to defend himself against a conceptual shark that, swimming the "flows of human interaction," is after his mind and his memories. As the "earlier" Eric Sanderson, Eric had himself attracted the shark. A conceptual creature, the shark embodied an opportunity for him to store his memories of Clio in Un-space as his own memory was slowly disintegrating. Absorbing thoughts and memories of people, the shark had seemed an obvious, if also dangerous, external hard disk to store these memories: a predator appearing as a "self-contained living afterlife," an infinite, moveable memory container. However, the shark would turn against the earlier Eric and devour him, memories and all, allowing the future Eric to emerge. While his psychiatrist tells Eric he is suffering from fugue, Eric believes it is the shark that has emptied his mind and identity.

The connection between identity and memory that *The Raw Shark Texts* centrally explores has been established at least since John Locke's *Essay Concerning Human Understanding*. Here, elaborating on Plato's account of the soul ("Of Identity and Diversity"), Locke argues that personal identity is framed by the continued awareness and memory of oneself and one's actions in a chain of memories of past selves remembering past selves (rather than one uninterrupted super memory).[4] Furthermore, because for Locke the awareness and memory of (a past) self conditions identity, it also allows for potentially different persons within the same woman or man, since a person is tied to a current state of consciousness that (like Eric Sanderson's) may be interrupted, thus giving birth to a different person: one wo/man, different persons.

As we know, David Hume questioned the basic significance of awareness and memory for personal identity, arguing that just as no impression of self is stable and durable enough to become foundational for an idea of sameness, so no memory is extensive enough to cover all moments of self. According to Hume, what we (or Locke) think of as identity is merely a quality that we attribute to different perceptions—and the unity we impose on them.[5] Identity is thus fictitious—a projection at best. If Eric Sanderson's recurrences are reconsidered in this processual light, they highlight the effects of repeated interruptions of self-consciousness and memory less than they illustrate the *impossibility* of a personal identity based on the idea of sameness as a continued self-awareness. Eric's repeated episodes of amnesia, or fugues, could thus be seen as performing the basic, fragmentary flux of impressions.

However, I argue that it is the theories of consciousness and selfhood in German idealism, for which Hume's skepticism more or less paved the way, that most fully account for Eric's predicament. The idea of infinite reflexivity (Fichte, Novalis, Hölderlin)—that difference rather than sameness constitutes the self—here plays a central role. In Fichte's system, I can try thinking myself as myself, but I will never reach myself as a unity, since I approach myself by separating myself as other (subject-object). Hölderlin, of course, radicalized this potentially differential outlook by no longer positing a common ground but an *Ur-theil* or arche-partition at the "root" of the I and the not-I. As a result, the I as subject-object famously becomes the *effect* of this partition. Subject and object are instated by a separation inherent in reflection, when the self dissociates itself as an object to be pondered. There is no identity, no given basis out of which the I evolves; it is rooted in a quicksand of *différance*. In a similar fashion, Eric's dissociative fugues do not simply revolve around memory breaks, but rather *foreground* the differential process of the self as an effect of an arche-partition—his interrupted self thus becoming not so much an exception to the rule as the illustration of an inescapable condition.

On his way back to kill the shark, the "current" Eric Sanderson encounters Scout, who, for her part, looks like a second version of Clio (whose last name, Aames, echoes the surname of the protagonist of Cameron Crowe's *Vanilla Sky*, a remake of Alejandro Amenábar's 1997 *Abre los ojos*).[6] In turn, Scout wants to use the shark to reclaim a tiny part of her mind that has been colonized by a once-human computer database called Mycroft Ward (the pun on Microsoft Word is inevitable, although Mycroft also refers to Sherlock Holmes's even more gifted brother). She leads Eric into a paper-made un-space (one of many references to *Fight Club*, *House of Leaves*, and *Hard-Boiled Wonderland and the End of the World*), where doctor Trey Fidorous conducts his research into language viruses, turns of phrases, and word fish. Trey and Scout (for reasons of her own) help Eric to imagine and navigate a virtual world containing the sea, gulls, barrels, and a boat where the Ludovician will be faced in a final showdown that is a rehearsal of the final scene of Spielberg's *Jaws* (but not Benchley's novel).[7] (See Figures 4-1 and 4-2.)

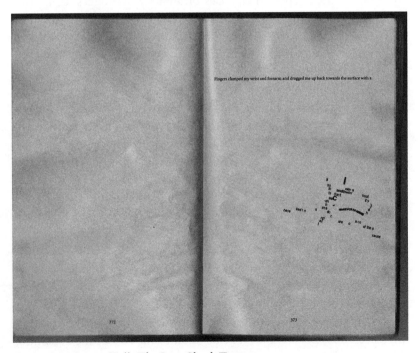

Figure 4-1. Steven Hall, *The Raw Shark Texts.*

Figure 4-2. *The Raw Shark Texts*: When the page is flipped, jaws open.

In the end, Eric and Scout remain in un-space, heading for the island of Naxos, where the earlier Eric Sanderson and Clio had spent their last holiday together.

Like *The Raw Shark Texts*, *Woman's World* is thoroughly "secondary," thoroughly derived from existing text fragments, and so thoroughly the result, to use de Certeau's term, of poaching. Readers, de Certeau suggests, are nomads who traverse a myriad of other texts in their engagement with a single one: "readers are travellers; they move across lands belonging to someone else, like nomads poaching their way across fields they did not write." Yet instead of being overruled by the cultural claims to those fields (claims involving meaning and intention, for instance) readers can actively, if only provisionally, appropriate these fields, bending them to their own needs. It is this kind of creative appropriation that the "graphic" novel *Woman's World* foregrounds by being composed of forty thousand cut-and-pasted fragments (all visible as such, including chapter headings and page numbers) from 1960s British women's magazines.[3] (See Figure 4-3.)

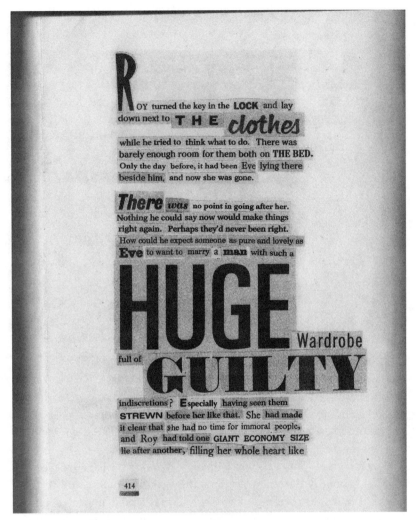

Figure 4-3. Graham Rawle, *Woman's World*.

Within the constraints of these coercive prefab discourses the plot unfolds: Norma Little, whose brother Roy is "on vacation" in the Himalayas, is a patchwork version of Brett Easton Ellis's Patrick Bateman in her fascination with brands, stylistic prescriptions, and cosmetics—a fascination appropriately voiced in assembled contemporary advertisement texts. Pining for an admirer and looking for a job, Norma dates photographer Mr. Hands. When he assaults her in his apartment, she hits him with her Cinderella slipper and leaves him for dead ("There was a HARD crack as the tip dug into his SCALP").[8] Meanwhile, Roy has returned and falls in love with another character named Eve. However, it turns out that Norma and Roy are the same person, since—in (what Judith Butler calls) a gender-melancholic way— Roy has internalized the gender identity of his sister, who died in a car accident when they were children. Because of the crisis with Hands (who does not die), but also on account of the lovely Eve, Norma "must go." However, she fails repeatedly to depart. Norma survives another car accident, and the novel ends with Norma imagining Roy and Eve reunited in the manner of a standard romance.

Both *The Raw Shark Texts* and *Woman's World* are print-based novels that nevertheless participate (directly or indirectly) in a network aesthetic of the digital age: these are not unified "works" but rather verbal-visual conjunctions defined by their connections and interactions with other texts. *They* occupy an in-between space where visual, textual, and graphic figurations interact and resonate. There is nothing that is not already prosthetic in these texts. Totalizing and originary, the prosthetic here exceeds the postmodernist literary play of intertextuality as we have known it since Roland Barthes and Julia Kristeva. If the novels rehearse the idea of text as a node in a network of other texts, they also explode the signifying potential of the space in between texts by totalizing that space as a norm. As a result, these texts become quasi-generative displays that reassemble other texts and images.

GENERATIVE TEXTUALITIES: BETWEEN PRESENTISM AND NOSTALGIA

Generative textuality is a subcategory of electronic textuality. It boils down to the programs or codes used, as Katherine Hayles puts it, "either to generate texts according to a randomized scheme or to scramble and rearrange pre-existing texts." Gnoetry is by now a familiar example: out-of-copyright texts are fed into a program that analyzes how words appear relative to each other in these texts. The program then yields randomly selected language in accordance with the rules it has observed within a predetermined frame of, say, a sonnet, a haiku, or blank verse (one can indicate the relative percentage of the source texts one wants to use). Gnoetry thus works like a computational scrambling machine, offering poetry that is part machine-made and part human-made, hence in part impersonal. Because of this machinic intervention and the use of found material, it is not possible to read these poems as poems in the romanticist-humanist tradition—that is, as vehicles of expression, building on the assumption of an inner voice speaking in self-reflection. No longer starting from a subject-centric perspective, Gnoetry no longer revolves around expressive models of mediation, but rather around mimicry: the reiteration and incorporation of used modes and models.

Evidently, Gnoetry and other scrambling and mimicking digital textualities (such as Jim Andrews's *Stir Fry Texts*, David Link's *Poetry Machine 1.0*, or spamoetry) derive at least in part from twentieth-century collage and assemblage techniques in paper-based literature and the arts. Feeding on the "new" media (newspaper, phonograph, or cinema), during the early twentieth century avant-garde collage (whether cubist, futurist, or surrealist) typically cut up found material to disfigure, interrupt, and thus critically incorporate mass mediations. F. T. Marinetti's words-in-freedom, Kurt Schwitters's Merzbau (though this is more like a mini-Wagnerian *Gesamtkunst*), and surrealist newspaper poems as promoted by André Breton are a case in point. As Tristan Tzara put it in his "Dada Manifesto of Feeble Love and Bitter Love," cut out the words of an article you would like to make a poem with, shake them gently in a bag, and then reassemble them in the order you have removed them from the bag—the poem will "reassemble you."[9]

Randomness instead of intentionality, bricolage instead of authority, ready-mades instead of inventions, simultaneity instead of linearity: these indicate the counterdirections of collage art and literature in the modernist age. Later, in the late 1950s and 1960s, Brion Grysin and William Burroughs intensified these directions with the cut-up and fold-in methods. Cut-ups are passages of text cut by oneself and/or others and regrouped in random order. Fold-ins, by contrast, amount to folded passages of texts, cut in half and subsequently rearranged. As is well known, in *Nova Express* and *The Ticket That Exploded*, Burroughs aimed to use words to derail conventional modes of perception, thinking, and writing. If in linear print and mass communication words were just another mode of mind-lock, in cut-ups or fold-ins they realized their viral, wrecking potential. In this way, collage-as-cut-up became a political tool used both to reveal the strategies and interpellations of mass media and to unsettle them in dislocated word groups.

As a generative method, collage rerendered texts as word constellations that were mechanic rather than organic. Yet today such constellations are no longer as disruptive as Burroughs imagined them to be. Since the 1960s collage as remix or sampling has increasingly become a norm in popular music and visual art in the form of DJ and VJ culture, digital culture, and (as we will see) textual culture.[10] Indeed, cutting and pasting—though not precisely in random order—are now routinely used icons on our computers, while sampling in music, digital editing in film and video, and mainstream hypertextual structures on the net have rendered collage ubiquitous rather than antithetical. It is against this ubiquity that I position *Woman's World* and *The Raw Shark Texts*. How does collage "work" on paper in a digital age that has rationalized an artful juxtaposition that was once radical?

Woman's World is a paper-based collage that has internalized digital textual technologies indirectly and after the fact. Precisely because it is paper-based and so constrained by linearity, it foregrounds collage as a material intervention that fragments processes of reading *within*, rather than outside of, a linear setup. The text obstructs, delays, distracts—not because text passages have been randomly or senselessly juxtaposed (on the contrary, their juxtaposition is painstakingly precise), but because they constitute a relentlessly interrupted yet constant sequence—a discontinuous continuity. There are "proper" sentences, although visibly composite, and there is a "proper" story with a beginning, middle, and end, but the stitched words always unsettle that propriety. One can never escape the gaps and cuts in between words or word groups; nor can one ignore the material singularity of these words and word groups. Because the recurrence of signifiers in different contexts and positions is made visible through a constantly changing graphic materiality (font, style, size, and so on), we now see what we normally pass over.

As a result, the text passages in *Woman's World* always remain alien bodies, stubbornly retaining a visible connection to an anterior site and time. *Woman's World* is never "its own"; it is a *prosthetic text*, simultaneously an amputation and an extension, without an "originary integrality."[11] As such, it embodies an irresolvable paradox. On the one hand, it is structured by a linear storyline (despite a tendency toward circularity); on the other, it is fractured by a visible, material multiplicity that cannot be contained, covered, or passed over (see Figure 4-4).

In contrast to Gnoetry, where the font, size, and style of collected text fragments can be seamlessly assimilated and the semblance of a generated, instead of prosthetic, textuality can easily be created, the singular materiality of words here reveals a resistance to sampling.

Would this resistance then perhaps indicate that paper books may still have some "radical" reading practices in store, that the future of the literary is not digital alone? Is it more than simply nostalgic to use

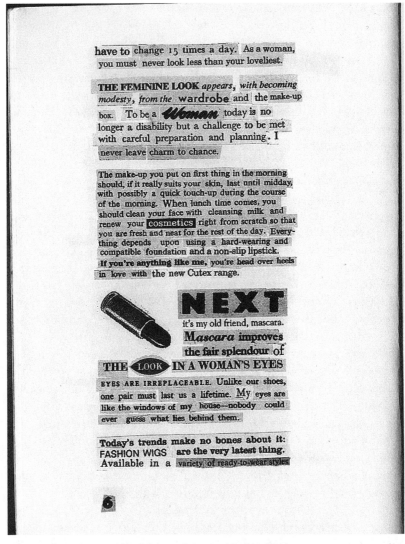

Figure 4-4. *Woman's World*: A visible, material multiplicity.

earlier twentieth-century methods of composition for the twenty-first century? *The Raw Shark Texts* likewise asks what it means to be analog in the digital age. The "old" medium of paper-based writing (and others like video tapes, dictaphones, telephones) plays a decisive role in the novel, as Eric Sanderson receives all crucial information about "himself" and his adversaries in letters, written notes, and postcards. Indeed, in my "undexed" edition, *The Raw Shark Texts* concludes with a post-card sent by Eric to Dr. Randle, his psychiatrist—although the last image is of Ingrid Bergman and Humphrey Bogart. Why old mail in digital times? Has the digital revolution made paper-based writing more authentic, so that Plato's old fears about writing are now redirected toward the digital? The earlier Eric believes that electronic communication cannot be trusted: "remember there is *no* safe procedure for electronic information. Avoid it at all costs."[12] However, this mistrust is ironic. In the novel, what Eric calls "conceptual flows" or thought flows are just as contaminable as electronic flows, since the conceptual shark can catch your thoughts at any time:

> The animal hunting you is a Ludovician. It is an example of one of the many species of purely conceptual fish which swim in the flows of human inter-action and the tides of cause and effect . . . The streams, currents and rivers of human knowledge, experience, and knowledge which have grown throughout our history are now a vast, rich, and bountiful environment. Why should we expect these flows to be sterile? . . . in the wide, warm pools of society and culture, millions of words and ideas and concepts are constantly evolving.[13]

One cannot control the fertile interstices, the in-between spaces that give rise to becoming and signifying. These (un-)spaces are generative spaces, liquid flows that recall Derrida's recurrent metaphor of liquid forces in "Force and Signification": forces of a seemingly interminable or "infinite implication"—excessive, for never wholly containable, energy or virtuality. This is precisely why these flows—or volumes, as Derrida might say—breed monsters. The shark is an embodiment of the profound depth and endless movement into which this energy taps (many sharks, after all, live at great depths), as well as of the surplus of signifying possibilities haunting the conceptual flows that first destroyed and then resurrected paper-made Eric Sanderson—overkill and breeding ground, destruction and generation, in one and the same current. Thus, even though in *The Raw Shark Texts* (as in "Memento Mori" and *Memento*) paper-based writing is (re)produced as more authentic and more intimate than its digital counterparts, written words also already harbor the dangers of digitization.

As a monster, the shark is also a thief. Indeed, it is through this thieving, and the careful coding used as a precaution against it, that *The Raw Shark Texts* displays a certain anxiety with respect to the generative spaces of signifying. Thus earlier Eric Sanderson takes meticulous care that later/future Eric Sanderson receives his text messages in their pure, unadulterated form: doubly, triply codified so that they cannot be contaminated. Indeed, future Eric Sanderson takes on different simulative identities to divert the shark from stealing thoughts and memories and feeding on an "intrinsic sense of self."[14] Whence the anxiety and the coding? Together, they point to a felt loss of authorial intention, the inevitable gap between sender and message, message and reader, sender and reader. The shark personifies that gap; it is a container in which stolen words and ideas take on meanings and directions beyond the reach of their author and are disseminated so radically that they can never be recollected (first Eric Sanderson and his thoughts and memories are, after all, gone beyond retrieval). While we know this is a necessary dissemination, a condition for signs to function outside of their "first" appearance, it is also a lethal intervention: authors must be killed for signs to emerge. It is as such a lethal apparatus that the shark resembles the scrambling machines that have appeared on the Internet since the 1990s. Like other conceptual fish, it is visibly a composite and emptying out of the words and thoughts of others.

The Raw Shark Texts repeats the antagonism of the shark as a scrambling machine in its own endless appropriating and resetting of texts. This antagonism betrays an uneasy relationship to the digital and the ways in which digitized textuality has automatized and normalized assemblage. The novel interrupts that practice by foregrounding the fate of an author—first Eric Sanderson—desperately protecting his copyrights (for lack of a better word) by means of old-medium-style firewalls. However, just as Eric Sanderson is not a given entity but rather a text-generated effect, so The Raw Shark Texts does not simply offer a resurrection of old-time conventions. Although there is a nostalgic gesture toward print-based novelistic and poetic "currents" that have been formative in the prehistory of cyberspace and electronic literature, and even toward impossible authorial intentions, The Raw Shark Texts also reanimates and redesigns the novel as a prosthetic text through quasi-electronic techniques. Once we understand the logic of this reanimation, it is possible to recognize the ways in which The Raw Shark Texts presents a passage from human to posthuman subjectivities that are mediated, inherited (indeed, sent by mail), fragmented, and dispersed.

Woman's World performs a comparable double resurrection of the paper page. As in The Raw Shark Texts, there is the palpable trace of an authorial presence through the visibly hand-pasted texts. Indeed, the author is included in the text through an appendage entitled "The Making of the Book," where Rawle reveals that he first wrote a rough draft of the story and then collected and cut out substitute ready-mades. This translation is, however, precisely where presence becomes absence: "Little by little, my original words were discarded and replaced by those I'd found."[15] That is to say, the prosthetic text usurps the typed words, so that the former at once affirms (as "homemade" materiality) and wipes out (as found materiality) the author's hand or coding: as generative text, it is personal and impersonal, authorial and procedural at the same time. In an age where the digital mode has become a culturally dominant mode, this procedure of scrambling, stitching, and overwriting conjures up not only "old" assemblage methods, but also electronic text-generating procedures—as if the stitched text passages ironically return these procedures to analog form, rendering them uneasy and more difficult.

RAW SHARKS AND HYBRID DISCOURSES

Recently, Katherine Hayles has shown how Mark Danielewski's *House of Leaves* mimics the computer's all-consuming hunger for multimedia:

> As if learning about omnivorous appetite from the computer, *House of Leaves*, in a frenzy of remediation, attempts to eat all the other media. This binging, however, leaves traces on the text's body, resulting in a transformed physical and narrative corpus. In a sense, *House of Leaves* recuperates the traditions of the print book—particularly the novel as a literary form—but the price it pays is a metamorphosis so profound that it becomes a new kind of form and artifact. It is an open question whether this transformation represents the rebirth of the novel or the beginning of the novel's displacement by a hybrid discourse that as yet has no name.[16]

A monster—in Derrida's sense of an omen, a sign of the future that cannot yet be decided: what will become of the novel? Like *House of Leaves*, *The Raw Shark Texts* and *Woman's World*—as different as these texts may be—indicate that this is not only a question of the future (a move toward a network aesthetic), but also a return of the past: back to paper, back to handmade materiality, and even back to linearity. It is the mixture, the ambiguity that counts.

The Raw Shark Texts embodies this ambiguity by reworking in a codex book the instability attributed to electronic texts. As Mark Poster has claimed, written traces on the computer screen are radically alterable: "The writer encounters his or her words in a form that is evanescent, instantly transformable, in short, immaterial."[17] Hayles has argued convincingly that this idea of immateriality is problematic, that, indeed, electronic texts have their very own medium-specific materiality. Instead of existing in an immaterial form, she proposes, electronic texts exist in an emergent or "dispersed fashion"; their source (code) and the display mode do not coincide, so that the display may produce different textualities (insofar as changes in font, color, screen, and so on are concerned) in different settings for different users. Electronic texts have no existence as such (strictly speaking, as the display we perceive) before they are activated by a reader and the program on which they are running: they are plural, animated, and cannot be reduced to the mimicked scrolls we generally see on screen; these are phantom appearances.

The Raw Shark Texts rematerializes this emergent electronic textuality by means of an "ancient" paper-based technique: the flipbook. Consider, to this end, how the shark never appears in exactly the same form to readers of *The Raw Shark Texts* (compare the sharks in Figures 4-1 and 4-2). Rather, it reshapes itself with ever-new thoughts and words, thus mirroring Eric's recurrent self-transformations. The predator never appears as more than a shifting shape of scrambled word-patterns, which are animated when the pages are flipped. In flipping through pages 335 to 373, the reader engenders the shark's approach.

By incorporating the flipbook technique, *The Raw Shark Texts* mimics the instability that Hayles attributes to electronic textuality: Because one never flips these pages in quite the same way, the inscriptions emerge differently with each reading. They may be durably inscribed, yet the dynamic of manually mediated reading/viewing renders the inscriptions unpredictable given the possible differences in a next reading (slower, faster, complete, skipping a page, etc.). This is, I believe, not just a remediation of the instability of electronic textuality; the flipbook technique is all too evidently present for that. Rather, by emphasizing its materiality through animation techniques dating back to the nineteenth century and before, *The Raw Shark Texts* shows how, in an age of electronic dominance, paper-based writing challenges binary distinctions between old and new, durable and flexible modes of inscription and display. Indeed, ancient flip techniques now serve as modes of remediated print on the Internet: digital flipping reenacts the gesture of the hand turning pages; it performs a memory of handheld paper and its reading conventions as manual activity. *The Raw Shark Texts* taps into that memory and resituates it in a paper-based inscription that is neither entirely durable nor wholly flexible: it moves in between both.[18]

Flipbooks have their own mode of flickering; Hayles reserves a special mode of flickering for electronic textuality: It is only the latter that allows the signifier no longer to be "understood as a single marker. . . . Rather, it exists as a flexible chain of markers bound together by the arbitrary relations specified by relevant codes."[19] That is, it exists in fluctuation. Conceptually, flickering signifiers are derived from Jacques Lacan's idea of floating signifiers—signifiers without stable signifieds that, like driftwood, float without an anchoring point. Flickering signifiers are floating signifiers whose drifting has assumed a material dimension. This materiality is not given, but results from the interactions between writers (and programmers), readers, and the operations of an intelligent machine; it is a provisional materiality without continuity over time. Thus, Jim Andrews's *Spastext* offers itself relative to the user's interactive movements: What at first seems a single-level text in fact partakes of five texts (each presented in a different font hue) that can be read consecutively if one clicks the bluish arabesque logo. However, once the mouse of the user moves over the text, it transforms spasmodically, uncontrollably. It thus becomes impossible to speak of "the" text; instead, *Spastext* performs itself as other and plural: every movement of the mouse brings forth a transformative invasion of the other four texts, which now appear as layers of an assemblage. They eat into each other and infect each other at the faintest touch, becoming less and less intelligible in the process.

The Raw Shark Texts mimics such flickering on two levels. First, and most obviously, it has a virtual, cognitive flickering that recalls symbolist experiments such as Stéphane Mallarmé's "Le vierge, le vivace et le bel aujourd'hui." Here, it is the materiality of the signifier as a spoken signifier (cf. *cygne/signe*) that allows words to flicker (as swan/sign) incessantly. In *The Raw Shark Texts* this is most obviously at issue in the title, which, as we have seen, sounds like, and thus includes, *The Rorschach Tests*. (Mycroft Ward is another instance, and similar language games occur at various levels.) The novel thus foregrounds the Derridean notion of language as an uncontrollable organism, as a force field that is constantly shifting due to the productive tension between signifiers, and in which the duplicitous meanings of words can radically alter sentences. This once more suggests an implicit claim that "new" textualities feed on "old" signifying habits.

Second, like *Spastext*, *The Raw Shark Texts* revolves around the fluctuating interplay of multiple implied (or explicitly referenced) texts: it is palimpsestic, to recall Genette. As such, it also approaches what

Joseph Tabbi has called the electronic processual page. "What is distinctive of this newly dynamic page," he writes, "is the ability to not so much stack texts one on top of another, but to enfold various texts into each other."[20] Such a page has no stable textual basis, a dimension that *Spastext*, for instance, performs by being coded as hypersensitive (although the text *can* be reset).

The Raw Shark Texts evokes such a dynamism indirectly through the excessive intertextual and generic vantage points it offers: a well-informed reader experiences a restlessness comparable to reading *Spastext*, as the narrative seems continually to invoke different generic categories—road novel, romance, orphic quest, quasi-cyberpunk novel, and *Bildungsroman*-turned-Enactornovel—or yet another of the innumerable intertexts that inform it as a generative text. It, too, is hypersensitive in an associative sense. As an "electronic" dimension, this hypersensitivity relates to the status of *The Raw Shark Texts* as if an open nerve center. Thus, in my edition, the text reveals its own incompleteness through its undex, which refers to chapters and passages not included in the book. They can be found on the Internet or in, say, a Greek translation. For instance, the "Aquarium Fragment" can be accessed on the website www.rawsharktexts.com, where one can obtain the necessary password by winning a digital game of Memory within two minutes. The fragment contains vital information about Eric's first descent into the shark: "—and living, the thing obviously alive and with will and movement. Coming oddly towards me through the space in the room and the gaps, chains and blinking-light links in my memory, swimming hard upstream against the panicking fast flow of my thoughts" ("Aquarium Fragment"). Linked to "un-spaces," images, and texts on (and off) the Internet that may or may no longer be available, *The Raw Shark Texts* behaves—so to speak—in the manner of hypertext.[21] Indeed, since Hall's novel has appeared in different and incomplete paper editions, there is no definitive version of it. This no doubt reinforces the novel's urban myth–like status: It's a rumor spreading around.

Hypertext, as processual text, is of course not only unstable but also fundamentally unfinished because infinitely connected. For some (conservative) critics, the ascendancy of this kind of text and the "new" reading strategies it has heralded signal the ascendancy of a different type of subjectivity. For example, Birkerts has linked the instability and allegedly flashy aspect of electronic texts to a fateful distractedness in contemporary Western culture. Indeed, he foresees a possible dissolution of the printed book in an all-consuming electronic network that will effectuate the disappearance of the individual self as we have known it: "we will conduct our public and private lives within networks so dense . . . that it will make almost no sense to speak of the differentiated self."[22] The "self must change as the nature of subjective space changes," and if that space no longer fosters seclusion, safe from distraction, we will witness a waning of the private self. Such dystopian views are of interest to me because they assume a correspondence between printed book and private self, between electronic text and networked, decentered self. Both *The Raw Shark Texts* and *Woman's World* tap into that correspondence by presenting a "posthuman" protagonist in printed texts that start to behave in the manner of electronic texts.

"ELECTRONIC" TEXTUALITIES AND POSTHUMAN SUBJECTIVITIES: STITCH BITCH TO SHARK QUARKS

In *Woman's World* there is likewise an evident, and almost inevitable, interaction between the identity of Norma/Roy and the materiality of the text: both are patched, so that the being-assembled of the latter is reflected and reinforced by that of the former, and vice versa. Indeed, Norma/Roy is *made* of the magazine fragments stitched together into a material confession, while the fragments betray her transvestism before Norma has confessed to being Roy in the first place. In this respect, *Woman's World* seems a paper-made answer to Shelley Jackson's classic hyperfiction *Patchwork Girl*, which likewise questions the integrity of cultural and bodily identity. Like *Woman's World*, *Patchwork Girl* textually performs the impossibility of such identity in a monstrous—that is, hybrid—constellation, "seamed and ruptured," as Hayles has put it, "comprised of disparate parts with extensive links between them."[23] While this performance is specifically linked to *Patchwork Girl* as an electronic text, with its consequent foregrounding of a multiplicity at the heart of the "screenic" body-texts we get to see, *Woman's World* remediates such multiplicity through polyvocal effects. Just as *Patchwork Girl* offers a monster—the promised bride for Frankenstein's monster, torn apart by the doctor himself and, in Jackson's rewriting, stitched back together by Mary Shelley—composed of the fragments of others whose stories we get to read, so Norma/Roy carries with her/him

a multiplicity of found voices cut and reassembled from the magazines.[24] This multiplicity makes it impossible to discover Norma/Roy's
"own" voice, because her/his voice is always already spectral, prompted
and inhabited by magazine styles, tones, and typefaces.[25] There is an
interiority that is at once alterity here—indeed, an artificiality (textual
prosthesis) that undoes distinctions between interiority and exteriority.

If the sampled textuality of *Woman's World* thus corresponds to the
paper-made subjectivity it portrays—a paper trace, so to speak, of
cybernetic transformations of subjectivity—*The Raw Shark Texts* follows a more ambiguous path. One can easily see how cybernetic concerns (networked, viral communication, for one) are here absorbed in
an "old" paper materiality and how an assembled textuality comes to
perform a posthuman subjectivity that is quasi-machinic, thoroughly
artificial, and thoroughly textual at its core. Thus, Eric realizes himself
in the interaction with a prescriptive text (the instructions in the letters
passed on to him) and a ready-made history (the so-called Light Bulb
Fragments recounting the last holiday of Eric and Clio). Others make
his memories (the first Eric Sanderson's textual heritage), others steal
his memories (the shark). Another even *becomes* Eric, and vice versa,
the very first time he becomes aware of himself:

> The man in the wardrobe mirror carefully touched his fingers over his thin
> cheeks, his nose, his mouth, his short crop of dirt brown hair. He was in his
> late twenties, pale and a bit sickly looking . . . The man was a stranger and
> his expressions were written in a language I couldn't begin to understand.
> We reached out to each other and our fingertips met . . . I drew my hand
> back and called the reflection by his name. And he said the same thing back,
> but silently, just moving his lips: *Eric Sanderson*.[26]

This first imaginary contact—rehearsing the famous scene from Nolan's
"Memento Mori"—acts out the fantasy (Lacan) of a primary identification that is at once a differentiation. (Note that the text immediately
performs what the protagonist/enactor is described to be doing: com-
posing itself through a process of doubling.) To fully understand this, it
is important to realize that Eric's quest against oblivion easily collapses
into an unwillingness to remember given the relentless pursuit of the
shark: there is a dissociated memory in search of its author here—the
memory of Clio—that the shark verbally embodies. As a "self-contained
living after-life," the shark's incessant hunting after Eric signals a process of unconscious remembering that should be familiar from Freud's
reading of trauma in *Beyond the Pleasure Principle*: the monster is the

demon that returns; the inability to forget is due to a fatal process-failure. Consequently, it persists as a fateful haunting, a haunting that *instates* the later/future Eric.

Signaling a return both from a primordial past and Eric's (imaginary) past self, the shark in *The Raw Shark Texts* functions as an embodiment of the trauma of which Eric's self-forgetfulness is but a symptom. Indeed, his very self is a symptom of that trauma if we conceive of trauma not simply as a breach in the protective shield of a psychic apparatus, but a fateful openness to mimicry. As Ruth Leys has suggested in elaboration of Mikkel Borch-Jakobsen's mimetic model of trauma: traumatic shocks rehearse a shock of identification preceding the coming into being of the subject. Viewed from this perspective, the relation between the earlier and the later Eric Sanderson involves an endless mediation or reflexivity generated by an original difference that prevents a merging of self and other. For who is that former self but an assemblage of printed matter, codes and instructions sent in advance of a reader? As the ghostly presence mediated through this assemblage, is not the "first" Eric Sanderson also already an effect of the "second," rather than only the reverse? One way or another, dead matter is at the origin of Eric as a subject, the inheritance that sets him going as a "blank" empty subject.

Yet if such a state of affairs invokes the specter of a critical posthumanism abandoning the idea of an anterior and interior self, a self that could migrate integrally into another sphere, there is nevertheless always the trace of another posthumanism in Eric. If he seems to act as the inverse of Mycroft Ward, who feeds on and infinitely expands himself through the minds of other people to become immortal, Eric is nevertheless just as gregarious and vampiric; like the shark, like Ward, he feeds on others. As an impersonator, he not only usurps the earlier Eric Sanderson, but also Ryan Mitchell and Mark Richardson as paper-based personae. Similarly, his performance as a coded self links Eric to the networked, artificially operating minds reembodied transhumanistically within electronic circuits in such recent fictions as Richard K. Morgan's *Altered Carbon*, Robert Sawyer's *Mind Scan*, and Scarlett Thomas's *The End of Mr Y*.[27] Just as *The Raw Shark Texts* hovers in between modes of paper-based and electronic textuality, so Eric Sanderson oscillates between the embodiment of a critical and a utopian posthumanism, between an internally differential and an infinitely replicating self.

Indeed, I read the novel as an intervention that forces us to rethink binary oppositions between "good" and "bad" posthumanisms and, thus, between humanism and posthumanism, since the utopian mode intensifies and extends humanist conceptions of selfhood. If Eric Sanderson is composed out of dead matter, if his very core or interiority is but an infolded exteriority, that matter nevertheless consists of a mode of inscription traditionally associated with the building of selfhood in the humanist age—that is, with writing as a mode of self-composition and self-survival. Eric is thus an incorporation of a posthuman subjectivity that cannot shed, or wholly control, its humanist trace. One might even conclude that the digital technologies channeling posthumanist subjectivities have in fact reproduced paper-based writing as an authentic medium bearing the close and direct imprint of an author authoring him/herself.

III

Both *The Raw Shark Texts* and *Woman's World* perform on a textual level the thoroughly prosthetic subjectivities of their respective enactor-protagonists, Eric and Norma/Roy. In both texts, identity is thus doubly performed as an entity no longer purely and durably interior, but rather the provisional effect of an infolded exteriority. As a porous tissue imbued with a literary and cinematic heritage, *The Raw Shark Texts*'s strategy of absorption is symptomatic of the ways in which Eric absorbs his several identities through textual mediation. Thus, a critical posthuman subjectivity is echoed in an experimental "posthuman" textuality, and vice versa—although a trace of a utopian posthumanism and a humanist composition of selfhood uneasily persists. Neat and comforting distinctions between critical and utopian posthumanisms ("right" and "wrong") become slippery as the one easily coexists with, and indeed feeds on, the other. Likewise, posthuman textuality in *The Raw Shark Texts* is a textuality that moves in between (remediated) print and electronic materialities.

Woman's World* similarly refashions the digital along "old" print lines: it offers an assemblage within the confines of linearity, even while this is a linearity that constantly interrupts itself in the infinite connectivity of pasted words from other settings. At the same time, the pasted word-text functions as a screen text, with the originally word-processed text functioning as the code text—the latter programming, as it were, the former, and the former overwriting the latter. As the author confesses: "I started writing the book in the usual way [i.e. the basic code of the story] . . . I then searched through hundreds of women's maga-zine, cutting out anything that seemed relevant to the scenes I'd written . . . Little by little my original words were discarded and replaced by those I'd found."[28] Thus, *Woman's World* embodies the digital as a text becoming screen-text.

In its turn, and like *Woman's World*, *The Raw Shark Texts* taps into the digital age by refashioning modernist techniques of concrete poetry, collage, and assemblage, techniques rooted in the print age. Both texts thus remind us that in literary criticism binary oppositions between electronic and paper-based writing are not very helpful.[29] Because the one cannot be thought without the other, there is an inevitable, and indeed productive, trace of the one within the other—a productivity illustrated by *The Raw Shark Texts*'s and *Woman's World*'s inventive refashioning and reanimating of—by now—standard inscription proce-dures in hypertexts and electronic generative texts. In the end, such nov-els bring to the fore an ambiguity that is, I believe, symptomatic of current cutting-edge paper-based writing, a writing that hovers between futurism and nostalgia, between modes of mediation that at once link up with "new" electracies and look back at "old" strategies of printing, cutting, and assembling.[30] In this way, it reinvigorates the field of litera-ture, which as recently as the 1990s seemed to have been consigned to the past.

PART TWO

Digital Reflexivities

Prose, Poetry, Code

CHAPTER FIVE

Intermediation

The Pursuit of a Vision

N. KATHERINE HAYLES

Literature in the twenty-first century is computational. Almost all print books are digital files before they become books; this is the form in which they are composed, edited, composited, and sent to the computerized machines that produce them as books. They should, then, properly be considered as electronic texts for which print is the output form. Although the print tradition of course influences how these texts are conceived and written, digitality also leaves its mark, notably in the increased visuality of such novels as Mark Danielewski's brilliant hypertext novel *House of Leaves*, Jonathan Safran Foer's *Extremely Loud and Incredibly Close*, and Salvador Plascencia's *The People of Paper*.[1] The computational nature of twenty-first-century literature is most evident, however, in electronic literature, literature that is "digital born," created on a computer and meant to be read on it. More than being marked by digitality, such works are actively formed by it. For those of us interested in the present state of literature and where it might be going, electronic literature raises complex, diverse, and compelling issues. In what senses is electronic literature in dynamic interplay with computational media, and what are the effects of these interplays? Do these effects differ systematically from print as a medium, and if so, in what ways? How are the user's embodied interactions brought into play when the textual performance is enacted by an intelligent machine? Addressing these and similar questions requires a theoretical framework responsive both to the print tradition from which electronic literature

necessarily draws and the medial specificity of networked and programmable machines. Computation is not peripheral or incidental to
electronic literature but central to its performance, play, and interpretation.[2] Consequently, we will begin our interrogation by considering the
cognitive capacities of computation for participating in the kind of
recursive feedback loops characteristic of literary writing, reading, and
interpretation.

DYNAMIC HETERARCHIES AND FLUID ANALOGIES

Many scholars in the humanities think of the digital computer as an
inflexible, brute force machine, useful for calculating but limited by its
mechanical nature to the simplest kind of operations. This conception
is both true and false—true in that everything computable must be
reduced to binary code to be executed, but false in the belief that this
inevitably limits the computer to simple mechanical tasks with no possibility for creativity, originality, or anything remotely like cognition.
From the field that includes artificial intelligence, artificial life, neural
connectionism, simulation science, and related computational research,
I will focus on two central concepts to develop the idea of intermediation: dynamic heterarchies and fluid analogies as embodied in multi-
agent computer programs.

The simple computational devices called cellular automata, as Stephen Wolfram's research demonstrates, can create complex patterns
that emerge from local interactions between individual cells (or
agents).[3] The problem then becomes how to bootstrap such results into
increasingly complex patterns of second-, third-, and n-level emer-
gences. One proposal is intermediation, a term I have adopted from
Nicholas Gessler, whereby a first-level emergent pattern is captured in
another medium and re-represented with the primitives of the new
medium, which leads to an emergent result captured in turn by yet
another medium, and so forth.[4] The result is what researchers in artificial life call a dynamic hierarchy, a multitiered system in which feedback
and feedforward loops tie the system together through continuing interactions circulating through the hierarchy. Because these interactions
go up as well as down, down as well as up, such a system might more
appropriately be called a *dynamic heterarchy*. Distinguished by their
degree of complexity, different levels continuously in-form and mutually determine each other. Think, for example, of a fetus growing inside

a mother's body. The mother's body is forming the fetus, but the fetus is also reforming the mother's body; both are bound together in a dynamic heterarchy, the culmination of which is the emergent complexity of an infant.

The potential of this idea to explain multilevel complexity is the subject of Harold Morowitz's *The Emergence of Everything: How the World Became Complex.*[5] Its glitzy title notwithstanding, Morowitz's book is essentially a revisioning of well-established domains of scientific knowledge such as cosmology, the origins of life, and molecular biology into a unified scenario in which, at every level from the beginning of the universe through complex human social systems, complexity emerges through dynamic heterarchies interacting with one another. For example, atoms consist of dynamical systems in which electrons interact with the nucleus comprised of protons and neutrons (in the simplest account) to form more or less stable units. When atoms combine to form molecules, the nature of the dynamics changes, and the patterns created by the interplay of atomic forces is transformed into a different system in which the emergent results of the first system are re-represented in the different medium of molecular interactions. These are captured and re-represented in turn when molecules combine to form macromolecules such as proteins. At this point the interplay between digital and analog processes enters in decisively important ways. DNA sequences can be understood as primarily digital systems of base pairs, represented by the discrete letters of the DNA code, *ATCG*. But when the sequences are folded into proteins—the process responsible for determining functionality—the analog processes of topology become crucial as they continuously interact with the genetic sequences.

As this example suggests, digital and analog processes together perform in more complex ways than the digital alone, for each has strengths complementary to the other. Digital processes, because they are discrete, give much finer error control than analog processes. By definition, analog processes vary continuously along a spectrum; rectifying small errors is difficult because all real points along a number line can theoretically be occupied. This is the main reason why analog computing, which flourished until the 1950s, lost out to digital computing. Nevertheless, analog processes have strengths of their own. They excel in transferring information from one medium to another through morphological resemblance, and the complexity of continuous variation allows them to encode information in more diverse ways than digital encoding. In dynamical heterarchies, analog and digital processes can be expected to perform synergistically with one another, as they typically do in biological processes.

Now let us make a speculative leap and consider the human and the digital computer as partners in a dynamic heterarchy bound together by intermediating dynamics. Do these components satisfy the requirements for a dynamic heterarchy? They are obviously at different levels of complexity, the human being immeasurably more complex than the computer. Just as obviously, they exist as different media, with the human a carbon-based entity with complex electrochemical and neuronal feedback loops, whereas the computer's dynamics are based on relatively simple electro-silicon circuits. Differences in complexity notwithstanding, the human and computer are increasingly bound together in complex physical, psychological, economic, and social formations.

Increasingly, the environments people create for themselves include a diverse array of intelligent machines, especially in developed countries such as the United States. As computers proliferate, they are endowed with increasingly powerful networking capabilities; they are also moving out of the box into the environment through ubiquitous computing, embedded sensors and actuators, mobile technologies, smart nanodevices embedded in a wide variety of surfactants and surfaces, real-time sensors and data flows, and a host of other developments. As a result, people in developed societies are surrounded by smart technologies of all kinds, from the virtual online world Second Life to intelligent toasters that decide when the bread is brown. In light of these developments, it seems reasonable to assume that citizens in technologically developed societies, and young people in particular, are literally being reengineered through their interactions with computational devices. A survey by the Kaiser Family Foundation entitled "Generation M: Media in the Lives of 8–18 Year-Olds" reports that young people between the ages of eight to eighteen spend an average of over six hours *per day* (including school days) consuming media.[6] While the lion's share goes to television, significant chunks are also consumed by surfing the Internet, playing video games, sending email, and otherwise interacting with computers.

Anthropologists have long recognized that humans have been biologically, psychologically, and socially shaped by their technologies at least since Paleolithic times.[7] The new wrinkle is the power of computers to perform cognitively sophisticated acts. Compared, say, to a hammer or stone ax, a computer has much more flexibility, interactivity, and cognitive power. In addition, computers are able to handle both natural language and programming code, capabilities that allow them to function in complex human-computer networks. Humans are routinely considered to be distinguished from other species by their intelligence and particularly by their ability to use language, making it possible for them to develop complex social formations. Computers are crucial components of those structures, from international banking protocols to air traffic control at LAX to twelve-year-olds IM-ing their friends. In developed societies, it is not merely a metaphor to say that (some) humans and computers are bound together in dynamic heterarchies characterized by intermediating dynamics. Humans engineer computers and computers reengineer humans in systems bound together by recursive feedback and feedforward loops, with emergent complexities catalyzed by leaps between different media substrates and levels of complexity.

What evidence is there that computers can function as cognizers, that is, as agents capable of intentionality, the "aboutness" that makes a subject (or an agent) capable of referring to something outside of itself? Recalling John Searle's Chinese room analogy, we may also add the requirement that in some way the computer must *understand* what it is about in order to be considered a cognizer in the strong sense.[8] Here I turn to the research program of Douglas Hofstadter, who in collaboration with several generations of graduate students has devoted himself to investigating this issue.

In *Fluid Concepts and Creative Analogies: Computer Models of the Fundamental Mechanisms of Thought*, Hofstadter details this research.[9] His mantra, "cognition is recognition," posits that cognition is built upon the ability to recognize patterns and extrapolate from them to analogies (pattern A is like pattern B). Once analogies can be formed, the process can theoretically be extended to analogies between analogies (between analogies . . .), a progression capable of leapfrogging between levels in recursive cycles of increasing complexity. The first necessarily modest step is to create a computer program capable of recognizing a pattern. Hofstadter's test case was inspired by the "Jumble" puzzle that appears in newspapers, in which the reader is challenged to unscramble a sequence of letters to form a recognizable word. The idea is to construct the program (dubbed Jumbo) using a wide variety of "codelets," small programs that function as independent agents performing specific tasks. The emergent result from the interactions of all the agents is the successful construction of a word.

The codelets function by randomly putting together pairs of letters or larger strings in a process that includes parameters indicating how strong are the letters' affinities for each other and how "sticky" that string is, that is, how much those particular letters want other letters to join them. Another feature of the program is the "coderack" (an allusion to the coatrack in a checkroom), a sequencer that determines which codelet runs next. As a codelet moves from random assemblage into strings where the bonds between letters are strong, its urgency rating increases so that it will be run more frequently. Hence, the closer it comes to assembling a recognizable word, the greater the likelihood it will have the processor time to finish the task. Although the programs necessarily run sequentially, this mode of sequencing simulates multi-agent parallel processing because all programs are given some opportunity to run, albeit in an evolutionary environment where fitness is defined in terms of creating recognizable words. This programming structure creates a milieu in which the program can "understand" the words it assembles—that is, understand not semantically but philologically and linguistically in terms of grapheme and syllable formation.

Another program (Copycat) seeks to complete an analogy by performing a transformation like a given transformation of a sequence of letters (or numbers), for example $abc \to abd$ is "like" $wxy \to$? The answer would be immediately obvious to a human ($wxy \to wxz$), but the point is to use local interactions between diverse agents to arrive at an analogy that reveals the deep structure of the situation. In this example, the deep structure is the linear sequence of the alphabet. A more challenging analogy is this comparison: $abc \to abd$ is "like" $xyz \to yz$? Faced with this challenge, the program evolved through local interactions three emergent results. The first, $xyz \to xy$, implies that the alphabet is a line segment with nothing beyond its terminus. The second, $xyz \to xyzz$, suggests a deep structure in which the line segment may be extended by repeating elements. The most elegant solution, $xyz \to xya$, implies that the alphabet is circular, with the end cycling back to the beginning.

Despite the apparent simplicity of the challenges, the programs' virtue is that they accomplish their tasks not by applying a rigid set of rules but rather through fluid exchanges between many codelets that progress from random forays in the possibility space to increasingly "informed" guesses about possible answers. Because the dynamics are emergent and interactive, the programs create the computational equivalent of "understanding" the problem, unlike programs that merely encourage the illusion of comprehension while understanding nothing (which Hofstadter calls the Eliza effect, after Joseph Weizenbaum's well-known program that mimics Rogerian psychoanalysis).[10] Hofstadter's inspiration for his research came from introspection about his own techniques for solving similar problems. Following subtle clues and momentary glimpses into his perceptions as they surfaced into consciousness, he became convinced that his cognition emerged not from rigid rules but flexible analogies that could branch in several different directions; hence his name for the method he instantiated in the programs, fluid concepts and creative analogies. As we will see, this work is particularly appropriate for thinking about intermediation between humans and computers as a framework for understanding electronic literature. The programs that perform electronic literature are generally quite different from those created by Hofstadter and his collaborators, but nevertheless Hofstadter's programs nicely capture their spirit. Because literature works through metaphor, evocation, and analogy, it specializes in the qualities that programs like Jumbo and Copycat are designed to perform.

In the context of electronic literature, intermediation has two distinct ways in which it might be understood: as a literal description of the dynamics of human-computer interaction, or as a metaphor for such interactions. Hofstadter's programs add the possibility of recursive loops between these binaries, loops that entangle the literal with the metaphoric, so that the binaries operate as a spectrum of possibilities rather than as polar opposites with an excluded middle. As subcognitive systems, Hofstadter's programs provide the matrix from which higher cognitions can emerge. For example, they have no capacity for semantic recognition, but the humans interpreting their results might see interesting patterns in, say, the set of recognizable words generated from a given anagram. The more complex cognitive system, the human who gains insights from the program's results, might complete the loop by tweaking the program. In this case, the program functions literally as an adaptive system bound together with the human through intermediating dynamics, the results of which are emergent realizations. The program can also operate as a metaphor for other computational systems less intelligent and adaptive that similarly spark insights in the humans who use them. Framed like this, the literal/metaphoric binary becomes a spectrum along which a variety of programs can be placed, depending on their cognitive capacities and the ways in which the patterns they generate and/or recognize are structurally coupled with humans.

In electronic literature, this dynamic is evoked when the text performs actions that appear to bind together author and program, player and computer, into a complex system characterized by intermediating dynamics. Generally, the performance is metaphoric rather than literal because the programs are not nearly as cognitively sophisticated as those Hofstadter created. Nevertheless, the performance is designed to elicit emergent complexity in the player, who possesses much more powerful and flexible cognitive powers than the computer. If this is indeed the result, then the program's *effects* are no longer simply metaphoric, for it has literally changed the human's perceptions and, to the extent that perceptions provide the scaffolding for cognition, cognitive processes as well. The cycle operates as well in the writing phase of electronic literature. When a programmer/writer creates an executable file, the process reengineers the writer's perceptual and cognitive system as she works with the medium's possibilities. Alternating between writing modules and testing them to be sure they run correctly, the programmer experiences creation as an active dynamic in which the computer plays a central role. The result is a meta-analogy: as human cognition is to the creation and consumption of the work, so computer cognition is to its execution and performance. The meta-analogy makes clear that the experience of electronic literature can be understood in terms of intermediating dynamics linking human understanding with computer (sub)cognition.

Crucial to the formation of this analogy is the sense that the human is interacting not exclusively with a rigid rule set (although for most of the programs currently used to create electronic literature, such rule sets exist in abundance), but rather with a fluid mix of different possibilities. For the player, the sense might come from a program designed to encourage this orientation by having parameters vary continuously to produce unexpected results. For the programmer, the fluidity might arise from unexpected effects possible when different functionalities within the software are activated simultaneously. However the effects are achieved, the importance of fluidity to the analogy-forming process is evident in the richly diverse senses in which flow has become central to narrative thematics, design functionalities, and literary dynamics for contemporary electronic literature.

At this point it may be instructive to compare the processes described above with what happens when a person writes and/or reads a book. The book is like a computer program in that it is a technology designed to change the perceptual and cognitive states of a reader. The difference comes in the degree to which the two technologies can be perceived as cognitive agents. A book functions as a receptacle for the cognitions of the writer that are stored until they are activated by a reader, at which point a complex transmission process takes place between writer and reader, mediated by the specificities of the book as a material medium. Although authors have occasionally attributed agential powers to the book (in Jorge Luis Borges's fantastical "The Book of Sand," for example, the letters shift into new positions every time the book is closed),[11] the letters in actual books never shift once ink has been durably impressed upon paper. But in many electronic texts, words and images do shift, for example, through randomizing algorithms or programs that tap into real-time data flows to create an infinite number of possible recombinations.[12] Recombinant flux, as the aesthetic of such works is called, gives a much stronger impression of agency than does a book. Displays of the computer's agency are common in electronic literature, including animated Flash poems that play by themselves with little or no intervention by the user, generative art such as Loss Pequeño Glazier's poems that disrupt the narrative poetic line every few seconds, and interactive fictions such as Emily Short's *Galatea*, a sophisticated program that produces different responses from the Galatea character depending on the precise dynamics of the player character's actions.[13] Because the computer's real agency, as well as the illusion of its agency, is much stronger than with the book, the computer can function as a partner in creating intermediating dynamics in ways that a book cannot.

When literature leaps from one medium to another—from orality to writing, from manuscript codex to printed book, from mechanically generated print to electronic textuality—it does not leave behind the accumulated knowledge embedded in genres, poetic conventions, narrative structures, figurative tropes, and so forth. Rather, this knowledge is carried forward into the new medium, typically by trying to replicate the earlier medium's effects within the new medium's specificities. Thus, written manuscripts were first conceived as a visual continuity of connected marks reminiscent of the continuous analog flow of speech; only gradually were innovations introduced such as spacing between words, indentations for paragraphs, and so forth. A similar pattern of initial replication and subsequent transformation can be seen with electronic literature. At first it strongly resembled print and only gradually began to develop characteristics specific to the digital medium, emphasizing effects that could not be achieved in print. Nevertheless, the accumulated knowledge of previous literary experiments has not been lost but continues to inform performances in the new medium. For two or three thousand years, literature has explored the nature of consciousness, perception, and emergent complexity, and it would be surprising indeed if it did not have significant insights to contribute to ongoing explorations of dynamic heterarchies.

I propose to put the idea of intermediation in conversation with contemporary works of electronic literature to reveal, in a systematic and disciplined way, how they achieve their effects and how these effects imply the existence of entangled dynamic heterarchies binding together humans and intelligent machines. In *My Mother Was a Computer: Digital Subjects and Literary Texts*, I explored intermediation by taking three different analytical cuts, focusing on the dynamics between print and electronic textuality, code and language, and analog and digital processes.[14] Such wide-ranging analyses are beyond the scope of this essay, so I will limit my examples to the interplay between print and electronic textuality, with the understanding that the other dynamics, although not foregrounded in this discussion, also participate in these processes.

FROM PAGE TO SCREEN: MICHAEL JOYCE'S *AFTERNOON, A STORY* AND *TWELVE BLUE*

When electronic literature was in its infancy, the most obvious way to think about screens was to imagine them as pages of a book one turned by clicking, a tendency visually explicit in the short-lived Voyager experiments with electronic books. Nothing comes of nothing, as King Lear observes, and electronic literature was not born ex nihilo. Especially in the first generation of electronic literature the influence of print was everywhere apparent, much in the way the first automobiles were conceived as horseless carriages. In retrospect, early claims for electronic hypertext's novelty seem not only inflated but misguided, for the features that then seemed so new and different—primarily the hyperlink and "interactivity"—existed in a context in which functionality, navigation, and design were still largely determined by print models. As the field began to develop and mature, however, writers, artists, designers, sound artists, and others experimented to find out what the medium was good for and how best to exploit it.

That evolution is richly evident in the contrast between Michael Joyce's seminal first-generation hypertext *afternoon, a story*[15] and his later Web work, *Twelve Blue*.[16] Both are authored using Storyspace

(Eastgate System's proprietary hypertext authoring program), but the ways in which the medium is conceptualized are startlingly different. In the few years separating these two works, we can see a steep learning curve in process, a curve that represents one writer's growing realization of the technology's resources as a literary medium. *afternoon* has received many excellent interpretations, so its effects can be briefly summarized.[17] It works through a branching structure in which the reader is offered alternative plot developments, depending on which sequences of lexias she chooses to follow. In different plot lines, Peter, the protagonist, discovers that his son either died that day or did not die. The ambiguity is not so much resolved as illuminated when the reader comes upon "white afternoon," a crucial lexia surrounded by a "guard field," a program conditional that prevents a reader from accessing it until certain other lexias have been opened. In "white afternoon," the reader discovers that Peter may have been the driver of the car that collided with the vehicle in which his son and ex-wife were riding, with the possible result that he himself caused the fatal injury of his son. This discovery explains the approach-avoidance pattern Peter displays in attempting to find out where his son is; he does not want to face what in some sense he already knows. As Jane Yellowlees Douglas explains in her fine reading of the work, once the reader reaches this lexia she is apt to feel that she has in some sense "completed" the work, even if all the lexias have not been discovered and read. The work is thus driven by a mystery that, once solved, gives the reader the satisfaction normally attained through a conventional Aristotelian plot structure of rising complication, climax, and denouement.

The technique of conflicting plot lines is, of course, not original with Michael Joyce. Some two decades earlier, Robert Coover experimented with similar techniques in short stories such as "The Elevator" and "The Babysitter," print fictions that, like *afternoon*, are broken into brief segments relating mutually contradictory details.[18] These stories are often identified as precursors to electronic hypertexts, for like *afternoon*, they employ branching structures that create irreconcilable ambiguities centering on violent events. In some ways, Coover's stories are more daring than *afternoon* for they contain no kernel that invites the reader to reconcile the contradictions through a psychological interpretation. Comparing the two works reveals how print-centric *afternoon* is, notwithstanding its implementation in an electronic medium. It uses screens of text with minimal graphics, no animation, no sound, no color, and no outside links (a possibility that only came into existence with the World Wide Web). Navigation proceeds by using the Story-space navigational tool showing what links are available from each lexia, or by clicking on "words that yield" within each lexia. The linking patterns create short narrative sequences, also identifiable through the navigation tool that allows the reader to follow a given narrative sequence through the similarity of the lexias' titles. The writer's control over these sequences is palpable, for several of them do not allow any exit (short of closing the program) until the reader has clicked through the entire sequence, creating an oppressive sense of being required to jump through the same series of hoops numerous times. Although the reader can choose what lexias to follow, this interaction is so circumscribed that most readers will not have a sense of being able to play the work—hence my repeated use here of the term "reader" rather than "player."[19]

Twelve Blue, by contrast, makes playing into one of its central metaphors. Significantly, it is not conceived as a work driven by the reader's desire to solve a central mystery. There is no mystery here, or more precisely, there are mysteries but not ones that can be solved in any conventional sense, for they open onto unanswerable questions about life and death. ("Why do we think the story is a mystery at heart?" the lexia entitled "Riddle" asks, following that with "Why do we think the heart is a mystery?")[20] Other central images, playing on the etymology of "text" as "weaving," are threads that come together to form patterns and then unravel to come together in different ways to create new patterns. "Twelve Blue isn't anything," Joyce writes in his introduction. "Think of lilacs when they're gone" ("Introduction"). Compared to *afternoon*, *Twelve Blue* is a much more processual work. Its central inspiration is not the page but rather the flow of surfing the Web. The work is designed to encourage the player to experience it as a continuous stream of images, characters, and events that seep or surge into one another, like tides flowing in and out of an estuarial river. In this sense, although it has no external links, *Twelve Blue* is Web-conceived as well as Web-born.

Two seminal intertextual works illuminate the difference between *afternoon* and *Twelve Blue*. The epigraph, taken from William Gass's *On Being Blue*, signals that the strategy will be to follow trails of associations (as Gass says) "the way lint collects. The mind does that."[21] Every screen contains at least one instance of the word "blue," in a range that parallels Gass's own capacious repertoire. The second, less explicit intertext is Vannevar Bush's seminal essay "As We May Think,"[22] in which he argues that the mind thinks not in linear sequences but in associational links, a cognitive mode he sought to instantiate in his mechanical Memex, often regarded as a precursor to electronic hypertext. In *Twelve Blue*, Joyce takes up Bush on his speculation by creating a work that, much more than *afternoon*, instantiates associational thinking and evokes it for the player, who must in a certain sense *yield* to this cognitive mode to understand the work (to say nothing of enjoying it). The player who comes to *Twelve Blue* with expectations formed by print will inevitably find it frustrating and enigmatic, perhaps so much so that she gives up before fully experiencing the work. It is no accident that, compared to *afternoon, Twelve Blue* has received far fewer good interpretations and, if I may say so, less comprehension even among people otherwise familiar with electronic literature. Like sensual lovemaking, the richness of *Twelve Blue* takes time to develop and cannot be rushed.

Let us begin, then, with a leisurely embrace that wants to learn everything it can about this textual body, with an intention to savor rather than attack or master it.[23] The surface that first presents itself already invites us to play, for it consists of twelve colored threads in different hues, predominantly clustered at the blue end of the spectrum, against a deep blue background. The threads, which are interactive and change orientation according to how we play them, are divided into eight "bars," suggesting the measures of a musical score. By playing this score we are also weaving the threads into patterns, a metaphor not so much mixed as synesthetic, for sight is mixed in with sound, texture with vision. As we open the screens by clicking on the threads or choosing to play one of the bars, the mix we have chosen is imaged on screen left, representing the orientation the threads have in that bar. The URL, shown at screen bottom, indicates the bar and thread respectively of that sequence (for example, 4_10). Repeated exploration could theoretically locate each sequence within a two-dimensional grid indicating its position in time (the bar number) and space (the thread number).

Entering the flow of the screen narratives, one cannot help noticing how difficult it is to identify the characters. Pronouns abound while proper nouns appear sparsely, teasing the player with ambiguities and arousing the desire to probe further into the work, to anchor the actions to terra firma. Gradually, as the player enters the flow and lets it enter her, she comes to recognize patterns and sees them emerge into recognizable shapes. Think of staring at a random dot image; if one strains one only delays the emergence of the pattern, but if one relaxes and lets it take over, the subconscious puts together the information and suddenly the patterns leap out.

So now with *Twelve Blue*. Javier, the cardiovascular surgeon, was married to Aurelie, but they were "unmarried" ("Blue mountain," 2_5) when she chose to "run off" ("Run off," 3_8) with her daughter Beth's swim coach, a woman named Lisa, who "didn't do mother" ("Fierce eyes and a mother's fears," 7_8). Nevertheless, Aurelie cannot help associating Beth and Lisa, these apparent antinomies flowing together in her thoughts. Divorced from Aurelie, Javier has fallen in love with Lisle, a Canadian virologist who also has a teenaged daughter, Samantha. Lisle and Samantha live by Wappinger Creek. When a deaf boy drowns in the creek while his girlfriend, who cannot sign, sits helplessly by on a creekside log, Samantha is the one to find his body as it floats down to her and Lisle's house.

This is the picture that emerges, but as with a random dot image, the picture itself is unremarkable. The interest is rather on the picture's emergence, the mysterious subconscious and unconscious processes that, out of a chaos of seemingly random information, mysteriously assemble a coherent whole. Central to these processes is the flow of images, like streams coming together, joining, separating. Images caress one another by fleetingly touching, sometimes through the juxtapositions created by links, sometimes by sparking a momentary conflagration in a player's receptive mind. An example or two will illustrate the process (although, since the flows are continuous, one or two has a way of modulating into eight or twelve).

One of Lisle's memories from her childhood is of Delores Peters, whose father on impulse bought a carnival ride in which blue cars, like "stubby little shoes" whirl around ("white moths," 4_10). He sets it up in his farmyard and his wife invites her daughter's girlfriends over to play on it. The mother tries to make the occasion festive by making a cake and bringing out a jug of lemonade, which she sets on a tub of ice. As day fades into evening, the ice melts and white moths settle on the dark liquid, some to struggle and escape, others to die ("white moths," 8_10). The farmyard whirly flows into Lisle's memory of the carnival ride on which she whizzes with her carny boyfriend, after which they have furious sex ("Alpine," 5_9); the blue cars flow into the blue leather Mary Janes that she wore as a child, which she remembers carrying her to the parochial school where she was embarrassed to tell the Sister she had her period ("Long time after one," 2_10). Menstrual blood links this memory to her daughter's poetic image of the damp creekside soil smelling like blood, which she narrates to Lisle in a story that has a boy named "Henry Stone" coming to her ("waters of resurrection," 6_6). This pattern flows into the deaf boy's girlfriend, who refuses to join him in the water on the day he drowns because she is having her period. Samantha sees the moon whitely reflected on the dark creek water and imagines it is like a photograph ("Li Po," 6_12); she is startled when the deaf boy's body surfaces in the middle of this image, in a pattern that recalls the white moths struggling on the dark water. Another lexia entitled "white moths" has Lisle explicitly making the connection to the boy's death, thinking "the world was a drum of dark water where we sometimes caught our wings like moths" ("white moths," 7_10).

Like Hofstadter's codelets that have varying degrees of affinities for different letters, the images are constructed to "stick" preferentially to other image-sequences to form larger patterns such as the one discussed earlier. Metapatterns emerge through the process of forming analogies between analogies. For example, the associations comprising the Lisle/Samantha group are linked with another group centering on Eleanore and Ed Stanko, connected to Lisle/Samantha through the overlapping character of Javier. Long ago Javier met a woman named Elli in the Blue Ridge Mountains of Virginia and had an affair with her; the woman is (perhaps) Eleanore, who now lives in a seedy hotel-turned-apartment building owned by Ed Stanko, an unremittingly mean and hard man. Eleanore has a shaky grasp on reality (not to put too fine a point on it, she is nutso) and, having long ago lost a baby girl who may (perhaps) be Javier's illegitimate child, somehow blames Ed Stanko for her loss. Luring him into her apartment with the offer of a quickie, she knifes him in the gut while he is in the bathtub, which she afterwards cleans, along with herself, in a strange ritual involving flowers and skins of blood oranges.

The moon-reflection-as-photograph image from the Lisle/Samantha group connects with the photograph of Javier's great-grandmother, Mary Reilly, that he discovers in the lobby of Ed Stanko's ex-hotel, the only image of her known to exist. Through pure meanness Ed Stanko denies even a copy of the image to Javier, who therefore undertakes a pilgrimage with his daughter, Beth, back to the hotel so she can see it. When they arrive, Eleanore (who on Javier's previous stop at the hotel had hitched a ride with him to Roanoke, perhaps to buy the blood oranges she uses in her cleansing ritual) tells him that Ed Stanko is "indisposed," a pattern that flows into the body of the deaf boy, who like Stanko dies in water. The silence in which the deaf boy had lived in turn flows into Eleanore's silence when she is told (presumably by the police) that she has the right to remain silent.

Such play as this has no necessary end, especially when the player accepts the flow as fulfilling desire rather than insisting on the sharper, more focused, but also briefer satisfaction of a climax, no sooner reached than replaced by the legendary sadness of the denouement. Here the pleasure is more diffuse but also longer-lasting, ending only when the player closes the work, knowing that if she were to linger, still more flows could be discovered, more desires evoked and teasingly satisfied. As Anthony Enns points out in his reading of *Twelve Blue*, this work challenges Frank Kermode's criterion for "the sense of a ending" that helps us make sense of the world by establishing a correlation between the finitude of human life and the progression through a beginning, middle, and end characteristic of many print narratives.[24] Here there is no inevitable progress toward the death of the plot. Does that mean *Twelve Blue* fails in the archetypal narrative purpose of establishing a correlation between its sequentiality and human mortality? I would argue rather that *Twelve Blue* makes a different kind of sense, one in which life and death exist on a continuum with flowing and indeterminate boundaries.

In a lexia representing in free indirect discourse the thoughts of Ed Stanko, the narrator links him with the deaf boy, a character already dead by drowning, while the other is soon to meet his death in a bathtub. "No consciousness in the grub or maggot, none in the fallen bird, the grain of wood, the drowned boy. And yet for all of your life you have wondered, redeeming that word: a wonder. . . . Do we live beyond our breath?" ("Wonders never cease," 5_11). The deaf boy becomes a metaphor for the divine in a linked pair of lexias connecting the "minor character" of his girlfriend (whose name we never learn, she being minor in our story, though undoubtedly major in her own) with another young woman marked for life by the drowning of her mother: "Consider the mind of god a drowning boy" ("naiad," 2_11). Deconstructing the boundary between the mindlessness of inanimate objects, the once-mindfulness of the newly dead, and the infinite mind of God, the analogy-between-analogies that emerges from these flows suggests there are no sharp distinctions between the noncognitive, the subcognitive, and the fully cognitive.

In one of the few perceptive interpretations of *Twelve Blue*, Gregory Ulmer relates it to the shift from a novel-based aesthetic to a poetics akin to the lyric poem.[25] He also relates it to a change from literacy to "electracy," arguing that its logic has more in common with the ways in which image and text come together on the Web than to the linearity of alphabetic language bound in a print book. The graphic qualities of the work indeed play a larger role in *Twelve Blue* than in *afternoon*, from the sensuous deep blue background to the interactive threads with their changing spatial orientations. Undoubtedly Ulmer is correct; the publication of *Twelve Blue*, Joyce's first work available on the Web, occurred during the time the Web was exploding from curiosity to daily necessity. The leap from *afternoon* to *Twelve Blue* demonstrates the ways in which the experience of the Web, joining with the subcognitive ground of intelligent machines, provides the inspiration for the intermediating dynamics through which this literary work creates emergent complexity.

MARIA MENCIA: TRANSFORMING THE RELATION BETWEEN SOUND AND MARK

In Maria Mencia's work, the emphasis shifts from the mixing of human and machine cognition to reconfigurations possible with digital technologies of the traditional association of the sound with the mark. It was, of course, this association that inaugurated literacy and, in the modern period, became deeply identified with print technology. In "Methodology," Mencia comments that she is particularly interested in the "exploration of visuality, orality and the semantic/'non semantic' meaning of language."[26] With graduate work in English philology, she is well positioned to explore what happens when the grapheme and phoneme are detached from their customary locations and begin to circulate through digital media into other configurations, other ways of mobilizing conjunctions of marks and sounds. Digitality assists in the process by providing functionalities that enable new conjunctions and unsettle the established conventions of print. With traditional print literature, long habituation causes visuality (perception of the mark) to flow automatically into subvocalization (inaudible sound production), producing the recognition of words (cognitive decoding) that in turn is converted by the "mind's eye" into the reader's impression that the words on the page give way to a scene she can watch as the characters speak, act, and interact.

"Worthy Mouths" demonstrates how Mencia's reconfigurations trouble this process.[27] The video shows a mouth articulating words, but no sound emerges; rather, text phrases flash at a pace too rapid to allow them to be read completely, although not so fast that portions cannot be deciphered (one such phrase, for example, is "lips pushed outwards closed"). By the time the phrase is decoded, the mouth is already forming other words, no sooner pursued than they too are dislocated from the mouth's movements. The effect is both to mobilize the viewer's desire to connect mark with sound and discombobulate it, forcing a disconnect that unhinges our usual assumptions about the connection between sound and mark. In "Audible Writing Experiments,"[28] video projections covered the gallery's four walls, so that the spectator was surrounded by writing and immersed in a soundscape in which a voice articulated English phonemes. The writing quickly became illegible as it proceeded down the space, transforming into wavy lines that forsook their graphemic vocation and instead began to resemble the threads of a woven fabric. Mencia notes that the illegible writing was "quite textural," a phrase that recalls the etymology of "text" as "knitting" or "weaving." Although the connection between text and vocalization remained intact, the visual perception of the mark registered its gradual divorce from phonetic equivalent into purely visual form.

In Mencia's "Things come and go . . . ,"[29] digital projection showed an animated calligram composed of pieces of paper inscribed with letters moving through the sky, initially legible as a poem about the ongoingness of things as they come into being, change, and go, a process humans resist as they attempt to hold onto them. As the calligram shifted and reformed into new shapes, the initially coherent phrases of the poem were broken and reconfigured while a computerized voice articulated the changing configurations. In her documentation of the work, Mencia comments that "the spectator can either love or hate" this voice, or accept it as it moves "from one state to another."[30] We may wonder if her comment about hating the voice reflects feedback from spectators who found the work frustrating because they yearned for the durably inscribed marks of print that have the decency not to mutate while one is reading them.

In "Birds Singing Other Birds' Songs,"[31] a work shown as a video installation and now available as a Flash version on the Web, birds' sounds were transcribed into morphemes representing human perception of their songs and represented as the corresponding graphemes. These graphemes were then animated to form the bodies of birds flying, with human voices, tweaked by the computer, articulating the sounds denoted by the marks. In the complex processes of translation that the work instantiates, the human is mixed in with nonhuman life forms to create hybrid entities that represent the conjunction of human and nonhuman ways of knowing.[32] The work can also be understood as a reenactment of the history of literacy through different media as it moves from sounds present in the environment to written marks (orality/writing), written marks to the iconographic shapes of the animated avian bodies (writing/digital images), accompanied by the re-representation of human speech as computerized voice production (digital multimodality).

The ways in which Mencia's works go in search of meaning create analogies between human and nonhuman cognizers, on the one hand, and, on the other, analogies between different media transformations. The analogy-between-analogies suggests that media transformations are like the dynamic interchanges between different kinds of cognizers, thus revealing a deep structure of intermediation that encompasses the history of media forms as well as the emergent complexities of interactions between humans, animals, and networked and programmable machines. Although Mencia's works can be classified as electronic literature, they are fundamentally about literacy as such rather than any given literary form. Reenacting media transformations and the conditions that make literacy possible, they are appropriate complements to the comparison between the print-inflected aesthetic of *afternoon* and the "electracy" of *Twelve Blue*.

RUPTURING THE PAGE: *THE JEW'S DAUGHTER*

Judd Morrissey's *The Jew's Daughter*, like the works discussed earlier, both references the print page and profoundly alters its dynamics.[33] In an interview with Matthew Mirapaul, Morrissey commented that because *The Jew's Daughter* "takes the paradigm of the page, you can see that it's not a page."[34] The entire work exists as a single screen of text. Reinforcing the page metaphor is a small box at the upper right corner, which when clicked indicates the current screen's number as well as a box in which the player can type to indicate what screenic text (as indicated by "page" number) should come up next. Within the screen text, a few letters (from part of a word to a sentence or two) appear in blue, seeming to reference the clickable links pervasive on the Web. The blue letters are not links in the conventional sense, however, but rather screen locations of mouseovers. When the player mouses over the blue letters, some part of the text, moving faster than the eye can catch, is replaced. Reading thus necessarily proceeds as rereading and remembering, for to locate the new portion of the page, the reader must recall the screen's previous instantiation while scanning to identify the new portion, the injection of which creates a new context for the remaining text.

For example, the beginning screen narrative is focalized through the young male writer and student whose voice is the predominant, though not the only, narrator for the text.

> I wrote to you that it would not be forgivable, that it would be a violation of our exchange, in fact, a criminal negligence were I to fail to come through. To hand to you the consecrated sum of your gifts, the secret you imparted persistently and without knowledge, these expressions of your will that lured, and, in a cumulative fashion, became a message. In any case, the way things worked. Stops and starts, overburdened nerves, cowardice (Is this what they said?), inadequacy, and as a last resort, an inexplicable refusal. You asked could I build you from a pile of anonymous limbs and parts. I rarely slept and repeatedly during the night, when the moon was in my window, I had a vision of dirt and rocks being poured over my chest by the silver spade of a shovel. And then I would wake up with everything. It was all there like icons contained in a sphere and beginning to fuse together. When I tried to look at it, my eyes burned until I could almost see it in the room like a spectral yellow fire.
>   A street, a house, a room. (*JD* 1)

Mousing over "criminal," the word in blue, changes the text to this:

> To hand to you the consecrated sum of your gifts, the secret you imparted persistently. June through clouds like sculpted snow demons. My fortune had said, you are about to cross the great waters. But how, now, to begin? After stops and starts, overburdened nerves, cowardice, inadequacy, inexplicable refusal, after everything, she is still here, dreaming just outside the door, her affirmed flesh beached in bed as the windows begin to turn blue. And what can now be said about this sleeping remainder? Her face is a pale round moon. She had a vision of dirt and rocks being poured over my chest by the silver shape of a shovel. (*JD* 2)

While in the first screen the "I" who has a "vision of dirt and rocks" is the male writer, in the new context the pronoun shifts to "she," his lover and girlfriend who is sometimes called Eva. The shifting antecedents are embedded within intertextual allusions that recall Shelley Jackson's *Patchwork Girl*, in which the female creature from Mary Shelley's *Frankenstein* is reassembled to become the principal narrator, as well as the original *Frankenstein*, with its allusions to graveyard robbing to

obtain body parts. The play here between the male and female characters sets up an ambiguity similar to that instantiated in *Patchwork Girl*,
where the female creature displaces the male scientist as the focalizer.
Also resonating through the passage is the "spectral yellow moon," an
image that recalls the "dull yellow eye" of the male creature that Victor
sees open in *Frankenstein* (in chapter 5), a detail Jackson repeats in
Patchwork Girl. In the second screen, however, the "pale round moon"
of her sleeping face becomes a second source of light competing with
the "spectral yellow fire" representing the emergent realization the male
writer can almost, but not quite, achieve. This gesture toward some
looming synthesis evoked only to be postponed is the work's central
dynamic, instantiated in both its thematics and functionalities. As each
screen modulates into the next, the pattern of overlapping repetition
and innovation propels the text forward through a series of disjunctions
and connections, as if it were perpetually in process, driving us toward
a synthesis inevitably delayed as the text transforms once again.

In the interview with Mirapaul, Morrissey commented that in conceptualizing *The Jew's Daughter*, "I wanted a fluidity that I haven't seen
in hypertext." The fluidity is indeed there, but so are ruptures and discontinuities created by disjunctive syntax and wrenched contexts. The
effect is significantly different from the "stream of consciousness" associated with modernist texts, including the work alluded to by Morrissey's title, James Joyce's *Ulysses*.[35] In chapter 17 ("Ithaca") of *Ulysses*,
the anti-Semitic ballad "The Jew's Daughter" appears during the course
of a conversation Bloom and Stephen have in the kitchen after Bloom
has invited Stephen home. Unlike the shifting pronouns and sliding
antecedents of Morrissey's work, chapter 17 takes the form, unique in
Ulysses, of an ultrarational catechism in which an interlocutor asks
questions and another voice answers using the "objective" language of
the "view from nowhere."[36] To visualize the scene, readers are forced
to translate from the style's pretentious objectivism back into the language of everyday perceptions. Whereas *The Jew's Daughter* has an
excess of "stickiness" that facilitates ambiguities and multiple syntactic
combinations, the *Ulysses* chapter performs the opposite extreme, articulating facts with a pseudo-precision associated with the scientist goal
of eliminating ambiguity altogether.

The "stickiness" of phrases that can ambiguously attach to different
sentences and phrases also enacts a difference between modernist
"stream of consciousness" and the kind of awareness represented in
The Jew's Daughter. As Molly Bloom's final passage illustrates, stream

of consciousness narration usually proceeds as a continuous flow of ideas, images, and language. In *The Jew's Daughter*, by contrast, narration is both belated and premature, early and late. Consider the following sequence. "Words are always only words, but these waiting words pause, are cautious, self-aware; know that what is said determines what is has been and will be, what has already not yet happened, what losses are taken and who gets what" (*JD* 7). This morphs to "Words are always only real-time creation, realized under the pressure of days, just as this once should have been realized under the pressure of days. Incipit. Three knocks" (*JD* 8), which morphs to "The fog-breath of the carriage horse on Michigan Avenue would rise impenetrably to obscure the city. Real-time creation, realized under the pressure of days, just as it once should have been realized under the pressure of days. Incipit. Three knocks" (*JD* 9). "Real-time creation" makes sense in the context of the fog-breath rising, but in the earlier context of *words* as "real-time creation" makes less sense, especially when one thinks of words as inscriptions that linger. Similarly, the comparison "just as *this* once should have been realized under the pressure of days" can be taken to refer to the present text's composition, but, when transposed into the next screen's context, results in a puzzling repetition as the relative pronoun mutates to the third-person singular pronoun: "Real-time creation, realized under the pressure of days, just as it once should have been realized under the pressure of days." As the phrase "what has already not yet happened" suggests, temporality has become fractally complex, no longer a uniform progression but a complex formation in which different strata overlap, diverge, and move with different tempos. This temporal complexity is reflected at the narrative level by the disjunctions, sometimes slight and other times more radical, that signal breaks in the text where a passage has inserted itself before its proper context or lingered after its conjoining phrases have mutated into something else. Taken as a representation of consciousness, the kind of awareness performed here is not a continuous coherent stream but rather multilayered shifting strata dynamically in motion relative to one another.

This kind of interaction is very similar to the "Multiple Drafts Model" that Daniel C. Dennett, in *Consciousness Explained*, argues best explains the nature of consciousness.[37] Dennett proposes that consciousness is not the manifestation of a single coherent self synthesizing different inputs (characterized as the Cartesian Theater, the stage upon which representations are played out and viewed by a central self);

rather, interacting brain processes, operating with varying temporal dynamics and different neural/perceptional inputs, *are* consciousness. In Dennett's model, time is represented by and instantiated in distributed brain processes and neural locations; as a result, perceived time is emergent rather than given, constantly modulating according to which processes and locations are dominant at a given instant. To explain the subjective impression of possessing a central self, Dennett argues that the self is not synonymous with consciousness as such. Rather, the illusion of self is created through an internal monologue that does not so much issue from a central self as give the impression a central self exists. Thus narrative, the emergent result from different processes interacting, sutures together discontinuities in time, location, differential inputs, and diverse perceptions to create a single stream of storytelling that tries to make sense and create coherence.

Seen in this perspective, *The Jew's Daughter* recapitulates the temporal and spatial discontinuities constitutive of consciousness through the (inter)mediation of computer software and hardware. The computer, programmed by the writer and designer, reveals to the human player the mechanisms whereby her interior monologue is (mis)taken as the production of a coherent self. The visual interface presenting itself as a print page can then be understood as a simulacrum in multiple senses. Possessing a fluidity and mutability that ink durably impressed on paper can never achieve, it simulates the illusion of a coherent stream-of-consciousness narrative (and by implication, a coherent self producing the narrative) while also making visible the temporal discontinuities, spatial dislocations, and narrative ruptures that subvert the premises underlying traditional ideas about consciousness, thereby pointing toward another model of consciousness altogether. Consciousness in this view is disjunctive, emergent, dynamic, and temporally stratified, created through local interactions between diverse agents/processes that together create the illusion of a continuous coherent self.

That the computer is intimately involved in the performance of this simulation is not coincidental, for similar fragmented, subcognitive processes take place within it, a mechanism that remains innocent of the experience of consciousness. Without knowing anything about *The Jew's Daughter*, Dennett sets up the comparison between human and machine cognition by likening the subcognitive agents from which consciousness emerges, and the even simpler processes that underlie them, to mechanical programs that could theoretically be duplicated in a computer.[38] This move enables us to give an account of *The Jew's Daughter* in terms that combine the computer's operation with the human player's cognitions. In the intermediating cycle as it occurs in *The Jew's Daughter*, mechanical computational processes perform a simulacrum of a narrative traditionally understood as the production of consciousness, thereby stimulating in the player subcognitive processes that dynamically produce consciousness as the emergent result, which in turn results in the player's mouseovers that, processed by the computer, perform the ruptures and discontinuities gesturing toward the emergent nature of the narrative and the consciousness with which it is associated, both within the diegesis and within the player herself.

"The Error Engine," a collaborative work coauthored by Judd Morrissey, Lori Talley, and computer scientist Lutz Hamel, carries the implications of *The Jew's Daughter* to the next level by functioning as an adaptive narrative engine that initiates a coevolutionary dynamic among writer, machine, and player. In "Automatic Narrative Evolution: A White Paper," Hamel, Morrissey, and Talley explain how the program works.[39] Each narrative node—that is, each textual passage—is assigned a list of keywords that may or may not appear explicitly but in any event reflect the node's thematics. In response to the player's selection of a given word in the screen text, the engine searches for the node whose keyword list most closely matches that choice and presents it as the next screen of text. The algorithm differs from a traditional link coded in HTML as <href> in that the link is not hardwired but rather chosen from a pool of possible candidates. In the next instantiation of the program, not yet implemented, the authors envision an algorithm whose selection criteria can itself evolve in relation to the player's choices. Such a program would deserve to be called a genetic algorithm, a complex adaptive system in which the user's choices and the algorithm responding to those choices coevolve together. Whether the present implementation is truly evolutionary may be debatable, but clearly the authors envision evolutionary computing as the appropriate context in which to understand their work.[40] In this sense, intermediating dynamics, whereby recursive feedback loops operate through the differently embodied entities of the computer and human, become an explicit part of the work's design, performance, and interpretation. Adaptive coevolution implies that real biological changes take place in the player's neuronal structure that result in emergent complexity, expressed as a growing understanding of the work's dynamics, thematics, and functional capabilities; these in turn change and evolve in interaction with the player's choices.

At this point readers who grew up with print and remain immersed in print aesthetics may object that this is merely a fancy way to say what literary criticism has said for a very long time—that literature functions as a technology designed to change the cognitions of readers. Certainly print literature changes a reader's perceptions, but the loop is not closed because the words on the page do not literally change in response to the user's perceptions. The new component possible with networked and programmable media is the cycle's completion, so that the feedback loops run in both directions, from the computer to the player and from the player to the computer. A perspective that takes this fully into account requires understanding the computer's processes and procedures, its possibilities, limitations, and functionalities as a subcognitive agent, as well as its operations within networked and programmable media considered as distributed cognitive systems. The danger in applying critical models developed for print is that the new possibilities opened for literary creation and interpretation will simply not be seen. Whatever limitations intermediation as a theory may have, its virtue as a critical framework is that it introduces computation into the picture at a fundamental level, making it not an optional add-on but a foundational premise from which to launch further interrogation.[41]

The implications of intermediation for contemporary literature are not limited to works of electronic literature but extend to contemporary print literature and indeed to literary criticism as a whole. They include the mixing in of human and machine cognition; the reimagining of the literary work as an instrument to be played, where the textual dynamics guide the player to increased interpretive and functional skills; deconstruction of the relation between sound and mark and its rearticulation within environments in which language and code are in active interplay; the rupture of narrative and the consequent reimagining and re-presentation of consciousness not as a continuous stream but as the emergent result of local interactions between various neural processes and subcognitive agents, both biological and mechanical; the deconstruction of temporality and its reconstruction as an emergent phenomenon arising from multiagent interactions; and the performance of an adaptive coevolution cycling between humans and intelligent machines envisioned as cognizers embodied in different media at different levels of complexity.

The urgent challenge digital textuality presents for criticism is to reenvision and rearticulate legacy concepts in terms appropriate to the dynamics of networked and programmable media.[42] No less than print literature, literary criticism is affected because digital media are increasingly essential to it, limited not just to the word processing but also the ways in which critics now access legacy works through digital archives, electronic editions, hypermedia reinstantiations, and so forth. Critical production is affected as online journals such as *Vectors* offer publishing venues for the development and dissemination of multimedia criticism—that is, criticism that is not just about multimedia works but itself uses the capabilities and functionalities of multimedia as essential components of interpretation and analysis.[43] The validation and review procedures of print criticism are also under revision, for example in the project sponsored by the Institute for the Future of the Book to reimagine how publication protocols should change for digital media.[44] These developments imply that critics, no less than writers, are increasingly involved with computation-intensive environments. Given as a truism that the technology one uses affects not only *how* work is produced but *what* is produced, the critical self-reflection that linked, for example, grammatological theory with changed modes of writing and thinking should result in further transformations that link computational theory with new ways of critical thinking, writing, and creating.

Literature, conceptualized not just as print books but as the entire complex system of literary production that includes writers, editors, publishers, critics, designers, programmers, booksellers, readers, players, teachers, copyright laws and other legal formations, Web sites and other electronic dissemination mechanisms, and the technologies that enable and instantiate all of the above, is permeated at every level by computation. The belletristic tradition that has on occasion envisioned computers as the soulless other to the humanistic expressivity of literature could not be more mistaken. Contemporary literature *is* computational.

CHAPTER SIX

Net.art: Dysfunctionality and Self-Reflexivity

MARIE-LAURE RYAN

Most cognitive scientists consider self-reflexivity to be a distinctive feature of the human mind. The concepts of the I, of the self, or of identity are the product of a process by which the mind looks back upon itself and tries to grasp how it relates to the world toward which it is normally directed.[1] Given the fundamentally self-reflexive nature of human intelligence, it is not surprising that many of its products should display the same property. According to Noam Chomsky, human languages distinguish themselves from animal communication through their ability to describe or define their own elements and to embed their own structures recursively.[2] Self-reflexivity is also found in all the representational arts, as well as in computer languages and mathematical systems. Whenever a type of sign or a medium can represent something external to itself, the human mind will find a way to redirect it toward its own capability to represent. In this chapter, I will focus on the patterns of self-reflexivity found in Web-based art (or net.art), arguably the form of new media that has pursued the scrutiny of its technological foundation the most persistently.

To prepare, theoretically, the ground for this investigation, I will start by distinguishing three concepts that are often used interchangeably, especially in literary theory: the concepts of feedback loop, recursivity, and self-reflexivity. A feedback loop is a process by which the output of an operation is used as input to this very same operation. Feedback loops occur in domains as varied as the ecology (for instance, the balance of predators and prey in a closed environment), finances (the fluctuations of the stock market), mechanical engineering (the design of a self-regulating heating system or of the flushing mechanism of your toilet), and last but not least in the relation between human user and machine in interactive computer systems. The second concept, recursivity, designates a pattern by which an object is made of smaller copies of itself. Recursion is illustrated in nature by the structure of trees (made of smaller trees) or by the anfractuosities of rocks, in mathematics by functions that generate fractal images, in optics by the images captured by two mirrors facing each other, and in computer programming, by functions that activate copies of themselves. In the cases of feedback loops and recursion, the examples I gave include both naturally occurring phenomena and human-made artifacts. By contrast, I would like to restrict the concept of self-reflexivity to products of the human mind. Self-reflexivity is the property of an object that brings attention to itself through an intentional design or through a deliberate interpretive act. On a planet without humans we would still have feedback mechanisms and recursive patterns, but we would have no self-reflexivity, because self-reflexivity is a semiotic phenomenon produced by a mental operation, while a feedback loop is a type of mechanism, and recursivity is a type of pattern.

But if they are theoretically distinct, the three concepts are often deeply entangled, and it may be very difficult to take them apart. For instance, the recursive patterns that characterize fractal images are the product of a function, and this function generally involves a feedback loop. Another form of entanglement comes from the fact that recursion and feedback loops are the most efficient ways to produce self-reflexivity. A visual artwork will for instance achieve self-reflexivity by recursively embedding a copy of itself. It is also very tempting for the human mind to interpret a recursive pattern in nature as being self-reflexive, though a tree made up of smaller trees does not say anything about itself intentionally. But as the sentence "this sentence has five words" demonstrates, we can have self-reflexivity without recursivity. In this case self-reflexivity is not triggered by a small copy of the sentence, but by a deictic element—"this"—that bears no resemblance whatsoever to the sentence it refers to. We can furthermore give a stable truth value to the sentence, without causing this truth value to curl back upon itself, while if we try to evaluate a sentence that illustrates the Cretan paradox, for instance "this sentence is false," we will create a feedback loop, because if the sentence is false, it is true, and if it is true, it is false, in a series of endless reversals.

TYPES OF SELF-REFLEXIVITY

The term "self-reflexivity" covers a wide range of phenomena diversified along three axes: the axis of explicitness, the axis of scope, and the axis of individuation.

The axis of explicitness concerns how strongly the text represents itself—how unavoidable is a self-reflexive interpretation. It runs from a strong pole of literal self-reference through an intermediary zone of self-reflexivity to a weak pole of artistic self-awareness. Genuine self-reference, which I consider to be a subspecies of self-reflexivity, is a feature limited to semiotic systems capable of making propositions or issuing commands. It is illustrated by the paradox-creating sentence "this sentence is false." Outside natural language, we find it in mathematics, for instance in Gödel's famous theorem, and in computer code. Images, by contrast, cannot literally refer, since they lack the indexical power of language, but they can represent themselves through recursive self-embedding. The closest we find to self-reference in the visual domain are consequently pictures that contain copies of themselves, as on the box of the Laughing Cow brand of cheese, where we see a cow with earrings representing the Laughing Cow box of cheese.

The middle of the spectrum of explicitness is occupied by works that present what I will call symbolic or emblematic forms of self-representation. This form is characterized by a double meaning: The self-reflexive elements represent both the text of which they are a part and something situated in the world created or described by the text. In a narrative text, for instance, the description of an object or a conversation between characters may both play a role within the plot and tell us how the text should be read, and in a poem, a metaphor may both participate in the concrete thematics of the text and offer a message about poetry.

At the weak pole of the axis of explicitness we find the kind of self-awareness that Roman Jakobson calls the "poetic function of language." According to Jakobson, this function focuses the reader's attention on the message—but it would be perhaps more appropriate to say on the text for its own sake. Verbal art is language that attracts attention to itself, but it can do so in a subtle way, through either pleasant sound patterns, creative imagery, or a narratively immersive content, without explicitly taking itself as referent.

The axis of *scope* diversifies self-reflexivity according to two variables: first, how much of the text functions self-reflexively; and second, how completely it represents itself. These two variables correspond to signifier and signified. To capture the difference, consider once more the case of "this sentence is false." Here only part of the signifier functions self-reflexively, but the scope of the deictic expression "this sentence" is the entire sentence; in other words, it mirrors itself completely.

On the Laughing Cow box of cheese, similarly, self-reflexivity is limited to the earring of the cow. It is because only part of the image is self-reflexive that it is able to represent anything at all: If the earring took the whole box, there would be no room for the cow or for anything else. As small as it is, the earring is supposed to represents the entire box, but it cannot do so completely, because in visual media, complete reflection would lead to an endless regression. If the self-representation were complete, the cow on the earring would need to have an earring that represents the box, and on this earring would be another cow, with another earring, that represents another cow, and so on ad infinitum.

Now let us take literary examples. It could perhaps be said that a symbolic poem that reflects on the nature of poetry, for instance a poem by Mallarmé, is self-reflexive throughout. When every word contributes to the global theme of poetry, the text becomes an allegory of itself. But no matter how much the text tells about itself or about poetry, there will always be aspects of its subject matter that it cannot represent. In other words, a text is always richer than what it says about itself. This is acutely the case in Marcel Proust's series of novels *A la recherche du temps perdu*. At the end, the narrator describes a book he intends to write, and the reader realizes that the description applies to the book he has just read—in other words, to Proust's actual work. But the self-reflexive passages occupy only part of Proust's novels; otherwise the novel would have no plot—it would be a gigantic meditation on literature. Moreover, the novel as a whole is much richer and much more diverse than what the narrator says about it in one volume, *Le temps retrouvé*; if it were not the case, we could limit our reading to the self-reflexive passages, and there would be no need to read the whole novel. Literary self-reference usually—or perhaps inevitably—focuses on some aspects of the text and leaves others in the shade.

Figure 6-1 situates the various types of self-reflexive texts mentioned above on a diagram with two axes. The origin of the axes corresponds

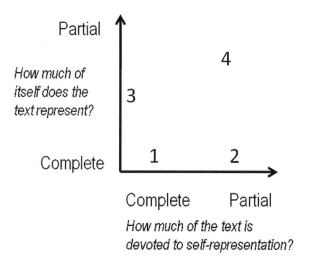

1. "This sentence has 5 words"
2. Laughing Cow cheese box
3. A symbolic poem about poetry (e.g. Mallarmé)
4. Proust's *A la recherche du temps perdu*

Figure 6-1. Types of self-reflexivity.

to the case of an image (or text) entirely devoted to a reflection of itself, and that represents itself in its totality. This area remains empty, because if a work did not capture anything external to itself, it could not represent anything at all. Similarly, if we place two mirrors facing each other perfectly, and there is nothing between them, there will be nothing to reflect.

The third axis concerns the *focus of the reflexive activity*. It runs from texts that reflect specifically on themselves, highlighting their own distinctive features, to texts that include a broader class in their self-mirroring, such as their medium or their genre. I will call these two poles individuated and categorial self-reflexivity. As an example of categorial self-reflexivity, consider the lexia "This writing" from the hypertext *Patchwork Girl*, by Shelley Jackson, which reflects on the difference between reading from a book and reading on a screen in a hypertext environment:

When I open a book I know where I am, which is restful. My reading is spatial and even volumetric. I tell myself, I am a third of the way down a rectangular solid, I am a quarter of the way down the page, I am here on the page, here on this line, here, here, here. But where am I now? I am in a here and a present moment that has no history and no expectations for the future.

But self-reflexivity in *Patchwork Girl* can also be individuated. For instance, the text map for the section "Crazy Quilt" is shaped like a patchwork quilt. This image alludes to the narrative thematics of the text, which describes how a fictional counterpart of Mary Shelley creates a female monster by sewing together the body parts of various women. The sewing activity of Mary Shelley functions in turn as an allegory of the writing activity of the author, Shelley Jackson, who stitches together the body of a text out of heterogeneous (and often recycled) textual fragments. In a movement leading from individuated to categorial self-reflexivity, the shape of the map allegorizes the particular story, but the story itself allegorizes the type of writing promoted by the Storyspace authoring system, with which *Patchwork Girl* was composed.

NET.ART

By net.art, I mean any artwork available on the World Wide Web that takes advantage of the computer, not only as a mean of production and dissemination, but also as a support necessary to the performance of the text. In other words, I restrict the category net.art to works that need to be executed by code.

Net.art was born in the 1990s, when the Internet developed from a resource mainly used by a technological elite into a widely accessible forum of mass communication, entertainment, and commercial activity. The hackers who previously owned cyberspace felt suddenly dispossessed. Their response to the invasion of the Net by clueless tourists was a fiercely anti-commercial and subversive form of art that requires some amount of technological literacy to be truly appreciated. The vast majority of the works of net.art give little pleasure to the eye, but the best of them stimulate the mind through the ingenuity of their generative idea. The response that net.artists try to generate is not "how beautiful," nor "how moving," as is the case for novels, but "how clever."

PARODY

Richard Powers, the author of my first example of self-reflexivity in net.art, is not a specialist in digital media but a distinguished novelist with a predilection for technological subjects. In "They Come in a Steady Stream Now," he tackles the proliferation of spam in email, and he does so through a Web-based story that mimics the interface of a standard email program.

When we first open (or rather, execute) the text, we are faced with a display that looks like a mailbox with various folders: "inbox," "drafts," "sent," and "trash." As the reader clicks on a mail to read it, another message (or rather, its headline) appears on the screen. At the end of the reading process, there will be seventeen emails in the inbox, but, ironically, none in the trash can, even though ten of them are spam: The user's agency is limited to reading the inbox, and in keeping with the theme of the story, the fictional system is unable to filter out the junk. The spam letters run the familiar gamut of pornography, drug offers, and investment opportunities. There is, for instance, "Iris Suarez," who peddles a catalog of singles available for dating, "Can-drgs," an outfit that sells six thousand medicines at "substantial price savings," "Evidence Eliminator," a company that warns you that you are "in serious trouble—it's a proven fact," but offers an absolutely safe protection against this danger, and a spam letter from "Christian Mortgages USA," which tells the user "Jesus loves you—refinance now!" In addition to the junk mail, the mail program is plagued by pop-up messages, which readers must close one by one before opening a new mail (Figure 6-2).

In contrast to the humor of the junk mail, the seven "legitimate" letters, addressed to the reader by Richard Powers himself, contain a melancholic meditation on aging. This meditation is triggered by the incessant hawking of drugs that promise to reverse the damage of time. The narrator sees himself on the brink of a brave new world inhabited by a posthuman species that enjoys eternal youth, a constant state of sexual arousing, and perfect memory. But he realizes that, like Moses, he will never enter this Promised Land:

> Lifestyle drugs, they're called: and who is going to argue? Not you, at 65, the last member of the last generation of humans still barred from returning to the garden, the last who will have to grow old, with nothing to look forward in retirement but Internet come-ons from the eternal future. . . . What will it feel like, to be another species? Nothing that your species might compare it to. Soon we'll be whatever comes after people. And puzzled by the hunger that we've finally outgrown.

The spam outlines a dystopic future for those who value our present condition of pre-posthumans. But it also opens windows onto the past

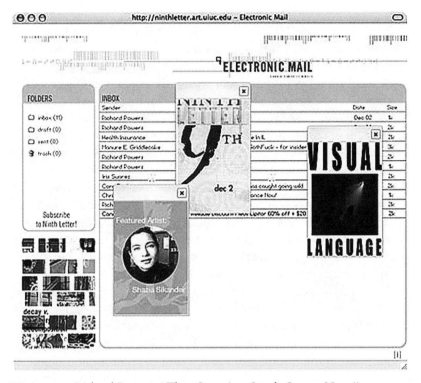

Figure 6-2. Richard Powers, "They Come in a Steady Stream Now."

by refreshing the memory of the narrator, not through drugs, but, quite inadvertently, though the names of the fake senders. One of the junk mails bears the name of a childhood friend of the narrator, a boy from his confirmation class who was struck by lightning when scrambling out of a lake during a summer outing. At the end of the story, the arrow of time will be reversed, and the narrator will relive the glorious afternoon by the lake before the boy was struck.

But first the reader must submit to a familiar Internet ritual. In the last of the seven letters we read: "PLEASE REGISTER. The content you requested is available only to registered members. Registration is FREE and offers great benefits." The user is asked to enter his or her email address in a box and to submit it by clicking a button. Those who dare follow these instructions (mindless of the risk of viruses) are rewarded with a response that read: "Thank you! You will receive your confirmation e-mail shortly." This is followed by an email from Richard Powers himself with a link to an Adobe file that can be downloaded and then printed. This file contains the text of the previous six fake mails, together with a very Proustian conclusion in which the present absorbs the past and the past becomes present. By including all the previously read installments, the final delivery invites the reader to reflect on the difference between the reading experience of the print and the electronic medium. In the email simulation, the text comes to the reader as a collection of fragments that create distraction through their many windows, through frequent interruptions, and through the obsessive need to click. The printable text gives rise to an entirely new reading experience. Now we can hold the entire text in our hand, a tactile relation that enhances concentration; we can read it without interruption, and we do not have to worry about competing windows nor about the order in which the text should be read. All these features, by freeing our attention from the interface and from the material conditions of reading, allow us to pay greater attention to the poetic quality of language. (It also helps, of course, that we are rereading rather than reading for the first time.) The originality of Powers's achievement lies in the complementarity of the comic experience of the screen version and of the lyrical experience of the print version. In its play with two media, the text is truly more than the sum of its parts. It manages to be at the same time emotionally moving, as good stories are, and clever, as net.art prides itself to be.

Where is Powers's text situated with respect to the three axes of self-reflexivity that I have defined above? On the axis of explicitness, I place it on the literal side. On the axis of scope, it is partial on both counts: On the side of the signifier, the self-reflexive components do not fill the whole text, since there is also the theme of the recapture of time, while on the side of the signified, the text reflects only on one specific feature of email, namely its invasion by spam, leaving out of its scope the more beneficial aspects of the technology. And finally, on the axis of focus, it represents a categorial rather than an individuated form of self-reflexivity, since it reflects on a use of digital technology, rather than being specifically about itself.

CODEWORK

My second type of self-reflexivity is represented by codework, that is to say, by works that draw attention to the machine language that controls their own performance. This emphasis on code can be seen as a reaction to the so-called WYSIWYG (what you see is what you get) aesthetics that has dominated the design of software and operating systems since the introduction of the so-called graphic user interface by the Macintosh in the early 1980s. The icons of the graphic interface are perfectly opaque buttons, and clicking on them requires no more knowledge of the inner working of the machine than choosing an item on the touch-operated menu of your microwave oven. Codework is an attempt to restore the user's awareness of the hidden layers of machine instructions that make it possible for data to travel from computer memory to the surface of the screen.

The example of codework that I will discuss here comes from Code-Doc, an exhibition organized in 2002 at the Whitney Museum of American Art in New York City. The curator, Christiane Paul, gave a dozen artists the assignment to write a computer program whose purpose was to connect and move three points in space, a theme that could be interpreted either literally or figuratively. The works bring attention to code by making visitors scroll through the code file, until they reached a button at the bottom that triggers the execution of the program.

In John Klima's "Jack and Jill," the code produces an imitation of the low-resolution computer games of the eighties, such as Loderunner or Donkey Kong. Another intertextual allusion is to the character Mario of the Super Mario Brothers series of games. The task of connecting and moving three points in space is ingenuously and humorously fulfilled by turning the three points into the protagonists of the well-known nursery rhyme "Jack and Jill." The purpose of the game is to enact the plot of the nursery rhyme, by taking Jack and Jill up a slope to fetch a pail and by making them tumble down the hill, once the pail has been reached (Figure 6-3). In contrast to standard computer games, users cannot use the keyboard to control the characters, but they can influence their movements indirectly by assigning values to a number of variable parameters: the choice of a "Chauvinist" or "Feminist" attitude decides which character is ahead of the other; the assignment of an intensity value to Jack's and Jill's desire controls the speed at which the characters climb the hill (with a low desire, they never get to the pail); and the specification of "pail allure" (which gives a choice of repulsive, moderate or undeniable) dictates the magnetic force exercised by the pail. To win the game, the user must find the proper combination of values for the parameters.

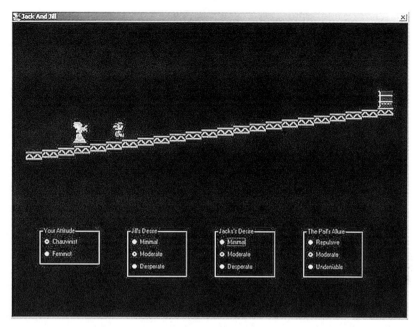

Figure 6-3. John Klima, "Jack and Jill."

The game is too easy to really challenge the player, but the real programming coup lies in the duplication of the game story by the text of
the code. This duplication means that the story is both dramatically
enacted on the screen, and verbally narrated in the code.

```
Sub Main()
    The_Story.Show
    While True
    If YourAttitude = CHAUVINIST Then
    If Fetch(pail, jack, jill) then Gouphill jack, jill
    If Felldown (jack) and Brokecrown(jack) then Tumblingafter
    jill, jack
    Else YourAttitude = FEMINIST Then
    If Fetch(pail, jill, jack) then Gouphill jill, jack
    If FellDown (jill) and Brokecrown(jill) then Tumblingafter
    jack, jill
    End if
    The_Story.Draw
    Wend
End Sub
```

What enables digital code to be read as a story is the fact that computer languages consist of two types of elements: names and operators. The operators are expressed through a fixed vocabulary of reserved words specific to the language, but the programmer can freely choose the names. For the computer, they stand for variables, constants, programs and subprograms. Here the variable names Jack, Jill, and Pail refer to the characters, and the subprogram names Fetch, Felldown, Brokecrown, and Tumblingafter describe the narrative events. But not all of the code could be used as storytelling device: For instance, the operator *If . . . then* is detrimental to narrative meaning, because a story is a report of facts, and as such, it cannot be told, at least not literally, in the conditional mode. It would be an extraordinary achievement to enroll both names and operators in the production of a story, and Klima can be forgiven for not achieving what is probably an impossible feat.

The status of "Jack and Jill" with respect to the axis of explicitness is debatable. The names of variables and subprograms refer explicitly, but what they refer to are addresses in memory and modules of code, not to the characters in a story. We must give them an emblematic reading, and we must ask the imagination to provide lots of information if we want to see the code as a narrative text that represent the adventures of Jack and Jill. The position of the text on the axis of scope is more straightforward. As I have already mentioned, only part of the code can be used for storytelling, and its representation of the game action is very schematic. "Jack and Jill" consequently illustrates the case of partial-partial. And finally, the text clearly occupies the individual pole of the axis of individuation.

MAPPING

My third example of self-reflexive net.art, Lisa Jevbratt's *1:1*, is an attempt to produce a map of cyberspace that gives access to every existing web site. The title *1:1* refers to a paradox that has fascinated authors as illustrious as Lewis Carroll and Jorge Luis Borges: the paradox of the map that achieves perfect self-reflexivity by becoming indistinguishable from the territory represented.

This idea is a theoretical problem of representation and not a practical problem in geographic visualization because such a map would be totally useless as a tool of navigation. A fusion of map and territory would necessitate a complete image of a territory at a 1 to 1 scale, and the territory should include the map itself. Why 1 to 1? Because any reduction would require the omission of some features. And why should the map be part of the territory? Because if it were not, it would point to something external to itself: one can, for instance, imagine a complete map of the earth at a 1 to 1 scale spread out on another, larger planet. Both of these conditions lead to paradoxes. As Borges has argued in "Partial Magic in the Quixote," if a map is part of the world, it can only represent the world completely by representing itself, which means that it must represent its own self-representation, in an infinite regression similar to the case of the Laughing Cow box of cheese. Moreover, if the map were at a 1 to 1 scale, it would cover the whole world, and according to Lewis Carroll this would lead to inevitable contradiction. A perfect map should contain an image of every blade of grass, but if it were spread out over the world, the sun would be blocked, the grass would die, the farmers would be mad, and the map would become unfaithful. Lewis Carroll suggests, tongue in cheek, a luminously simple and delightfully absurd solution to this problem: "So we now use the country itself as its own map, and I assure you it does nearly as well."[3]

If the fusion of map and territory cannot be achieved for physical space, would it be possible to resolve the paradox for the abstract territory known as Cyberspace? In "Every," one of the five visualizations that make up *1:1*, Jevbratt proposes a mapping of the Internet that aims at exhaustive coverage without sacrificing functionality. According to comments by Jan Ekenberg posted on the project's Web site, *1:1* "becomes not only the map, but the environment itself." Referring to Lewis Carroll, Ekenberg concludes: "Let's hope the farmers don't object." Jevbratt's own online description of the project concurs with Ekenberg's assessment: "The interfaces/visualizations are not maps of the Web, but are, in some sense, the Web. They are super-realistic and yet function in ways images could not function in any other environment or time." I agree with the second sentence, but I find the first one very problematic, unless "in some sense" means "in a very loose sense."

The project that inspires these rather hyperbolic statements is an attempt to visualize the Web as a system of IP addresses. The IP address of a Web site is the numeric translation of its domain name; in other words, what is for human users www.amazon.com could be for the computer 217.170.37.221. If IP addresses are made of four eight-bit words, for a total of thirty-two bits (as they were 1999 and 2001, when "Every" was created), there could be as many as 2^{32} distinct pages on the Web. But many IP addresses are not claimed, and attempts to reach them leads to the message "cannot find server, or DNS error." Other addresses are claimed, but the user is not authorized to access them.

To produce her map of the Web, Jevbratt used Web crawlers—programs that search the Web address by address—to determine which IP numbers have active servers. The crawlers returned all the active addresses for the sampled areas, for a total of 180,000. The pixels are color-coded on the basis of the numerical value of the address they represent, so that, by looking at the image, one can tell the "distance" (in numerical value) between occupied addresses: sharp contrasts in color mean that there are large intervals between active IPs, gradual contrast means that a region is densely populated (Figure 6-4). Each pixel is a hot link, and by clicking on it the user can reach the corresponding IP. This provides an interface to the Web radically different from the modes of navigation offered by standard browsers. As Jevbratt explains, "Instead of advertisement, pornography, and pictures of people's pets, this Web is an abundance of inaccessible information, undeveloped sites and cryptic messages intended for someone else." The user gets an idea of how small the proportion of the information stored on the Web is publicly accessible, and of how much the Web has changed since the creation of the project. I clicked about twenty times on the visualization, and my random selection yielded only one accessible website: the home page of "Marjorie Orr, top international astrologer."

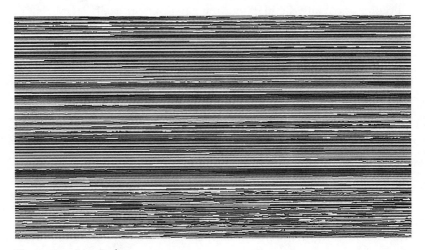

Figure 6-4. Lisa Jevbratt, *1:1*.

How should we understand the title *1:1*? One obvious interpretation is that each unit on the screen corresponds to a distinct IP address, in a one to one relation. But this relation is very different from the scale of a map, where 1:1 means that a certain area of the map corresponds to the same area in the world. The units on the screen are made of one pixel, but they stand for addresses made of thirty-two bits. Nor can we interpret *1:1* as meaning that the design represents the information available on the Net in its totality. First, the image shows only a section of the Net—there are not enough pixels on the screen to represent all the active Web addresses. We could admittedly imagine that the image is scrollable, and does cover the entire Net—it is just that it does not make it all visible at the same time. But even in this case, the visualization would not show what makes the Web a web: the complex system of links that interconnects its various elements.

All this should make it clear that *1:1* remains a long way from achieving the perfect self-referentiality presupposed by the claim that it is the Web itself. Conceptual artists have a tendency to produce auto-descriptions of their works, and commentators have a tendency to take these descriptions at face value. But nothing guarantees the validity of an auto-description, and there is consequently no reason to exempt artist's comments from critical examination. (One of the few commentators who dared to challenge Jevbratt's auto-comments is George Dillon.) But even if *1:1* does not live up to the hype of the author's description it remains an impressive achievement in data visualization, because its combination of representation and active interface to Web sites creates a type of image that could only exist in a digital environment.

Let us once again map this project with respect to my three axes. I am not sure that the contrast explicit vs. implicit is applicable to *1:1*, so I will leave the question open. In the matter of scope, we should distinguish Jevbratt's ambition from what she actually achieves. Her ambition is certainly to create a work that realizes the impossible, namely a work entirely devoted to its own self-representation. As I have suggested, this would be a blank image capturing its own void. *1:1* does not capture a void, because it represents only a limited aspect of the Web—the numeric distribution of its addresses, but we can safely say that it devotes itself entirely to this partial representation. And finally *1:1* practices a categorial rather than an individuated form of self-representation, since it displays the Web, of which it is a part. It only represents itself individually if one takes at face value the claim that it *is* the Web.

CONCLUSION

Let me return, in conclusion, to the question of what makes self-reflexivity so dominant in net.art. The rationalist will say that the Web is a tool designed by humans for the storage and exchange of information. We can turn this tool upon itself and play with it, just as we can do with many other forms of representation, because we are essentially self-reflexive animals. The relativist or postmodernist will object that we do not think about our technological systems as much as *they* think through us, because we are an inevitable part of their organization. Computer networks are the manifestation of a collective intelligence, and it is through net.art that this intelligence reaches self-awareness.

The interpretation that I personally favor is a compromise between these two positions. It borrows from the postmodernist position the idea of a feedback loop between human intelligence and the technological tools that it creates: We make and use these tools to solve our own problems, but in return they shape our life and our consciousness, and they create new problems to solve. Yet it is our innate propensity for self-reflexivity—as the rationalist position assumes—that enables us to deliberately turn digital technology upon itself, in order to explore to which extent we control the computer, and to which extent the computer controls us.

All three of the works I have discussed reflect on the issue of control by creating dysfunctional uses of digital technology. For Richard Powers, dysfunctionality is an email system paralyzed by spam; for John Klima, it is a game that nobody would buy, because it is too easy to win and visually too outdated; for Lisa Jevbratt, it takes the form of an interface to the Net that wastes most of the user's time, and when it gets the user somewhere, the process is so random that it cannot be used for practical interests.

By filling the Web with dysfunctional images of its own utilities, these works undermine the kind of immersion in digital technology that limits our attention to the surface of the computer screen. When we use digital technology, we may be driven by our own desires, but our agency is limited by code, and code is determined by the commercial interests of those who designed the software. Net.art resists this commercial control by choosing playful dysfunctionality, the epitome of a nonutilitarian activity. In this sense, all of net.art can be said to involve some form of self-reflexivity, whether implicit or explicit, partial or global, categorial or individual. For net.art, reflecting on its medium is not so much a search for identity as it *is* identity.

CHAPTER SEVEN

Moving (the) Text

From Print to Digital

KATALIN SÁNDOR

In the field of printed visual poetry, provoking and unavoidable theoretical questions about the digital medium have been raised, because printed visual literature—a corpus of medially hybrid texts at the margins of the literary canon—is familiarly reread and repositioned through questions, concepts, and metaphors that are constructed for theorizing the digital or the hypertextual. From this perspective, printed visual poetry seems to be a productive, though not unproblematic, reference point for critical discourses that do not reiterate dichotomies and canons, such as the (old) book versus the (new) Net, print versus digital, and linear versus nonlinear. Such dichotomies, as András Müllner points out, favor totalizing structures and the construction of an evolutionary history in a diachronic perception of media, and this concept of evolution is invested with certain values and ideologies.[1] This is, then, how techno-optimists praise the electronic medium for its flexibility, variability, nonlinearity, interactivity, and indeterminacy; its (apparently) more democratic way of distributing knowledge; and, for its technical potential to "put into practice" the poststructuralist notions of endlessly dispersed and decentered textuality. On the other hand, as Bolter observes, skeptics worry about the culture of the book: They deny that physical aspects of technologies of writing might determine its actual practice and instead argue that these technologies can be described only along social needs and preferences. Both discourses, however, seem to lack critical potential and perpetuate a "false"[2] and counterproductive dichotomy: counterproductive, because social needs and technological constraints are interrelated and conditioned by each other in a way that makes it impossible to separate them according to the logic of causality. The question I want to raise here, then, is: How does twentieth-century printed visual poetry look forward to, and affect the conceptualization of, the hypertextual, the digital, and the nonlinear?

VISUAL PRINTED POETRY, THE NONLINEAR, AND THE DIGITAL

Espen Aarseth, in his attempt to outline a theoretical framework for nonlinearity (mostly, but not exclusively, for hypertextual and cybertextual constructions), acknowledges that certain computer-mediated digital texts might show more resemblance with printed texts than with their own digital "relatives."[3] Aarseth's matrix of textual variants and user-functions describes textual formations without linking their nonlinearity to their medium in an essentializing way. In his typology, four types of nonlinear texts exist: simple nonlinear text, hypertext, determined cybertext, and indetermined cybertext.[4] Some printed visual poems—even if not explicitly mentioned—might be discussed within the first type as simple nonlinear texts, since their scriptons (textual sequences) are not presented in a determined linear order, their textons (the basic elements of textuality) are static, open, and can be configured by the reader/user.

In his study on digital literature, Péter Józsa points out that Aarseth's approach replaces the opposition between print and digital by the dichotomy of ergodic versus nonergodic (and, I add, linear versus nonlinear). The ergodic refers to the "nontrivial effort to traverse a text," while the trivial one consists of following the lines and turning the pages; it is not necessarily linked to the mediality of the text. However, Józsa also argues that in order to avoid a diffuse terminology, it is more productive to restrict the use of the term hypertextual to nonlinear digital texts, whereas nonlinear print texts should be called proto-hypertexts or quasi-hypertexts.[5]

Recent theoretical perspectives, such as those by Péter Józsa and Anna Gács, show that visual print poems, pattern poetry, or concrete poems (together with lexicon novels, multilinear narratives, collage-like texts, self-generating texts, and so on) can be conceptualized as proto-hypertexts. Like hypertext or cybertext, visual print poetry rhetorically works through configurative writing functions and through a nonlinear or multilinear textual body that has no predefined pattern for readability and sequence, and is also open to remaking and reconfiguration. Yet we should be prudent to build a new print canon—or at least a genre—on the basis of the concept of the hypertextual. It is instructive to consider Müllner's reservations with respect to intertextuality in literature here: for him, in the poststructuralist perspective, *all* texts are intertextual as the latter is a precondition for meaning to arise in the first place. Thus, one text cannot be "more" intertextual than another.[6] How then to use the intertextual as a generic concept? The same argument goes for nonlinearity or nonlinear literature: all texts and all reading can be considered nonlinear in one way or another; for example, through the dialectic of prospective and retrospectively overwritten expectations (or the Iserian protension and retension in the act of reading), the continuous revision of semantic constructions, and the associative, multilinear, intertextual practice of reading delinearize the process of meaning-making. Thus, linearity and nonlinearity cannot be exclusively restricted to the modality of presenting the scriptons of a text in a specific order. András Kappanyos, for example, approaches the question from the perspective of perception and comprehension/interpretation in the process of reading. He comes to the conclusion that the interpretive/meaning-making level of reading has never been linked to linearity, though the perceptive level of decoding graphic signs in a certain order most probably works in a linear(izing) manner.

While fully agreeing with András Müllner about the instability of canons based on concepts like intertextuality or nonlinearity—as probably Aarseth himself would do, too—I still think that foregrounding the "hypertextual" or the "nonlinear" in analog texts, may be productive as a strategy to think of media in nonessentialist terms (linear versus nonlinear, print versus digital, fixed versus open, and so on) and to avoid conceiving of media in a totalizing paradigm (for example, the culture of the book versus the culture of the Net). What is so interesting about visual print poetry is its possibility to undermine such essentialist terms and, at the same time, to question the idea of a radical historical shift from the culture of the allegedly linear, totalizing book to that of the seemingly nonlinear, nontotalizing hypertext. Visual print poetry—like the experimental and concretist image-texts of the Noigrandes group—and its rhetorical preoccupation with the mediality of text, disbands the representational transparency of the linguistic sign, and interrogates the materiality of language and the way it "collaborates with," or destabilizes processes of, signification. In this way, the artistic practices of visual print poetry, of pattern poems, calligrams, concrete poetry, lettrism, and collages have come to function as a continually recycled "resource" for digital poetry.

Digital poetry, we could in fact say, is visual poetry in print plus time and intervention. As Roberto Simanowski has shown, while concrete poetry "combines linguistic and graphic qualities of letters, in digital media time and interaction are two additional ways of expression."[7] Friedrich W. Block argues that the experimental and conceptual visual poetry of the 1950s and 1960s is programmatically continued in the digital space with significant poetic changes: For example, movement becomes animation and processuality, the intermedial shifts toward a so-called *diabolisierung* of the signifier and the signified, and interaction becomes participation in the process of making the artwork.[8] In other words: In visual print poetry and digital poetry the seemingly invisible medium of writing is thematized and rendered visible, becomes its own object, but visual print poetry is also *transformed* and *displaced* as digital text, as the "traits" of the former return with a difference in new medial, technological, and interpretive contexts.

ICONICITY, ANIMATION, AND DISPLACEMENT

The idea of kinesis and temporality has been a central poetic challenge for the medium of printed visual and concrete poetry. Charles Olson's poem "The Motion," for instance, verbally (and metaphorically) thematizes and, at the same time, visually traces a process of *movement* and differentiation, a displacement of identities from the "I" or the word "I" toward the "not I," toward the Other "you," a process from identity to difference in the white space of the page.[9] This process also reflects on the way in which the verbal medium configures and is configured by its own Other, by the nonverbal difference of its own inscription, foregrounding the visuality and medial heterogeneity of the linguistic. Thus the downward, segmented motion in this poem may function as a space for (ontological) displacement: the process in which the medial homogeneity of the verbal is dispersed and delinearized by the nonphonologic, nonverbal Other.

The lettrist poem "Csúszás" ("Slide") by the Hungarian poet János Géczi also "provokes" the print medium and deals with the problem of movement: We see (only) the traces, the effects of a slide, of a technical process of manipulation; namely, the disfiguration of the letter "A" or "a" by the photocopy machine, the process of erasing its codified identity or form. The poem can also be read as an ontological "slide" or shift from the understanding of the grapheme as a phonologically functional and secondary signifier (with a codified form) to its perception as a nonreferential and nonrepresentational image. The idea of movement and dislocation is significant as a poetic experiment to challenge the limits of the medium, but also as a possible trajectory for meaning-making practices.

In these visual poems, the text does not actually "perform" any kinesis; rather, the reading eye acts on the traces of some movement, often directed by nonlinear verbal-visual patterns or maps. Such trajectories easily become patterns of and for a disturbed cognition or interpretational indeterminacy, since these nonlinear texts do not offer one fixed reference point or one predetermined sequence for their own reading.

The concept of movement here questions the idea of writing as a fixed, imprinted entity, which also fixes the reader's position. Kinetic poetry (for example, the works of Ian Hamilton Finlay) also flirts with the idea of displacing the text, of dissolving the fixed position of the text and the reader, making the latter aware of her own spatial position, and the way this affects perception and the practices of meaning-making. Still, the letters here remain materially imprinted, and only the surfaces on which they appear perform aleatoric movements (for example, letters on water).

Today visual poetry has entered the digital space: not only does the reading eye or the imprinted surface move, but the text is also programmed by an invisible code-text to act as the "doer" of kinesis. Nevertheless, animated texts, which do not require the reader's intervention, are not a poetical novelty: They are reminiscent of the text-movies or television poetry of the 1960s and 1970s, as Simanowski observes.[10] The various intermedial discourses of film titling (long before the digital medium) also used complex, nonlinear surfaces and modalities of animated writing that possessed qualities of temporality and depth. In such film titles, writing is both language and image, both discursive and nondiscursive, and it often anticipates the visual rhetoric or some narrative aspect of that film.

Alex Gopher's *The Child* can, I suggest, be read within a framework outlined by such filmic traditions. *The Child* is actually a ludic textual music video that is part of an anthology of digital literature (*Hermeneia*). The video narrates a somewhat predictable story about the nonetymologic birth of the word "child," and its characters are animated words and letters. The background music is an electronic remix of Billy Holiday's classic song "God Bless the Child." The ludic narrative is programmed according to filmic conventions such as a steady cam, zooming in, and long takes and cuts, and it uses few words with little or no syntax. In this respect, it is clearly reminiscent of concrete poetry, pattern poems, and film titles.

The first image from this animated dictionary of New York—that of clouds and skyscrapers shown from a distance—is a scene on which the camera gradually zooms in before it is disrupted into separate signs, letters, and words, which dissolve the analogous continuity and the transparent representationality of the picture. Foucault's "thing," assumed to be caught by the double trap of calligrammatic figurality (in the famous study *This is not a Pipe*), is here overwritten by language and disrupted into writing, digits and letters, and into signs, which behave like images or pixels of an image. These letter-pixels foreground the textuality, and thus, the constructedness of the digital moving picture. The discontinuous letter- and pixel-fragments of the image here undermine the work of iconicity and seeing-through. By zooming in, the iconic image-text is not only brought closer, but also disrupted as image and thus exposed as an iconic configuration of linguistic signifiers. Like Foucault's conception of the calligram as an impossible double—verbal and pictorial—trap, the image as iconic representation is here always already dissected by the lines of writing. The signified, which cannot be read and looked at simultaneously, slips away from this double trap of representation and signification.

Gopher's work not only plays with the calligrammatic, iconic aspect of writing (for example, the expression "Very very long Cadillac" is indeed a long line forming the image of a Cadillac), but also with the way in which these word-images are programmed to "use" the virtual space as they "behave" in an anthropomorphic or object-like manner. Thus, it is possible to omit verbal syntax and linguistic connectors in favor of a visual narrative and sequence: we see, for example, the word "taxi" crossing the words "Brooklyn Bridge." The choreography of writing here reenacts a calligrammatic tradition in print, but the iconicity of visible language is exchanged for the iconicity of *performed acts and processes*: the figure of the word "taxi" does not resemble an image of a "taxi," but *acts* like one. This also happens in Augusto de Campos's animated concrete poem "Bomba," which does not form the image of a bomb, but performs the act of explosion annihilating the word itself by dispersing it into letters, and erases itself as its own referent. In these animated texts, reading becomes *screenic*. By this, I mean a mode of reading that takes place *in the instant*, rather than in a sequence, in the interaction with a coded interface. If the digital adds the dimension of time to visual poetry, the temporal in *The Child* becomes the time of the momentary: it plays with the experience of a flash of recognition or a sudden insight, rather than that of a sequence. Here, reading no longer *takes time*, but occurs in a minimal instant.

ANIMATION, PROCESSUALITY, AND INTERVENTION

As we have seen, in digital poetry readers not only respond to but also intervene in animated texts. As Shuen-Shing Lee puts it, referring to Aarseth and Ryan, the reader here performs ergodic actions identified as a complex form of interaction and expression.[11]

Jim Andrews's poem "Seattle Drift" addresses the reader by a somewhat limited interface-rhetoric: "I am a bad text. I used to be a poem but drifted from the scene. Do me. I just want you to do me." The reader has three options: to do, to stop, and to discipline the text: "do the text" means to launch the dismantling of the text, which starts to fall apart into disconnected words; "stop the text" means to end this process at a certain moment, which results in a nonlinear disjointed linguistic material; and "discipline the text" means to restore the initial cohesive version of the text. According to Simanowski, "the irony intermedially results from the contrast between the naming of the lost original disposition (which the reader reads) and the result of restoring it (which the reader sees): I drifted from the scene, says the poem when it is in proper order, but ends up all the more in the void when you try to help it. As if the order of the lines went against the real order of being, an order of permanent shifts and of the unspeakable. As the theory of différance, whose playful adaptation 'Seattle Drift' seems to be, tells us, to name something is to reduce it."[12]

I want to add to this reading that the intermedial rhetoric, as it dismantles and disperses the text, offers the reader ambiguous options of intervention. Thus "Seattle Drift" exposes language in its rhetorical-tropological elusiveness, which makes any (authorial, interventional) control over the text illusionary. For instance, the expression "bad text" can be read as commenting both on nonpoetry and on having lost the status of poetry: It plays ironically with the notion of literariness—a notion being constructed by various modes of reading, disciplining, and canonization. The option of "doing the text" launches, in fact, a process of undoing it, of loosening its fixed grammatical and syntactical connections (in a neo-avant-garde conception of the text, this grammatical disconnectedness might actually unleash the discursive indeterminacy and productivity of language). In this case, "drifting from the scene" (of poetry) could be the result of disciplining the text, which is an action performed by the reader: interpretation, reading, reduction, or any other intervention.

Disciplining may thus be the metaphor of a reading practice that reduces the elusiveness of the text to nonpoetry, but this disciplining is also something that can never be fully achieved. After all, what it restores is once more . . . a "bad text" again asking for some readerly interference. With the figure of apostrophe ("Do me. I just want you to do me.") the text interpellates a quasi authorial subject-position, but, at the same time, the elusive figurativeness of language undermines the possibility of a completed performative act: "Doing" the text will actually result in undoing its structure. In this way, the expression "bad text" can also be the metaphor of a rhetorically evasive text: a text that resists being disciplined, that both invites and eludes reading and intervention, while questioning and destabilizing the reader's sense of control and authorial function.

Marko Niemi's "Concrete Stir Fry Poems" exemplifies another modality of intervening into the textual-graphic process: one of intermedial mimicry. Moving the cursor, the reader visually manipulates the letters, erasing, covering, uncovering, disfiguring, and eventually recovering their form. In the poem "four musicians," the four letters of the word "echo" can be visually maneuvered. The words "musicians' and "echo" invoke the audible, the multiplication and rupture of sounds and words. The intermediality of the rhetoric consists precisely in transmuting and remediating the audible effects of the echo into visible figurations: The audible is visually "echoed" by letters whose unfixed, fractured forms produce and multiply other letters or fragments, each letter containing and mediating another. Reminiscent of the nonsemantic use of language in lettrism, the letters are detached from phonological and representational functions. The graphemes—disturbing the transparency of language—become self-referential, images with fluid margins and unpredictable structures. *Yet*, like signs, they continue to invoke the audible.

The fact that such digital texts are codependent on the user's intervention and manipulation questions the boundaries of the text as object in favor of a textual processuality without a definable identity and finality. This displacement, paradoxically, not only confers the reader/user certain authorial functions but also suspends the illusion of the user's control over a predictable process of participation in the "making" of the text. Such a poetics of intervention is familiar from the (open) works and performances of experimental and conceptual poetry, which all seek to destabilize the institution of authorship (and even that of the art system), the traditional roles of the reader, as well as the medial borders of artworks. For critics like Friedrich W. Block the electronic space (*elektronische Raum*) realizes in full the transgressive modes of textuality that analog art already projects. However, as I have been at pains to point out here, the authorial and participatory position of the reader as a subject position, often uncritically welcomed by techno-optimists and associated with empowering and individualizing functions, cannot be fully sustained when we consider works like "Seattle Drift" and "Concrete Stir Fry Poems." For here, the reader is *programmed* to intervene into the text—and, indeed, the text works as much on the reader as the reader works on the text. How far does intervention go, how free can reading be, when it is predetermined?

ANIMATION AND TEMPORALITY

We have already briefly seen above that animated texts foreground issues of temporality and the manipulation of time in the process of reading. Thus, we have shown how reading is transformed into the experience of an instance, instead of a sequential experience, in *The Child*. We now have occasion to consider the temporal dimension of digital poetry in more detail. In Raine Koskimaa's view, the rhetoric of temporality and timing is a specific quality of digital media. Koskimaa distinguishes four modes of manipulating time: digital texts can limit reading time; delay the time of reading; restrict the reading period; and behave like "living" texts in time. In other words, they can change and be updated at various intervals.

The manipulation of time can be the result of the user's intervention: in Kenji Komoto's "Life," the user can shorten the prolonged, empty time between the words "birth" and "death" and thus can bring the end of the text closer. However, digital poetry also subjects readers to time, limiting the time of reading by excluding any form of intervention. A fine example of this is Brian Kim Stefans's "Star Wars, One Letter at a Time," which rewrites the entire script of the fourth episode of *Star Wars*. The reappropriation itself is a double citing process: The reinscription of the text is done by invoking an older apparatus of inscription—namely, the typewriter—and thus the older medium becomes the remediated content of the newer one. The fonts, letters, the typical knocking and ringing sound of the machine, and the segmented appearance of the letters all materially invoke the typewriter. As we know from Friedrich Kittler the typewriter marks the separation of writing from the authorial hand (or voice) and control, as well as the break in the continuity body-nature-culture guaranteed by handwriting.[13] Stefan's poem remediates this separation.

In "Star Wars," the process of inscription is disturbed and made partially inaccessible: The letters do not remain imprinted on a flat surface as the material traces of the apparatus occupying physical space—as with the typewriter—but instead they flash and disappear one by one as they are, as it were, dematerialized in the virtual, apparently immaterial depth of the electronic space, almost like speech sounds, which appear too fast to be deciphered. The flashing text plays with the real-time aspect of retyping the whole *Star Wars 4* script and the reader's inability to catch up with temporality, exposing an anxiety of not possessing an unfixed, electronic, text. This sort of writing seems to "remember" and, at the same time, to "forget" and undo what the typewriter "did": namely, dissecting the continuity of (hand)writing, objectifying and codifying the letters, splitting the text from the authorial hand, and fixing it as a durable construction in a redistributed space. By remediating the practice of typing, the writing of disappearance in Stefan's text, becomes a process without a product, a (re)inscription without a definite place, without depth and finality, without a material archive, stored in codes and programs awaiting activation.

Nevertheless, it would not be productive to simply reinforce an assumed binary opposition between the alleged immateriality of the digital text and the materiality of the book here. As András Müllner observes, the hypertext and computer work themselves on hard material grounds, viruses, and power cuts, which can make the immaterial hypertext unreadable, and this confronts us with its materiality and with its hardware.[14]

As far as signification and reading practices are concerned, the digital retyping of the *Star Wars* script dematerializes the text because it loses its tactile and imprinted aspect; it moves away, alluding to an invisible code-text or program-text lying behind the animated signs on the screen. The knocking sound that accompanies the heavy imprinting work of the typewriter in an indexical manner is deferred here as a medial citation, and so is typing, which is reinscribed in the digital medium as absence. Katherine Hayles observes: "In the computer the signifier exists not as a durably inscribed flat mark but a screenic image produced by layers of code precisely correlated through correspondence rules. Even when electronic hypertexts simulate the appearance of durably inscribed marks, they are transitory images that need to be constantly refreshed to give the illusion of stable endurance through time."[15] We might thus say that Stefans's text does not conceal its own transitory existence, but foregrounds it in a reflective way that hinders the process of reading.

Perhaps there are few readers who have the patience to watch/read the digital "retyping" of the whole script of *Star Wars 4*. If and when they do, their reading will oscillate between recognition and misreading, readability and unreadability, the cultural familiarity of the text and the material alienation of its reinscription. In these conditions, even for a short time, reading becomes a process of deciphering and decoding. This process, I suggest, here exposes our cultural ambitions for reading as a reading for meaning, which is perhaps even more emphatic when made impossible.

REMEDIATION

Retyping the script of *Star Wars 4* is interesting not only within the esthetics of meaning-making, but also within the esthetics of the conceptual work, which displays technologies of writing, reading, and meaning-making precisely by disabling them (as in Ryan's dysfunctional net poetry), as well as modalities of citing and remediating other media. The way the typewriter is "cited" here reflects on the mode in which digital media iterate and reposition other (traditional) media. The typewriter as an apparatus is detached from its work of inscription, the sound and the imprinted writing is apparently delayed within the work that produces it because the letters seem to be digitally dematerialized. Typing is cited as a historical mode of inscription: it becomes part of the software. Jay David Bolter also draws attention to this iterative, remediating aspect of the digital; in his view, the computer as a manipulator of symbols remains a technology of writing and fits into the tradition of the papyrus scroll, the codex, and the book, but as a sensual-perceptive manipulator the computer enlarges the tradition of television, film, photography, and even representational painting.[16] In the process of remediation, then, the digital medium repositions these different traditions, simulating, incorporating, and (historically) displacing certain technologies, conventions, and features of various media.

If we think of the digital medium as a remediation of old and new media, we can say that it not only stores all the other media as an archive but also cites and repositions them, which exposes their historicity within altered conditions and contexts of meaning-making. This double function of storage and repositioning/rewriting, displays the digital not as a compound, but rather, as an intermedium and a metamedium, into which other media are reinscribed as forms, as absences, and as figurations of difference. Joachim Paech, referring to Niklas Luhman, states that the medium which is transparent in the process of mediation, can only be observed in the contingency of forms it enables to appear, thus only in the self-observation of observation.[17] If we accept Paech's understanding of intermediality as a process of transformation, as the reinscription of the medium into the text, the imitation of the technology of typing is an event of intermedialization, in which the older medium is deferred and repositioned by the digital in a new or "interim" space: a space of indeterminacy. Thus, both media appear as "other": The simulated reinscription of the typewriter also exposes the *differences* of the digital. The reinscription is performed in a pointedly disturbed, dysfunctional manner, since it does not permit for an immediate access to the historically "cited" absent apparatus—or to the text.

INSTEAD OF CONCLUSIONS

Without trying to map out all the significant interactions between printed and digital visual poetry, this chapter has traced some typical poetical displacements in paper and digital textuality. First, we have explored the extension of the static-compositional calligrammatic iconicity in concrete poetry toward the temporal iconicity of performative acts in digital texts. Second, we have addressed the issue of textual movement and the high difficulty degree of temporal reading in digital poetry. Third, we have seen how the reader participates in the configuration of a digital text, which transforms the latter into a process rather than a fixed object. In addition, this chapter has discussed works in which the digital cites other media as "absences" and as historical modes of inscription. In itself, this may be a citation of the book, which, once aspired to, includes all other arts.

Roberto Simanowski points to another shift in the relation between printed and digital poetry (especially the concretist one): the move away from a spectator-reader experience based on symbolic and semantic manipulation toward the esthetics of the sensual, the mannerist surface spectacle.[18] What I want to add to this observed shift is that as far as poetic language is concerned, too much preoccupation with the code, with the program, with the sensual, material aspect of language might lead toward a total metapoetry. The esthetics of the surface, the language of concrete, postconcrete, and visual poetry in the digital medium might prove to be a self-referential, hermetic, politically weak poetic discourse. This, I believe, can be remedied only when an open display of the materiality of language is used to expose (and open up to contestation) the discursive and medial conditions within which we play our political language games.

CHAPTER EIGHT

Technology Made Legible

Software as a Form of Writing in Software Engineering

FEDERICA FRABETTI

The main goal of this chapter is to propose an analytical framework for the cultural understanding of the group of technologies commonly referred to as "new" or "digital." I aim to dispel the opacity that still surrounds new technologies and that currently constitutes one of the main obstacles in their conceptualization. I argue that such demystification is essential if we are to take new technologies seriously and to engage with them on both a cultural and political level. To achieve this, I will look at software as a particular manifestation of what we commonly refer to as "text" in the digital age.

My understanding of new technology is that of technology based on software. The ubiquity of software does not need to be demonstrated here. According to Katherine Hayles (to quote but one source), the importance of software resides in its capacity to control the behavior of digital computers, which in turn "permeate nearly every kind of advanced technology." Software "can set off missiles or regulate air traffic; control medical equipment or generate PET scans; model turbulent flows or help design innovative architecture. All of these tasks are binary code and logic gates that are intolerant to error."[1] Software is the regulative technology of the present.

An in-depth understanding of new technologies and of their role in contemporary culture and society therefore requires, as a preliminary step, an investigation into how software operates. Indeed, I want to suggest that it is possible to understand technology by focusing on its basic function rather than on the intertwined processes of production, reception, and consumption of technology (processes that typically constitute the focus of media and cultural studies). It must be recalled at this point that, from the perspective of media and cultural studies, to study technology "culturally" means to follow the trajectory of a particular "technological object" (generally understood as a technological product), and to explore "how it is represented, what social identities are associated with it, how it is produced and consumed, and what mechanisms regulate its distribution and use."[2] Such an analysis concentrates on "meaning" and on the way in which a technological object is made meaningful. Meaning is understood not as arising from the technological object "itself," but from the way it is represented in the discourses surrounding it. By being brought into the arena of meaning, the technological object is constituted as a "cultural artifact."[3] Thus, meaning emerges as intrinsic to the definition of "culture" deployed by media and cultural studies.

In the approach to new technologies, media studies and cultural studies have therefore predominantly been focused on the intertwined processes of production, reception, and consumption, that is, on the discourses and practices of the new technologies' producers and users. From this perspective, even a technological object as mysterious as software is analyzed in terms of how it has been made into a significant cultural object. For instance, in his 2003 article on software, Adrian Mackenzie demonstrates the relevance of software as a topic of study essentially by examining the new social and cultural formations that surround it.[4]

Although I recognize that this perspective remains important and politically meaningful for the cultural study of technology, I suggest that it should be supplemented by a more "immersed" investigation of technology. In other words, as I suggest, to understand the role that new technologies play in our lives and world, we also need to shift the focus of the analysis from the practices and discourses *concerning* them to a thorough investigation of how new technologies *work*, and, in particular, of how software *works* and of what it *does*. Therefore, I seek a way to access the ever-present but allegedly invisible codes and languages that constitute software. In this way, I am attempting to reformulate the problem of understanding software-based technologies as a problem of making software *legible*.

By arguing for the importance of such an investigation, I do not mean that a "direct observation" of software is possible. In fact, I am

well aware that any relationship we can entertain with software is
always mediated, and that software might well be "unobservable." In
fact, I intend to take away all the implications of "directness" that the
concept of "demystifying" or "engaging with" software may bring with
itself. I am particularly aware that software has never been univocally
defined in any disciplinary field (including technical ones), and that it
assumes different forms in different contexts. For instance, a computer
program written in a programming language and printed on a piece of
paper is already what we call software. When a computer executes such
a program, it is no longer visible, although it might remain accessible
through changes in the status of the machine (such as the blinking of
lights, or the flowing of characters on a screen)—and it is still defined
as software. According to Matthew Fuller, software is an "object" that
is not "static." Rather, it operates "in participial terms."[5] The term
"participial" was first used by Elaine Scarry in her 1994 work *Resisting
Representation*.[6] As Fuller explains, the term "simply means a word
that is both a verb and a noun, a thing and a motion."[7]

In this chapter, I start from a widely accepted definition of software
as the totality of all computer programs as well as all the written texts
related to computer programs. This definition constitutes the conceptual foundation of software engineering, a technical discipline born in
the late 1960s to help programmers design software cost-effectively.
Software engineering describes software development as an advanced
writing technique that translates a text or a group of texts written in
natural languages (namely, the requirements specifications of the software "system") into a binary text or group of texts (the executable computer programs), through a step-by-step process of gradual refinement.[8]
For instance: "software engineers model parts of the real world in software. These models are large, abstract and complex so they must be
made visible in documents such as system designs, user manuals, and
so on. Producing these documents is as much part of the software engineering process as programming."[9]

The essential move that such a reformulation allows me to make is
to transform the problem of engaging with software into a problem of
reading it. Moreover, since software engineering is concerned with the
methodologies for writing software, I will also ask to what extent and
in what way software is a form of writing. Such a reformulation enables
me to take the textual nature of software seriously. In other words, I
aim to show that concepts such as "reading," "writing," "document,"

and "text" are no mere metaphors. Rather, they are software engineering's privileged mode of dealing with software as a technical object. It could be said that in software engineering, software's technicity is dealt with as a form of writing.

Software was already conceptualized as writing when software engineering was still in its infancy—when it constituted itself as a discipline at the end of the 1960s, and continued to map its future developments.[10] Two conferences organized by NATO in 1968 and 1969 mark the official start of software engineering both as a field of research and as a profession. This founding moment was connected with the so-called software crisis—a turning point in software production, when the international software community started worrying less about productivity and more about software quality. The NATO conferences are well documented (transcripts are widely available), and they included many of software engineering's "founding fathers."[11] The most controversial issues at the origin of software engineering are discussed in these papers. A genealogy of software engineering is particularly important to understand in what way writing was assumed as the privileged instrument for dealing with technological complexity.

Before examining a specific example of the interplay between "software," "writing," and "code" as they were understood in the early days of software engineering, I want to point out that my approach to software gives rise to two major questions: First, to what extent and in what way is software legible, or in what way is one supposed to read software, including code? Second, how is "writing" to be understood in the context of programming and, more broadly, of digital technologies?

As for the first question, which I can address only briefly here, I argue that, in order to make software legible, the concept of reading itself needs to be problematized. In fact, if we accept that software presents itself as a distinctive form of writing, we need to be aware that it consequently invites a distinctive form of reading. But to read software by conforming to the strategies it enforces upon its reader would imply reading it as a computer professional would, that is, in order to make it function *as software*. I argue that reading software on its own terms is not equal to reading it functionally. For this reason, I develop a strategy for reading software by drawing on Jacques Derrida's concept of deconstruction. However controversial and uncertain a definition of "deconstruction" might be, I am essentially taking it up here as a way for stepping out of a conceptual system by continuing to use its concepts while at the same time demonstrating their limitations.[12] "Deconstruction" in this sense aims at "undoing, decomposing, desedimenting" the conceptual system underlying software, not in order to destroy it, but in order to understand how it has been constituted.[13]

WRITING AS MODERNITY

According to Derrida, in every conceptual system we can detect a concept that is unthinkable within the conceptual structure of the system itself—therefore, it has to be excluded by the system, or, rather, it must remain unthought to allow the system to exist. A deconstructive reading of software therefore asks: What is it that has to remain unthought within the conceptual structure of software?[14] In Derrida's words, such a reading looks for a point of "opacity," for a concept that escapes the foundations of the system in which it is nevertheless located and for which it remains unthinkable. It looks for a point where the conceptual system that constitutes software "undoes itself."[15] For this reason, a deconstructive reading of software is the opposite of a functional reading. For a computer professional, the point where the system "undoes itself" is a malfunction, something that needs to be fixed. From the perspective of deconstruction, it is rather the point where the conceptual system underlying software is clarified.

Furthermore, revealing the hidden assumptions that have made technology what it is today does more than just contribute to its demystification. In fact, deconstruction allows not only for the desedimentation of fixed structures and meanings but also for their rearrangement. Such a rearrangement can enable us to see technology differently; it can also allow for something unexpected to emerge. This is precisely what is meant by the "affirmative" aspect of deconstruction. Therefore, I argue that, ultimately, being able to put into question at a fundamental level the premises on which a given conception of technology relies would expand our capacity for thinking technology on a political level.

What is "writing" in a deconstructive reading of technology? My analysis is tightly related to the debate around materiality and information that has recently gained a central importance in the cultural studies of technology. This debate is characterized by a growing awareness of the inseparability between materiality and signifying practices in the realm of digital technologies. In *My Mother Was a Computer*, Hayles repositions materiality in relation to textuality and, particularly, in relation to "the traffic between language and code."[16] Specifically, she argues for a sophisticated understanding of the interaction between language, writing, and code. She writes:

> Unnoticed by most, new languages are springing into existence, proliferating across the globe, mutating into new forms, and fading into obsolescence. Invented by humans, these languages are intended for the intelligent machines called computers. Programming languages and the code in which they are written complicate the linguistic situation as it has been theorized for "natural" language, for code and language operate in significantly different ways.[17]

What is interesting for me about this quote is that Hayles identifies throughout history three main "discourse systems"—namely, the system of speech, the system of writing, and the system of digital computer code, all of which are still active in contemporary culture. According to her, each of these systems is associated with a specific "worldview"— that is, a specific set of premises and implications which can be detected, exemplarily and respectively, in the semiotic theory of Ferdinand de Saussure, in the grammatological thought of Jacques Derrida, and in the theories of thinkers such as Ellen Ullman and Matthew Fuller, who have dealt with programming languages.[18] For Hayles, language and writing (albeit code) work together in a complex process of "intermediation," and code has a very specific relation to metaphysical thought: It actually minimizes the need for ontological presuppositions, and in so doing it offers different answers to metaphysical questions from the ones grammatology proposes.

And yet this presupposition is not without problems. In order to demonstrate why, I here propose a rereading of Derrida's understanding of writing that differs slightly from Hayles's interpretation. I also want to push my understanding of writing a step further so as to show how Derrida's conceptualization of writing could also be put to work in the interpretation of code. Since his earliest works (particularly *Of Grammatology*), Derrida has defined writing as a material practice. As is well known, for Derrida the subordination of writing to speech (or seeing writing as a representation of speech) has meaning only within the system of Western metaphysics. According to him, the premises of Western metaphysics have been inherited by human sciences, and particularly by linguistics. In Richard Beardsworth's terms, for Derrida, "the theory of the sign is essentially metaphysical."[19] In *Of Grammatology*, Derrida focuses on the deconstruction of linguistics from this viewpoint. More precisely, for Derrida the deconstruction of linguistics and of its central concept, the concept of the sign, is exemplary for the deconstruction of metaphysics. Moreover, the sign is so important because it is exemplary of the metaphysical devaluation of materiality.

As Beardsworth points out, "the very possibility of the sign is predicated on an opposition between that which is conveyed (the signified, the *logos*, the non-worldly) and the conveyor (the signifier, the worldly)."[20] The signifier is a material entity, such as a sound or a graphic sign; the signified belongs to the realm of concepts. For Derrida, this opposition is the foundation of all the other oppositions that characterize Western metaphysics (infinite/finite, soul/body, nature/law, universal/particular, and so on). Deconstructing the sign is thus a fundamental and exemplary move for him precisely because "metaphysics" is derived from the domination of a particular relation between the ideal and the material, which assumes definition in the concept of "sign."[21] The sign is central because it constitutes the foundation of the distinction between signifier and thing, a distinction that in turn is the basis of *epistemē* and therefore of metaphysics. Again, in Beardsworth's words, "metaphysics constitutes its oppositions (here: the non-worldly/worldly and the ideal/material) by expelling into one term of the opposition the very possibility of the condition of such oppositions."[22]

For Derrida we therefore need to have an understanding of writing in order to grasp the meaning of orality. For him, "writing" takes precedence over orality not because writing existed "before" language, but because we must have a sense of the permanence of a linguistic mark in order to recognize and identify it. Ultimately, a sense of writing is necessary for signification to take place. But we can have a sense of the permanence of the mark only if we have a sense of its inscription, of its being embodied in a material surface. In other words, although we recognize the written form of a grapheme (say, *t*) only by abstracting it from all the possible empirical forms a "t" can take in writing, we need such an empirical inscription to make this recognition possible. This is what Derrida means when he says that the transcendental is always impure, always already contaminated by the empirical. In other words, language itself is material for Derrida; it needs materiality (the possibility of an "inscription") to function *as* language.

This interpretation contrasts with the consolidated (Anglo-American) reception of poststructuralism and of Derrida's thinking as allegedly unaware of the material aspects of culture, society, economics, and politics (according to his famous statement, "There is nothing outside of the text"). But we have already seen that, for Derrida, textuality and materiality are not opposed. There is no actual need—as it is often claimed—to "go back to materiality" after the "linguistic turn" in cultural studies, because materiality has always been there. Writing is material because materiality is the condition of writing itself, and of signification.

WRITING AND SOFTWARE

If materiality is the condition of signification, then every bit of code is material. More precisely: The possibility of inscription as a condition of code's functioning is material. This is not the same as to say that technology always has material and semiotic characteristics, or that technology involves physical apparatuses and information, microcircuits and Boolean logics, the social and the conceptual. Of course this is all true, but what a material understanding of software as writing means in addition is that, in the first instance, software can function only through materiality—not only because it has to run on a processor, or because there are economic forces behind it, but because it is (also) code, and code functions only through materiality, because materiality is what constitutes signs (and therefore codes). Second, writing is based on the same possibility of material inscription, and the fact that it has been chosen as the privileged way of accessing digital technology by software engineering should come as no surprise at this point. Paraphrasing Bruno Latour, we can say: We have never been immaterial.

But if every bit of code is material, and if the material structure of the mark is at work everywhere, how are we supposed to study software as a historically specific technology? I propose that software's specificity as a technology resides in the relationship it entertains with writing, that is, with a historically specific form of writing. It is in this relationship that software—as Gary Hall would have it; see Chapter 14—finds its "singularity." Such coemergence of software and writing (or, better, of "software," "writing," and "code," which actually constitute each other as constantly shifting terms) can be found in the discourses and practices of software engineering. Here I argue that there is no writing prior to code—that is, there is no *such* writing as the one that emerges *in* and *with* software engineering. Such kind of writing emerges *only there*, and only in relation with software and code. One cannot exist without the others. Although this coemergence constitutes the historical specificity of software engineering, it is not to say that it also constitutes the specificity of "all software," since the definition of software varies in time and space. This is why ultimately I prefer to speak of the "singularity" of software (as Hall does) rather than of its historical "specificity." The singularity of "writing software"—as a singular practice distinct from other kinds of singular practices, such as writing literature or writing electronic literature—is precisely this: that it emerges in relation to software and code in the (again, singular) context of software engineering.

To give but one example of such coemergence of software, writing, and code, let me now analyze briefly the model of the process of software development proposed by Calvin Selig during the NATO conference held in Garmisch, Germany, in 1968.[23] One must be reminded here that software engineering made its appearance in the context of the early industrialization of software production, and that its main interest as a discipline was the formalization of the process of software development precisely in order to industrialize it. With little variation, Selig's scheme was to become the typical representation of what would later be called the "software life-cycle."

According to Selig, the process of software production is the sequence of different stages. Each stage can be described as a period of intellectual activity that produces a usable product that constitutes the point of departure for the subsequent stage. At the beginning, a problem is identified, to which the software system will be the answer. The first stage of intellectual activity, named "analysis," produces a description of the identified problem—which is substantially a document written in a natural language. The stage of analysis is variously enmeshed with the phase of design (the two terms are used quite interchangeably in the report of the Garmisch conference), which constitutes a refinement of the problem description in order to propose a system that solves it. The phase of design produces a complete system specification, which is a stable description of *what* the software system is supposed to do. The system specification is the point of departure for the stage of implementation, which basically determines *how* the system will do what it is supposed to do. As rapidly became clear in the course of the Garmisch conference debate, the boundaries between all these stages get quite blurry, and the terminology itself is rather unstable. The most important reason for this is that feedback loops are necessary between the different stages of software development: For instance, the actual production of code can make apparent some inconsistencies "hidden" in an earlier understanding of the system, and therefore the process of software development unavoidably involves a number of iterations.[24] However, the stage of implementation "translates" (Selig's term) the specification of the system into the actual system or working system, that is, a software system that can be installed on a computer. Before the system can be delivered to the final user, it needs to be tested, which basically means that one must verify whether the system actually does what it is meant to do and, second, whether it does it in the way it is meant to. This stage is variously called "testing" or "acceptance," or—as in Selig's case—it can be incorporated in a general stage of "maintenance," which comprises all the activities performed on a completely operational software system (such as corrections and modifications that might become necessary even after the system has been delivered to its users). As soon as it becomes operational, the system is obsolescent, and it will finally be abandoned in favor of newer systems.

Two important points must be emphasized in Selig's model: First, it explicitly refers to documentation, that is, the body of written texts produced in the course of the whole process of system development, and second, software development itself allegedly covers a longer time span than the "traditional" one (that is, the one antecedent to software engineering). As for the former point, it is worth noting that the definition of documentation will remain an open problem of software engineering for decades, and the use of the term itself will continue to shift from user documentation (that is, the user manuals provided to final users as an explanation of the software system) to technical documentation or internal documentation (both of which describe the system and serve as a means of communication between software developers). As for the latter point, Selig comments that, although programming has traditionally been viewed as the production of code, "in practice programmers perform duties over [the] span" that goes from the understanding of the problem to the obsolescence of the system. Both of these points actually concur in elucidating how the formalization of the process of software development is attained in software engineering. In order to be controlled, the process of software development is broken up into periods of activity, each of which produces, as a result, a written text. Each written text is the point of departure for the following phase, and it is supposed to be used as a tool for developing further writing. Thus, the organization of time is carried out through a practice that I here call "writing," since it produces "written texts." Some of these written texts are called "documents," while others are referred to as "software" or "programs" or "code": These terms keep shifting.

A significant example of this shift can be found in Peter Naur's conference paper, where he writes:

> Software production takes us from the result of the design to the program to be executed in the computer. The distinction between design and production is essentially a practical one, imposed by the need for a division of the labor. In fact, there is no essential difference between design and production, since even the production will include decisions which will influence the performance of the software system, and thus properly belong in the design phase. For the distinction to be useful, the design work is charged with the specific responsibility that it is pursued to a level of detail where the decisions remaining to be made during production are known to be insignificant as to the performance of the system.[25]

It is not necessary to enter into the detail of Naur's technicalities here. What must be kept in mind is that here "design" can be broadly understood as the stage of system specification, and "production" as a synonym for coding. According to Naur, the decision to break down the process of software development was made in order to favor the division of labor. He introduces a very subtle point here: The level of detail in the description of the system (at the design level) aims at maintaining the division of labor. In other words, a sufficient level of detail would completely erode the space left for implementers (that is, for the programmers who produce the actual code) to make decisions of their own, and thus their ability to influence the software system. The detail given in the documents produced during the stage of design ultimately constitutes a means for the control of the workforce. But the most important point that can be drawn from Naur's observation is that there is actually no essential difference between design and production, and therefore between the written texts produced in these two stages, or between design documents (written in natural language plus different kinds of formal notation) and computer programs. In other words, *there is no essential difference between documentation and code.* The only apparent difference between these written texts is the introduction of a foreclosure: That is, the "practical" division of labor forecloses the possibility of decision at later stages of software development. What is already inscribed, or written down, at the stage of design cannot be changed at the stage of production, cannot be decided upon any more, cannot be undone, or unmade: It is subtracted from the process of decision, of change, of further inscription. Writing performs a foreclosure of time through what is already inscribed (that is, the level of detail of the design documentation). By foreclosing the possibility of decision, writing also forecloses responsibility in the stage of production. Finally, it prevents feedback from production into design, from the "how" into the "what"—a feedback that is, nevertheless, necessary. Thus, the differentiation of writing in software development is an attempt at foreclosing an unavoidable iteration. For this reason, such a foreclosure is destined to fail—and yet, the process of software development relies on it and tries to keep it in place all the time.

CONCLUSION: SOFTWARE AND DECONSTRUCTION

In the foundational texts of software engineering, we can see how "software" was constituted as a process of material inscription through the continuous unmaking and remaking of the boundaries among "software," "writing," and "code." Software's singularity as a technology resides precisely in the relationship it entertains with writing, that is, with a historically specific form of writing.

Let me now consider for a moment some of the consequences that a deconstructive examination of software might have on the way in which media and cultural studies deal with new technologies. We have already seen that the issue of technology has been present in media and cultural studies from the very beginning, and that the debate around technology has contributed to defining the methodological orientation of the field. For this reason, it is quite understandable that rethinking technology would entail a rethinking of media and cultural studies' distinctive features and boundaries.

Furthermore, a deconstructive reading of software will enable us to do more than just uncover the conceptual presuppositions that preside over the constitution of software itself. In fact, such an investigation will have a much larger influence on our way of conceptualizing what counts as academic knowledge. To understand this point better, we must be reminded that new technologies change the form of academic knowledge (through new practices of scholarly communication and publication) as well as shift its focus, so that that the study of new technology has eventually become a legitimate area of academic research. Furthermore, as Gary Hall points out, new technologies change the very nature and content of academic knowledge.[26] In a famous passage, Jacques Derrida wondered about the influence of specific technologies of communication (such as print media and postal services) on the field of psychoanalysis by asking, "what if Freud had

had e-mail?"[27] If we acknowledge that available technology has a formative influence on the construction of knowledge, then a reflection on new technologies implies a reflection on the nature of academic knowledge itself. But, as Hall maintains, paradoxically, "we cannot rely merely on the modern 'disciplinary' methods and frameworks of knowledge in order to think and interpret the transformative effect new technology is having on our culture, since it is precisely these methods and frameworks that new technology requires us to rethink."[28] According to Hall, cultural studies is the ideal starting point for a study of new technologies, precisely because of its open and unfixed identity as a field. A critical attitude toward the concept of disciplinarity has characterized cultural studies from the start. Such critical attitude includes cultural studies' own disciplinarity, its own academic institutionalization.[29] Hall argues that cultural studies has not always been up to such self-critique, since very often it has limited itself to an "interdisciplinary" attitude, understood as an incorporation of heterogeneous elements from various disciplines that does not deeply question the structure of disciplinarity itself (what has been called the "pick 'n' mix" approach of cultural studies). Rather, he suggests that cultural studies pursue a deeper self-reflexivity, in order to keep its own disciplinarity open and shifting. This self-reflexivity would be enabled by the establishment of a productive relationship between cultural studies and deconstruction. The latter is understood here, first of all, as a problematizing reading that would permanently question some of the fundamental premises of cultural studies itself. Thus, cultural studies would remain acutely aware of the influence that the university, as a political and institutional structure, exercises on the production of knowledge (namely, by constituting and regulating the competences and practices of cultural studies practitioners). It is precisely in this awareness, according to Hall, that the political significance of cultural studies resides. It seems clearer now why a reconceptualization of technology based upon a deconstructive reading of software entails a reflection on the theoretical premises of the methods and frameworks of academic knowledge.

To conclude, in this chapter I propose a reconceptualization of new technologies, that is, of technologies based on software, through a close, even intimate engagement with software itself, rather than through an analysis of how new technologies are produced, consumed, represented, and talked about. In what way and to what extent this intimacy can be achieved and how software can be made available for examination are the main problems opened up by this approach. Taking into account some possible difficulties resulting from the working of mediation in our engagement with technology as well as technology's opacity and its constitutive, if unacknowledged, role in the formation of both the human and academic knowledge, I have argued that such an engagement is essential if we are to take new technologies seriously, and to think them in a way that affects—and does not separate—cultural understanding and political practice.

PART THREE

Intermedial Reflexivities

Film, Writing, Script

CHAPTER NINE

Cinema as a Digest of Literature

A Cure for Adaptation Fever

PETER VERSTRATEN

According to a well-known definition introduced by Ricciotto Canudo in 1923, film is the seventh art. The cinema owes this label to its heterogeneous nature. Film is not the seventh art because it is the successor of six other arts, but because, according to Canudo, it is a synthesis of three rhythmic and three plastic arts. The rhythmic arts are dance, music, and poetry; the three plastic ones are architecture, sculpture and painting.[1] It is remarkable, to say the least, that theater and literature fall outside the scope of the definition, since they are generally considered the sister arts of cinema. The exclusion of literature and theater, however, is due to the idea that these two arts risk pulling film into the swamp of storytelling. The familiar argument runs that film can develop into a "true" art form only on the condition that it avoid the pitfall of narrativity. In short, a film can stake an artistic claim on when it distances itself from literary and theatrical influences.

According to a strictly esthetic vision on cinema, literature works like a kind of poison. In spite of this vision, film is still all too often compared to literature. The logic resides in the destination that, willy-nilly, has been attributed to the cinema. Those who pioneered with moving image at the end of the nineteenth century, such as Étienne-Jules Marey and the brothers Lumière, were merely interested in scientific applications. They were hardly enthusiastic about the possibility of reproducing lifelike scenes on the screen. If one goes back to the originating years of the medium, the technological aspect tends to be stressed. The new invention was seen as a device to marvel at for the sheer fact that moving images could be projected, and the status of cinema had best be compared to a fairground attraction.[2] Cinema was predicted to have a poor future around the date of its birth, and it could turn into a seminal medium of the twentieth century only thanks to its potential for storytelling, which was recognized only with the advent of cutting. Since the first cut, cinema has been dominated by a constant narrative pressure; as Seymour Chatman observes, story time in film is always "ticking away."[3] In the words of André Gaudreault, cinema is a "machine which is doomed to tell stories 'for ever.'"[4] And as a narrative medium, film is both a companion and a rival to literature.

Jan Simons once wrote that film and literature are caught up in a "tragic-comical" competition. As a verbal medium, literature is usually automatically privileged over an audiovisual medium. Film is the underdog that time and again has to undergo a decisive test in order to prove its worth. The rivalry between the two media has a tragic-comical dimension, Simons argues, because each time film is able to stand the test, literature is reintroduced as an arbiter to another trial.[5] Critics who discuss the battleground between film and literature usually remind us that film can never carry the day, since literature can always appeal to a rich tradition. The Bible clearly favors words over images: the word was God, according to St. John's Gospel, and the Second Commandment forbids the production of idols. Moreover, the conventional argument of seniority also privileges literature over film: Thanks to its longer history, literature would be the better art form, because the older, the more prestigious. Furthermore, the idea runs that words and literature stimulate our thoughts, while images and film provoke our senses. And whereas a novel can dedicate ample space to describe characters or landscapes, a film can show them at a glance. In contrast to the presumed cultivated nature of literature, the cinema is at times considered as potentially vulgar.[6]

From this perspective, film has lost the "battle" in advance unless we change our policy. To adopt a new approach, I return to the ideas of André Bazin, who wrote about film in the 1940s and 1950s. He was opposed to the notion of film as the seventh art, and he suggested that it would be wise were film to "digest" the traditions of theater and literature. As a case study, I use Spike Jonze's 2002 film *Adaptation*, which has "digested" literature to the maximum degree possible. As such, this self-reflexive film offers us—as good as it can get—a "theory" of adaptation.

TWO TYPES OF ADAPTATION FEVER

Adaptation is a film that drives you crazy. Not only do the characters themselves turn mad, but the spectator himself becomes dizzy as well—and for this reason I cannot restrict myself to a brief summary of Jonze's film. The main protagonist is scriptwriter Charlie Kaufman (Nicolas Cage), who is unanimously praised for his keen script for *Being John Malkovich*, a 1999 film directed by Jonze. At the beginning of *Adaptation*, film executive Valerie Thomas (Tilda Swinton) requests that Charlie turn the nonfiction bestseller *The Orchid Thief* (1998), written by Susan Orlean, into a screenplay. Charlie announces enthusiastically that he will opt for a different approach than the usual Hollywood method: no thefts, no sex, no car chases, no profound life lessons. He wants "a movie simply about flowers." The book has no structure, so the film has to do without as well, he reasons. This consistent choice results into a serious writer's block, and it gradually makes him madder and madder.

In between scenes we see Charlie's flagging writing process intermingled with events from years before. On one hand, these inserted fragments show how Orlean (Meryl Streep) is writing her book; on the other, they show her experiences with the subject of her book, a sexy orchid thief named John Laroche (Chris Cooper). This Laroche is a low-class guy who is intellectually miles away from her own circle of highbrow friends. Laroche is a man who can be passionately dedicated to his leisure interests and can quit with them rigorously after some time. He switches from fishing to orchids to porno websites. He makes it into a habit to constantly challenge the borders of what is legally permitted. Next to these scenes, which are analogous to the events from *The Orchid Thief*, the last quarter of *Adaptation* contains a spectacular supplement to Orlean's book. Charlie's twin brother Donald has a shrewd suspicion that the "relation" between the writer and her subject did not end at the very last page.[7] At the initiative of Donald, the brothers start an investigation as to the whereabouts of Orlean and Laroche. Their examination results into a sudden twist in the last part of the film.

The narrative levels are intricately connected to one another, and this turns *Adaptation* into an extremely tight movie. This tightness is even reinforced because the film's title evokes a triple meaning: adaptation as a biological process, as the capacity for adjustment, and as the case of novel made into film. All three meanings are relevant, but I am predominantly concerned with the last option. Initially, Charlie tries for a "pure" transcription from book into film. Since *The Orchid Thief* lacks a clear storyline, he thinks that he himself should not think in terms of a plot either. His attempt to remain faithful to Orlean's book will become the source of his writer's block, however. The fact that the perspiration stands out in beads on his brow can be seen as signs of what we may call "adaptation fever."[8] This fever is a well-known disease within the tradition of film adaptations and concerns the presumed necessity to reveal the secret behind the "original" text. One supposes that the only way to do the source text justice is to decipher the codes of its words. In that case, the script is a mark of honor to the "true" meaning of the text.

By contrast, Donald is a representative of the modern adaptation fever. Because of the success of his brother with *Being John Malkovich*, Donald is inspired to start scriptwriting himself. He has attended a three-day seminar by the script guru Robert McKee, who teaches his pupils to search for originality within the limits of an existing genre. To Donald, each script is a supplement by definition; a script merely elaborates upon previous ones. This becomes evident in the judgment of his mother after reading Donald's first scenario. She describes his attempt as "*Silence of the Lambs* meets *Psycho*." Donald just aims at a variation on established conventions. He is content to linger in the gap between two famous films.

Adaptation is not brilliant because it juxtaposes the old-fashioned and the modern adaptation fever, but because it plays explicitly against each other these two diseases. And this clash results in a cross-fertilization that sheds the notion of adaptation itself into a different perspective.

OUROBOUROS IRONICUS

The shortcoming of the old concept of adaptation is that the source text is considered as untouchable. The original novel counts as the privileged point of reference, and the film is only its derivative in an audiovisual medium. This presupposition will lead into an inevitably hierarchical comparison between novel and film that triggers the law of communicating vessels: The higher the book is valued, the more the film risks being trashed by the press and those people among the audience to whom the novel is particularly dear. As a consequence, film adaptations are usually only discussed generously in case they are inspired by trivial fiction or totally unknown texts. A film can be better only on the condition that the novel happens to be a failure. Alfred Hitchcock wanted to film Dostoyevsky's *Crime and Punishment*, but because he considered the novel a true masterpiece, he turned down the idea. According to him, his film would "betray" the brilliant nature of the book.[9]

An adaptation is all too often bedeviled by the so-called fidelity issue.[10] As long as fidelity is regarded as an adamant standard, one wonders whether the film is analogous to the book in terms of spirit and theme. Is the setting in accordance with the location in the novel, are the events told in the same order, and does the mental image that the reader has of the protagonist correspond to the facial expression and attitude of the actor? Or, to be more concrete: Is James Cazievel convincing as Jesus in Mel Gibson's *The Passion of the Christ* (2004), and is Nicole Kidman imaginable as Isabelle Archer in Jane Campion's 1996 adaptation of Henry James's *Portrait of a Lady*? Hitchcock retorted with an apparently jesting solution to adaptations: throw the book away after a first reading. In short, a director should grab the basic idea and then take a distance from the literary language in order to develop a specific film language.[11]

In his essay "In Defense of Mixed Media," written in 1952, Bazin makes a distinction between an original masterpiece and a film that is inspired by another text. According to him, masterpieces such as Sergei Eisenstein's *Battleship Potemkin* (1925), F. W. Murnau's *Sunrise* (1927), and Jean Renoir's *Rules of the Game* (1939) are inimitable. Their brilliance is a matter of timing; a masterpiece is produced at exact the right the moment and could not have been made at a later stage, let alone copied.[12] A masterpiece is so unique in tone and style that it cannot generate equivalents. To the studio executive who had approached Charlie to turn *The Orchid Thief* into a film script, the arthouse success *Being John Malkovich* perhaps counts among the superior category of masterpieces. She tells him that the film struck her because of its "unique voice." She probably has selected him with the unvoiced wish that he will repeat his original touch of genius. Charlie suffers from cold perspiration all the time, because he experiences that a unique voice is only a one-off and cannot be reproduced.

Next to original masterpieces there are, according to Bazin, those films that do not shy away from "digesting" the traditions of art forms with a richer history than the cinema. He draws upon an analogy with translations: You can make a perfect translation into English of a German text only on the condition that you can handle both languages properly. Hence, film can benefit from absorbing influences from an art form such as literature, since both use narration as a structuring device. Correspondingly, films that rely on a stage play should be prepared to incorporate the conventions and language of theater to develop the potential of cinema. Bazin even claims that film is better capable of developing its own language when it is inspired by a "supercinematic" literary style or when film has to bend itself to theatrical conditions.[13] The problem with Charlie is that he has to remember to remain faithful to the general purpose of Orlean's book, including its content. Bazin, however, does not argue for similarities in content, but for an influence in terms of style.

Just as there are no generally applicable guidelines for a good script in the eyes of Charlie, there are no set procedures for the "digestion" of literature. Bazin's essays are written in a period in which the aversion to sound in the cinema had not completely vanished among film critics. The "silent film aestheticians" were reluctant to embrace sound because film would bargain away its presumed essence as a medium of moving images. With the addition of sound, film might become too literary or too theatrical. In his essays, however, Bazin aims to neutralize this skeptical attitude, first, by qualifying the coming of sound as positive, since it brings the cinema closer to its "destiny" as a recording machine of reality. Second, he advocates the usefulness of a cross-fertilization among media for a new film language. Bazin did not yet illustrate how such a process should be enacted successfully.

Lacking a clear guideline, Charlie gradually shakes off the self-imposed pressure to stick close to the book and be creative at the same time. His "journey into the unknown" turns into a "journey into the abyss." First, he has in mind just to adapt a motif. He reads in *The Orchid Thief* that Orlean was hardly interested in the issue of orchids, but that she was preoccupied with the unimpeded passion of the main protagonist for these specific flowers. His preference for orchids is subordinated to the idea of a craze. Keeping this incentive in mind, Charlie decides that he will focus upon an unstoppable passion himself. Excited by her photo on the cover of her book, he turns Susan Orlean herself into the main character. While doing so, he actually thinks that the only topic he can write about is himself, but he rejects this idea as narcissistic and pathetic. It would make him into too much of an *ourobouros*, the snake swallowing its own tail. This ascertainment is followed by one of the many scenes between John and Susan that are inserted in between the episodes about Charlie's reflections. We see John and Susan wade through a river looking for a ghost orchid. Then John snarls at her that she is like a leech, a parasite upon the preoccupations of others. In turn, by transforming her book into a film script, Charlie acts like a leech himself. As a consequence, he realizes that he is caught in an impasse. His tendency to remain faithful to the book hampers him to reawaken his unique voice, while a looser adaptation threatens to turn him into a narcissistic person who just misuses the craziness of someone else. This impasse seems to suggest that the fever is incurable.

"WORSE THAN BAD"

The ridiculous suggestion by Charlie's agent that his twin brother might be of use is a turning point in the movie and will offer a way out for Charlie's problem. The unconcerned good-for-nothing Donald—in everything the opposite of his brother—has, to the utter surprise of Charlie, received enthusiastic response to his "smart, edgy script," written according to the Ten Commandments of Robert McKee. Charlie renounces his artistic principles and decides to visit a seminar, lectured by the script guru. McKee promulgates a ban against the voiceover, a device that is frequently used up to that point in *Adaptation*. In a bar, he provides Charlie with an important practical tip: "The last act makes the film. You can have an uninvolving tedious movie, but wow them at the end, and you've got a hit!" And he also confides him into an absolute "do not": "Don't you dare bring in a deus ex machina. Your characters must change, and change must come from them."

Thereafter Charlie takes the advance of "the great Donald," and at that point the modern adaptation fever becomes a companion to the old one. In his *The Fright of Real Tears*, Slavoj Žižek has criticized films such as Gus Van Sant's *Psycho* (1998) and Anthony Minghella's *The Talented Mr. Ripley* (1999) as examples of the postmodern disease of "filling in the gaps."[14] Van Sant's film is bashed as a "cold shower," since his *Psycho* is an almost complete shot-by-shot copy of Hitchcock's original version from 1960. Film critics were puzzled why Van Sant had opted for such a deliberate imitation of the horror classic, but Žižek's problem with the film is precisely that the new version is not a hundred-percent remake of the predecessor. Van Sant has inserted a scene in which Norman looks at Marion through a peephole and starts to masturbate. The new *Psycho* imitates the Hitchcock horror and supplements some typically contemporary accents. These extras display, according to Žižek, the postmodern tendency to provide additional commentary and offer the illusion of completeness. Minghella's *The Talented Mr. Ripley* may even be a stronger case. In the 1955 novel of the same title by Patricia Highsmith, Ripley is a cold and enigmatic main character. In the first adaptation from the book, René Clement's *Plein Soleil* (1959), this role is magnificently played by a young Alain Delon, with his slick but nevertheless mysterious appearance. By contrast, in Minghella's version from 1999, repressed homosexuality is inserted as a motive to explain Ripley's misdemeanors. As opposed to the nonpsychological nature of the Ripley of Highsmith and Clément, which gives the protagonist a chilling edge, Minghella's version cannot resist offering us a psychological legitimization of Ripley's behavior. And hence, the film version of *The Talented Mr. Ripley* answers to the need in postmodern times to improve the original. The present-day film fills in what it presumed could not be addressed in films from the past: It "repairs" what is missing from the past.

Donald's first comment upon Charlie's scripts is: "I feel you're missing something." In the spirit of the disease of "filling in the gaps," he thinks he can trace what is missing if he has a talk with Orlean about her book. During the interview, Donald hints at an intimacy between Susan and John that underlies the book as a whole. She, however, insists that there is no relation toward the protagonist beyond the final pages of the book. Nevertheless, Donald remains convinced that she is misleading him, and the final part of *Adaptation* is triggered by his imagination. He presumes that Susan and John have been seeing one another even after the failed expedition to search for the ghost orchid. The final episode is not a part of the book and it is to be taken as a supplement that should overpower the spectator, according to McKee's dictum. Donald finds a photo of Susan on a porno website supervised by John, and he discovers that she is on drugs. This discovery by the Kaufman brothers is the start of an exciting car chase, to the utter dismay of Charlie. The excitement brings the brothers closer to one another, and their bonding results in a wise life lesson by Donald after he is fatally wounded: "You are what you love, not what loves you."

Having elaborated on this keenly structured movie, I can now spell out why the film is so important as a reflection upon the relation between literature and film. The first joke of *Adaptation* has to do with the spectator's horizon of expectation. Because of the success of *Being John Malkovich*, Charlie has a reputation of inventing the most absurd and smart twists. As spectators, we are initially curious after the matchless narrative skill that Charlie will certainly have in store for us. The last part, however, is filled with spectacular events and cheap turns that are far from unconventional. Due to the sensational plots, we are disappointed in our initial expectations about the originality Charlie had announced that he was yearning for. In his case, we did not reckon on a whole range of prescribed rules from screenwriting handbooks. But at precisely this point we should acknowledge a stroke of genius on the part of Charlie Kaufman: The fact that he regales us with a plenitude of script stereotypes is so contrary to our expectations that his approach becomes teasingly "original" on the rebound.

The second big joke of *Adaptation* concerns the notion of adaptation itself. At the end of the film, Charlie explains the difference between himself and his brother. He has a hesitant nature and acts bashfully out of fear of the opinions of others. By contrast, Donald is "just oblivious," totally carefree. As if it costs him no effort, Donald takes up the art of scriptwriting. He can easily keep company with women despite his poor jokes and feeble anecdotes. He even plays a game of Boggle with Charlie's favorite actress Catherine Keener from *Being John Malkovich*. Donald has a built-in capacity to adjust himself to circumstances, while Charlie lacks this quality. His inflexibility seriously hampers Charlie in his adaptation of *The Orchid Thief*. So far, the scenes with Laroche have been clearly derived from Orlean's book. From the moment Donald interferes with the script, though, the scenes with John go beyond the final page of the best-seller and seem inspired by the "reader's guide" in the form of a conversation with the "real" Susan Orlean at the end of the book.

The pattern of questions and answers in the reader's guide provides the book with meta-reflexivity. Orlean has to answer questions like, "How can you transform a small news item into a full-fledged novel?" and "Are you yourself not the protagonist of the book instead of John Laroche?" The marvelous gesture of *Adaptation* is that the film does not restrict itself to sketching the main events of the book, which is customary in the case of adaptations. The film is above all an adaptation of similar problems from the reader's companion: "How can we construct a script from a book about flowers with a thin plotline?" Moreover, the fact that the reading of the book is like the peeling of an onion, finds a parallel in the multilayered nature of the film: Charlie and Donald each are writing a script; Donald contributes to Charlie's script; and we see Susan doing research as well as writing her book that is the basis for Charlie's scenario. All these various stages finally make up *Adaptation*. Furthermore, the assertion by the interviewer in the reader's companion that *The Orchid Thief* is a form of autobiography corresponds to the way Charlie has written himself as a character into his own script. On top of that, Orlean claims in the reader's guide that she is best at writing about things she is not too involved with: "Orchids were to me a complete cipher—just flowers, how could anybody care about them?" For Charlie as well, orchids are an absolute riddle. And as Orlean focuses on the world of orchids, the scriptwriter focuses on her book about flowers. In short, Susan's struggle with her subject has a strong analogy to Charlie's struggle with the book that has been palmed off on him. The film does not imitate the book as a *product*, but it reproduces the *process* of creation: The writing of the book keeps track with the making of the film. This shift from product to process is helpful in combating the old adaptation fever. By thrusting himself forward, Charlie does not attempt to imitate the *content* of the original as faithfully as possible, but he aims at an identical *effect* of (the subtext of) Orlean's book.

That the author confesses in the reader's companion that she has used John for her own benefit illustrates once again that content is subordinate to effect. She did not convey a flattering portrait of him, but she nevertheless owes her success to him. Not for nothing does one of the questions in the reader's guide run like this: "Are you not living off the desires, aspirations, happenings of others? That is how you make your living. As a common parasite, really." The reader appreciates Orlean's book because of her "unique voice," according to the studio executive in *Adaptation*, and because her main protagonist is a "fun character." Her role as a parasite is even mentioned by Laroche himself as he tells her that she sucks him dry and spits him out. In a similar way, Charlie misuses his twin brother. He himself is disgusted by the Hollywood methods practiced by McKee, but his attempt to stick to his own creative criteria lead to a dead end. Just as Laroche lacks moral qualms, twin brother Donald does not bother about matters of ethics and originality. Charlie can use Donald as a disguise for all the commonplaces about a sinister love relation between the author and her protagonist.

The last act of the film seems to imply that McKee and Donald have carried their point over the old adaptation fever that holds on to the principle of fidelity. However, the film has not simply turned into a Donald-movie. Toward the end, *Adaptation* becomes even worse than the worst clichés. At the moment Laroche threatens to kill Charlie, an alligator suddenly appears from the swamp as a typical deus ex machina, a device that goes against McKee's principles. And just before the final credits we hear Charlie's voiceover verbalizing his thoughts: "Shit, this is voiceover," he remarks. "McKee would not approve. Who cares what McKee says? It feels right."

Adaptation has become a movie that constantly swallows its own tail. The film opens and ends with a lengthy voiceover. It opens with the expectation that we will hear a "unique voice" and follows a trajectory through McKee's handbooks in order to close with feeble film clichés that, paradoxically, live up to the expectation. *Adaptation* links so many commonplaces together that the film becomes "worse than bad," and this superlative is the key to its "unique voice." Scripts that are written according to handbooks show a pattern of "success A meets success B," just like the script Donald has handed in. The originality of Jonze's film is precisely the self-reflexive multiplication of this meeting: "success A meets success B meets success C meets . . ." The structure of *Adaptation* is based upon the Mobius strip, where you go one way and end up on the other side. Or, even more appropriate, the structure of the film is the trademark of the *ourobouros*. Because the old style of fidelity drives Charlie mad, he switches to a modern method of adaptation. Thanks to his forbidden, far too vulgar stylistic devices, this method is neutralized, or rather, digested completely.

Adaptation seemed to become a Donald-movie, but because Charlie sinned against McKee's commandments, the film nevertheless carries the latter's signature. To break his own writer's block, Charlie has acted as a parasite on his twin brother's urge to sensationalism. And since the relation between Charlie and Donald is a mirroring of the way Orlean has used her protagonist, *Adaptation* is to be seen as an ironic "digestion" of *The Orchid Thief*. In no way is the adaptation an attempt to translate the novel into an audiovisual text as accurately as possible, but it relies upon an underlying process of analogy. *Adaptation* is an adaptation in the true sense of the word, because the film does not aim to be faithful to the content of the novel, but the film imitates in the exchange between Charlie and Donald the parasitical effect Orlean has had upon Laroche. Being concerned about a similarity in effect rather than in content is the best guarantee that the two media can influence one another fruitfully. Or, to stay in tune with the song by The Turtles: In *Adaptation*, literature and film are living apart, but they are nevertheless happy together.

CHAPTER TEN

Cinematography as a Literary Concept in the (Post)Modern Age

Pirandello to Pynchon

LOVORKA GRUIC GRMUSA AND
KIENE BRILLENBURG WURTH

Long live the Machine that mechanizes life!

Do you still retain, gentlemen, a little soul, a little heart and a little mind?
—LUIGI PIRANDELLO, *Shoot!*

In the Zone, all will be moving under the Old Dispensation, inside the Cainists' light and space: not out of any precious Gollerei, but because the Double Light was always there, outside all film.
—THOMAS PYNCHON, *Gravity's Rainbow*

Since long before the invention of cinema, literary writing has been engaged in the mediation of moving images. Indeed, as Sergei Eisenstein once intimated, literary writing has in crucial ways premediated cinematographic techniques, especially that most cinematographic of arts: montage.[1] Montage may be tied to D. W. Griffith, but as Eisenstein famously observed, "Griffith arrived at montage through the method of parallel action, and he was led to the idea of parallel action by—Dickens!"[2] The link between cinema and the realist novel has by now been well established. In the 1970s, Alan Spiegel proposed to read Gustave Flaubert's *Madame Bovary* (1857) as a protocinematic (or, more precisely, "scenographic") novel that anticipated the special visual effects of film.[3] Such special effects, Robert Stam has noted, include the detailed notation of objects, gestures, and attitudes in the novel, literary props, verbal long shots (the scene of the Rouen cab), and so on.[4] Eisenstein had, of course, already celebrated the famous scene of Emma and her lover Rodolphe at the Yonville agricultural fair as an instance of vertical montage: a technique allowing various impressions, movements, stories, or dialogues to become present at the same time, rather than one after the other.[5] Spiegel, however, tried to show how cinematographic techniques evolved in nineteenth-century fiction—not only in Flaubert, but also in Henry James and Joseph Conrad—and culminated in modernist works such as James Joyce's *Ulysses* (1922). Such techniques, for Spiegel, boiled down to showing instead of telling, and in particular a showing of how things are seen: This pertained to visualizations of objects *and* to the ways in which such objects are perceived.[6]

In the 1990s, critics such as Irina Rajewski and P. Adams Sitney continued to debate cinema and literature in terms of transmediation or the transfer of techniques among different media, arguing that film makers were just as much influenced by literary writing (and literary scopic regimes) as modernist writers were affected by film.[7] More recently, Susan McCabe's *Cinematic Modernism* and Laura Marcus's *The Tenth Muse* have mapped the tracks between film and poetry (Williams, Moore) and early twentieth-century literary (Woolf, Joyce) as well as critical writing respectively. How have film's techniques helped to shape literature in the modernist age—and how has modernist literature affected film?[8] Similarly, Julian Murphet and Lydia Rainford's *Literature and Visual Technologies* traces the impact of twentieth-century visual technologies on literature, showing how such technologies have informed "new" literary modes and techniques, and vice versa.[9]

As an alternative to such medial histories of analogy and transaction, critics such as Garrett Stewart and David Trotter have proposed to analyze modernist techniques in literature *and* film as parallel manifestations of a shared "textuality" ruled by automatism.[10] "Modernist writing," as Stewart argues, is "neither predominantly impressionist nor expressive (since both imply the intervening subjectivity of an author) but in some new way strictly technical, a prosthesis of observation in the mode of inscription."[11] In this approach, modernist literature and film share a discourse network, rather than being separate modes of art affecting each other: the discourse of technologically mediated, depersonalized realities and subjectivities.[12] In this chapter, we follow this framework of contiguity as suggested by Stewart and seek to add to it through a comparative analysis that extends beyond the modernist age into the sphere of the postmodern. As we show, the issue of prosthetic perception is foregrounded in modernist as well as key postmodernist texts that take film as their primary cue.[13] We focus on Luigi Pirandello's *Shoot!* (1915) and Thomas Pynchon's *Gravity's Rainbow* (1973) as representative twentieth-century "cinematographic" texts in Europe and the United States that critically incorporate the power of film not only to mechanize perception, but also to mechanize or substitute for the real.[14] This comparative analysis lays bare the modernist "cinematographic" mechanisms at the heart of the postmodernist simulacrum: The one cannot be thought without the other. The parallel is extended to Pynchon's *Vineland* (1990), which processes and addresses the medium of television: Does this domestic mass medium signal a change, a radicalization, or an undermining of the patterns and discourse of automatized perception?

MEDIATED WORLDS, MEDIATED SUBJECTS: CAMERATIC PERCEPTION IN *SHOOT!*

The emergence of the modernist novel is roughly contemporaneous with the birth of film—and with a modernist "frame" of mind that casts the mind as "cinematographic." In 1907, in the final chapter of *Creative Evolution*, Henri Bergson invoked the cinematographic apparatus to capture the ways in which the intellect approaches reality: as movement rendered static rendered dynamic once again, as in filmic recording and montage. Thus, the intellect re-renders reality-as-movement as a discontinuous continuity:

> Instead of attaching ourselves to the inner becoming of things, we place ourselves outside them in order to recompose their becoming artificially. We take snapshots, as it were, of the passing reality. . . . We may therefore sum up . . . that the mechanism of our ordinary knowledge is of a cinematographical kind.[15]

For Bergson, while the intellect thus freezes moments of the flux that reality embodies, it is by contrast through intuition that one may penetrate and participate in that flux, rather than capturing this flow in snippets and reassembling it as a mechanical whole.[16] The implication is that film, as an embodiment of mechanized perception, cannot cater intuition.[17]

Pirandello's *Shoot!* (first translated into English in 1927) enacts this association between film and "inhuman" mediations of reality flows through its first-person narrator who is at once a cameraman. Because of this double bind, narration is framed within a cinematically mediated focalization,[18] so that the distinction between writing and filming, between reading and viewing, is problematized from the start—however much the narrator wants to artificially uphold the distinction between paper and celluloid. *Shoot!* offers the fate of Serafino Gubbio, who negotiates between old and new media by being an "operator" or cameraman for the film studio Kosmograph by day, and the writer of his memoirs by night.[19] Yet, even as a writer he cannot disengage himself from his perspective as a cameraman. His hand, operating the handle of the camera and holding his pen, which records the melodramas unfolding before and behind the camera, becomes a prosthetic device, as if attached first and foremost to the machinery Gubbio is operating, rather than to his body. This is precisely what *Shoot!* is about: the relegating of perception to the focus of a machine, an adaptation of a special kind.

Like other major Italian authors in the early twentieth century, such as Giovanni Verga, Guido Gozzano, Marco Praga, and Gabriele D'Annunzio, Pirandello was engaged in the emerging Italian film industry as a writer. Of these writers, it was Pirandello who became specifically concerned with the aesthetics and cultural implications of film, and who also became a source of inspiration for film "authors" such as Jean-Luc Godard.[20] *Shoot!* draws on Pirandello's experiences in the film business, offering the familiar story-within-a-story (and more) that takes on the shape of a melodrama typical of silent film: There is a diva, the Nestoroff, her lover, Carlo Ferro, a jilted lover, Aldo Nutti, two other rejected lovers (Duccella and Giorgio Mirelli) and a suicide (Giorgio), a caged and condemned tiger, and two murders in the end. As a subplot, there is the case of scenario writer Cavalena and his jealous wife—and their daughter Luisetta who is secretly, and impassively, loved by Gubbio. One way or another, these characters are all fed to Gubbio's camera, voracious and vampiristic like the other machines of the modern age:

> Long live the Machine that mechanizes life!
> Do you still retain, gentlemen, a little soul, a little heart and a little mind? Give them. Give them over to the greedy machines, which are waiting for them! . . .
> The machine is made to act, to move, it requires swallowing up our soul, devouring our life. And how do you expect them to be given back to us, our life and soul, in a centuplicated and continuous output, by the machines? Let me tell you: in bits and morsels, all of one pattern, stupid and precise, which would make, if placed on top of another, a pyramid that might reach to the stars.[21]

In Gubbio's camera perspective, it is not only perception but also life as a whole, indeed the life of the soul, which is mechanized: devoured, partitioned, carved out, made to fit. It is as if Bergson's "cinemato-graphic" knowledge has colonized experience, subjectivity, and materi-ality, and no room is left for intuition—however feeble the pyramid of morsel-souls may be.

This all-pervasiveness of the cinematographic outlook at once implies a blurring of the "given" and the "mediated"—the latter rather always already frames the former in a world where, as Gubbio suggests, the speed and noise of machination format our experience:

> Do you hear it? A hornet that is always buzzing, forbidding, grim, surly, diffused, and never stops. What is it? The hum of the telegraph poles? The endless scream of the trolley along the overhead wire of the electric trams? . . . Of the cinematograph?
>
> The beating of the heart is not felt, nor do we feel the pulsing of our arteries. The worse for us if we did! But this buzzing, this perpetual ticking we do notice, and I say that all this furious haste is not natural, all this flickering and vanishing of images; but that there lies beneath it a machine which seems to pursue it, frantically screaming.[22]

The machine becomes like a Schopenhauerian life-Will, subtending and informing all "this flickering and vanishing of images": this phenome-nal world that has been cut to pieces and reassembled in a furious haste.[23] My reference to Arthur Schopenhauer is not incidental—and not only because the machine operates in the manner of the Will as a force at once productive and constructive, a condition of possibility and a condition of death; an undercurrent of the world of ideas, in Schopen-hauer's terminology, objectified in perceivable forms and, indeed, our very own bodies. It is not just the aimless movement of this Will that Gubbio's machine resonates with, but its very inevitability: We cannot escape it, since we cannot but feel the movements within our bodies reminding us of our own "superfluity": our own, fateful, capacity for reflection that, for Gubbio, renders us chronically dissatisfied. *Shoot!* could thus be said to recast Schopenhauer's unconscious Will as a mechanical force impregnating all aspects of modern life.

The machine feeds, but also itself feeds on, life: This double bind epitomizes the paradox foregrounded in *Shoot!* How precisely does Pir-andello thus move beyond a binary opposition between the human and the machine in *Shoot!*? And how, in turn, does this condition the idea of the "cinematographic" in the novel?

The complexity of the relations between human and machinic worlds in *Shoot!* is reflected in the degree to which reality and fiction here inform and produce each other, rather than being separate categories.

Thus, on one level, there is the repeated reference to a drive of "making it real" in the film industry with props and decors ("Scene painters, stagehands, actors all give themselves the air of deceiving the machine, which will give an appearance of reality to all their fictions")—and the intrusion of a living prop, a tiger to be shot in actual fact, in the film Gubbio is shooting: *The Lady and the Tiger*: "India will be a sham, the jungle will be a sham, the travels will be a sham, with a sham Miss and sham admirers: only the death of this poor beast will not be a sham."[24] Life is sacrificed to the demands of machinic mimesis, and in this sacrifice displays its slippery demarcations as a material reality: that materiality is equally fictitious in, what will become, a snuff movie. In the movie's final scene a plurality of stories behind and before the camera fatefully intertwine: the tragedy of Duccella and Giorgio Mirelli, who lost their respective lovers to these lovers, and Nutti, who lost the Nestoroff to Carlo Ferro afterward. While Nutti is supposed to shoot the tiger, he shoots the Nestoroff and himself; Carlo Ferro will be devoured by the tiger, and the tiger will be shot. Thus, the genre of the melodrama inhabits different ontological planes that are always already intertwined: Narrative patterns of love and death format actual love affairs, while the consequences of these affairs are played out in the film as melodrama.

During the execution of these patterns, Gubbio continues to "turn the handle," and in this continuation a position is revealed that is at once "human and inhuman." As noted earlier, Gubbio has adapted himself to the camera in such a way as to have become its extension. As a character and a narrating voice, he is first of all a "hand" ("my soul does not serve me. My hand serves me, that is to say, serves the machine"), an operator whose vision is mediated by the camera. In turn, the characters, impressions, and events he narrates are specifically framed as passing projections in a flux: "on nothing, nothing at all ought we fix our attention. Take in, rather, moment by moment, this passage of aspects and events, and so on, until we reach the point when for each of us the buzz shall cease."[25] Gubbio *sees* cinematographically. This not only means that his perceptions mimic camera positions and movements, or that his visualizations foreground a "cameratic" play with light and colors in virtual close-ups:[26] "a wonderful sight was the play, on [the Nestoroff's] face, of the purple shadows, straying and shot with threads of golden sunlight, which lightened up now one of her nostrils of her upper lip, now the lobe of her ear and a patch of her throat."[27] Rather, the intensity with which Gubbio perceives the "external aspects of things" renders his vision cinematographic—it is a perception that is as distracted as it is dedicated to fleeting appearances; a perception that, as such, remains as impassive, detached as the camera-machine.

Detachment is a key concept in *Shoot!* It is present as much in the operator Gubbio as the faces and figures he projects on screen. In a famous passage that Benjamin used for his *Work of Art*, Gubbio relates how film actors are exiled from the public as much as from their voices and their bodies: "it is *their image* alone, caught in a moment, in a gesture, an expression, that flickers and disappears."[28] Here, already, one can see the apparition of the posthuman: a body transported on screen, a spectral presence projected primarily as a grimacing face, which extends and substitutes the Nestoroff as a material presence.[29] The difference between such a spectrality and materiality is, however, not a difference in kind but a difference in degree: already in real life, as we have seen, the Nestoroff is interpellated as a melodramatic subject, mediated by the scripts she performs onscreen (and vice versa). Insofar as the posthuman involves a technological contamination, this contamination becomes originary here: the Nestoroff is "in essence" an after-effect of the imaginary.

Likewise, Gubbio's detachment as a cameraman/narrator is never simply a machinic alienation: In his detachment there is, as Allesandro Vettori has argued convincingly, a display of humanness in terms of an almost mystic disinterestedness.[30] Thus, it seems as if Gubbio's humanness is only preserved in his writing and corrupted by his work as a cameraman, as it is through his writing that Gubbio revenges himself on a world of automatized perception: "I satisfy, by writing, a need to let off steam which is overpowering. I get rid of my professional impassivity, and avenge myself as well."[31] Yet precisely through the camera Gubbio attains a selflessness that approaches the kind of disinterestedness which has been celebrated since the eighteenth century as a sign of cultivation, of human distinction: the art of willing desire away in the face of objects of sense; the art of no longer willing such objects to satisfy one's own needs and wants—of becoming purely, "objectively" cameratic.

Interestingly, therefore, in *Shoot!* the camera can be seen not only as a metaphor of the modern machine age, an age of alienation, but also as an escape route from this very same alienation through an alienation of a different kind: through the aesthetic gaze that, as a gaze subjecting experience to the mould of a synthesis in Kant's third critique, is constitutive of a shared sensible world that is here at once projected as the a priori or prestructuring power of the machine. This "double dealing" of alienation allows the "human" and "inhuman" to collapse into each other in *Shoot!*: The reduction of the one to the other at once becomes its own inverse.[32] Indeed, Gubbio's passivity becomes the perfect antidote against the human superfluity that is a constant impediment to human happiness—and a motor of the machine age.

Seen in this light, the "cinematographic" in *Shoot!* incorporates a beyond of the human that is imagined as a synthesis: the synthetic gaze of the machine and a synthesis of the senses that regulates reality as a scopic regime. On one hand, this synthesis involves the camera and editing techniques of early film, and the modes of automatized perception framed by it,[33] insofar as film represents a vision machine. On the other hand, transmediated (transmediation being the transference and transformation of one mode of mediation into another) techniques of early film in *Shoot!* as a print-based text blur distinctions between writing and this vision machine, that is, between a medium familiarly associated with "humanness" in the modern age and one perceived—in the earlier twentieth century—as a medium of the future (see Filippo Marinetti) and beyond of the human: as speed, projection. Yet precisely *as* a regime of visibility, "cinematographic" in *Shoot!* invokes a whole network of associations with selflessness, disinterested contemplation, and silence (what Gavriel Moses has called the film medium's "central metonomy," in the end inversed as Gubbio's very "physical reality"): in short, a strangely aesthetic-existential dimension that is both self and other to a voracious machine.[34] (And yet we may wonder whether Gubbio's indifference is not, in effect, an indifferentism that, as Jacques Rancière has noted, is potentially fatefully aligned with indistinction). Thus, "cinematographic" in *Shoot!* is never simply a given, a stable category outside of the text, but is rather made manifest *as an effect of* that text—after the fact—as a multifaceted dimension of the visual (perception) and (appropriate to the period) of the silent (impassive).

GRAVITY'S RAINBOW AND "THE PHANTOM OF THE MOVIE PALACE": PRERECORDINGS AND REASSEMBLAGES

The case of *Shoot!* already suggests that we had better use the concept of the "cinematographic" in literary studies not as a fixed or general but a singular concept, that is, always within the framework of a specific text using specific techniques, offering different meanings and concepts of cinema. There is, after all, a huge difference between "cinematographic" techniques in texts by H. G. Wells, Luigi Pirandello, John Dos Passos, James Joyce, or Alain Robbe-Grillet—as a concept it emerges anew, opening a field with every cultural and literary negotiation. Literature, too, shapes and affects the cinematographic.

At the same time, the instability of the cinematographic as a concept is obviously due to developments in the medium of film in Europe and the United States. Thus, in the postmodern age "cinematographic" has connotations different from Bergson's idea of the intellect carving up the flux of reality, or Eisenstein's notion of montage as a montage of attractions. Indeed, Stanley Solomon has argued that "cinematographic" in a postmodern sense bears most significantly on surface play or "texture," and an absence of classical narrative structures:

> Plot is being replaced by texture. By texture I mean incident or event or conversation—as distinct from structured action that has beginning, middle, and end. An incident is not sustaining in itself, but many incidents and many conversations strung together may resemble something like a traditional narrative. Texture includes tone and spectacle, and if it is constantly applied it is another principle of organizing narrative art.[35]

Cinematography has become special effects since, roughly speaking, the late 1970s, insofar as it revolves around visual texture in major Hollywood productions ranging from *Star Wars* (1977–2005) to *Titanic* (1997), *The Mummy* (1999), and *The Core* (2003), which mostly build a narrative with the mere purpose of fitting it in between scenes of special effects and violence.

This paradigm shift, if one may call it thus, is also felt at one remove. Thus, in novels like Robert Coover's *Gerald's Party* (1986), the plot revolves around the murder of the character Ros and a detective's attempt to solve it. The novel can be perceived as texture of numerous (in)consistent conversations that interrupt one another or occur simultaneously with violent events and dead bodies piling up as the evening wears off, parodying detective fiction and mimicking spectacle movies. This emphasis on spectacle inevitably invokes Guy Debord's idea of the society of the spectacle, where social relations are mediated by images, and the spectacle becomes a manufacturer of alienation.[36] We have already seen this process at work in Gubbio's camera perspective— though alienation here always has the double connotation of becoming machine and becoming transcendent at once—yet even in Debord's evocation as a Situationist the spectacle is not necessarily triumphant: there is still a place from which to combat the spectacle, just as Gubbio inhabits and instrumentalizes this space by using the camera as a means of surrender to and escape from the machine. As we know, the finality of the spectacle only becomes pressing in the perspective of postmodernist philosophers like Jean Baudrillard, where opposition to the spectacle is impossible as the spectacle reinforces itself with every repetition of itself as flashy mass-mediation.[37] It is this total surrender to the spectacle that is enacted but also problematized in postmodernist novels like Thomas Pynchon's *Gravity's Rainbow*.

Much has been said about cinematographic references and techniques in *Gravity's Rainbow*. Indeed, Charles Clerc has noted that *Gravity's Rainbow* "brings to bear the imprint of cinema on modern life. It demonstrates the pervasive influence of movies in all facets of our culture, down to indelible effects upon individual sensibilities."[38] Even in the 2000s cinema as a cultural influence is still present in novels like Danielewski's *Only Revolutions* and Hall's *The Raw Shark Texts*, with fragments of film patterning the texts: Cinema continues to be a powerful cultural metaphor in American and European literature. The "cinematographic" texture of *Gravity's Rainbow* may consist of references to films and of mimicking their mode of presentation, but it is given full force in the novel as a discourse that has co-shaped modern consciousness and storytelling: the images that cinema provides are the archetypical images once provided by myth. Scott Simmon observed long ago that "the complexity of *Gravity's Rainbow*'s film-form comes from Pynchon's awareness that our whole way of approaching narrative itself has been altered by film."[39] Or most tellingly, the complexity of *Gravity's Rainbow* comes from Pynchon's characters, whose minds function "cinematographically" in the old Freudian sense of cinema as a dream sequence, fading in and out as ghosts on screen. Likewise, the plot is framed cinematographically, as if derived from screen, which gives the novel the semblance of being a *novelization* at its core: it presents itself as a transcription, "always already," just as *House of Leaves* had done over a decade earlier.

Copy and origin, technology and fantasy: they have become co-dependent and indistinguishable in this novel opening with a dream and ending in a movie theater. Like other modern technologies, cinema controls minds in *Gravity's Rainbow* and gives rise to reality effects of a very special kind, such as the imaginary Schwarzkommando in Gerhard von Göll's ("der Springer") fake documentary, which turns out to be a real African rocket unit serving under Germany, and Springer's belief that his film has brought these men into being (as German cinema in *Gravity's Rainbow* is accused of bringing certain realities into being). Cinematographic control does not exclude the reader, who in the end is caught as a viewer in the act of reading in front of a big, empty screen. As in *Shoot!*, where writing and recording become conflated, so in *Gravity's Rainbow* reading is repositioned within the frames of the imaginary. We cannot *but* be looking at a screen.

This inescapability of cinema as a "paranoiac" medium, shaping reality, and absorbing culture, epitomizes *Gravity's Rainbow*.

The cinematographic space-time frequently merges with the System- and Zone-realities of the characters respectively, at times drastically changing their lives. One example is the figure of Ilse—a child put into a concentration camp to blackmail her father, Franz Pökler—who was conceived after the screening of Pökler's film *Alpdrücken*: "how many shadow-children would be fathered on Erdmann that night?"[40] The star of the same movie, Margherita Erdmann, became pregnant during the shooting of the film, presumably due to a gang rape. Franz wonders if the "movie-child" whom the Nazi archvillain Lieutenant Weissmann sends him is, in fact, his daughter: "*Isn't that what they made of my child, a film?*"[41] Thus, the birth of Ilse and Bianca (Margherita's daughter) coincides with an act of filmic mediation. Bianca dies horribly on the ship *Anubis*, and Ilse's presence then assumes an episodic character:

> So it has gone for the six years since. A daughter a year, each one about a year older, each time taking up nearly from scratch. The only continuity has been her name, and Zwölfkinder, and Pökler's love—love something like the persistence of vision, for They have used it to create for him the moving image of a daughter, flashing him only these summertime frames of her, leaving him to build the illusion of a single child . . . what would the time scale matter, a 24th of a second or a year.[42]

Pökler's "24th of a second" here refers to Jean-Luc Godard's dictum that a film speed of twenty-four frames per second is ideal for accommodating "persistence of vision." Thus, in the novel, what connects Ilse and her father in "reality" has become a replica of the scenes from *Alpdrücken*—an effect of automatized perception related to "cinematography" as a freezer and reassembler of the flux of the real. As in numerous other scenes, cinema here conditions perception and apparitions of reality "itself" (see Von Göll's subsequent determination to "sow in the Zone seeds of reality" with images of his phony Schwarz-kommando footage).[43] Thus, the "cinematographic" in *Gravity's Rainbow* emerges as a prerecording of the real: formative and inevitable.

CINEMATOGRAPHIC AND TELEVISUAL MODES OF PERCEPTION

As a "cinematographic" text, *Gravity's Rainbow* still participates in a modernist discourse of automatized perception, while at once radicalizing that discourse: It further destabilizes ontological differences between "real" and "mediated" worlds—these worlds interact with, and collapse into each other. While *Shoot!* already stages such interactions, and thus likewise problematizes distinctions between filmed worlds and worlds captured by an I/eye that is nevertheless also a camera I/eye, the cinematographic in *Gravity's Rainbow* regulates a regime of visibility that *becomes* the real. Indeed, it is the very possibility of a cinematographic regulation of the real as an illusionist and uncontrollable regulation that connects *Shoot!* to *Gravity's Rainbow*. The emphasis on calculated effect plays a central role in this, not only in *Shoot!*, where "real life" starts to adapt itself to the melodramatic formats of silent film, but also in *Gravity's Rainbow*, where films in a way animate life.

What is more, both novels critique the effects of the cultural colonization of cinema as a "mainstream" machine while at the same time drawing on the more experimental techniques of avant-garde cinema (as the numerous references to German expressionist film in *Gravity's Rainbow* attest to) to *materialize* that criticism in literary writing. This critique should be read, we feel, in the context of the precariousness of the literary with respect to cinema in the twentieth century—a similar precariousness as has been observed for literature in the digital age. While the transmedial adaptations of film in twentieth-century literature were frequent and fertile, film also threatened to suppress older media such as the theater and literature as dominant cultural media.

As for literature, the threat to its marginalization at once entailed a threat to literacy—and this threat moved far beyond the realm of the aesthetic into that of the social-political: democracy and the vote. Thus in 1940, George Duhamel's *In Defense of Letters* (1940), anticipating Sven Birkerts's *The Gutenberg Elegies* (1995), points to the centrality of print in Western culture, the vitality of literacy to democracy, and its possible erosion due to the perceived, imperialist expansion of film and radio in the twentieth century. In nineteenth-century Western Europe and the United States, as Robert Morss Lovett paraphrases Duhamel in a contemporary review, "an immense reading public was called into being [in direct relation to the liberal struggle for the extension of suffrage], and to this public literature became a religion."[44] In the twentieth century, for Duhamel, it is not so much the threat of illiteracy as the threat of new media (which carries for him another, repeated threat of illiteracy) that undermine the scope and depth of this reading public. According to him, print has been degraded into "popular" forms, while the mass mediations of film and radio undermine a culture of solitude that would lie at the foundation of the culture of reading since the Renaissance—a culture fostering autonomous thought and individual, reflecting minds. Even today, apocalyptic critics like Birkerts uphold this view, arguing that the electronic media have corroded humanist developments of print and after, and that privacy and autonomy, are now "values" of the past—as films such as *The Truman Show* and *Eternal Sunshine of the Spotless Mind* and novels such as Steven Hall's *The Raw Shark Texts* and Paul Auster's *Travels in the Scriptorium* might illustrate.

In different ways, *Shoot!* and *Gravity's Rainbow* perform this tense opposition between solitude (literature, literacy) and mediated minds (film, radio) and mourn the "lost" humanist values this opposition favors implicitly: Solitude in these novels never again is an unproblematic, nor even an attainable, state. Though in *Shoot!* the undecidability of "alienation" in terms of machinic isolation on one hand and aesthetic indifference on the other undermines a stable opposition between the automaton and human values, this is less ambivalent in *Gravity's Rainbow*. *Gravity's Rainbow* still offers an escape from the System, yet it is but a marginal escape from what Tony Tanner has called a "world of non-being, an operative kingdom of death, covering the organic world with a world of paper and plastic" ran by anonymous forces.[45] In the Zone, all meaning collapses, all becomes disconnected—an alienation of the drifting sort that is a far cry from the autonomous solitude of humanism. Conversely, in the System individual minds are framed and formatted by official meanings and narratives, thus likewise undermining the possibility of a freely thinking, individual mind that is at the core of the humanist tradition.

Is this how literature, or at least a certain literature, announces its "defeat," and the "defeat" of print literacy, in the twentieth century? By tapping into a discourse network of automatized perception that it presents as omnipresent, as an enemy to be fought in a cultural war? Kathleen Fitzpatrick has noted in this respect that what she calls late-twentieth-century "novels of obsolescence," novels announcing, in one way or another, the "end" of literature in an age of mass mediation, are implicated in an ideology of their own. Counting among its practitioners authors such as Pynchon and Don DeLillo, Fitzpatrick argues that the anxiety of literary obsolescence focuses typically on dehumanization, propaganda, and (once more) loss of individuality. While her analyses are framed not so much by the "cinematographic" as by the televisual, not so much in a specific as in a broad sense of multimodal, networked mass mediation, she also finds that anxieties over the imminent death of literature interact with other anxieties: those of white males who have been losing their privileged position within the domain of literature to female authors and those of other ethnicities. Thus, "the threat that television poses to the [white male] novelist functions as an acceptable cultural scapegoat for that much stickier social issue: the perceived dominance of the contemporary literary scene of fiction by women and racial and ethnic minorities."[46] What poses as the threat of new media only hides, for Fitzpatrick, the threat of the Other.

In Pynchon's *Vineland*, published one year before the first Gulf War, this threat of the televisual is, indeed, emphatically (one might almost say: predictably) rendered. Set in 1984, and revolving around California-based old hippie Zoyd Wheeler, his daughter, Prairie, and her vanished mother Frenesi (and—like *Shoot!*—around a snuff movie), *Vineland* displays and reflects a world modeled by TV programs, a world where television shapes the protagonists' desires, expectations, and behavior. There is a narcotics agent, Hector Zuniga, who tries to behave like cops he sees on TV, while at the same time persuading Zoyd that the model's representation is nowhere near the real undercover cop's life. Conversely, there is Frenesi, who encounters a "real" policeman after having masturbated in front of her favorite cop show, seeing him *through the screen of the door*, which functions in the geography of private spaces as an "outlook" on the world. This outlook is thoroughly mediated, since TV controls her response to the world outside: The cop show conditions her emotional state and submissive stance toward the policeman.

Everybody in the novel is shaped by the Tube—indeed, as Brian McHale has pointed out, the world in *Vineland* is divided into different TV genres, to which different characters and their worlds correspond (Zoyd and sitcoms, Prairie and soaps).[47] Switching from one world to the other is like switching channels—which situates the novel typically outside the linear domain of traditional narrative. Pynchon grotesquely depicts this TV-based culture through Thanatoids, a community of neither fully alive nor fully dead people, due to karmic imbalances: "like death only different," moving but motionless (like Benny and the Crew from Pynchon's earlier novel *V*), who watch TV all the time. Indeed, due to its (much-problematized) dimension of simultaneity or liveness, TV in *Vineland* acts as a household presence that people relate to, chat with, and masturbate with.[48] Culture in *Vineland* is a culture of reruns: an endless repetition of scopic regimes, constituting a virtual death-in-life, and hence a virtual timelessness, encapsulated in an eternal return. Seen in this light, it is not only the tube, but also technologies of video recording that recast the texture of reality in *Vineland* into tape materiality of endless replay.

And yet, if film and the even more menacing, domestic presence of TV here act out the perceived threats of a culturally diversified literary field, and if white male authors of the 1980s and 1990s—knowingly or unknowingly—use film and TV as a screen on which to project their anxieties of "best manhood" (in Kathleen Fitzpatrick's phrase), the very nature of TV mediation at once deconstructs this very projection. Let us, to this end, and near the end, go back to the beginning: to Henri Bergson's observations on the intellect and cinematographic mediation. For Bergson, as we have seen, the intellect makes snapshots of the flux of reality, rather than participating in that flux, which is the province of intuition. If film thus cannot cater intuition in Bergson's perspective, we may make a possible exception for TV. After all, if we elaborate on Raymond Williams's famous dictum in *Television: Technology and Cultural Form*, the experience of watching TV has been associated with flux or flow. While in literary and theater culture, the reading and viewing audience was accustomed to "discrete" entities such as books or pieces, TV offered an experiential flow that was to change cultural perception—and the cultural conception of sequence.[49] Fixed endings and intervals, such as the intervals in cinema, virtually disappeared in this technology.

Watching TV can thus be compared to stepping into a river—always *in medias res*—even though it is a rigidly scheduled river, and the river is in the plural.[50] Though the flow may in fact be a segmentation without end, Cecilia Tichi has emphasized print novels of the later 1980s and 1990s, absorbing the medium of TV, typically mimic this open continuity: "Readers are made to feel that, instead of a beginning, there is a point of entry. We are joining a program in progress, i.e., in process. We move into a sequence of events which are to be represented in a continuous flow."[51] Tichi refers to fictions by Ann Beattie, Brett Easton Ellis, or David Leavitt as "enacting the traits of broadcast television in the very form of their fiction"—offering narratives with no clear entry and exit points, a pervasive sense of the present, and moveable contexts or settings of focalization. Precisely for this reason, texts such as Bret Easton Ellis's *Less than Zero* have been typically downplayed as "shallow," but it is a shallowness attesting to a significant transmedial transfer: Framed by a dominant, televisual medium paradigm, the protagonist in such televisual fictions is "constructed as a figure in transit, and the reader also. Both are mobile figures, true to the cognitive experience of television. . . . The mobility of televisual "flow" is the fundament of fictional form."[52] If this is indeed the case, then the discontinuous continuity of cinematographic perception—revolving around the constant freezing, cutting, and reassembling of the real—has in the televisual era been replaced by a continuous discontinuity: a flow of infinite parts, beams. It is this continuous discontinuity that reapproaches Bergson's mode of intuition, if in a deeply synthetic way, at once "doing" and "undoing" the forms of automatized perception. The "end" of the novel, in this paradigm, is nowhere in sight: it has adapted itself to, and creatively absorbed the latter in a discourse of fluidity, impermanency, and simultaneity.

CONCLUSION

In this chapter, we have seen how the concept of the cinematographic works as a literary concept in modernist and postmodernist fictions. In *Shoot!* the cinematographic becomes the framework for rethinking the relations between humans and machines: to think a beyond of the human that is imagined as a synthesis—the synthetic gaze of the machine and a synthesis of the senses that regulates reality as a scopic regime. Yet if we think that cinema represents a disembodied, machinic perception here, while literary writing is attached to some kind of lost humanity and individuality, and the kind of solitude and privacy attached to this humanity, the very transmediation of the cinema in *literary writing itself* blurs binary oppositions between the two. Such blurring defines our reading experience of *Shoot!*, as the literary and the cinematographic here affect and contaminate each other.

Likewise, in *Gravity's Rainbow* the cinematographic and the novelis-tic—and all the values attached to both—spill over into each other. As we have seen, the novel still participates in a modernist discourse of automatized perception, but it also radicalizes that discourse: *Gravity's Rainbow* further destabilizes ontological differences between "real" and "mediated" worlds, as these worlds interact with, and collapse into each other. Here, daily life does not just adapt itself to cinematographic life—here, the cinematographic formats the real itself.

Is this, we have wondered, how literature, or at least a certain litera-ture, announces its "defeat," and the "defeat" of print literacy, in the late twentieth century? By tapping into a modernist discourse network of automatized perception that it presents as omnipresent, as an enemy to be fought in a cultural war? With reference to Fitzpatrick, we have observed that there might be another enemy at work in these novels of obsolescence: the Other writing back to the center—the Other pre-sented in the guise of new media that move "beyond" humanism. Cin-ema and, even more menacing, the domestic presence of TV may here be acting out the perceived threats of a culturally diversified literary field: White male authors of the 1980s and 1990s—knowingly or unknowingly—use film and TV as a screen on which to project their anxieties of "beset manhood." Yet if TV is used as such a screen, its particular mode of mediation may take us back to the very patterns of intuition that, in Henri Bergson's writing, film would not be able to cater: patterns of flow, of a continuity that mimics "becoming." *These* patterns, we have suggested, have helped to reinvigorate the form of the novel in the 1990s and 2000s.

CHAPTER ELEVEN

Novelizing Tati

JAN BAETENS

Novelization, the "translation" of an original movie in a novel, seems to be the perfect victim for adaptation studies.[1] It does not come as a surprise, therefore, that one of the most recent overviews of adaptation and intermediality studies, Linda Hutcheon's *A Theory of Adaptation*, pays attention to the genre, if indeed it is a genre (which I think it is).[2] One of the striking features of this current interest for novelizations is the fact that nowadays—in contrast to "classical" adaptation studies (if they exist)—these works are studied in a broader cultural perspective. This is clearly influenced by the shift from literary to cultural studies, which impelled a stronger emphasis on issues linked with contextualization on one hand, and on topics allegedly marked as "unsophisticated" (but, as Stanley Cavell has taught us in his book *The Pursuit of Happiness*, no serious knowledge really holds if it is incapable of understanding the unsophisticated).[3] Deborah Cartmell and Imelda Whelehan's seminal reader *Adaptations*, which can be read also as a manifesto in defense of the cultural studies approach of the genre, takes all these issues and questions wonderfully on board.[4]

However, this broadening of the scope should invite us to raise a more radical question, namely, is novelization really an instance of adaptation if we understand adaptation in terms of a process, a transformative reworking, of a story or subject in one medium (film) into another (text)? In other words: Is adaptation a transmedial affair, whereby transmediation is understood in terms of a transfer from one medial regime to another? When one analyzes the way many (though not all) novelizations are made, there are good reasons to doubt this. As I have argued on other occasions,[5] novelizations may be adaptations, but they are not necessarily transmedial adaptations, that is, involving the transfer from one medium to another. Novelizations lack such a crucial transfer. Contrary to the adaptation of a book in a cinemato- graphic process, most novelizations are not based on an "alien" medial regime, a visual source, but on a screenplay or scenario: a *verbal* pre- text, which entails, among other things, that the problem of the "trans- lation" from one regime to another is systematically eluded. Second, because novelizations are based on an often almost prenovelized screen- play version, they also skirt the major challenge of filmic adaptation, namely, the equilibrium between the two forces that Brian McFarlane has termed *transfer* and *adaptation proper*.[6] To the extent that novel- izations restrict themselves to the textual transposition of an already written scenario and to the novelistic transposition of an already emphatically narrative structure, the genre can comfortably be an adap- tation that skirts almost all the traditional problems of cinematographic adaptation. However, I would no longer infer from this that noveliza- tions are anti-adaptations, but only not necessarily transmedial.

If one rejects transmediality as the key to novelization studies, other readings become possible or even necessary. Thus, though the notion of transmediality has persisted in current research into novelization, it is now no longer restricted to the semiotic analysis of the transformation of a movie into a book, but opened up to the cultural analysis of the relationships between media in the media ecology of a given period and a given context. Let me briefly and very generally mention two new types of questions that may emerge within this perspective.

My first example is that of the well-known notion of *remediation*.[7] If we follow Bolter's and Grusin's theory, it is difficult to understand why movies are novelized, since the remediating powers of the noveliza- tion are weak: this is a transfer between texts and a movie in-between. Yet novelizations have always existed, from the very beginning of the movies, and they are far from dead (most Hollywood films that are not already book adaptations will be novelized: Such films are couched in between paper-based cultural products). What makes the genre so inter- esting is the new light it may shed on the relationships between litera- ture and cinema, books and films, words and images in our culture. Novelizations help contesting the linear vision of a global shift from textual to visual culture. They help also to decipher the media network as a heterotopic field (in the sense coined by Foucault),[8] as a space where evolution from A to B is always contested by the active survival of all kinds of anachronisms.[9] In other words: With novelization, we can enlarge the notion of transmediality and transfer it from the field of translation and adaptation studies to the field of mediascapes.

The second example I would like to give concerns the relationship between film and literature. If the cultural studies-approach that surfaces in adaptation studies helps to abandon the linear and chronological vision of a movie (step A) transformed into a book (step B), it should become possible to proceed beyond this critique of source and target relationships and to see how novelizations can enable us to reread both singular movies and the film industry in general. The main idea here is that a reading of the historical changes of the novelization genre does not simply reflect a previous change in film, but offers on the contrary new insights in the way films were made. In many cases novelizations influenced the actual reception of a movie (think of the novelization of *King Kong* in 1932, before the movie opened)—or of a certain type of movies, since novelizations are not always one-shots, but are part of larger series which interact with certain categories of movies—just as they interfered with the production of new movies. In other words: Thanks to the novelization, and the critical positions it has yielded, it may become possible to rewrite the history of film form the viewpoint of its book adaptations.

The perspective I will defend in this chapter will be mixed. Given the complexity of the object, I believe that one should approach it in a mood that is as interdisciplinary as possible, with an eye for the semiotic and literary as well as for the historical and contextual aspects of the corpus. I will therefore not completely reject the classic transmedial approach, with its emphasis on the close reading of adaptation transfers from one medium to another (what does the novel do that the film does not do?). Yet I will also frame my reading contextually, a context that is equally part of the object that cultural studies has enabled us to interpret in terms of "cultural form."[10] In this regard, I can only express my admiration for scholars such as David Trotter and Tom Conley, who, despite their deep mistrust of traditional adaptation studies, succeeded in maintaining the double perspective of semiotic close reading and cultural and historical contextualization.[11] It is this type of reading that gives the horizon to which I try to go myself.

It is often said that there are two types of novelizations: the bad ones and the good ones, the commercial ones and the literary ones, those written before the film is starting to get shot and that have to be available worldwide in the airport and supermarket stands the very day of the film release and those written many years later, in a gesture of cinephilic nostalgia, by "great authors" who accept the challenge to compete with the images that are haunting them, and so on. This opposition is not false, but it is very relative, and one of the reasons why I dwell on the novelization of Jacques Tati's 1953 film *Les vacances de M. Hulot*, by Jean-Claude Carrière, is the fact that this book, published in 1958, happily deconstructs the distinction between the good and the bad. The novel did not have the ambition to be art (although it is, definitely, or at least it will not deceive those who are looking for the aesthetic in popular fiction), yet it also obeys clear commercial strategies (although it was published five years after the movie's release).

WHY *LES VACANCES DE M. HULOT*?

Tati's novelization is certainly appealing for having boosted the career of Jean-Claude Carrière (no pun intended), a young novelist and scriptwriter who had won the literary contest organized by the publisher when he was looking for a writer capable of transposing *Les vacances de M. Hulot*. It was Tati himself who chose Carrière, for he considered the pilot chapter written by the young novelist as the most original of all the samples that had been presented.[12] Carrière would become rapidly famous in various regards: as a scriptwriter (among others for Luis Bunuel and Milos Forman), as a film director, as a playwright, and as a "novelizer," among other things. Although the novelization did not fall into complete oblivion after its publication, it is curious to see that it hardly received any critical attention. One of the major books on film and literature in French devotes only one line to it,[13] defining the work not as a novelization but as an adaptation (but that is not unusual, since the label "novelization" is of recent use in French criticism) and describing it as a "*texte comique de Jean-Claude Carrière, alors au début de sa carrière de scénariste.*"[14] Jacques Kermabon's book on *Les vacances de M. Hulot* contains a detailed study of Carrière's book, but only from the viewpoint of a comparison of the scenes that have been added or deleted in the four known version of the movie: screenplay, first version, final version, novelization.[15] Carrière's book is here reduced to a narrative skeleton, as if one prefers a screenplay in disguise. In addition, Tati's biographer, David Bellos, mentions the novelization, but without analyzing it.[16] Finally, the author himself, despite his huge production in the novelization field and despite the new 2006 edition, does not mention the book on his site, and even his quite complete Wikipedia entry, which includes his recent novelization of *Goya's Ghosts* (2007), remains silent on the existence of the book. The most plausible explanation of this silence, besides the fact that Tati's movie is considered a masterpiece and that our stereotyped views of novelization make us believe that only bad movies can be satisfactorily novelized, is probably the fact that the book is so atypical, and that it does not obey the formats that were available in those years, and that have survived from these years: the highly commercial and streamlined novelization (often called "Hollywood novelization," but obviously present in France too), the experimental "ciné-romans" of that period (represented mainly by Alain Robbe-Grillet and Marguerite Duras), and the various types of novelization adopted by the type of cinema that Tati had helped preparing. (I will come back on these types.) Carrière's novelization does not fit completely into one of these categories, and this may be the main reason why his book was much less noticed than others.

But let us have a closer look the moment in which the book appeared. In 1958, French cinema was about to live one of its major revolutions, namely the emergence of the New Wave (*Les cousins/The Cousins*, Claude Chabrol, 1959; *Les 400 coups/The 400 Blows*, François Truffaut, 1959; *A bout de soufflé/Breathless*, Jean-Luc Godard, 1960). This New Wave, however, did not appear in a void, but was the creative continuation of a series of critical discussions on, or rather against, mainstream French cinema of the postwar years, the "French quality" system.[17] Besides being old-fashioned and corporatist, "French quality" had the major flaw in the eyes of their opponents of doing away with was "typically cinematographic": the image on one hand, the film director on the other hand. "French quality" films were indeed in general literary adaptations, and both words, "literature" and "adaptation," are equally important here. The fact that most films were based on a literary text meant that screenwriting became the most essential part of filmmaking: The director was a kind of technician who was supposed to follow the screenplay as closely as possible, and in such a perspective it is not unsurprising that shooting a movie became close to staging; the director filmed an action staged in front of the camera, and the actors, often coming from the world of drama, read their lines and performed their roles as if they were on stage.

The fact that most films were adaptations also had a specific implication. Two authors, Jean Aurenche and Pierre Bost, dominated the world of French scriptwriting in an almost monopolistic way, and they had imposed a type of adaptation that fitted perfectly the literary model. An Aurenche and Bost adaptation involved a double operation. First of all, the rewriting of the book in such a way that equal attention was given to story and dialogue, the importance of the dialogues transforming the adaptation into a kind of text drama. Second, the replacement of the scenes of the original book that resisted adaptation, since Aurenche and Bost believed that the only way to be faithful to the book even when it proved impossible to adapt it was to invent new equivalents for what had to be abandoned. And as François Truffaut's famous polemic "D'un certaine tendance du cinema français" (1958) has demonstrated, these operations are far-reaching, technical and artistic as well as ideological, and the impact of the Aurenche-Bost model explains why French cinema, despite its "quality label" had entered such a deep crisis.[18]

For the novelization genre, this discussion on the techniques, the aim, and the status of adaptations is crucial, for if it is easy to understand why French quality movies can easily be novelized, even when they are based themselves on literary source texts (see *La chartreuse de Parme*), it is no less easy to recognize why the New Wave films will force the publishers both to emphasize the practice of novelization and to modify it in a radical way (which moreover will have a certain impact on moviemaking itself). New Wave films are as literary as French quality movies, both in the traditional and the nontraditional sense of the word: First, New Wave films are stuffed with literary allusions, literary props, and acts of reading and writing, second, they are no longer satisfied with adapting literature, but they consider themselves the new literature. New Wave movies are however suspicious of too adequately well-staged screenplays, since they want to give maximal freedom to the director. Hence the use of improvisation, which is a way of radically doing away with literary declamation and the pressure of literary dialogues, which represent the core of the French quality adaptation business. Improvisation can thus be read as the attempt to establish film as an independent language, using the "camera" as a "pen." Most New Wave directors came from the seminal magazine *Cahiers du cinema*, where they had promoted the so-called auteur theory, a theory based on the idea that the film director is not just the professional who shoots the screenplay, but the artist who succeeds in shaping the film's *Gesamtkunstwerk* in order to communicate a certain way of seeing.

For all these reasons, one could imagine that New Wave movies would be ignored, at least in the beginning, by novelization: on one hand, because the role of the screenplay had become quite different (it was a starting point, a tool, and no longer a bible, an aim in itself); on the other hand, because the dominant aspect of the movie is no longer the story (or no longer the story in its abstract, nonvisual, rephrasable form) but the visual form the story takes and the way this form expresses the worldview of the director. Both elements complicate the task of the novelizer. Nevertheless, the New Wave appeared to be a very heavy user and promoter of novelizations, but not in a homogeneous way. All New Wave directors had a very keen sense of publicity and promotion (after all, they had moved from the world of the press to the world of moviemaking), and for this reason, the very existence of a novelization—and of an immediately available novelization—was of vital interest to them. Yet their artistic and ideological sensibilities were too different to select one single mood of novelization.

Claude Chabrol, for instance, has no less than four different novelizations, all very close to the release of *Les cousins* on March 11, 1959: a short story in the weekly *Cinémonde* (April 22); a photonovel in the July issue of the monthly *Nous deux film*; a novelization, also in July, in the famous collection Romans-choc (specializing in sensationalist rewritings of contemporary movies on the "youth problem"); and another photonovella version, published in the September and October issues of the weekly *Festival* (the most popular feature of the many publications offering this type of material).[19] François Truffaut, probably the most "literary" of the New Wave directors, if we take "literature" here in the traditional sense of the word, wanted to write his own novelization of *Les 400 coups* (here still in collaboration with his co-screenwriter Marcel Moussy; later he would write some "autonovelizations" without further help). Yet invited to contribute a volume to the Romans-choc series, he seems to have declined the invitation, preferring to give his text to the most prestigious of French publishing companies, Gallimard (ironically enough, this book would continue its life in the much less prestigious domain of children's literature, and its only available edition is in a pocket series for younger readers). Godard, finally, accepted a novelization of *Breathless* in the Romans-choc series, but the possibly pseudonymous author, Claude Francolin, succeeded in giving a particular twist to the tone and the scope of the series: instead of focusing on the sociological aspects of the story (the "youth problem," juvenile delinquency, the generation gap, and so on), he appropriated quite a lot of the literary style of the hard-boiled detective novel, which was immensely popular in France through the *Série noire* publications and whose influence on Godard, on *Breathless*, and on the New Wave in general was decisive.[20]

Les vacances de M. Hulot seems very far from all this: no scandal book, no self-novelization, no colloquial language, as far as the New Wave novelizations are concerned; nor is it a mainstream commercial novelization or an experimental book. Yet at the same time, it is a blend of all this: although it does not want to provoke, it contains quite some social critique; although it is not a self-novelization, it is clear that the book has been written under the control of the director who also imposes the presence of the illustrator, Philippe Etaix; although there is no colloquial language, there is a great effort to invent new dialogues; although it is a mainstream novel, the book innovates the novelization formula in many ways, which makes it, to a certain extent, also experimental. And this is, of course, why *Les vacances de M. Hulot* matters for us today: The novel is a fascinating attempt to novelize a story that at first sight seems to be impossible to novelize in a traditional, mainstream way, for it lacks the twofold basis of the average novelization: a real storyline on one hand, dialogues on the other hand.

In Tati's movie many things happen, of course (it is not a minimalist movie), but the events are not part of an overall narrative. They are sketches that simply follow each other, instead of being part of one encompassing thread. Tati's background is the burlesque mime and his great ambition was to reintroduce this tradition, which had been crucial for the development of a certain type of silent cinema, to the domain of sound cinema: Tati's cinema is not a nostalgic attempt to recover the lost mythical purity of the early period, but an attempt to revalorize the visual burlesque in a cinema that is not talking cinema but sound cinema. In *Les vacances de M. Hulot*, we see what happens in a small hotel and on the beach where a certain Mr. Hulot and many other guests are staying for the summer. The whole film is a chain of small sketches, but the absence of a larger narrative and of real dialogues does not mean that the film is not constructed on a temporal level and that we just see "images" (or even immobile images, following a tendency that will haunt all ambitious moviemakers of that period). Yet the constructing principles have become different. First of all, there is of course sound, which replaces dialogues. The montage of the shots obeys sound structures, each scene has its own sound effects, and the development of these effects contributes to the composition of the scene. Second, each scene, often filmed with a rather static camera which avoids any foregrounding of cinematographic effects, is filled with time in very resourceful ways: On one hand, there is never just one focus point, for instance, from the center of the screen, there are always many different things to see in different places of the screen, so that the eye can never totally grasp what is happening; on the other hand, many paces are also gradually filled with people, things, and events, and then emptied again.[21]

REWRITING TATI: A NEW WAY OF TELLING?

Not surprisingly, the reader of *Les vacances de M. Hulot* finds in the book "the real film." Except for some small scenes that have been added or deleted, Carrière follows the various scenes of the film, just as he maintains the quasi-totality of the characters—a feature that is quite rare in novelizations, which tend to simplify the filmic material. More generally, the reader is directly aware of the fact that Carrière does not want—or did not have the freedom—to revolutionize the genre of the novelization itself. If his book can be distinguished from many others, it is not negatively, by its refusal of a given format. *Les vacances de M. Hulot* does not contradict Jeanne-Marie Clerc's global assessment on the genre's conservatism between the 1920s and the 1950s:

> Il est curieux de constater que, malgré les bouleversements qui, durant cette période, ont affecté le cinéma comme le roman, l'évolution subie par l'adaptation romancée reste minime, ne portant souvent que sur des points de détail comme la disposions typographique, ou des caractères inhérents au film muet et que l'apparition du parlant rend caducs, ne modifiant rien en profondeur à la structure romanesque de l'adaptation.[22]

According to the same author, the major distinctive feature of the traditional novelization of this period concerns the attempt to add what is supposed to be missing: psychological motivations of the characters, on one hand, and a recognizable narrative voice, on the other hand:

> La spécificité romanesque semble donc se concentrer dans cette élaboration d'un personnage autonome, le narrateur, et de son discours propre, qui sert de médiateur absolu à l'histoire empruntée au film. . . . Le récit romanesque tire sa valeur, non de ce qu'il montre ou raconte mais de la communication

qu'il établit avec son lecteur grâce à un discours qui affiche sa présence: cel-le-ci agit comme un filtre permanent à l'égard de l'image qu'il est censé restituer.[23]

And this narrative voice, which offers not just a representation of the images, but a real interpretation, is considered by Clerc a double of the spectator himself of herself:

> On assiste, dans ces textes, à la façon dont ce dernier reconstitue, somme toute pour lui-même, son propre "cinema" à partir d'un film qui sert de point de départ à sa récréation imaginaire. En cela, il agit comme tout spectateur. . . . En fait le véritable héros du roman tel qu'il est mis en lumière par ces textes; c'est le narrateur, et les personnages n'existent que dans la mesure où il peut en faire ses créatures.[24]

What Carrière is doing is exactly that. He shifts the focus from the "objective" representation of the image to its "subjective" reinterpretation through a narrative voice. Something has thus been withdrawn: the visual excess of Tati's images. And something is replacing it: the point of view and the idiosyncratic language of a narrator. Yet Carrière's narrator is not at all a "modern" one (the book bears no relationship at all with the experiments of the New Novel of that era); he is a "round" character, he claims omniscience, and he is even capable of organizing his story in such a way that he can host embedded narratives told by other characters.

But if one takes a closer look, it soon appears that the narrator is quite unconventional. For instead of producing a narrator who can be a substitute for the spectator of the movie, Carrière selects as his first-person narrator one of the very characters of the movie, and even the most apparently insignificant one: it is the character called Arthur in the movie (in the book he does not name himself), an older man who does nothing else than following his wife on her ceaseless walks ("*Ma femme continue, et je vais son chemin, qui est aussi le mien*"). Since his character plays no active role, he becomes of course the perfect observer. Technically speaking, Carrière rejects thus the invention of an extradiegetic narrator (who is not part of the fictional world) and promotes a character in homodiegetic narrator (who is part of the fictional world, but not at the center of the action). This capital difference between book and film (which has no such narrative voice) is however also a very faithful transposition of what happens in the movie itself, where Jacques Tati combines the two roles of extradiegetic director and intradiegetic character. By transforming a character into narrator, the novelization subtly underlines the plural logic of the cinematographic agent, who has to play various roles, as well as Tati's attempt to do away with the differences between all these roles. From this point of view, significantly enough, the novelization of *Les vacances de M. Hulot* accentuates and exemplifies in its own way what is meant by the auteur's cinema.

Carrière's Arthur, however, is not the same Arthur as the pale character we observe in the movie. Contrary to the film, the book becomes quite sarcastic in its portrait of the French (and European) middle-class that is gathered at the beach. Through Arthur's commentaries on his neighbors, Carrière can make a crude satire of a very specific type of character: civil servant (hence lazy), Parisian (hence snobbish), married (hence misogynistic), and so on. Yet at the same time, Carrière's Arthur is open to changes: He gradually becomes aware of his superficial and boring life and slowly starts revolting, for instance against his wife (in a scene added in the book, he stops following his wife at the beach, and even if at the end of the day she has not even noticed her husband's absence, we know that Arthur has been "contaminated" by Hulot, who represents in the movie as in the book the sense of freedom and anarchy that all characters are looking for but that nobody dares to assume).

The novelization takes the form of a diary, which regularly includes a dialogue with a second person. This "you," however, is not the imaginary double of the narrator or the diary itself, but, given the play on the various roles and the various narrative levels, an extradiegetic reader, actually the reader of the book itself. Carrière's Arthur does not stop saying things like "I am like you," and this "you" is in his or her turn a double "you," too. On one hand, as I said, the reader of the book, but on the other hand also the spectator of the film, both the real spectator of *Les vacances de M. Hulot* and the virtual spectator of the new film by Tati, *Mon oncle*, announced on the back cover of the book and to be launched at the Cannes Festival some weeks later.

If one accepts this interpretation, Carrière's narrator becomes even more complex and multilayered. By becoming the narrator of the book, Arthur does not only modify the meaning of the film (the social satire which remains very soft in the movie turns out to be much more direct in the book), he also intervenes in the reception of Tati's work. By addressing directly the actual and future spectators of Tati's movie, and by saying that he is just like them, he tries indeed to impose his reading of *Les vacances de M. Hulot*, preparing the spectators of the new Tati movie, *Mon oncle*, to the more satirical vein that this work will explore. With Carrière, we are very far away from the traditional novelization, whose impersonal and anonymous narrator simply wants to tell the story in a way that will help the spectator to prepare for or to relive the film experience (or even to be a substitute for it). Here, the novelization addresses the future spectator in such a way that he or she will know in advance how to read the new film of the director. In other words, in the case of *Les vacances de M. Hulot*, the novelization is as much prospective than retrospective; it is as much an announcement of *Mon oncle* as a double of Tati's previous movie, and it is therefore a very active part of the global intermedia construction of "cinema in action."

A LITERARY NOVELIZATION

The analysis of narrative structures has demonstrated the possibility to take into account the broad frame of transmedia culture in which the novelization has its role to play. But also from the viewpoint of transmedial operations in the narrow sense of the word, *Les vacances de M. Hulot* is a captivating object. The narrator of the book is indeed not someone who is talking, but someone who writes. He keeps a diary, and his verbal and literary choices reveal a sharp awareness of what novelizations can or should do.

As I said, one of the main problems for the novelizer of this film is the apparent shallowness of its content matter. Even if the book can reuse almost all of the scenes, the story is rather thin, and there are hardly any dialogues that can be recovered. Given the utterly visual dimension of the sketches and the relative absence of words in the soundtrack, Carrière has been obliged to invent, whereas the average novelizer's principal job is to select and to arrange the story and dialogues of the screenplay. Instead of adding new scenes (there are some additions, but very few) or complete dialogues (the words that can be heard in the movie are there, but they remain just that: words), Carrière has created humoristic effects with purely verbal means, which enable him to transpose Tati's visual adventures at a textual level. Once again, Carrière's approach is cautious (as "invisible" as Tati's camera), and it is mostly by excellent timing that he succeeds in exploring the comical side of the following techniques:

> The parody of stereotypes (the narrator's wife is, for instance, always repeating clichés such as "*Que de vert*" ("what to do" [*faire*], parodied as "what to green" [*vert*]), "*Il faut chaud*" ("it is [*il fait*] hot [*chaud*]," parodied as "it must [*il faut*] hot").

The use of a wide range of metaphors to name the same object (for instance, the noise made by Hulot's antique car, and by extension Hulot himself: "*coups de feu*" [gunshots], "*cyclone*" [cyclone], "*coup de vent*" [gust of wind), and so on].

The choice of one style, one vocabulary, one syntax for each embedded narrator.

The play with specific sound effects. For example, when Smutte, the Belgian businessman, is called on the phone, which happens every three pages, the stuttering repetition of words with "*b*" express the surprise as well as the painful effort of the character: "*Le Belge bondit, court. Ah! Business, business.*"

The elaboration of very dense paragrammatic networks. Hulot's name, for instance, is systematically "disseminated" each time the character appears, with an clear overrepresentation of the vowels U/O and the consonants L/T are everywhere: "*Butor . . . Malotru . . . bougonnait l'officier. Ce malotru qui s'appelait Hulot.*"

And, of course, the combination of all these techniques, as in the following exchange, which also contains a fine parody of Flaubert's typical syntax:

> Mais déjà jaillissait au loin, dans la direction de l'hôtel, un cri qui se répétait:
> Monsieur Smutte! Té . . . Téléphone!
> Le garçon, la voix du garçon!
> La chaise longue craque. Le Belge bondit, court. Ah! Business, business . . .
> Notre train-train quotidien. Une mer grise, quelques embarcations craintives. Des pêcheurs de crevettes, là-bas, près des rochers.

A second mechanism that Carrière's novelization investigates in depth is the issue of what Jean Ricardou calls the "chronical disease" of the text, which wants to transpose the spatial simultaneity of the visual to the temporal succession of the verbal.[25] Given the paramount importance of visual copresence in Tati's images, Carrière has been obligated to elaborate a certain number of "tricks" capable of attenuating the conflict between the simultaneity of the visual referent and the linearity of his means of expression. In this regard, one should foreground all of the aforementioned techniques. First of all, there has been the decision to include a broad set of illustrations, which not only remember the film's iconography (the illustrator of the book was also the designer of the extremely successful film poster) but also try to visualize as much as possible the content of the movie. Second, there is also Carrière's play with alternative montage, which is a useful tool for the representation of sound simultaneity: Various conversations that are overheard or conversations mixed with radio programs are reproduced in this way, which "naturalizes" their elliptic and often incomplete structure.

Besides the verbal sound humor and the play with simultaneity, Carrière is also fond of the "impressionistic" or "artistic" style when it comes to rendering sound (independently from the sound of the characters' speech). Aimed at giving first the overall visual effect of an object before giving the details of what is seen, the impressionistic style foregrounds perception at the expense of the things seen and underlines this effect with the systematic use of certain stylistic "tics"—for instance the use of the plural, the absence of the definite article, the fragmentation of the referent in a myriad of small objects and notations, and, most significantly, the nominal style. Carrière draws heavily on these techniques, often very rare, like the nominal style, in ordinary novelizations, and he succeeds in transferring this particular style from the domain of images to that of sound. The opening of the book is extremely telling in this regard:

> Sacs tyroliens et cannes à pêche, contrôleurs ahuris qu'on houspille et dont on secoue, dont on arrache les boutons dorés, coups de sifflet, piétinements, appels, enfants giflés, chuintements des machines . . .

Finally, Carrière adjoins a fourth mechanism, which helps him to create even stronger simultaneity effects. This technique concerns the combination of simultaneity with syntactically symmetrical enumerations. Since it is so hard to write down in a string of words what happens to a whole set of characters copresent in the same place, the traditional novelist will generally use an enumeration, yet this technique has an inevitable tendency to break the visual simultaneity. As a compensation for this rupture, Carrière multiplies all types of symmetry at syntax level, which diminish the effect of linearity and sequentiality. Once the reader understands that a first item is repeated with variations in the other items of the enumeration, he or she will produce a kind of overview by linking each item to an implicit model—more or less as what happens with the synthetic capacities of a title. The examples of this technique are numerous:

> —Silence! demanda monsieur Smutte.
> Le commandant baissa la voix. Ceux qui lisaient ne levèrent pas les yeux de leurs livres. La dame qui brodait resta tout entière à sa passementerie,

l'intellectuel à son journal, monsieur Fred à son apéritif. Le garçon jeta un regard à l'extérieur, en écartant le rideau d'une fenêtre.

Le commandant au garde-à-vous près de sa chaise. Monsieur Smutte qui consulte une dernière facture. Une dame assez jeune et assez jolie, mais piquée d'élégance, se repoudre les joues.

To conclude, it is of course not sufficient to argue that Carrière's novelization is (almost) as intelligent and profound as Tati's movie. What matters is the fact that this novelization tackles the basic issue of the genre, namely the clash between the visual enunciated and the verbal enunciation. Many novelizations try to avoid this clash, either by copying the film's storyline (at the expense of the film's visual dimension) or by simply forgetting the film. *Les vacances de M. Hulot* takes the challenge as directly as possible. Carrière's work confronts all major aspects of novelization as a transmedial cultural form: it addresses the impossibility of any literal transmedialization; it demonstrates in an exemplary way that novelization should not be reduced to a question of storytelling; and it suggests that to novelize is always an act, which both changes the source text and influences the cultural context in which it appears. The result may seem a very classic novel, yet the close analysis of it has demonstrated, I hope, that this novelization should be studied closely by all those who have a serious interest in the genre.

CHAPTER TWELVE

Copycat-and-Mouse

The Printed Screenplay and the Literary Field in France

MATTHIJS ENGELBERTS

One of the many effects that the birth of a medium is liable to produce in its medial environment is (predictably, for once) new competition. In the arts, this has especially been the case, in the last century or so, for film and literature; it did not take long before the relations between these two art media, or at least between film and the novel, became fraught with rivalry. Even today, in an almost entirely different setting, they continue to be so more often than might be expected after more than a century of competition, but also expansion of both these art media as well as of cooperation and transmediation. Criticism on the relationship between film and literature has, surprisingly, for a long time taken over this competitive stance in describing the relations between the two arts. Analyses of one of the aspects of this question, the connections (or absence thereof) between the film script and litera-ture, for instance, consist usually, as we will see shortly, of succinctly argued, normatively oriented positions about the screenplay in general, cast in a combative terms pro or contra the literary aspect of the film text, that leave little space for research on specific questions or a partic-ular corpus that could, presumably, lead to less general and perhaps less dogmatic stands.

This still tends to be the case today. In what is certainly one of the best books published on the film/literature issue in recent years, *Rethinking the Novel/Film Debate*, Kamilla Elliott admirably dissects the topics and strategies in the field; however, even here the rivalry implicitly resurfaces in the way some stances are described—albeit far less blatantly than has happened elsewhere. When the author writes, in a section on proponents of "Film Words as Literature," that "the film-words-as-literature analogy disowns film's actual language as literary other," she accurately describes one of the strategies in the field, which claims the dialogue, the screenplay, or even film itself as literature.[1] However, in opposing the terms "film's actual language" and "literary other," and in claiming that a literary stance toward film texts "disowns" the film's "actual" language, she nevertheless discredits the idea that film words can ever be considered as literary, in whatever sense.[2] This amounts to a more or less implicit ban on considering the literary aspects of film texts, a ban that contradicts the author's later, explicit and in my view convincing wish to recognize the "more complex word and image engagements both within and between . . . media."[3]

Such recognition indeed seems not very frequent in comments and studies on the screenplay and its relations to literature. The long debate on this issue is largely a general debate on "the" film script in which two positions dominate and usually lead to a normative stance: The movie screenplay should, or should not, be considered as a literary text. Since the question of publishing screenplays in print plays an important role in the debate,[4] it should be interesting to take a close look at the institutional production side of the printed film text. How often have screenplays in fact been launched on the book market by publishing houses, in a particular culture? Furthermore, since we are interested in the literary orientation of the screenplay, the second question would be to what extent the published scripts have been produced by houses that are equipped to position screenplays as literary texts. This empirical and institutional approach to the relationship between the screenplay and literature will, hopefully, contribute to shift the basis of the argument over the supposed (non)literary nature of the screenplay and perhaps, more generally, help to establish a different view on the relations between literature and film, or between media as such.

REFLECTIONS ON THE SCREENPLAY

Before taking a close look at a particular situation and its quantitative particulars, it is useful to look at some of the more or less authoritative positions on the vexed question whether the screenplay can be literature, in order to gauge the history of the debate and to identify in more detail one of the aspects that could be fruitfully worked out so as to cast new light on the question. Here are a few voices, in chronological order—and as ever so often, they do not all speak the same language.

"The screenplay, in contrast to the theater play, *has no aesthetic existence independent of its performance*."[5] Such is the verdict of the art historian Erwin Panofsky, who published the second, enlarged version of his now often reprinted essay "Style and Medium in the Motion Pictures" in 1947, while living in the United States after having fled from Germany. Early on in his text, Panofsky had already broached the subject of the film script by giving what he called "another empirical proof of the coexpressibility principle" (that is, the fact that the word and the moving image depend on each other in film): "Good movies are unlikely to make good reading and have seldom been published in book form."[6]

This pronounced judgment notwithstanding, in the mid-1940s the question was far from being settled. Here is another voice, in English translation: "By now many scripts are available in print and soon they may be more popular reading than the more abstract stage play. It is difficult to say how much time must elapse before our literary critics finally notice this new phenomenon before their eyes."[7] Such is the position of Béla Balázs, writer and also one of the prominent film theoreticians of the first generation. He discussed the script in his last book, first published in Russian in 1945—about the time Panofsky was revising his only film essay. It is quite clear that the assertions made by these two theorists are quite far apart, both normatively as well as empirically. Not only do they take opposing views on the literary nature of the film script, but they also assert that the same empirical evidence—the supposed number of published screenplays—supports their opposite views on the aesthetic value of the printed film text as such.

This is not to say that in the same period there were no middle positions in what we might today call an intermedial (here used in a general, media-comparative sense) debate on whether texts written for other media than the printed word can also function autonomously as print literature. At the time Balázs and Panofsky were unwittingly in the heat of the battle, the foremost French film critic André Bazin prudently made the following suggestion: "*Verra-t-on naître à côté du théâtre un cinéma 'littéraire' dont le synopsis et les dialogues supporteraient la publication?*"[8] As his American-German and Hungarian-Austrian colleagues, Bazin compares the film script to drama, but he is much more hesitant to make general claims; hence he does not state that *all* film scripts (or none) qualify as literature. To some degree, this also holds true for John Gassner's position, notably in the preface to the first volume of his collection of *Best Film Plays*, first published in 1943. Despite the title of the introduction, "The Screenplay as Literature," Gassner occasionally departs from his general defense of the "film play"—here, too, as the last term indicates, the stage play serves as a guarantee for the literary nature of the film script. Not only does his selection of "best film plays" already suggest that some screenplays are better—more literary—than others, but he is also much more concerned than most theorists with questions such as which version of a screenplay is published and which form it should take in print to be as "rewarding as reading literature."[9]

Starkly opposing and often quite belligerent declarations have not ceased to be expressed, even as other voices replace Panofsky and Balázs; and, as in their case, they will mostly talk without directly responding to each other. Larry McMurtry states in "The Screenplay as a Non-Book," an article that appeared in *American Film* in 1976, that the screenplay is "a publication in book form that need not and should not be read," and that it cannot be justified "on grounds either of utility or pleasure."[10] The famous Italian director Michelangelo Antonioni would not have objected, since he formulated this same position ten years earlier, albeit in a more eloquent fashion. The French translation (published a year after the publication in Italian) of the unfilmed screenplay *Tecnicamente dolce* (1976) contains a preface with this quote from the 1960s: "*Les scénarii ne font que présupposer le film, ils sont sans autonomie. Ce sont des pages mortes.*"[11]

The screenplay posed as a nonbook echoes—unwittingly, in all probability—the screenplay as "dead pages"; however, the opposite position was far from becoming scarce. In the early 1970s, American academia had produced a book entitled *The Screenplay as Literature*, by Douglas Garrett Winston (1973)—a telling yet ambiguous title, since for Winston "screenplay" refers not only to the written script of a film but also to film itself. His thus holds a quite peculiar position; yet his voice was heard and answered, for a change, when a Belgian critic explicitly quoted this book in a note, but also implicitly in the perhaps unintentional reference in the programmatic title of a comparative literature article: "Le scénario comme genre littéraire," the screenplay as literary genre.[12]

A few years later in Tübingen, Claudia Sternberg published *Written for the Screen* in which she inadvertently engaged in a dialogue with her French colleague, in which she summons the aid of an American critic.[13] These are the closing sentences of that 1997 study:

> It is of the utmost importance that the screenplay is not pushed back into its traditional niche, because it is, as I hope to have shown here, a multi-dimensional, multi-functional and independent text deserving of the critical attention that is taken for granted in the study of literary texts:
>
> > A screenplay is a separate entity; it is not film, dialogue or outline, or a cinematic tool. It is a literary structure written first to be read and then produced. . . . And while it is, perhaps, understandable that the business mind of Hollywood overlooks the literary contributions of the screenplay writer, that the literary world should abandon and neglect one of its own is near sinful.[14]

Near or not, it is no great effort to commit such a sin. Recently, a literary review in academic France sinned according to a long-standing tradition by candidly rejecting the idea that it is "of the utmost importance that the screenplay is not pushed back into its traditional niche." That niche (traditional or otherwise) is indeed ardently defended by yet another Belgian critic, but not one who seems to speak the same language as her Walloon predecessor: "*Le scénario ne peut, en aucun cas . . . être considéré et étudié comme de la littérature.*"[15]

My aim is not to add yet another voice to this concert and defend either one of the positions. Instead, I would like to look at the publication of film scripts empirically. It may indeed seem quite puzzling just how little attention has been paid to empirical questions in this debate, such as: how often have scripts functioned as "literary" texts, have particular (kinds of) texts functioned as such more often than others, and whether there have been changes in the situation over time. The vast majority of stances are indeed both normative and general positions, sometimes adorned with (often sweeping) statements on empirical matters, which are almost always limited to the supposed number of "available" film scripts—and these loose, cursory quantifications are always in accordance with the normative views of the beholder.[16] Here it is obviously impossible to give an answer to all the empirical questions related to the publication of screenplays and their place within the literary field. Instead, I propose to look at the number of published screenplays in France from 1945 until 2005, and especially at the relation between these screenplays and the literary field.[17] I would also like to be able to provide a tentative answer to the question whether there are any variations over time. I will focus on the institutional production of the printed text, particularly on the aspect of the publishing house and its collections. The premise is that it is more likely for a printed text to function in the literary domain if it is published by a well-known literary house than if it is published under other circumstances.

FILM TEXTS INTO THE LITERARY FIELD

The largest specialized collection of published film scripts in France is held at the Bibliothèque du Film (Bifi); one of the next largest in a specialized library is in the Bibliothèque du Cinéma François Truffaut in Paris. I have based my research on these two collections,[18] which overlap to a large extent, and which, in my experience, yield a near-complete file of French screenplays published since 1945.[19] Since I am focusing on France and its literary field, the first step is to exclude foreign scripts, that is, texts published in other languages than French, and texts translated into French. The first result is that approximately six hundred French film scripts have been published between 1945 and 2004.[20] That is much more than the 110 complete screenplays of classic, English and American, and other foreign films that Dudley Andrew was able to find in print in the 1970s, at the time of the McCarty *Checklist* of published screenplays, which has four hundred entries but also contains a lot of published passages of scripts.[21] However, these figures from one of the very few existing quantitative inventories are from the middle of the 1970s and can thus only be partially compared to more recent data.

In an analysis of the published film scripts and their relation to the literary domain, the first striking fact is the sheer number of texts that have appeared in specialized reviews or series. There are two very different cinema series, each of which publishes issues that contain the script of a film. First, about three hundred of the published French scripts in the collections have appeared as issues of *L'avant-scène cinéma*. This monthly periodical, founded in 1961, publishes postproduction scripts, or *découpages techniques*, as they are sometimes called in French. Due to the nature of these texts, the publisher, and the periodical, which is clearly connected to cinema and *not* to the literary field, the issues of *L'avant-scène cinéma* have to be set apart in an analysis of the circulation of film texts on the literary market. The other case is the Petite bibliothèque des Cahiers du cinéma, which has been publishing film scripts since 1996. This series has published more than forty scripts in separate volumes, both French screenplays and translations. The Petite bibliothèque is a more complicated case than the monthly magazine *L'avant-scène cinéma*, but since it is a cinema review that publishes these texts, these can be set apart as well.

The inventory now yields slightly fewer than three hundred French screenplays[22] that are possibly geared toward the literary field. In order to pinpoint any historical shifts that have occurred in the publication of screenplays and their relation to the literary field, I have drawn up a table of these that comprises six decades from 1945 onward (first column).[23]

Published screenplays and the literary field

Dates	Screenplays After First Selection	Screenplays by Literary Publishers	*Percentage of 1st Selection*	Screenplays by Renowned Literary Publishers	*Percentage of 2nd Selection*	*Percentage of 1st Selection*
1945–54	27	22	*81*	1	*5*	*4*
1955–64	22	20	*91*	13	*65*	*59*
1965–74	51	48	*94*	27	*56*	*53*
1975–84	36	32	*89*	10	*31*	*28*
1985–94	55	41	*75*	16	*39*	*30*
1995–2004	95	51	*54*	10	*20*	*11*
Total	286	214	*77*			

In this first selection, however, not all publishers are equal: There are a certain number of small publishing houses that do not (primarily) aim at upholding a literary reputation, and occasionally organizations whose main activity is not publishing, such as film production or distribution companies (for example, MK2). For our purposes, these can be discarded in a second selection, since, institutionally, they are not geared toward the literary domain or are not in a position to have any impact on it. This second selection includes not only the larger, more conspicuous candidates, such as Gallimard, Grasset, and Seuil, but also well-known houses of pocket editions and smaller publishers whose collections are manifestly geared toward the literary field (such as Losfeld, Quai Voltaire, or Hors Commerce).[24] Approximately 210 film texts have been published by institutions that are equipped to position them in the literary field.

Furthermore, for a more detailed and reliable answer to the question whether film scripts circulate as literary artifacts on the level of their institutional production, a third selection should be useful, taking into account those screenplays that have been published by renowned literary companies (third column). I have included "Galligrasseuil"[25] and five other renowned literary publishers: Flammarion, Mercure de France, Minuit, Seghers, and Stock.[26]

A first analysis of the data in these three selections yields a few clear results. What should be noted first is the increase in the total number of published screenplays in the first selection (first column): From the 1940s onward, the tendency is toward growth, with important rises in the decades around 1970 and around 1990. This increase in the number of screenplays launched by publishers other than those of specialized reviews[27] is an interesting fact for proponents of the thesis of the dominance of a supposed visual culture in our era. In jest, it could be said that video and DVD have apparently not made print culture obsolete. This all too general statement is, nevertheless, to some extent legitimate in the specific context of the publication of screenplays. One of the explicit arguments posited by the early defenders of script publication indeed used to be that printed screenplays would allow for a more detailed and accurate study of films—in an age when these could only be viewed in theatres and were thus not readily available.[28] On the basis of this argument, one should indeed expect that publication would plummet after the introduction of video and DVD—which is clearly not the case (at least in France). This fact manifestly corroborates the thesis that the rise and continuing expansion of a medium, or a conglomerate of media, does not necessarily and perhaps not generally lead to the downfall of another medium. That proposition is certainly not new; but it is no easy task to find such a clear and specific demonstration of the fact that written culture, and more specifically print culture, is far from being mutually exclusive with what I would prefer to call (with W. J. T. Mitchell) "audiovisual culture" (instead of the more widespread term "visual culture").[29] The case is all the more clear since the inclusiveness even counts for a cultural practice that is so clearly part of the audiovisual field: film. As the first column shows, publishing screenplays as printed texts does not seem to be endangered so far, and it is certainly not limited to the first decades of the spoken film—in which case it might have been regarded as, say, a last gasp of print culture in its struggle to maintain a shadow of its old influence.

But print culture is not synonymous with literary culture, and we can now look more specifically at the second and third columns in order to see how the printed film script relates to the literary field. Considering the absolute numbers (roman type in all columns), the second selection shows that the number of screenplays published by literary publishers also increases, at least until the mid-1970s, and more irregularly afterward. Nonetheless, it should be noted that from the 1980s onward, the growth is not proportionate to the increase of the published screenplays of the first selection. In the last two decades included in the survey, the number of published screenplays in the first selection increases by more than 50 percent, but only by about 25 percent if we consider literary houses (second column) exclusively. As for the texts published by renowned literary houses (third column), it is not possible to speak in terms of a steady growth in absolute numbers anymore: Between 1945 and 1974, the figures rise significantly, but there is a clear drop after 1974, the pattern is irregular afterward, and the number of screenplays published between 1965 and 1974 is not equaled in later decades.

Moreover, turning to the results of the last two columns in terms of *percentage* of the total number of published screenplays (in italics), it is clear that the relative number of texts published by literary presses generally tends to decrease. This is the case from the 1980s onward for all literary publishers (second column); it more specifically holds true for the best-known houses, since the percentage drops from the early 1960s onward, whether we compare the number of scripts to those of the first or of the second selection.

The overall picture that emerges from this analysis thus points in two directions. On one hand, the number of published scenarios is increasing incessantly, as is the number of screenplays that do not immediately fall outside the literary institutions. Moreover, the absolute number of screenplays published by literary houses was growing until the mid-1970s. On the other hand, in terms of percentages, the role that the literary presses play in publishing scripts has been far from negligible for more than two decades, but it has nevertheless tended to decrease considerably since the 1970s. Taken together, these figures thus seem to indicate that, whereas print culture as such is not on the wane in the specific audiovisual sector of contemporary culture that is surveyed here, the extent to which these printed film texts have been integrated in the literary field, as far as their production by publishers is concerned, was rather high until the mid-1970s but has generally been shrinking ever since that turning point.

It is interesting to add that the decade around 1970 occupies a special place in the survey. The number of screenplays published by renowned literary presses is the highest in absolute terms in those years (third column), although the number of screenplays published by literary houses (second column) does not drop importantly after the 1970s. However, *in percentage*, the number of screenplays published by literary houses is consistently high in the decade between 1965 and 1975, both for literary houses generally and, to a somewhat lesser degree, for renowned literary publishers. This is admittedly also true, and to a higher degree for the known houses, for the decade around 1950; but here the number of published screenplays is much lower in absolute terms all round—that is, for all three selections. If the decade around 1970 thus appears rather exceptional, one might obviously be tempted to conclude that this is so because of the publication of screenplays by literary authors who were already known as *nouveaux romanciers*. In those years, Robbe-Grillet indeed published *L'immortelle* (1963) and *Glissements progressifs du plaisir* (1974), and Marguerite Duras's *India Song* (1976) and *Nathalie Granger* (1973) appeared. However, of the twenty-seven texts published by renowned literary houses between 1965 and 1974, about ten were written by "literary" authors such as Robbe-Grillet, Duras, and Jorge Semprun, including noncontemporary scripts by Robert Desnos and Marcel Pagnol. The other scripts are mainly texts by authors who are known primarily as filmmakers: Louis Malle (*Le soufflé au coeur*, 1971), Francois Truffaut (*Les aventures d'Antoine Doinel*, 1970; *Jules et Jim*, 1962; *La nuit americaine*, 1973), Luis Buñuel (*Le journal d'une femme de chambre*, 1964), Jean-Luc Godard (*Deux ou trois choses que je sais d'elle*, 1966), Jean Renoir, Orson Welles (*Le procès*, 1962), and Costa-Gavras. Incidentally, this observation allows a tentative refutation of a rather widespread view, since it invalidates the idea that film scripts written by literary authors are the only ones that get published, at least by literary publishers, as is indeed rather often suggested.

CONCLUSION

If, in conclusion, we look back at the contrasting assertions in criticism about screenplays that have been quoted at the beginning of this paper, can these usefully be measured against the results of the analysis of published screenplays in France? In my view, the analysis of the French situation does not simply corroborate a particular stance toward the relations between the film script, publishing, and literature. It would rather appear that the general stances as they continue to occur in the debate tend to reduce a multifaceted reality, in what can seem an offhand manner, to what may be called a conceptual straightjacket—one that is in line with what the particular author would like to make of the relations between media (in this case "film" and the printed book) or arts (in this case, cinema and literature). This reduction becomes all the more apparent if one notes that the aspect that has been examined here is of course only one of the many sides of the topic that can be foregrounded. The light shed on the relations between the screenplay and literature in a particular culture will not produce the same results if one examines, instead of the production by publishers, the reception of screenplays, or, for instance, their current circulation (legal or not) in digital or photocopied form, or the aesthetic question of the literary qualities of particular film texts. It might be constructive for all these questions if critics did not copy the competitive drive that sometimes still governs the relations between film and literature, but instead paid more attention to specific questions, even—or especially—those that might undermine the relevance of prevailing general views.

PART FOUR

New Literacies, Education, and Accessibility

CHAPTER THIRTEEN

The New Literacies

Technology and Cultural Form

WILLIAM URICCHIO

Given the centrality of the word *literacy* in this essay's argument and the sense that its meaning has changed to the point that it must be invoked in the plural (even at the risk of creating a neologism), tracing its historical contours seems a useful place to begin. The *Oxford English Dictionary*, that chronicler of changing language usage, has something rather interesting to say about the terms "literate" and "literacy." The former first appeared in English in the mid–fifteenth century, only a few years before Gutenberg's demonstration of the printing press, and underwent significant modulation in the seventeenth century—a pattern of definitional activity that can easily be read against the very different explanatory backdrops offered by Adrian Johns, Natalie Zemon Davis, and Elizabeth Eisenstein.[1] If the fifteenth-century usage of the term called into relief the strict demarcations between those who could read and had access to the written word and those who could not or did not, the seventeenth-century sense of the word was more concerned with letters and literature and assumed not only more widespread functional literacy but also hierarchies of readerly taste and relevance.

Key usages of "literacy," by contrast, appear in two clusters: one in the late nineteenth century and one in the mid– to late twentieth century. In the case of the late nineteenth century, the term's definitional activity must be read against the period's great movement of populations, its project of urbanization, and the notions of social and national cultural coherence that accompanied these changes. Such occurrences as the publication of Matthew Arnold's *Culture and Anarchy* (1869), the rise of the public library movement, changes in the rotary press, and the panic over "dime novels" all, in various ways, testified to the potential social impact of literature—and literacy—as a forces for maintaining social stability or undermining it.[2] By the mid- to late twentieth century, the project of rationalization and specialization seen by Weber as characterizing the modern age seemed well established, with various new media channels and newly relevant cultural competencies (from "television literacy" to "economic literacy") rising to the fore. Yet the relative stability of the definition of literacy (as the reading and writing of words) until this point seems curious. In the West at any rate, our long-term shifting and accreted emphases on the spoken word, the written and printed word, the photographic and acoustic trace, and most recently data sets and algorithms, all testify to an ongoing series of transformations, and not merely the changes introduced in the mid- to late twentieth century. The coincidence of photography and phonography, for example, with the theories of signs discussed by Charles Sanders Peirce and others by the end of the nineteenth century offers early precedents for a more embracing sense of the term "literacy."

The histories of both "literate" and "literacy" map onto explicit social dynamics. This should not surprise us, given the inherently social dimension of any language-based system of expression. In any case, this realization helps to recall the residue of power and hierarchization that lingers on in these historically encrusted terms. And it provides one compelling reason to rethink these notions through our contemporary reorganization of social power, whether something as "simple" as shifting reader-writer relations or as diffused as globalization. There is also a second compelling reason to reconsider and perhaps redefine these terms. If we, like the *Oxford English Dictionary*, take literacy to mean "the quality or state of being literate; knowledge of letters; condition in respect to education, esp. ability to read and write," then it is not at all surprising that the meanings of the word continue to shift, reflecting, in the case of our present, the demands of the digital media environment and the affordances it has provided for new forms of social interaction. Networked computers; data streams of word, image, and sound; the breakdown of traditional cultural filters and brokering mechanisms; the blurring of producer and user in some settings; and the rise of new collaborative literary forms such as wikis, bulletin boards, and blogs have all contributed to new and widely embraced practices.

Rather than offer a new definition, this essay will mark its departure from the established meanings of the word "literacy" by using the word *literacies*—a term still rejected by my word processing software's spell check—to refer to the multiple competencies required by today's cultural environment. The term is put forward as inclusive of both traditional modes of literacy and the new ones; of word-based modes of expression and the broader array of affordances associated with text, image, sound, and data in digital media. Lest there be any doubt about the relationship between shifts in media apparatus and literacy, this essay's title references Raymond Williams (technology and cultural form),[3] and it seeks to underscore an axiomatic assumption regarding the interdependence of the cultures of technology and letters.

CONDITIONS OF CHANGE

Talk of rupture and radical change invariably generates skepticism. Apocalyptic claims seem to greet every change in the status quo, and the so-called digital turn has been no exception. But this time, there may be good reason to think that something quite distinct is at hand. First, to put things in perspective, we need to recall that digital technologies have been deployed more or less continuously since the fifteenth century (mechanical chimes; spiked drum assemblies for music boxes; perforated rolls for pianolas, organs, and monotype print systems; semaphore codes; even punched-card data-processing technology, deployed in the 1890 U.S. census). The digital is not in itself the agent of change; rather, it is an affordance that has recently been made use of in ways that are transformative.

On one hand, processing capacities and transmission speeds have looped back upon themselves, stimulating intensive development. Consider Moore's law, which took as its starting point the invention of the integrated circuit in 1958, and which stated that the number of transistors that can be placed on an integrated circuit will double approximately every two years. It remains valid today, and manifest in the rapid growth of memory, processing speed, and ever-greater strides in miniaturization. Or consider optical data transmission, which has also undergone rapid change. In March 2007, Alcatel-Lucent broke the 25.6 terabit transmission rate, or—as explained in the company's press release—something on the order of transmitting the content of six hundred DVDs in under one second. At this writing, breaking the 100-terabit barrier seems immanent, meaning the equivalent of transmitting the printed contents of the Library of Congress in just over four seconds. Although technologies capable of these capacities and speeds will not appear in our homes anytime soon, if we consider the future of networked computers in the light of these ongoing transformations of processing capacity, memory, and speed and consider the distance we have covered since the introduction of the World Wide Web in 1992, we can reasonably anticipate continued exponential change.

On the other hand, these steady improvements in computational technologies have enabled us to embrace a new approach to calculation evident in the intensive use of algorithms—a mathematical principle known since Euclid's time, but only effectively deployed with processing machines. Algorithms offer a fundamentally different approach to representing the world (as dynamic, process, procedure) than the *algorismic* regime that dominated the modern era (characterized by precision and fixed sums). Descartes epitomized the algorismic era, which manifests itself in precisely demarcated subject-object relations, the calculation of three-point perspective, and certainty. One might contrast the fruits of the algorismic and algorithmic eras by comparing Diderot's *Encyclopedia* with the algorithmically enabled Wikipedia; or three-point perspective to Photosynth; or Mercator's parallel grid cartography system to dynamic location-based navigation systems. In each case, computers enable the algorithmic processing and reassembly of multiple subjectivities and data streams into new composites, which, though lacking the old certainties, mathematical grids, and authority of fixed subject positions, enable dynamic new possibilities for manipulating data and even deploying our subjectivities.[4]

These factors, combined with a steady increase in the online population and its global reach (even if weighted toward developed and developing nations), have given rise to ever-more complex and innovative social forms. Whether taking advantage of the network's affordances for fast and cheap communication, or its potentials for anonymity, or the logics of "long tail" economics, or the various practices clustered together as Web 2.0 or "algorithmic culture," such as Wikipedia, many people have used the web for their own purposes, despite the availability of traditionally structured systems of interaction. And yet, the most striking of these developments seem to hark back to community practices that lost ground to industrialized culture at the start of the twentieth century. Cultural practices such as collaboration, participatory communities, and aggregation are by no means unique to digitally networked environments; they can be found in earlier texts such as the

Bible and folksongs, in traditions such as quilting, and in community activities such as barn raising. Yet the prominence of terms such as "participatory" in new media discourse points to their rapid acceleration, a shift in scale enhanced by their spread beyond embodied communities. Indeed, as Internet-enabled communities of interest continue to grow, opportunities for conflicts between the conditions of cultural citizenship (say, exchanging music—copyrighted—if one is a member of a music file exchange group) and national citizenship (obeying the nation's intellectual property laws) continue to increase.[5] If, as the fate of the recorded music industry suggests, the twenty-first-century state of these and related practices has threatened to overturn several of the twentieth century's dominant creative industries, one can only imagine how these activities will fare with the ongoing transformation of environmental conditions. The point is simple: The pace of technological change continues to develop exponentially, both driven by and enabling a new configuration of cultural production and circulation.

In medias res as we are, it is difficult to assess the import and character of the networked and collaborative practices so much a part of the lives of those under thirty (and many of us over thirty as well), but the data point to a significant increase in the posting of items—blog entries, photos, music—into publicly accessible places.[6] Recent data in the United States suggest that some 57 percent of American teens post artifacts in public online spaces. Given the control strategies that have accompanied the dominant culture industry throughout much of the twentieth century, is it any wonder that the contemporary remixing of cultural texts necessarily impinges upon the corporate claim to ownership of much of our common and public culture? If some of these remixing practices transgress legal code, do they constitute piracy? Or do they mark a return to age-old folk traditions of collaborative modification, recycling, and repurposing, temporarily suppressed by the intellectual property regimes of the culture industry during the twentieth century? Regardless of how we answer the questions, the simple fact is that the new technologies have afforded their users greater agency than previous media technologies. Although digital production technologies have some advantages over their analog forbears (including 8mm movie cameras, 35mm still cameras, typewriters, and tape-recording equipment), their real impact has been their ability to facilitate distribution and direct exchange and to both construct and maintain a (dispersed) collaborative community. Digital networks have broken the distribution barrier, and with it, the monopoly and the primary control system of the traditional cultural industries.

READERLY COMPETENCIES

As suggested before, the appearance of the word *literate* in English roughly coincided with the last major shift in technologies of the printed word—the fifteenth-century printing press. This technological advance, long understood by scholars such as Elizabeth Eisenstein as facilitating the comparison, stabilization, accretion, and spread of knowledge, occupied a key position in the linear regime of truth so important to the modern (algorismic) era. Eisenstein's softly technological determinist stance is familiar to those who see in the Internet an equally striking instrument of change in social structures, the distribution of power and the spread of knowledge. And yet, there are good reasons to challenge this view—as much for the introduction of the book as for networked computers. Adrian Johns, for one, offers a sharp counterpoint to Eisenstein in his examination of the practices behind the material culture of the book during its first century or two. Johns's *The Nature of the Book* argues that widespread social practices such as piracy, misattribution, and distortion introduced substantial noise into the system—not stabilization and the accretion of knowledge. Not only were such practices rife (the pirated edition of Martin Luther's translation of the Bible, according to some sources, appeared on the street before the authorized version), their very existence undermined the veracity of *any* text—a problem that would exist into the eighteenth century. Johns tells the story of Theophilus Desaguliers, lecturer in Newtonian philosophy in the 1720s, who became so fed up with the countless fraudulent books that bore his name (and the countless others that contained his work but not his name) that he circulated an announcement that only books bearing his handwritten inscription were to be credited by readers. The handwritten word, at least for Desaguliers, trumped the aura of the print and binding.

Johns's argument does much to restore social relations and readerly competencies to the definition of what it means to be literate. Literacy, Johns demonstrates, meant far more than reading and writing the word—it also involved understanding the status and provenance of the word. A reader may have been able to decode a text, but whether it was read as dogma or heresy, as fact or fiction, as authentic or fraudulent, had everything to do with its meaning and implications. His study goes on to show the strategies for textual stabilization and authenticity that emerged in the nascent publishing industry, emphasizing that these, too, were driven by social needs and enabled by human intervention.

Those of us who have been the beneficiaries of the ensuing regime of textual stabilization and who take for granted the authenticity of what we read in the form of published books probably have a far more circumspect view of digital publications. The transition that we have experienced as we have moved from the certainty of provenance and authority associated with the authored and printed book to the uncertainties and manipulability of the algorithmic text (say, a Wikipedia entry) or something posted with an unknown attribution plays itself out in ritualistic warnings to our students and a reflexive wariness of Internet citations. The intrinsic superiority of the *Encyclopedia Britannica*, with its attributions and editorial board, over the anonymously authored, collaboratively sourced, and ever-changing algorithmic composite Wikipedia seems obvious and immediate. And yet, to those digital natives who have grown up online, the situation is much more akin to those readers of texts during the book's first centuries. Then as now, to be literate in this challenging environment requires far more than just mastery of the mechanics of reading and writing.

Over the long haul, we have seen a shifting set of competencies inscribed within the domain of literacy, and they have changed over time and across culture. At times, only specific linguistic competencies (Latin) counted; at times, various degrees of writerly competences were needed (from mastery of writing one's name to writing as we know it); and at times, certain social groups found themselves categorically excluded from consideration as literate. Today's challenge is somewhat differently constructed. With higher levels of education and access than in the past, citizens in most developed societies are expected to have multiple literacies—cultural, visual, informational, mathematical, and the rest. Historically situated, these competencies have been (re)defined relative to changes in technology and cultural practice. We can describe these shifts in many different ways: from the scribe to the printing press to the computer circuit; from unique to multiple to on-demand; from inscribed to printed to digitized; and so on. But as Johns reminds us, more important and more determining than technology are the uses to which technologies are put. Consider the just-mentioned transformations reframed in terms of embodied authority (scriptorium); legal and corporate institutional authority (the publishing house); and the disembodied authority of the algorithm (processing any and all opinions into new composites). Were one to trace a pattern across these changes, one might argue that we have seen steady erosion in the authority, provenance, and traceability of the written word. And yet, as the early history of the book so vividly demonstrates, this is less a technologically determined view than a testament to social demands and tolerances.

The historical accretion of literacies can be tracked through the changing nature of its practitioners: from a small priest and clerical class; to an ever-expanding array of reading classes, with a relatively small cohort of publicly producing members; to a broad array of digitally enabled readers and public producers. Such a perspective permits us today to redefine the pubic from the "reading" public (whose writing is largely "private" and takes the form of letters, memos, diaries, and bank drafts) to the "participating" public (whose online postings are potentially, and sometimes embarrassingly, "public"). This latter group benefits from significantly lower publication barriers (vetting and cost) and enhanced potential for expression and reach in e-environments. Just as important, opportunities for participation include interaction, collaboration, accumulation, and reappropriation, again, as potentially public acts. This writing public, however, often lacks the visibility and authority of authors from earlier eras, particularly when algorithmically enabled in settings such as Wikipedia (where the submitted text is effectively anonymous, combined with the texts of others, and subject to ongoing change); or when it appears through blogs (where it is part of a discursive ebb and flow, and again, as often as not anonymous).

THE PARTICIPATORY TURN

In 2007, Mieko Kawakami won the Akutagawa Literary Prize in Japan for her *Breasts and Eggs*, a novel written as a blog largely using a cell phone. While this might seem to be an anomalous instance, Japan is a world leader in the social use of new technologies, accounting for 37 percent of blog posts worldwide. In 2007, half of Japan's top ten novels originated on the tiny screens of mobile devices, and novice mobile authors wrote the top three. The Japanese example not only suggests the rapid rate of change in some cultures, but underscores the notion that literacy, even defined as "the mastery of reading and writing the word," is alive and well and has been extended to forms such as texting, blogs, SMS messages, and wikis. But this is only half the story. In a recent online literature search, I came across a link to a possibly relevant thirteen-year-old, two-page-long article from a traditional (printed) academic journal. In order to read it, I first had to make a $31 payment to the publisher. Although this example took place in a digital environment (PayPal accepted!), the logics of scarcity, commodification, and control characteristic of the traditional print industry dominated.[7] The disjunctions between cultures of openness—openness to new authors, to new modes of writing, new technologies and audiences, new modes of circulation—and control are striking.

At stake here is far more than coping with new forms of textuality (hypertext, image-word relations, or even the aesthetics of code), more than the introduction of new literary genres and transformations of spelling and syntax. We are witnessing a paradigm shift in the nature of cultural production. Growing evidence suggests that the use of networked computers is facilitating new cultural practices and new types of participation, as just mentioned; new types and sources of cultural texts; and new logics of distribution and access. It is no exaggeration to say that the "heavy industries" of "mass" culture that have dominated since the end of the nineteenth century—the recording, publishing, press, film, and broadcast industries—are facing significant challenges and even collapse in some sectors as a networked public increasingly circumvents old industrial models and generates its own alternatives (fan fiction, garage band music, YouTube videos).[8] We can discern a discursive shift from an individual (one to one: the letter; or one to many: the publishing industry) to a networked model, with its own "spreadable" logics of circulation and its own systems of algorithmic aggregation (evident in various models from Wikipedia to Flickr to Google). These developments have shifted the position of agency and access, and made new forms of collaboration—even unconscious collectivity—possible. We are seeing the outlines of a major cultural struggle; the old cultural aristocracy (high culture) is as much under siege as the old twentieth-century cultural industries (popular culture). And what is under siege is a model of production: from the few (the taste-elite or cultural industry) to the many, to the many to the many.

We inhabit a moment of transition, and just as the first decades of the printed word gave rise to curious hybrids and saw the persistence of handwritten manuscripts, we too feel the presence of long-dominant industries, routinized ways of operating, and the stubborn residues of the familiar. Paradoxically perhaps, the convergence and concentration of media ownership accelerated greatly in the early 1990s just as the Internet grew in popularity. The Internet, too, has given rise to massive new corporate presences such as Google and Microsoft, and with them, new tactics for control. And old industrial giants such as those represented by Rupert Murdoch have quickly repositioned their might, spending fortunes to acquire social networking sites such as MySpace. Issues of power and dominance continue to appear in the uneven distribution of computers, network access, and speeds, and like other inequities, we can expect them to remain in place until more balanced regimes of wealth and power emerge. These contradictions testify to the momentum of the past as embedded in our institutional cultures, our legal systems, our communication infrastructures, and our memories. But the affordances of networked digital media, like those of the book, permit many new alternatives. Raymond Williams offered an apt description of this dynamic, noting how an era's dominant mode of engagement is informed by the lingering strategies of the past while imposing itself on newly appearing ideas, in his description of culture as "residual, dominant and emergent."[9] The developments that I have been describing are emergent, and as often as not, they are reinscribed within the terms of the dominant; in the process, their radical potential tends to get suppressed. But such is the nature of transition, and we should not misread the "taken-for-grantedness" of the dominant for the failure of an emergent cultural practice.

The new logics of space bound up in micro-level interpenetrations of private and public and macro-level globalization; new distributions of algorithmically mediated agency; new social forms; and a landscape characterized by what Colin McCabe calls the "promiscuity of media," all require new literacies. Networked culture brings new conditions to the project of reading and writing, including the means for greater participation, enhanced ease of interaction, new modes of distribution (person-to-person, viral), mobility, immateriality, mutability, and of course the previously discussed collaborative dimension.

LITERACIES MATTER

Richard Hoggart's 1957 book *The Uses of Literacy*—originally titled *The Abuses of Literacy*—took up the issue of mass literacy and popular culture in ways that resonate with our present. His project, and that of some colleagues associated with the British brand of cultural studies, sought in part to reveal the working of power in the marginalization of the popular. And although written more than fifty-five years ago, some of Hoggart's key observations ring true. Consider the past one hundred years of mass nonprinted media (film, recorded music, radio, television). These media forms enjoyed participation rates that consistently superseded those of the printed word; and yet, despite their centrality as expressive and communicative forms, they generated virtually no interest in audio or visual literacy. Harvard, Yale, and the leading universities of the Netherlands did not formally include film studies in university curricula until the medium was a respectable one hundred years old—and fast waning as an industry and cultural force. But fewer than twenty years into the era of networked computers, "new media" have been finding widespread curricular presence and support. While one might speculate about many reasons for this disjunction (perhaps we really do learn from our past mistakes!), surely concern about the circumvention of cultural and industrial filters, and the empowering of a new public in cultural production and distribution, must be central among them.

Dutch coffeehouses and cafes generally have a table stacked with newspapers and magazines—a tradition going back to the eighteenth century and called upon by Jürgen Habermas in his discussion of the emergence of the public sphere.[10] The combination of caffeine (or alcohol), a social space, the news of the day, and a literate readership triggered the shift from a "representational" culture of absolutism to a "critical" culture—the democracy that we take for granted today. Literacy provided a key means for staying critically informed, for enabling contributions to the public sphere and participating in the politics of self-rule. Although Habermas, consistent with critical theorists such as Adorno and Horkheimer, sees much twentieth-century popular culture and mass media as complicit in a culture of passivity and consumerism, it is difficult not to wonder if such perceptions attest to widespread illiteracy in domains *outside* the printed word. We certainly lack the refined critical instrumentarium for analyzing sound and image that we have long enjoyed for assessing the word. But as we enter an era in which the once-dominant media industries and state organizations are struggling to concentrate their holdings in the face of the Internet's dispersed logics and rapidly growing participation rates, one suspects that even a critical theorist would see the wisdom of advocating multiple literacies, and seizing the opportunity to enhance the critical participation of the public.[11] Add to this the affordances of computer networks for grass-roots distribution and deterritorialized community formation, and the civic implications of the new literacies also loom large.

Just as Johns tracks the slow shift toward stabilization of the publishing world, and with it, a particular regime of knowledge and expertise, we too are witnessing a new set of social dynamics emerge, a struggle between vested interests and newcomers, between an industrial elite and elements within the mass. On one hand, we can discern strategies for control (the actions of MySpace, Google, and their handmaids in the regulatory sector); on the other, new practices that have yet to be scaled, and that may yet hold the seeds of an unseen future. These new practices range from purpose-made (MIT's Open Course Initiative, Brewster Kahle's Internet Archive, *korişhin* and other forms of collaborative news networks) to the—at some level unintended—social and informational aggregates that can be found online. Again, we are only two decades into this process, but already we can see needed competencies. As we move toward increased cultural participation (*productive* participation, not just participation through consumption), we need to rethink the domain of literacy (literacies) and revamp our research agendas and curricular processes accordingly.

The old certainties—the truth of the vetted, authorized written word in the book (where we only had to master the codes that Gérard Genette calls paratexts)—are past; like the literacy of the sixteenth and seventeenth centuries, today's literacies require the assessment of uncertain utterances, the ferreting out of provenance and reliability, and the critical understanding of point of view. The great difference between the advent of the book and today's new media technologies regards participation. While the book opened the way to vast new readerships and facilitated authorship as well, networked computers have opened the way to vast new authorships (while enhancing access to the text), have enabled unfiltered distribution, and have stimulated suggestive new collective cultural and social forms.

CHAPTER FOURTEEN

Visibility, Blogging, and the Construction of Subjectivity in Educational Spaces

ASUNCIÓN LÓPEZ-VARELA AZCÁRATE

As part of a blogging project on personal democracy, Julie Barko Germany wrote in 2008:

> Four years ago, in the middle of the 2004 primaries, the online political community heralded the rise of the political blogosphere as an evolution in—and improvement upon—the printing press. Political bloggers became the new pamphleteers, and more than one journalist compared online political discussion groups, blogging communities, and listservers to coffee houses, where people go to get their daily fix of information. It is not a coincidence that we embraced the metaphors of the printing press, which once led Western Europe to question the traditions established by religious and political authorities, and coffeehouse, where so many connections were made, business transactions were conducted, and ideas were debated during the Enlightenment.[1]

Barko regards the rise of the blogosphere as being part of an ongoing development of free speech and education since the Enlightenment. The dawn of digitization has, for that matter, always carried with it the legacy of Enlightenment ideals of free speech, accessible education (Condorcet), and democratization. Has the digital age, with its transhumanist or posthumanist explorations into the improvement and extension of human life as a radical realization of individuality thus more or less materialized the seeds of Enlightenment? The question may be too broad to answer here—and it may be an all too problematic question, since the opposite can be (and has been) formulated just as easily: that the age of digitization and "googlefication" may have endangered the legacies of the Enlightenment by endangering the future of the book as a cultural medium, copyrights, and, precisely, the open access to books and information safeguarded by libraries.[2] Nevertheless, current debates on e-learning and, in relation to this, participation culture are informed by late-eighteenth-century ideals concerning the advancement of learning (only consider the encyclopedia, at once an icon of both the Enlightenment and, in its computerized version, the age of digitization, representing a pursuit of integrated but also democratized knowledge).

Here I raise the question if, and if so to what extent, new technologies have produced new media literacies and modes of learning, or if such technologies rather materialize ideas on education that have long been part of our Western cultural canon. The first part of this chapter is concerned with the effect of new media technologies on communication, subjectivity, and dialogic interaction (Bakhtin). In close connection with this, I then consider such technologies, and their uses, in the light of participatory culture (Jenkins). Elaborating on the growing body of literature on online education, literacy, and participation, I explore the uses of e-learning through blogging as an intermedial practice. If education produces subjectivities,[3] and if education is itself premised on particular subjectivities to be produced, what are the interrelations between e-learning and digital modes of subjectivity?

HUMACHINES AND HUMACHINE ENVIRONMENTS

As the result of technological developments in biology, the spheres of *techno* and *bio* have increasingly merged. According to Bernard Stiegler, subjectivity has always already been prosthetic, but during the last three to four decades the prosthetic has become more and more pronounced as a formative dimension of subjectivity in its posthuman configurations. The resulting integration of human and machine, as Mark Poster puts it, "constitutes an interface outside the subject/object binary."[4] Interfaces are devices or systems that allow unrelated entities to relate and interact with each other: interaction modalities. With the emergence of the information age, such interfaces can no longer be thought of as external to the subject, but rather signal a change in the relations between humans and machines. This change is enumerated in Poster's concept of humachines: a dimension in-between subject and object.

According to Poster, such humachines and the networks of digital information have profoundly changed the conditions of culture.[5] The

Internet no longer fits the frameworks of earlier modes of communication in real space, producing a new materiality of interaction where the virtual has taken on actual dimensions. Whereas "old" media such as print and radio are, for Poster, fixed outlets that typically lend themselves to state control, the Internet is ideally (though not in fact) decentralized and intimates a postnational future. Within this decentralized medium, "netizens" have emerged who answer to machines rather than to nature alone. Here, identity is dissociated from a biological substrate, rendering it flexible and vulnerable (to such things as identity theft).

If such humachines are intimately attached to digital media, how do these media operate as interfaces? In their foundational text *Remediation*, Jay David Bolter and Richard Grusin recognize that a certain awareness of the hypermediacy of the medium in digital formats acknowledges multiple acts of representation and makes them visible through plural, open-ended links and interrelationships. In other words, the awareness of hypermediacy allows us to see writing as both inscription and incorporation, never consigned to one mode of embodiment. Within the multiple layers of digital media, both meaning and data are contained. The first layer in digital media works at a binary machine level and according to generative Chomskyan patterns, while at the interface level, that of the visual image representation, new media open dialogical patterns between the cultural logic of the machine and that of the media (including the new kinds of relationships between producer/author and consumer/user as theorized by George Landow). The result is a mix of binary codes where the visible becomes increasingly rhetorical and the linguistic increasingly typographical. Thus, as interfaces, digital environments are both verbal (conceptual; based on arbitrary agreement of signs; linear/relational with intertextual-intermedial links) and visual (perceptual; based on resemblance of signs; relational—the distribution of information value or the relative emphasis among elements of the image). They are intermedial.

The World Wide Web has afforded new forms of reading and writing that allow networking dispersed across broad topographies. Blogs and personal web publishing systems, wikis or collaborative content management systems that allow the creation and editing pages instantaneously; distributed classification systems that allow the classification of items by associating them with any number of keywords or tags aggregated by the software for the benefit of the whole community, or rich site summary systems that alert the user when new content is available in blogs, wikis, and so forth have been among the self-exposing forms of visuality, both individual and communal, in the last years. Blogs especially have increased the accessibility and usability of the Web for non-professionals. Unlike traditional webpages, which required knowledge of HTML or the use of a specialized program such as Front Page, blogs are readily accessible to the general public through sites such as Blogger or WordPress. Although blogs can be customized, they all follow similar layouts and standards, and they are interconnected. Unlike linear printed texts, digital blogs can incorporate all kinds of media formats (image, audio, video) and include comments on the main body of the text written by authorized agents (individuals, institutions); they are multimodal. Multimodality is here a more inclusive and appropriate term than intermediality, since it does not refer to only the aspects of objects, or systems, but also to agents and users—to the way in which all their senses and modes of expression and response are addressed.

Most important, individual blogs afford a public space of exposure that allows "good" narcissist self-reflexive explorations as well as intermedial spaces of encounter with others. Thus, the new humachine environments include daily signifying practices that configure new, networked subjectivities while reconfiguring old modes of mediation ("the man on the street").[6] It must be recalled here that the very materiality of media changes over time, and can be manipulated in its own distinct way.[7] But we must also bear in mind that materiality is already culturally encoded and bears a certain institutional validation prior to the transmission of specific content. Thus, technological changes affect the way information is transmitted, emerge out of particular cultural conditions, and, in turn, result in new social and cultural situations. It is important to point out that technologies also produce relational positions of greater or lesser privilege as they regulate the flow of discourse in particular ways. Access, production, distribution, and use of new media are compromised inside and outside the Western world because of economic inequalities while, at the cultural level, the impact of Western media is felt as global. Thus, the visuality of certain local voices disappears under the excessive informational Western flow, a digital divide that becomes evident in the material and ideological differential outcomes between East and West, the rich and the poor, the able and the disabled (issues of accessibility), whose power and information vary with their relations of access, possession, and use of technology.[8]

If Poster is correct and networked digital information and human assemblages transform the fundamental conditions of culture, then how, precisely, can we imagine the construction of subjectivities, social

realities and culture formatted within specifically digital forms of materiality—forms that are, moreover, continuously changing (from Hyves
to Flickr to Twitter and so on)? By now, we have become familiar with
the idea and practice of reduplicated copied-and-pasted home identities
on the Internet that help people to transcend their very material/physi-
cal dimension. In particular, forms of social expression such as blogging
help the individual feel part of a larger whole, enabling a construction
of subjectivity within a greater networked community consciousness.[9]
According to Rebecca Blood, the explosive growth of blogs signals a
transition from "an age of carefully controlled information provided by
sanctioned authorities (and artists), to an unprecedented opportunity
for individual expression on a worldwide scale."[10] This problematizes
distinctions between individual and shared information, the private and
public sphere. The home becomes a primary environment of modern
public relations, where companies offer telecommuting options and
educational institutions opt for cheaper forms of e-learning and b-
learning.

Thus, the specific materiality of digital communication destabilizes
traditional conceptions of privacy and the individual as a private self—a
process that reactionary critics like Sven Birkerts have lamented as the
loss of one of the great values of the print and book age, with a self
bounded, so to speak, by the covers of a book. Most important, in the
age of blogging (roughly the last decade), this repositioning of "the"
individual is fundamentally *recursive*, that is to say: as we become
aware of ourselves in this teleconnected world, we also become aware
of our presence (inscription/incorporation) in the group. We acquire a
sense of being doxical agencies within the shared *habitus*: the constitu-
tional characteristics of an individual—that is, a set of (social) disposi-
tions that generate practices and perceptions.

As we have known since Bourdieu, *habitus* refers to "a socialized
body, a structured body, a body which has incorporated the immanent
structures of a world or of a particular sector of that world—a field—
and which structures the perception of that world as well as action in
that world."[11] For Bourdieu, the body is a cognitive space where culture
is inscribed and enacted. But he also claims that these internal dynamics
become naturalized and thus made invisible by their ubiquity, just as
code is hidden under interface surface (after all, this is the role of a good
interface: to create an illusion of transparency, a feature of the medium
that tends to blind its users to the part it plays in constructing their
experiential worlds). A good interface seeks to imitate the real so closely

as to allow an apparently unmediated experience. Early hypermedia theories studied how new media may function in a doxical way by appropriating space as a framing metaphor, proffering an ontology that escaped from embodiment and physical space. Only recently has the material dimension of mediation begun to acquire more importance in theory, for instance in the work of Mark Hansen, with the analysis of modes of embodied experience in digital surrounds, and in the work of Henry Jenkins, with its emphasis on media ecology and the "real" social networks involved and activated within digital communication networks. This is epitomized by Jenkins's concept of participatory culture, which roughly refers to the cultural competencies and social skills (rather than technologies alone) required for digital involvement.

PARTICIPATORY CULTURE AND EDUCATION ONLINE

In "Confronting the Challenges of Participatory Culture,"[12] Jenkins brings to bear his earlier conceptions of fan cultures and folksonomies on digital communication and education. In this important paper, he sketches the potential of online communities for learning and new media literacies: "a set of cultural competencies and social skills that young people need in the new media landscape." As Jenkins goes on to say, participatory culture "shifts the focus of literacy from one of individual expression to community involvement"—a shift he locates in the shift from old or analog to new or digital media ecologies. According to Jenkins, forms of participatory culture may typically include:

> Affiliations—memberships, formal and informal, in online communities centered around various forms of media, such as Friendster, Facebook, message boards, metagaming, game clans, or MySpace).

> Expressions—producing new creative forms, such as digital sampling, skinning and modding, fan videomaking, fan fiction writing, zines, mashups).

> Collaborative Problem-solving—working together in teams, formal and informal, to complete tasks and develop new knowledge (such as through *Wikipedia*, alternative reality gaming, spoiling).

> Circulations—Shaping the flow of media (such as podcasting, blogging).

Rather than focus on innovative technology in itself, Jenkins's idea of participatory culture firmly situates such technologies within "real" and specific social-cultural contexts of usage, circulation, materialization, adaptation (such as texting on mobile phones), and so on. It is these contexts, for Jenkins, that allow for the emergence of a "community involvement" on the net. For Jenkins, such an involvement or culture of participation is typically a culture:

1. With relatively low barriers to artistic expression and civic engagement

2. With strong support for creating and sharing one's creations with others

3. With some type of informal mentorship whereby what is known by the most experienced is passed along to novices

4. Where members believe that their contributions matter

5. Where members feel some degree of social connection with one another (at the least they care what other people think about what they have created).

Such a participatory culture may be an embodied culture insofar as it engages participants in both mind and body, allowing them, in the words of David Birchfield and colleagues, to "physically explore concepts and systems, by moving within and acting upon an environment."[13] Physically, because Birchfield's developments of new modes of interactive learning in SMALLab (*Situated Multimedia Art Learning Lab*, merging situated cognition, embodied learning, and collaborative learning), aim to "empower the physical body to function as an expressive interface." This means that the body becomes a mediator between augmented and "real" physical worlds—the point where the virtual and the material converge. One could say that participatory culture here refers not only to the participation of people in a group or network, but also to the participation or interaction of body and machine, as well as mind and body. Within this frame, SMALLab develops modes of learning that are "semi-immersive" and of "mixed reality." With respect to the first, the mediated or augmented world is always open to the surrounding world, actors freely moving in between both, and without needing any other extensions but their moving bodies to access the augmented world.

With respect to the second, actors in SMALLab environments use a mixture of devices to learn to cope with multisensory environments.

This amounts to "an integration of physical manipulation objects, 3D physical gestures, and digitally mediated components" (ranging from glowballs to dynamic texts and sounds). Digital culture being, according to Packer and Jordan, a new realization of old ideals of *Gesamtkunst*, SMALLab builds on this artistic heritage, providing synesthetic learning spaces where augmented realities interact with realities beyond, or bodies interact with machines, and the senses among each other.[14]

However, if SMALLab illustrates Jenkins's idea of participatory culture as an embodied culture, also in its reconceptualization of learning spaces as game spaces, it does not exemplify a major component of that participatory culture: the idea of networks. Again, it is important to emphasize that Jenkins ultimately derives his idea of participatory culture from his research into fan culture, a culture going back at least to the 1930s—if not to the nineteenth century or to medieval manuscript cultures—and that hinges precisely on an idea of circulation and flows: on forms of cooperation and interaction that were, in predigital times, dependent on mail and print circulation and that have now materialized in blogging, tweeting, or other social media. Networks are systems—nodes interconnected by communication paths—and social networks consist of persons acting as nodes, connected by what Manuel Castells calls "time-sharing practices that work through flows" (flows here referring to "purposeful, repetitive, programmable sequences of exchange and interaction between physically disjointed positions held by social actors"—the constant movement of information).[15] Networking logic privileges the spatial rather than temporal dimension of social relations, and the collaborative over the individual. As a form of network culture, participatory culture is embodied in its being part of a situated culture—of "real-time" users, and with "real-time" effects. That is to say, the open or porous augmented learning spaces developed by SMALLab, however localized they may be, are nevertheless illustrative of Jenkins's notion of participatory culture in relation to education as an embodied culture of flows: The digital and material converge.

BLOGGING, EDUCATIONAL SPACES, AND EMERGING SUBJECTIVITIES

Knowledge and information management are intimately linked to education as a transference motor of our shared cultural heritage. Technological applications play an important role in developing education and, hence, cultural policies and practices. The educational use of new media, particularly social software, and the emergence of constructivist approaches go hand in hand with a move toward greater flexibility, mobility, and tolerant attitudes.[16] In the European Union and elsewhere, particular attention is paid to competencies regarding the treatment of information, its transfer, and its use in responsible decision making and problem solving. There are innumerable examples of classroom experiences that state the benefits of social software systems and of working cooperatively with tools that facilitate the aggregation and organization of knowledge, while at the same time demonstrating that the diversity of individual research interests enhances learning for all (see, for instance, MIT's OpenCourseWare, MERLOT, and the Educause Learning Initiative, among others). These classroom experiences can help unveil the construction of posthuman subjectivities, since new technologies are not just tools or, in the case of social software, tools that can enhance social and collaborative abilities; they are also media that facilitate informational interchange and social connection, at once substituting for and making possible "human" communication. As such, these technologies can be considered as ecologies—literally, environments relating to living organisms—that mediate cultural practices. Within these parameters, networked education technologies frame subjectivities in different local environments that can connect to other local environments. Cooperative Language Quests and sister-classroom blogging are an example of such practices.

In the particular context of education, blogging offers a challenge to cultural analysis insofar as it can effectively function as a *dialogic* mediation: mediations of participation and reciprocity, whereby readers are openly and actively engaged in formulating a response. As Mikhail Bakhtin outlined in *The Dialogic Imagination*, dialogic texts are always already engaged in a communication with multiple other texts, hence becoming dynamic in a metaphoric sense; such texts continuously shift meaning in the framing and interaction with their intertexts, mutually affecting each other (see also Chapter 4 in this volume). This potentiality, so to speak, of novelistic texts—and in the spirit of Bakhtin it could be suggested that blogging is another instance of novelization—materializes as a convention in blogging: the open interchange between the public and the private. This exchange can help students develop practical research skills, involving the building of instructional modules for directive learning.[17] Because of their public nature, blogs kept by students themselves can be used as self-reflexive, directive learning tools. Taking the form of a diary, they can help expand students' understanding of specific issues. Blogs maintained by instructors also lend themselves well to the response strengthening inherent in directive learning because they can be arranged chronologically, and students' comments can be attached to each individual entry, added by the instructor. In this sense, blogging becomes a way of inscription/incorporation that helps mobilize students' motivation and, perhaps, social participation. Thus, the "narcissistic" nature of blogging can also be read as a move from individual consciousness toward forms of subjectivity increasingly collaborative and social. When exposed publicly and made visible, individual problems and concerns become part of the community, acquiring a measure of shared consciousness. The blogging subjectivities then become sites where inscription/incorporation of the self and other selves proliferate.

In the move toward European Higher Education Convergence, there are many initiatives that use blogs to help in the development of concepts, procedures, and attitudes. For instance, Complutense University of Madrid maintains a blog used to present classroom information and implement intercultural attitudes and encourage the development of interpersonal skills. This blog will soon be part of a larger Content Management System (CMS) hosted by Universidad Complutense within its Comparative Cultural Studies Organization.[18] Institutional evaluations through the Intercultural Observatory Project over the last two years have shown that the blog contributes to developing collaborative forms of relationship between the instructor and the students and among students themselves. The blog also helps stimulate creativity and encourages dynamic and relational argumentation, forcing students' participation in discussion and in the selection of pertinent informational resources, contributing to the transferability of learning results. Through blogs, dialogicity in education thus primarily revolves around the idea of participation—yet it remains to be seen if more radical dimensions of the "dialogic imagination" can also be at stake here. How, for instance, do students adjust themselves to the specific kind of dialogicity in the context, and how does this affect their use of language and learning skills? If blogs are participatory, to what degree are they—in educational contexts—conformative rather than dialogic? How do blogs relate to monologic educational modes? The answer to such questions is beyond the scope of this chapter, yet they are necessary to critically assess blogging as a realm of intersubjectivity.[19]

CONCLUSION

In Ian Watson's short story "When Thought-Mail Failed" (2000), nanobots have "rejigged the neural network" and "powerful microputers interfaced with the brain" so that a radically updated version of email, thought-mail, has become possible that allows for instant, mind-to-mind communication, making speech redundant. Thus, humanity became a "hive-entity . . . directed not by . . . instincts, but by self-generated thought-mail acting as a kind of overmind."[20] Though this is an extreme instance, networked machines—as I have argued—configure the outlook and "mentality" of humans in the posthuman age. As humachines, they are always already mediated, and this is not so much due to the computer as to its networked and networking potential. As Jim Porter has observed, if the computer has indeed occasioned a revolution, "the computer per se is not the revolutionary technology. Rather the revolution is the networked computer and the social/rhetorical contexts it creates and the way its use impacts publishing practices."[21] Networks invoke the metaphor of the text as an ever-expanding web, and it is within this metaphor that blogs have come to occupy a space in education: as tools of reflection, direction, and transfer. Ideologically, the uses of blogs in education remediate dialogic frames of pedagogy in the classroom. Blogs formally materialize such dialogicity, operating as they do in relation to other texts and authors. It remains to be seen, however, what the precise, and radical, implications of interactivity in education would thus be.

CHAPTER FIFTEEN

The Singularity of New Media

GARY HALL

> The metaphysicians of Tlön do not seek for the truth or even for verisimilitude,
> but rather for the astounding. They judge that metaphysics is a branch of
> fantastic literature. They know that a system is nothing more than the subor-
> dination of all aspects of the universe to any one such aspect.
>
> —JORGE LUIS BORGES, "Tlön, Uqbar, Orbis Tertius"

This chapter arises out of my research on specific forms and uses of new media. The particular form of new media I want to concentrate on here is that associated with open access, and my own involvement with a cultural studies open access archive called CSeARCH (which stands for Cultural Studies e-Archive).[1] For those unfamiliar with the term, open access can be defined as "putting peer-reviewed scientific and scholarly literature on the internet [in either open access journals or e-print repositories such as CSeARCH]. Making it available free of charge and free of most copyright and licensing restrictions. Removing the barriers to serious research."[2]

Although I consider open access to be an important topic in its own right, exploring it in detail as one specific form of new media also provides me with a way of responding to two main criticisms that anyone dealing with the impact of digital technology has risked facing in recent years. The first is that too "much writing on new media [is] concerned with other writing on new media rather than new media itself."[3] The second is that such writing tends to point to vague possible future consequences of new media, without examining specific material instances of it in any real detail.

Putting it all too crudely, we could say that a first phase of writing on new media, characterized by 1990s descriptions of the exciting future that was perceived as being ushered in by cyberculture, cyberspace, cyberpunk, virtual reality, artificial intelligence, artificial life, and so on, served to introduce the field to the academy, especially the humanities and social sciences. However, as Mark Poster's criticisms of Jacques Derrida's account of new media technologies, and of virtual reality especially, attest, new media theory at this point tended to be a little on the general and indeed transcendental side. For Poster, writing in his 2001 book *What's the Matter with the Internet?*, Derrida, although he senses the "need to account for differential materialities of the media," "tends to preserve the philosopher's taste for the general over the cultural analyst's penchant for the particular," providing "strings of hyphenated terms, 'tele-technology' or 'techno-scientifico-economico-media,' that vaguely point in a direction without guiding the virtual traveller in any particular direction."[4]

In recent years there has therefore been an interesting and, I believe, at times quite useful impetus in certain strands of new media theory to move away from the broad, hyperbolic, "the future is now" tendency of the 1990s, toward the development of a more focused, detailed and specific analysis of particular media platforms (websites, cell phones, MP3 players), application programs (word processors, Internet browsers, graphic design tools) and software (compilers, program text editors, operating systems). We can see Katherine Hayles arguing very much along these lines with regard to literature in her 2002 book *Writing Machines*: "We are near the beginning of a theory of media-specific analysis in literary studies," she writes. "Many people . . . are now . . . moving from print-orientated perspectives to frameworks that implicitly require the comparison of electronic textuality and print to clarify the specificities of each."[5] It is an approach that takes far more account of the materiality of digital media, even though it may see that materiality as an "emergent property," as does Hayles,[6] and that engages with specific instances of media technologies rather than with new media as a general category.

Yet even though this second phase, which Hayles characterizes in terms of "a theory of media-specific analysis,"[7] is only just beginning to emerge, I already want to make a case for the development of a third phase or generation of new media theory. I want to do so because, for all the emphasis on the "need to account for differential materialities" and specificities, it seems to me that insufficient attention is still being paid to the difference and specificity of much new media.

Let me illustrate what I mean in the following way. In *Information Please*, Mark Poster—attempting to provide precisely the kind of clear directions he sees Derrida's work as lacking—hypothesizes that it is very much possible that in the future the sharing or gifting ethos of peer-to-peer (P2P) networks will become a prominent, perhaps even the dominant, mode of cultural exchange:

> An infrastructure is being set into place for a day when cultural objects will become variable and users will become creators as well. Such an outcome is not just around the corner since for generations the population has been accustomed to fixed cultural objects. But as we pass beyond the limits of modern culture, with its standardized, mass produced consumer culture, we can anticipate more and more individuals and groups taking advantage of the facility with which digital cultural objects are changed, stored, and distributed in the network. A different sort of public space from that of modernity is emerging, a heterotopia in Foucault's term, and peer-to-peer networks constitute an important ingredient in that development, one worthy of safeguarding and promoting for that reason alone. If copyright laws need to be changed and media corporations need to disappear or transform themselves, this result must be evaluated in relation to a new regime of culture that is now possible.[8]

When it comes to digital culture, Poster is of course by no means alone in having such ideas. Many people have put forward similar hypotheses. They include the German Oekonux debate of 2000–2002, which attempted to develop the principles involved in the production of free software into a plan for the organization of society;[9] Brian Holmes with his slogan "open source for the operating systems of the earth" and the associated discussion of "open source as a metaphor for new institutions";[10] and Michael Hardt and Toni Negri's positioning of the decision-making capacity of the multitude as being analogous to the collaborative development of the open source movement, and their arguing for a form of "society whose source code is revealed so that we can all work collaboratively to solve its bugs and create new, better social programs."[11] And, to be sure, the idea that the relations of production and distribution associated with peer-to-peer networks can be scaled up to form a new regime of culture, or new kinds of networked institutions, or even a plan for the future organization of society in which cultural, political, and economic decisions are made in an open, distributed, participatory, cooperative, networked fashion, is a seductive one. No doubt grand historical narratives of this sort—in which the relatively fixed and stable imagined communities associated with classical ideas of the nation-state are regarded as gradually being superseded by more complex, fluid, and mobile networks of people that are frequently constituted strategically—also have a certain strategic value themselves. Certainly, if peer-to-peer networks and open source are to be considered two important ingredients in the emergence of any such new regime, I would insist upon open access being another. Nevertheless, there are at least two questions I want to raise as far as any such a hypothesis is concerned.

To begin with, if a new, post-"modern" (as distinct from postmodern) regime of this kind does emerge, what will it look like? Instead of being a realm in which culture in general takes on the distributed, networked, participative, collaborative character of much new media, I wonder if it is not more likely to assume the form of a mixed and (as Poster's reference to Foucault indeed suggests) heterogeneous economy, with different media, both "new" and "old," and the related infrastructures, operating in a relation of coexistence and even at times convergence, but also perhaps of divergence, competition, and antagonism.

This in turn connects to a further question. Even if such a new form of "public space"—different from that of modernity and derived at least in part from the gifting ethos of digital culture's peer-to-peer networks—is possible, would the various ingredients that go to make up this "heterotopia," in which we could perhaps include peer-to-peer file sharing, open source, free software, open content, the creative commons and open access, all contribute to such an open, distributed, networked, regime in more or less the same way? Or, just as there are obvious commonalities and points of connection between them, would there not be areas of friction, conflict, and even incommensurability, too? What is more, this is a possibility that need not necessarily be viewed pessimistically. In fact, I would argue that the specificity of politics, in a pluralistic, liberal democracy at least, is actually marked by a certain refusal to eliminate conflict and antagonism.[12]

Now, as you might imagine, I cannot answer these questions here. If for no other reason, their future-oriented nature makes that impossible. The point I am trying to make in raising them is that, if we *are* to substitute the literary and cultural critic's penchant for the particular for the philosopher's taste for the general, it is not enough to take account of the difference and specificity of the digital medium of reproduction: its material form and properties. Attention also needs to be paid to the many distinctions and divergences that exist between the various ingredients that go to make up digital culture at any one time. This is something I have tried to do in my research by emphasizing that the situation regarding the digital reproduction of scholarly literature is in many respects very different from that of the peer-to-peer sharing of music files. Open access is capable of working in the manner it does because of the specific character of both academia and open access at the moment: That is, because the majority of scholars do not expect, or need, to be paid directly or substantially for their writings (their reward comes more from the increase in feedback and recognition and enhancement to their reputation that publishing open access offers), which means they are happy to make their work available for free in a way many for-profit authors are not; and because the e-print self-archiving system enables academics to retain copyright over their work, or at least avoid infringing most publishers' copyright agreements, texts can be distributed freely, rather than being stolen or pirated, as is often the case with regard to music. In this respect one could say that the open-access publishing and archiving of academic scholarship and research constitutes a strategic use of a specific form of digital culture within particular institutional and sociopolitical contexts (although, as we shall see, it cannot be reduced to those contexts). It is not something that is necessarily generalizable or transferable to other forms and practices of digital culture—the peer-to-peer sharing of music and video files, the decentered electronic distribution of films, the digital storage of visual art, the online publication of science-fiction literature and so on—although it may be.[13]

This does not mean that all these various forms and practices are absolutely different and heterogeneous. The very weblike structure of the web often makes it difficult to determine where texts begin or end, all the cutting and pasting, grafting and transplanting, internal and external linking that takes place blurring the boundaries between the text and its surroundings, its material support, but also between other media and cultural texts, techniques, forms, and genres, making such boundaries almost impossible to determine. Indeed, many instances of digital media such as Amazon's peer-reviewing, Wikipedia's open editing, YouTube's video sharing, and Flickr's photo sharing have a number of features in common with both peer-to-peer and open access: not least that they all make use of digital networks; are dependent on an open, social process of collaboration and cooperation; are made up of user-generated content; and have the potential for the individual user to be able to create, alter, and modify that content as well as reproduce, store, and distribute it. Together with their material differences, however (as represented by the particular platform, hardware, software, operating system, programming code, graphical interface, and so on), I would argue that they also operate in different ways, situations, and contexts.

They are therefore not necessarily capable of having the same or comparable effects.

Wikipedia, for instance, in contrast to most other instances of Web 2.0, including both YouTube and Facebook, is controlled and run by a nonprofit organization (the Wikipedia Foundation), funded primarily through private donations, and releases its content under the GNU General Public License. Meanwhile Web 2.0 (including Wikipedia this time) tends to be different again from many peer-to-peer file sharing networks such as Kazaa, Gnutella, EDonkey, FastTrack, EMule, and BitTorrent, especially those that are peer-run and "pure" or decentralized in form, since the latter are distributed, commons-based systems which are not owned or controlled by anyone. This is why many more instances of Web 2.0 than peer-to-peer networking have been turned into a commodity and bought and sold by the likes of Rupert Murdoch, Yahoo!, and Google.[14] In fact some have gone so far as to characterize Web 2.0 as "capitalism's preemptive attack against P2P systems."[15] But even peer-to-peer networks are not all the same, for there are significant differences between them.[16]

So we cannot just say that the characteristics of much contemporary new media—their networked form, reliance on open, social processes of collaboration, use of user-generated content, and so forth—mean that it is going to lead to a new form of culture and society. Despite their similarities, Wikipedia, Web 2.0, peer-to-peer, and open access are not necessarily capable of having the same or comparable effects. Instead, those effects would have to be worked out by paying close attention to the specificity and indeed singularity of each in relation to a particular context. Obviously, this is not something I can do for all the examples of digital culture I have mentioned, not here, or even in a book-length project. That is why in the case of my recent research I have taken the tactical decision to focus on just one, which perhaps has the potential to be of most concern to the scholarly community: the open access publishing and archiving of research literature. Even here things are not simple, however, since the open access movement is itself neither unified nor self-identical. There are significant differences even among the various flavors of open access—John Willinsky has identified at least ten.[17] This is why I often focus on the model that is being invented and creatively explored by the specific digital repository I am involved with.

One of the things I am particularly interested in with this research is the way in which digital texts—with their lack of fixity, stability, and permanence relative to time and place, their undermining of the boundaries separating authors, editors, producers, users, consumers, critics/commentators, humans, and machines, and their ability to incorporate sound and both still and moving images—contain the potential, not merely to remediate older media forms, and thus deliver an unchanged and preexisting content, such as literature or cultural studies, albeit in a new way, but to transform fundamentally that content, and with it our relationship to knowledge. In this respect, the specificity of open access archiving resides for me, among other things, in the way it enables researchers to circumvent a lot of the restrictions placed on access to research and publications by copyright and licensing agreements, and thus provide a response to many of the issues and dilemmas that have been presented to scholars by an increasingly market driven and commercial academic publishing industry. Accordingly, openaccess archiving is able to offer a number of advantages and benefits to academics. As far as the cultural studies repository I am involved with is concerned, these include enabling authors to:

publish their research immediately upon completion, before it comes out in either journal or book form (which can take between nine months and two years from submission of the final manuscript, sometimes longer);

make their work available from (almost) any desktop, in any home, university, library or school, twenty-four hours a day, to anyone who has access to the Internet;

provide their audience, including fellow writers and researchers, undergraduate and postgraduate students, and the general public, with as many copies of their work as they need simply by supplying their readers with the URL where they can find them on the net and download them for free or print them if they prefer;

increase the size of their readership, and hence potentially both the amount of feedback and recognition they receive and the size of their reputation. As an increasing number of studies suggest, research published as open access is far more likely to be read and cited than if it is published in ink-on-paper form only;[18]

potentially increase reading figures, feedback, impact, and even sales of their paper publications: Rather than detract from them, as many commercial publishers fear, publishing on the web frequently increases sales of paper copies;

publish books and journals that have too small a potential readership, or too long a tail in terms of sales, to make them cost-effective for a paper publisher to take on;

make their research "permanently" available, so that authors no longer need concern themselves with the thought that their work may go out of print or become otherwise unavailable;[19]

republish texts that are rare or forgotten, or that have gone out of print;
revise and update their publications whenever they wish, so that authors need no longer be anxious about their work going out of date;

distribute their texts to an extremely wide audience, rather than reaching merely the specific audiences their publishers think they can market and sell their work to: in the case of cultural studies, often primarily the United States, the United Kingdom, and Australia;

link to underlying, background, and related research featured on blogs, wikis, and individual and institutional webpages;

fulfill their obligations to funding bodies easily and quickly. In 2006 the UK Economic and Social Research Council (ESRC) followed the lead set by the likes of the U.S. National Institutes of Health, CERN, and the Wellcome Trust, who have for some time now requested researchers to make their research available on an open access platform. The ESRC made the depositing of research in such an OA repository or journal a condition for the award of funding from October of that year onwards. Indeed, only one of the seven UK research councils has not established such an open-access mandate.

The specificity of open access also lies in the way an archive of this kind determines what can be collected, stored, and preserved, and the particular nature of the questions this determination raises. It is important to realize that an archive is not a neutral institution but part of specific intellectual, cultural, technical, and economic/financial networks. An archive's medium, in particular—be it paper, celluloid, or tape—is often perceived as constituting merely a disinterested carrier for the archived material. Yet the medium of an archive actually helps to determine and shape its content; a content, moreover, that is performed differently each time, in each particular context in which it is accessed or in which material is retrieved from the archive. An open-access archive is no exception in this respect. Its specific form, medium, and structure shape what it preserves, classifies, and performs as legitimate scholarship, in both time and scope. Consequently, a digital cultural studies archive is not just a means of reproducing and confirming existing conceptions of cultural studies: of selecting, collecting, gathering together, interpreting, filtering, organizing, classifying, and preserving what cultural studies already is or is perceived as having been. It is partly that. But it is also a means of producing and performing cultural studies: both what it is going to look like in the past, and what there is a chance for cultural studies to have been in the future.

Interestingly, this argument also applies to standards for preparing metadata, so that texts can be easily indexed and searched across a range of archives, journals, and databases. These, too, are never neutral, but help to produce (rather than passively reflect) what is classified as legitimate scholarship—and even more important, what is not. This is why, for me, the kind of fantasy that lies behind the Open Archives Initiative, or SHERPA's DRIVER project, or indeed Google Book Search for that matter, of having one place to search for scholarship and research such as a universal search engine, global archive, or international network of fully integrated, indexed, and linked academic work that can be centrally harvested and searched, must remain precisely that: a totalizing (and totalitarian) fantasy. Instead, I would argue for a multiplicity of different and perhaps at times conflicting and even incommensurable open-access archives, journals, databases, and other publishing experiments.

The determination of content by the archive's medium is of course a feature that digital repositories share with archives of other kinds. One of the issues that is specific to open-access archiving, however, is the way in which, as a result of the profound transformation in the publication of the academic research literature that is being brought about by the change in the mode of reproduction from ink-on-paper to digital, questions that were already present with regard to the print medium and other media, but that have tended to be taken for granted, overlooked, marginalized, excluded, or otherwise repressed, are now being raised more directly. As Adrian Johns reminds us in *The Nature of the Book*, right up until the middle of the eighteenth century the book was an unstable object, with Shakespeare's first folio including not only more than six hundred typefaces, but also numerous discrepancies and inconsistencies regarding its spelling, punctuation, divisions, arrangement, proofing, and page configurations. As a result, readers had to make critical decisions regarding particular manuscripts, their identity, consistency, dependability, and trustworthiness, on the basis of "assessments of the people involved in the making, distribution, and reception of books."[20] Early in the history of book, then, readers *were* involved in forming judgments around questions of authority and legitimacy: concerning what a book is and what it means to be an author, a reader, a publisher, and a distributor. The development and spread of the concept of the author, along with mass printing techniques, uniform, standard, multiple-copy editions, copyright, established publishing houses, editors, and so forth meant that many of these ideas subsequently began to appear "fixed." Consequently, readers were no longer asked to make decisions over questions of authority and legitimacy. Such issues were forgotten. The digital mode of reproduction, however, promises to place us in a position where readers are again called on to respond and to make judgments and decisions about the nature and authority of (digitized) texts, and of the disciplines, fields of knowledge, and registers these texts are supposed to belong to (or not), precisely through its loosening of much of this fixity. In this respect, open-access archiving has for me a certain tactical quality. For, as I say, we can now see that the destabilization created by the shift from print to digital offers us an opportunity and a chance, if only it can be taken, to approach academic research and scholarship anew, as if for the first time; and thus to raise precisely the kind of responsible questions concerning our ideas of knowledge, the discipline, and indeed the institution of the university that in many respects we should have been asking anyway.

Last but not least (for now, at any rate), the specificity of open-access archiving resides with the ethical issues it raises. How is it to be decided what is to be included in such an archive and what excluded? What categories of inclusion and exclusion should govern disciplinary protocols as far as the digital publication, transmission, dissemination, exchange, storage, and retrieval of academic research and scholarship is concerned? And with what authority, according to what legitimacy, can such decisions be made?

The ethical problems that an open-access repository enables us to bring to attention and emphasize were one of the main reasons I wanted to get involved in setting up an open-access archive specifically as opposed to a journal—and this is the case, even though with *Culture Machine* I have been publishing an open-access online journal since 1999. (I should stress that I am using the term *ethics* here not according to traditional moral philosophy, with its predefined codes and norms, but in the tradition of Jacques Derrida and Emmanuel Levinas. Ethics here is a duty and responsibility to what the latter terms "the infinite alterity of the other" who places me in question and to whom I have to respond.)[21] A "serious" academic journal, for instance, will primarily publish peer-reviewed articles that are recognizable as "proper" pieces of scholarly writing or research. Yet along with e-prints of peer-reviewed essays, an academic archive can also contain monographs, edited books, textbooks, book chapters, journal editions, out-of-print books, working papers, discussion papers, theses, bibliographies, conference papers, presentations, teaching material, and lectures. And that is before we consider artifacts of a more unusual nature, which can also conceivably be collected in even the most serious of academic archives. I am thinking of drafts of work in progress, manuscripts, leaflets, posters, "underground literature," photographs, sound recordings, film, video, multimedia resources, software, maps, letters, diaries, personal correspondence, and so on. But I also have in mind laundry lists and scraps such as one stating "I have forgotten my umbrella," which was found among Nietzsche's papers after his death and about which Derrida has written at length,[22] or even the content of dreams, such as those of Hélène Cixous, which are detailed in her notebooks and are now included as part of the Cixous archive at the Bibliothèque National de France.[23] And that is still to restrict myself solely to examples that, though perhaps unusual, are already authorized. Compared to a journal, then, which is commonly understood to be a serious, scholarly publication, an archive, which can be understood as both the objects and documents assembled and the place they are located, is by definition far more open—at least potentially—to the unusual and the quirky: the different, the foreign, the heterogeneous, the excessive, and so forth. It thus seems to me that an archive is capable of placing us in a position where we have to make ethical decisions over what can be legitimately included in it, and with what authority, in a way a journal simply is not.

What is more, if this is true of archives generally, it is even truer of open-access repositories. This is because another of the issues that is specific to open-access archiving (or certain instances of it anyway) is the extent to which the digital technology that enables it also makes it possible to multiply the permeability of its border control, thus bringing this problem of what can and cannot be legitimately included within such a repository to attention and emphasizing it. In other words, the speed of the digitization process, together with the sheer size, number, and variety of texts that can be produced, published, archived, preserved, and stored, the geographic range over which these texts can be distributed and disseminated, and the relative ease and low cost of doing all this, means that the need to make such ethical decisions becomes much more apparent—as does the difficulty involved in doing so. By providing us in this way with an opportunity to raise questions of academic legitimacy and authority that are often otherwise kept hidden and concealed (and in the process be potentially far more open, radical, and experimental when it comes to making responsible decisions about the quality and value of a piece of writing or research, and ask, following Derrida, what if Freud, or Hoggart, or Borges, had had not just email, but the web, a blog, a wiki, text messaging, Amazon peer-reviewing, podcasting, social networking, peer-to-peer file sharing?), an open-access archive is capable of having a much larger impact than an open-access journal, it seems to me. Indeed, we can now see that it is not just a matter of remediating the literary and cultural studies research literature: rather, an open-access archive places us in a position where we have to think about what literary and cultural studies is; how we are going to decide this; and with what authority and legitimacy such decisions can be made.

The fact that an open access repository such as CSeARCH is able to include books in particular (in both prepublication and postpublication forms) is especially significant as far as the raising of such questions for our ideas of knowledge, disciplinarity, and the institution of the university is concerned. The desire to broach issues of this nature is also why, when working on developing an open access archive, it was important to me that it have a cultural studies focus. A number of the queries this project raises regarding disciplinary and institutional legitimacy and authority may be applicable to other fields. And yet, as cultural studies is arguably the means by which the university currently thinks itself,[24] it provides a privileged mode of access to questions of this kind, in a way that physics, or the cognitive sciences, say, or even literary studies and philosophy, do not. There is certainly something specific about a cultural studies open-access archive, for me, then.

The posing of such questions—and the potential to do so that is created by the digitization of the research literature—has radical consequences for cultural studies in turn. The latter has tended to pride itself on its interdisciplinary approach. However, as I have shown elsewhere, cultural studies tends to sustain the identity and limits of those "legitimate" disciplines it is willing to include within its interdisciplinary repertoire as much as it challenges them.[25] Witness, most obviously, the manner in which cultural studies still endeavors to maintain its academic authority and professional legitimacy as a field by excluding,

more or less violently, what it regards as nonlegitimate or not yet legitimate forms of knowledge, including what might be called "non-
knowledge" or the other of knowledge (the apparently useless, unimportant, irrelevant, trivial or mistaken: hypnosis, for example, or projection, hallucination, illusion, transference, naffness, spectrality,
phantomism). This is not to say there should be no limits to cultural
studies (or any other field or discipline, for that matter). This is quite
simply not possible. Limitation is inevitable. There are always limits.
The point is rather to realize and acknowledge this process of limitation
(rather than try to avoid it and thus end up repeating it unknowingly,
as cultural studies frequently does now); and to think about how to
assume these limits, and with what authority and legitimacy. For me,
open-access archiving helps to put cultural studies in a position where
it becomes more difficult to avoid addressing questions of this kind: not
least because of its potential openness to the quirky, different, foreign,
and heterogeneous; that which is not necessarily, or not yet, legitimate;
and even the apparently useless, unimportant, obsolete, irrelevant,
worthless, trivial, or mistaken.

Now to have an effect on cultural studies and to raise ethical questions for its own thinking on the university, it is crucial to be able to
direct these queries at one of its main sources and criteria of value. This
is where the significance of books comes in. Books have an important
role to play as far as the institutionally pragmatic tactical use of open-
access archiving I am detailing here is concerned, since they are the
main criterion for employment, tenure, promotion, and so on in the
humanities in general and cultural studies in particular. We can thus see
that its ability to include books bestows upon an open-access archive
such as CSeARCH (which does include books) with the potential to
have a far larger impact—on cultural studies especially, but also the
humanities generally, and from there perhaps the institution of the university—than an open-access journal.

That said, I want to make it quite clear that the account of open
access and CSeARCH I provide in this research is not a case study—that
would imply I already have my theory of new media worked out and
decided in advance, and that I am merely using open access and
CSeARCH and this chapter, as a means of illustrating this theory. Sure,
such a media-specific analysis would enable us to detail the specificity of
open-access archiving—and in the process point out some of the ways in
which the current emphasis on the "need to account for differential

materialities" and specificities still pays insufficient attention to the difference and specificity of much new media. Such an approach certainly seems to offer a number of advantages. For one thing, it reduces the risk of producing vague, futurological generalizations about digital culture. For another, it also helps avoid falling into the trap of privileging one specific instance of digital media and assuming that a whole new cultural regime based on its particular principles and ethos is possible. As far as I am concerned, there is no system, set of principles, ethos, or philosophy that can necessarily be privileged and extrapolated out of open access—or any other example of new media, for that matter—and made to function as generally applicable to culture, or even digital culture, as a whole, either now or in the future.

Yet what is important about a cultural studies open-access archive is not merely the intended consequences and effects I can predict, foresee, and articulate on an individual level, consequences that are informed by my own theory and philosophy of new media and open-access archiving. To paraphrase Mark Poster, the way to understand the specific ethical (and political) effects of a digital archive for me is not just to analyze and critique it, but also to build the archive.[26] And by building it I mean devising, developing, constructing, and programming it; but I also mean inventing and creating it by using it, uploading and downloading texts and material into and from it, making the associated ethical decisions, setting "in place a series of relations," and otherwise "doing things *with* the archive," as Poster says, that may be unanticipated and unpredictable. Which means that there is always something that is going to resist theory and philosophy, something that can be engaged only in the archive's performance, and that therefore escapes or is in excess of any attempt to analyze it merely in terms of its specificity.

All of which means this chapter is no doubt going to prove a bit of a disappointment to some readers. For although I may have begun by giving the impression I was going to focus on open access and describe some of my own specific work in this area, this emphasis on not providing a "case study approach" means that I cannot quite do this. Certainly, part of my ethical project with this research has been to work out as rigorously as possible a new theory or philosophy of open-access publishing and archiving based on my own experience that others can then discuss, analyze, criticize, and engage with. Moreover, it has been crucial for me to have done so. We need to have a philosophy of open access if we are going persuade more academics and university managers, not to mention governmental, organizational, and institutional policymakers, to participate in publishing research in this fashion. To leave it at this, however, would be to imply that I already have my new theory or philosophy of new media thoroughly worked out and in place, and am merely using open access and this chapter as a means of illustrating it. It would therefore be to fail to remain open to the possible unintended and unforeseeable consequences and effects of the cultural studies archive; and thus to what takes us beyond theory and analysis—or at least beyond what can simply be discerned, discovered, and predicted by means of theory and analysis. In particular, it would be to fail to remain open to the temporal and affective poeticity and performativity of the archive's functioning: the ways in which the ethics of open-access archiving cannot be decided in advance but have to be created and invented by its users in a relation of singularity to finite, "concrete" conjunctions of the here and now.

It is the actual, singular points of potentiality and transformation that are provided by specific instances and uses of digital media such as an open-access archive that I am interested in—which means that there is always something that is going to escape or be in excess of or beyond the attempt to analyze new media in terms of its specificity. Consequently, as I say, even though this second phase of new media criticism envisaged by Hayles and others is only just beginning to emerge, I already want to make a case for the development of a third. This "new media theory 3G," or next generation of new media theory, would involve paying far closer attention to the affective, performative aspect of particular instances of new media in that relation of singularity to finite, concrete conjunctions of the here and now that I just mentioned. It would thus operate very much in the tradition of Heidegger, Derrida, Arendt, and Nancy, as well as that of recent work on the study of literature most notably by Derek Attridge and Timothy Clark,[27] in which singularity is understood in terms of a literary or poetic "event" that resists theory and is engaged only in the performance of a text. In short, as well as offering a "media-specific analysis," it would understand new media in terms of singularity, and would thus move toward developing a theory of media-singular analysis.

NOTES

INTRODUCTION
Kiene Brillenburg Wurth

1. Emily Apter, *The Translation Zone: A New Comparative Literature* (Princeton: Princeton University Press, 2006), 244.

2. Alberto Manguel, *A History of Reading* (New York: Penguin, 1996).

3. For this either/or position, see also the *Chronicle of Higher Education*, October 1, 2010.

4. Arguably, most experimental literature, from Laurence Sterne to Tom Philips, at once works within and resists the (constraints) of the paper page.

5. Lev Manovich, "Cinema and Digital Media," www.manovich.net/TEXT/digital-cinema-zkm.html (last visited October 2010).

6. See, for instance, the work of Mark Danielewski, Steven Hall, Tom McCarthy, and others.

7. Anne Friedberg, *The Virtual Window: From Alberti to Microsoft* (Cambridge, Mass.: MIT Press, 2006).

8. See Geert Lovink, *Dark Fiber: Tracking Critical Internet Culture* (Cambridge, Mass.: MIT Press, 2003).

9. Aya Natalia Karpinska's *The Arrival of the Bee Box* can be read/played at http://www.technekai.com/box/index.html. On that same site, Karpinska also offers a theoretical outline of—what she calls—her spatial poem.

10. Sylvia Plath, "The Arrival of the Bee Box," in *The Penguin Book of American Verse*, ed. Geoffrey Moore (Harmondsworth: Penguin Books, 1987), 534–535.

11. Ibid., 534.

12. See www.yhchang.com/DAKOTA.html.

13. Jessica Pressman, "The Strategy of Digital Modernism: Young Hae Chang Heavy Industry's *Dakota*," in *Modern Fiction Studies* 2 (2008): 302–319.

14. Ibid., 304.

15. Robert Stam, *Literature Through Film: Realism, Magic, and the Art of Adaptation* (Oxford: Blackwell, 2005); Linda Hutcheon, *A Theory of Adaptation* (London and New York: Routledge, 2006); Robert Palmer, ed., *Twentieth-Century American Fiction on Screen* (Cambridge: Cambridge University Press, 2007).

16. Distant and recent innovative studies include Alan Spiegel, *Fiction and the Camera Eye: Visual Consciousness in Film and the Modern Novel* (Charlottesville: University Press of Virginia, 1976); Keith Cohen, *Film and Fiction: The Dynamics of Exchange* (New Haven: Yale University Press, 1979); Richard Pearce, *The Novel in Motion: An Approach to Modern Fiction* (Columbus: Ohio State University Press, 1983); R. Barton Palmer, "Eisensteinian Montage and Joyce's Ulysses: The Analogy Reconsidered," in *Mosaic* 18 (1985): 73–85; P. Adams Sitney, *Modernist Montage: The Obscurity of Vision in Cinema and Literature* (New York: Columbia University Press, 1990); Garrett Stewart, "Cinecriture: Modernism's Flicker Effect," in *New Literary History* 4 (1998): 727–768; Deborah Cartmell and Imelda Whelehan, *Adaptations* (New York: Routledge, 2000); Julian Murphet and Lydia Rainford, eds., *Literature and Visual Technologies: Writing after Cinema* (New York: Macmillan, 2003); Susan McCabe, *Cinematic Modernism. Modernist Poetry and Film* (Cambridge: Cambridge University Press, 2005); Deborah Cartmell and Imelda Whelehan, *The Cambridge Companion to Literature on Screen* (Cambridge: Cambridge University Press, 2007); David Trotter, "T. S. Eliot and Cinema," in *Modernism/Modernity* 2 (2006): 237–265; Laura Marcus, *The Tenth Muse: Writing about Cinema in the Modernist Period* (Oxford: Oxford University Press, 2007); Tom Conley, *Cartographic Cinema* (Minneapolis: University of Minnesota Press, 2007).

17. Katherine Hayles, *How We Became Posthuman: Virtual Bodies in Cybernetics, Literature, and Informatics* (Chicago: University of Chicago Press, 1999).

18. See ibid.; Donna Haraway, *Simians, Cyborgs, and Women: The Reinvention of Nature* (1990); Bernard Stiegler, *La technique et le temps 1: La faute d'Epiméthée* (1994), as well as his *La technique et le temps 2. La disorientation* (1996).

19. An example is Sven Birkerts's *The Gutenberg Elegies* (New York: Faber and Faber, 1995). A perceptive deconstruction of this position is given in Alison Murri's *The Enlightenment Cyborg: A History of Communications and Control in the Human Machine* (Toronto: University of Toronto Press, 2007). There is more on this in Chapters 3 and 4 of this volume.

20. Jacques Derrida, "Paper or Me, You Know . . . (New Speculations on a Luxury of the Poor)," in *Paper Machine*, trans. Rachel Bowlby (Stanford: Stanford University Press, 2005), 41–66, 42–43; Jacques Derrida, *Papier Machine* (Paris: Galilée, 2003).

21. Derrida, "Paper," 46.

22. Ibid.

23. Ibid., 47.

24. Ibid., 57.

25. Derrida, *Papier Machine*, 15.

26. Ibid.

27. Pierre Levy, *Cyberculture*, trans. Robert Bononno (Minneapolis: University of Minnesota Press, 2001), 96.

28. Ibid., 99.

29. Walter Benjamin, *Der Begriff der Kunstkritik in der deutschen Romantik* (Frankfurt: Suhrkamp, 1973).

30. Zines are handmade, nonprofessionally produced and distributed personal manuscript channels of self-expression (diaries, journals, personal reflections) that are distributed by regular mail or on street corners. They are typically read and commented upon within a zine community: regional, national, international, or global. See Stephen Duncombe, *Notes From the Underground: Zines and the Politics of Alternative Culture* (London: Verso, 1997); Anna Poletti, *Intimate Ephemera: Reading Young Lives in Australian Zine Culture* (Melbourne: Melbourne University Press, 2009).

31. Jason Nelson, *Another Emotion* (2001), www.heliozoa.com/resume/color.html.

32. Ibid.

33. In this I elaborate on Katherine Hayles's critical position as outlined in *How We Became Posthuman* and *My Mother Was a Computer: Digital Subjects and Literary Texts* (Chicago: University of Chicago Press, 2005).

34. Loss Pequeño Glazier, *Digital Poetics: Hypertext, Visual-Kinetic Text, and Writing in Programmable Media* (Tuscaloosa: University of Alabama, 2001). Other important titles on electronic poetry and electr(on)ic writing are Michael Heim, *Electric Language: A Philosophical Study of Word Processing* (Yale: Yale University Press, 1999); Scott Rettberg, ed., *State of the Arts: The Proceedings of the Electronic Literature Organization's 2002 State of the Arts Symposium* (Los Angeles: Electronic Literature Organization); Katherine Hayles, *Writing Machines* (Cambridge, Mass.: MIT Press, 2002); Noah Wardrip Fruin and Nick Montfort, eds., *The New Media Reader* (Cambridge, Mass.: MIT Press, 2003); Teemu Ikonen, "Moving Text in Avant-Garde Poetry: Towards a Poetics of Textual Motion," in *dichtung-digital.de, Newsletter* 4 (2003); Brian Kim Stefans, *Fashionable Noise: On Digital Poetics* (Berkeley: Atelos Press, 2003); *Ästhetik Digitaler Poesie/The Aesthetics of Digital Poetry*, ed. Friedrich W. Block, Christiane Heiback, and Karin Wenz (Berlin: Hatje Cantz Books, 2004); Jerome McGann, *Radiant Textuality: Literature after the World Wide Web* (London: Palgrave, 2004); *New Media Poetics: Contexts, Technotexts, and Theories*, ed. Adalaide Morris and Thomas Swiss (Cambridge, Mass.: MIT Press, 2006); Katherine Hayles, "Electronic Literature: What is It?" *The Electronic Literature Organization* 1 (2007), http://eliterature-.org/pad/elp.html (last visited January 2009); Chris Funkhouser, *Prehistoric Digital Poetry: An Archeology of Forms* (Tuscaloosa: University of Alabama Press, 2007); Katherine Hayles, *Electronic Literature: New Horizons for the Literary* (Notre Dame, Ind.: University of Notre Dame Press, 2008); Matthew

Kirschenbaum, *Mechanisms: New Media and the Forensic Imagination* (Cambridge, Mass.: MIT Press, 2008).

35. Katherine Hayles, "Intermediation: The Pursuit of a Vision," in *New Literary History* 1 (2007): 99–125.

36. See Lynn Keller, "Fields of Pattern-Bounded Unpredictability: Recent Palimptexts by Rosmarie Waldrop and Joan Retallack," in *Contemporary Literature* 2 (Summer 2001): 376–412.

1. MEDIUM, REFLEXIVITY, AND THE ECONOMY OF THE SELF
Samuel Weber

1. Immanuel Kant, *Kritik der reinen Vernunft*, ed. Raymund Schmidt (Hamburg: Felix Meiner, 1990 [1781, 1787]), B35–36.

2. In *Politics of Friendship*, Derrida describes the history of friendship as a series of "zigzags" in which the "breaks" do not simply disengage with the past: "This History does not consist in a linear succession or in a continuous accumulation of paradigms but in a series of breaks that cut across (font angle) their own trajectories in returning, in anther manner, back: all the changes, all the new configurations repeat, in the new day that they open, some archaic motif from the day before, without which they would not even find their language." Jacques Derrida, *Politiques de l'amitié* (Paris: Galilée, 1994), 249; *Politics of Friendship*, trans. George Collins (New York: Verso, 1997), 221, translation modified.

3. All quotations from Benjamin are from *Der Begriff der Kunstkritik in der deutschen Romantik* (Frankfurt: Suhrkamp, 1973).

4. Emphasis added.

5. See *Benjamin's –abilities* (Cambridge, Mass.: Harvard University Press, 2008).

6. Hölderlin, *Werke und Briefe*, ed. F. Beissner and Jochen Schmidt (Frankfurt: Insel, 1969), 2:672.

7. Exception made, of course, for Benjamin's early (1915) essay, "On Two Poems by Friedrich Hölderlin." See my discussion of that essay in *Targets of Opportunity* (New York: Fordham University Press, 2005) and *Benjamin's –abilities*.

8. Emphasis added.

9. See his short fragment "Capitalism as Religion."

2. ANALOG IN THE AGE OF DIGITAL REPRODUCTION:
AUDIOPHILIA, SEMI-AURA, AND THE CULTURAL MEMORY OF THE PHONOGRAPH
Anthony Curtis Adler

1. Other TV shows and films featuring the LP include *Almost Famous* (2000), the Austin Powers trilogy (1997, 1999, 2002), *Ghost World* (2000), *American Dreams* (NBC), and *The Simpsons* (Fox). As David Hayes notes, "Many of these works romanticize the interaction between the listener and his

or her music, emphasizing the care required in removing a record from its cardboard jacket, placing it on the turntable and selecting a desired track. By contrast, when CD consumption is depicted in popular texts—a comparatively rare occurrence—the focus is almost always placed on sound rather than action, as if the disc magically cued itself." David Hayes, "'Take Those Old Records off the Shelf': Youth and Music Consumption in the Postmodern Age," *Popular Music and Society* 29, no. 1 (2006): 55.

2. Such claims go back to Edison and E. R. Finemore Johnson's report on the phonograph in *Scientific American*. See Colin Symes, *Setting the Record Straight: A Material History of Classical Recording* (Middletown, Conn.: Wesleyan University Press, 2004), 11–13.

3. For discussions of the role of nostalgia in the resurgence of vinyl, see Hayes, "'Take Those Old Records off the Shelf,'" 53–56.

4. See ibid.; Steven Threndyle, "The Vinyl Word in Music," *Canadian Business* 13 (1998); Chris Morris, "Audiophile Labels Put a New Spin on Vinyl," *Billboard* (August 17, 2002): 1–3; Ishinabe Hitomi, "Vinyl Turns the Tables on the Compact Disc," *Look Japan* (November 1997): 32–33.

5. The exchange between the editor of the audiophile magazine *Absolute Sound* and Larry Klein of *Electronics Now* gives a good sense for the character of these controversies. See Larry Klein, "Audiophile Silliness: Absolute Sounds Off," *Electronics Now* (February 1994): 80–81; see also Eric Rawson, "Perfect Listening: Audiophilia, Ambiguity, and the Reduction of the Arbitrary," *Journal of American Culture* 29, no. 2 (2006): 204.

6. For an accessible discussion of noise, see Rawson, "Perfect Listening," 210.

7. Ibid., 203.

8. Mark Katz, *Capturing Sound: How Technology Has Changed Music* (Berkeley: University of California Press, 2004), 5.

9. Walter Benjamin, "Das Kunstwerk im Zeitalter seiner technischen Reproduzierbarkeit (Dritte Fassung)," in *Gesammelte Schriften*, ed. Rolf Tiedemann and Hermann Schweppenhäuser (Frankfurt: Suhrkamp, 1991).

10. See Symes, *Setting the Record Straight*.

11. Rawson provides a vivid description of the "ideal" listening room. Ibid., 206.

12. For the importance of the distinction between analysis and synthetic for the early Romantic thought of Schlegel and Novalis, see Azade Seyhan, *Representation and Its Discontents: The Critical Legacy of German Romanticism* (Berkeley: University of California Press, 1992).

3. WHAT IF FOUCAULT HAD HAD A BLOG?
Joanna Zylinska

1. See Paul Rabinow's introduction to Michel Foucault, *Ethics: Subjectivity and Truth* (London: Allen Lane, 1997), xxv–xxvii.

2. Michel Foucault, *The Hermeneutics of the Subject: Lectures at the Collège de France, 1981–82*, ed. Frederic Gros and Francois Ewald (Basingstoke: Palgrave Macmillan, 2005), 36.

3. Ibid., 8.

4. Foucault, *Ethics*, 269–271.

5. Foucault, *Hermeneutics of the Subject*, 84.

6. Foucault, *Ethics*, 131.

7. Ibid., 163.

8. Ibid., 225.

9. Ibid., 225, 232.

10. As Foucault puts it, "Care of the self becomes coextensive with life." *Hermeneutics of the Subject*, 86.

11. Foucault, *Ethics*, 260.

12. Ibid., 235.

13. Foucault, *Hermeneutics of the Subject*, 125–126.

14. Ibid., 107–108.

15. Ibid., 227.

16. Gary Hall, *Digitize This Book! The Politics of New Media, or Why We Need Open Access Now* (Minneapolis: University of Minnesota Press, 2008).

17. Kris R. Cohen, "A Welcome for Blogs," *Continuum: Journal for Media & Culture Studies* 2 (2006): 164.

18. Academic blogs have also been described as "experiments in digital scholarship," or a testing ground for research in progress. See Craig Saper, "Blogademia," *Reconstruction* 6, no. 4 (2006), http://reconstruction.eserver .org/064/saper.shtml.

19. Jacques Derrida, "'There Is No *One* Narcissism' (Autobiophotographies)." In *Points . . . Interviews, 1974–1994*, ed. Elisabeth Weber (Stanford: Stanford University Press, 1995), 199.

20. Ibid.

21. See Emanuel Levinas, *Totality and Infinity: An Essay on Exteriority*, trans. Alphonso Lingis (Pittsburgh: Duquesne University Press, 1969); "Ethics as First Philosophy," in *The Levinas Reader*, ed. Sean Hand (Oxford: Blackwell, 1989).

22. Ewa Plownoska Ziarek, *An Ethics of Dissensus: Postmodernity, Feminism, and the Politics of Radical Democracy* (Stanford, Calif.: Stanford University Press, 2001), 39.

23. "Because it bears a relation to the outside, which is the experience of the limit of social regulation and thus of the historical constitution of the subject, the experimental praxis cannot be simply reduced to a goal-oriented activity. On the contrary, the outcome of such an experimental praxis aiming to surpass the historical limits of bodies, language and sexuality cannot be predicted in advance because it opens up a relation to a future that can [no] longer be thought on the basis of the present. . . . Foucault's invention of the improbable stresses the radical futural dimension of praxis beyond the anticipation of the subject." Ibid., 41.

24. Saper, "Blogademia," emphasis added.

25. Foucault, *Ethics*, 211.

26. Foucault, *Hermeneutics of the Subject*, 120.

27. The American Internet entrepreneur Alan Levy is rather explicit about the status quo: "The blogosphere is a world of haves and have-nots. Frankly,

about two bloggers out of every million have meaningful traffic and readership." Quoted in Hall, *Digitize This Book!*, 34.

28. Foucault, *Ethics*, 272.

29. Mark Poster, *Information Please: Culture and Politics in the Age of Digital Machines* (Durham, N.C.: Duke University Press, 2006), 38.

30. See Bernard Stiegler, *Technics and Time, 1: The Fault of Epimetheus*, trans. Richard Beardsworth and George Collins (Stanford, Calif.: Stanford University Press, 1998). I am indebted to Federica Frabetti for her discussion of the relationship between memory and technology in Stiegler.

31. Bernard Stiegler, "Technics of Decision: An Interview with Peter Hallward," trans. Sean Gaston, *Angelaki* 8, no. 2: 161.

32. Quoted in Ziarek, *An Ethics of Dissensus*, 41.

4. POSTHUMAN SELVES, ASSEMBLED TEXTUALITIES: REMEDIATED PRINT IN THE DIGITAL AGE
Kiene Brillenburg Wurth

1. See, for example, the work of Donna Haraway, Bernard Stiegler, Brian Massumi, and Katherine Hayles.

2. Allison Muri, "Virtually Human: The Electronic Page, the Archived Body, and Human Identity," in *The Future of the Page*, ed. Peter Stoicheff and Andrew Taylor (Toronto: University of Toronto Press, 2004), 251.

3. The term "rematerialization" is Alan Golding's, who defines it as "a shift in material medium or environment [e.g., paper page to screen] that raises a new set of aesthetic and theoretical questions about texts." Alan Golding, "Language Writing, Digital Poetics, and Transitional Materialities," in *New Media Poetics: Contexts, Technotexts, and Theories*, ed. Adelaide Morris and Thomas Swiss (Cambridge, Mass.: MIT Press, 2006), 252.

4. John Locke, *Essay Concerning Human Understanding*, ed. Kenneth P. Wrinkler (Indianapolis: Hackett, 1996).

5. David Hume, *An Enquiry Concerning Human Understanding*, ed. Peter McMillan (New York: Oxford University Press, 2008).

6. Philip Dick's *Ubik* may be farther down this intertextual line.

7. Because "graphic" novel is a label usually reserved for "serious" comic books, "graphical" would probably be more accurate here. Yet "graphic" conveys the playfulness of visual novels that is also present in *Woman's World* as a composite of magazine fragments.

8. Graham Rawle, *Woman's World: A Graphic Novel* (London: Atlantic Books, 2005), 225.

9. Tristan Tzara, "Dada Manifesto of Feeble Love and Bitter Love," in *The Dada Painters and Poets*, ed. Robert Motherwell (Cambridge, Mass.: Harvard University Press, 2007), 86–96, 92.

10. Telling, in this respect, are the numerous cut-up machines on the net inspired by the Gryson and Burroughs methods; see http://languageisavirus.com/cutupmachine.html and http://www.lazaruscorporation.co.uk/v4/cutup (last visited October 2010).

11. David Wills, *Prosthesis* (Stanford: Stanford University Press, 1995), 133.

12. Steven Hall, *The Raw Shark Texts* (Edinburgh: Canongate, 2007), 81.

13. Ibid., 64.

14. Ibid.

15. Rawle, *Woman's World*, 439.

16. Katherine Hayles, "Saving the Subject: Remediation in *House of Leaves*," *American Literature* 4 (2002): 781.

17. Mark Poster, *The Mode of Information: Poststructuralism and Social Context* (Cambridge: Polity Press, 1990), 111.

18. And is it not obvious that the materiality of paper is just as subject to change as electronic materiality? When my copy of *The Raw Shark Texts* accidentally fell—if appropriately—into the bathtub, it changed irreversibly. Along with Kirschenbaum and others, Golding has convincingly argued against making an easy distinction between "stable" paper-based print and "dynamic" electronic textuality. His strategy is not to oppose old and new technologies and materialities of inscription, but to place such "different materialities on a spectrum." Golding, "Language Writing," 277.

19. Katherine Hayles, *How We Became Posthuman: Virtual Bodies in Cybernetics, Literature, and Informatics* (Chicago: University of Chicago Press, 1999), 31.

20. Joseph Tabbi, "The Processual Page: Materiality and Consciousness in Print and Hypertext," in *The Future of the Page*, ed. Peter Stoicheff and Andrew Taylor (Toronto: University of Toronto Press, 2004), 207.

21. Un-spaces are unused spaces in the novel, just as they are in Palahniuk's *Fight Club*.

22. Sven Birkerts, "Into the Electronic Millennium," *Boston Review*, October 1991.

23. Katherine Hayles, *My Mother Was a Computer* (Chicago: University of Chicago Press, 2005), 247.

24. Compare this polyvocality to Juliet Davis's Web-based flash composition *Pieces of Herself*, which likewise configures the female body (or, more precisely, has the user/viewer make this configuration) as an intersection of inside and outside, private and public sphere. Embodiment only becomes possible through the introjection of the Other—an infolding of the "outside."

25. Often to humorous effect—as in the scene when Norma is assaulted by Hands: "I glanced at him drowsily through half-closed lashes and in one stark, mood-changing moment caught a horrifying glimpse of what he had been fiddling with. Man's sausage meat—stiff with outrage and frustration"—and Hands responds: "Barbie, will you kiss it better?" (221).

26. Rawle, *Woman's World*, 6.

27. Although in *The End of Mr. Y* this artificial intervention amounts to an old potion, recalling the days of Jekyll and Hyde rather than foretelling the days of human digitization, like *The Raw Shark Texts*, *The End of Mr. Y* invokes digital modes of mind extension without invoking the technology by describing mental migration through meditation or a "willing oneself" into an other, virtual habitable space. This points, in turn, to American nineteenth-century identity theft novels (*Sheppard Lee*, for instance) that likewise revolve around an

interminable consciousness that, like Mycroft Ward in *The Raw Shark Texts*, jumps from, and feeds on, one mind after another.

28. Rawle, *Woman's World*, 438.

29. Matthew Kirschenbaum argues likewise in his online riposte "Materiality and Matter and Stuff: What Electronic Textualities Are Made Of": "The opposition between fixed, reliable printed texts, on the one hand, and fluid and dynamic electronic texts, on the other—an opposition encouraged by the putative immateriality of digital data storage—is patently false, yet it has become a truism in the nascent field of electronic textual theory. . . . Ask a *Beowulf* scholar whether printed matter is really 'durable' or 'orderly' (the sole surviving manuscript of the poem was thrown singed and smoldering from a window during a library fire in the early eighteenth century, rendering portions of it illegible) or a Wordsworthean whether the texts of *The Prelude* (there are four of them, a two-book, a five-book, a thirteen-book, and a fourteen-book version) are 'static' and exhibit 'unity.' Those are *not* special cases (pedantic exceptions to some normative textual condition), and the tendency to elicit what is 'new' about new media by contrasting its radical mutability with the supposed material solidity of older textual forms is a misplaced gesture, symptomatic of the general extent to which textual studies and digital studies have failed to communicate."

30. "Electracy" is a term coined by Gregory Ulmer to replace "literacy" as a frame for thought that comes after literacy and the linear logic of the alphabet. While electracy is in some ways rooted in video, it is also specifically tied to the apparatus of digital writing. Ulmer argues that we have come to think and reason differently with new media, and that "electracy" captures this change from print to screen-based writing, reading, and research. One particular difference between literacy and electracy is that the boundary between the personal and the communal or social is lost in new modes of sharing and communicating.

5. INTERMEDIATION: THE PURSUIT OF A VISION
N. *Katherine Hayles*

1. Mark Danielewski, *House of Leaves* (New York: Doubleday, 2000); Jonathan Safran Foer, *Extremely Loud and Incredibly Close* (New York: Houghton Mifflin, 2005); Salvador Plascencia, *The People of Paper* (San Francisco: McSweeney's, 2005).

2. The field of electronic literature has recently been attracting much excellent criticism attentive to the media specificity of computational media. These include David Ciccoricco, *Reading Network Fiction* (Tuscaloosa: University of Alabama Press, 2008); Mark B. N. Hansen, *New Philosophy for New Media* (Cambridge, Mass.: MIT Press, 2004); Matthew Kirschenbaum, *Mechanisms: New Media and Forensic Textuality* (Cambridge, Mass.: MIT Press, forthcoming); Alan Liu, *The Laws of Cool: Knowledge Work and the Culture of Information* (Chicago: University of Chicago Press, 2004); Adalaide Morris and Thomas Swiss, eds., *New Media Poetics: Contexts, Technotexts, and Theories* (Cambridge, Mass.: MIT Press, 2006); Jessica Pressman, "Digital Modernism: Making It New in New Media," Ph.D. diss., University of California, Los

Angeles, 2007; and Marie-Laure Ryan, *Avatars of Story* (Minneapolis: University of Minnesota Press, 2006).

3. Stephen Wolfram, *A New Kind of Science* (New York: Wolfram Media, 2002).

4. Nicholas Gessler, "Evolving Artificial Cultural Things-That-Think and Work by Dynamical Hierarchical Synthesis," www.sscnet.ucla.edu/geog/gessler/cv-pubs/03naacsos.pdf.

5. Harold J. Morowitz, *The Emergence of Everything: How the World Became Complex* (New York: Oxford University Press, 2002).

6. "Generation M: Media in the Lives of 8–18 Year-Olds," Kaiser Family Foundation, www.kff.org/entmedia/entmedia030905pkg.cfm.

7. See, for example, André Leroi-Gourhan, *Gesture and Speech* (Cambridge, Mass.: MIT Press, 1993).

8. This argument has been published in various forms; see, for example, John R. Searle, "Is the Brain's Mind a Computer Program?," *Scientific American*, January 1990, 26–31.

9. Douglas Hofstadter, *Fluid Concepts and Creative Analogies: Computer Models of the Fundamental Mechanisms of Thought* (New York: Basic Books, 1995).

10. For a description of the Eliza program, see Joseph Weizenbaum, *Computer Power and Human Reason: From Judgment to Calculation* (New York: Freeman, 1976).

11. Jorge Luis Borges, "The Book of Sand," in *Collected Fictions*, trans. Andrew Hurley (New York: Penguin Books, 1999), 480–483.

12. It is no accident, then, that several electronic works inspired by "The Book of Sand" have been created; see, for example, Maximus Clarke for an interactive game based on Borges's work, "The Book of Sand: A Hypertext/Puzzle," http://artificeeterrnity.com/bookofsand; and Giselle Beiguelman, "the book after the book/o livro depois do livro," www.desvirtual.com/giselle.

13. See, for example, Loss Pequeño Glazier, *White-Faced Bromeliads on 20 Hectares*, http://epc.buffalo.edu/authors/glazier/java/costal1/00.html, and Emily Short, *Galatea*, http://www.mindspring.com/~emshort/galatea.htm. Both works can also be found in the *Electronic Literature Collection*, vol. 1, ed. N. Katherine Hayles, Nick Montfort, Scott Rettberg, and Stephanie Strickland, http://collection.eliterature.org.

14. N. Katherine Hayles, *My Mother Was a Computer: Digital Subjects and Literary Texts* (Chicago: University of Chicago Press, 2005).

15. Michael Joyce, *afternoon, a story* (Watertown, Mass.: Eastgate Systems, 1990).

16. Joyce, *Twelve Blue* (1991), www.eastgate.com/TwelveBlue. Although *afternoon, a story* has a publication date from Eastgate of 1990, Joyce was circulating copies of it at conferences as early as 1987. It is reasonable to assume, then, that something like four years separates the composition of the two works. Matthew Kirschenbaum in "Save As: Michael Joyce's *afternoons*," in *Mechanisms*, gives a detailed account of the different versions.

17. Particularly influential is Jane Yellowlees Douglas, "'How Do I Stop This Thing?': Closure and Indeterminacy in Interactive Narratives," in *Hyper/*

Text/Theory, ed. George P. Landow (Baltimore: Johns Hopkins University Press, 1994), 159–188; Jay David Bolter, *Writing Space: The Computer, Hypertext, and the History of Writing* (Hillsdale, N.J.: Erlbaum Associates, 1991), 123–28; and Jill Walker, "Piecing together and tearing apart: finding the story in afternoon," ACM Hypertext Conference (1999), http://jilltxt.net/txt/afternoon.html.

18. Robert Coover, "The Elevator" and "The Babysitter," in *Pricksongs and Descants: Fictions* (New York: Grove Press, 2000), 125–137, 206–239.

19. Noah Wardrip-Fruin, "Playable Media and Textual Instruments," in *dichtung-digital* (2005), www.brown.edu/Research/dichtung-digital/2005/1/Wardrip-Fruin, has an eloquent exposition of what it implies to consider a digital work as an instrument that can be played rather than simply a text to read; arguments such as his have bestowed added resonance on "player" as the term of choice for one who interacts with a digital work that has playable characteristics.

20. "Riddle," 8_4. The lexias of *Twelve Blue* are named, but occasionally two different lexias share the same name. Confusion can be avoided by also citing the numbers displayed in the URL, which indicate the thread and bar numbers, in that order, as indicated in the above citation (hereafter cited in text by lexia, thread, and bar number when appropriate).

21. William H. Gass, *On Being Blue: A Philosophical Inquiry* (Boston: David R. Godine, 1991), 7.

22. Vannevar Bush, "As We May Think," *Atlantic Monthly*, July 1945, 101–108.

23. "Attack" here is an allusion to Marie-Laure Ryan's aggressive reading of *Twelve Blue* in *Narrative as Virtual Reality: Immersion and Interactivity in Literature and Electronic Media* (Baltimore: Johns Hopkins University Press, 2003), where she comments, "The attitude with which I initially attacked the text—and I mean *attack* to be taken in its full force—had much in common with the frame of mind of the player of a computer game or the reader of a mystery novel. I was determined to 'beat the text' by figuring out what the system of links and the multiple ambiguities were designed to hide from me" (238). Her "quest for coherence" (226) and signature critical strategy of classifying texts through typologies are clearly at odds with the text's aesthetic, so that she finds the text's effect "is that of an amnesiac mind that desperately tries to grasp some chains of association but cannot hold on to them long enough to recapture a coherent picture of the past" (229), which is about as far from my own sense of the text as one could get. Nevertheless, she is too fine (and determined) a reader not to unearth many of the text's connections, and her reading is accurate and nuanced as far as it goes.

24. Anthony Enns, "Don't Believe the Hype: Rereading Michael Joyce's *afternoon* and *Twelve Blue*," *Currents in Electronic Literacy* (Fall 2001), www-.cwrl.utexas.edu/currents/fall01/enns/enns.html; Frank Kermode, *The Sense of an Ending* (New York: Oxford University Press, 1968).

25. Gregory L. Ulmer, "A Response to *Twelve Blue* by Michael Joyce," *Postmodern Culture* 5, no. 1 (1997), http://muse.jhu.edu/journals/postmodern_culture/toc/pmc8.1.html.

26. Maria Mencia, "Methodology," a brief explanation of the inspiration for her doctoral dissertation, "From Visual Poetry to Digital Art: Image-Sound-Text, convergent media and the development of new media languages" (2003), www.m.mencia.freeuk.com/Methodology.html.

27. Maria Mencia, "Worthy Mouths" (n.d.), www.m.mencia.freeuk.com/WorthyMouths.swf.

28. Maria Mencia, "Audible Writing Experiments" (2004), www.m.mencia.freeuk.com/AWE.html.

29. Maria Mencia, "Things come and go . . ." (1999), documentation at www.m.mencia.freeuk.com/video2.html.

30. Ibid.

31. Maria Mencia, "Birds Singing Other Birds' Songs," Flash version in *Electronic Literature Collection*, vol. 1, ed. Hayles and others; documentation of the video version (2001) at www.m.mencia.freeuk.com/birds.html.

32. Lori Emerson, in "Numbered Space and Topographic Writing," *Leonardo Electronic Almanac* 14, nos. 5–6 (2006), http://leoalmanac.org/journal/Vol_14/lea_v14_no5-06/Lemerson.asp, engages similar questions to the ones articulated here, asking "at what point . . . does digital poetry cross a threshold and break away from book-bound concerns, thereby also breaking away from the ways in which we normally account for texts?" (2). She rightly cautions that print poetry has also been concerned with movement, urging us not to extrapolate to digital poetry as the simple fulfillment of its teleology. To make the point, she instances Mencia's *Birds Singing Other Birds' Songs*; she finds that it "does not go beyond a transposition of book-bound concerns . . . neither does it demonstrate what the [digital] medium allows." I suggest that this reading, with its emphasis on spatiality, does not fully take into account the sophisticated translation processes discussed above and thus misses the play between different forms of cognition.

33. Judd Morrissey, *The Jew's Daughter*, www.thejewsdaughter.com (hereafter cited in text as *JD*). The credits specify that the work was "programmed and crafted by the author," Judd Morrissey, and that the "mechanics of reconfiguration [were] designed in collaboration with Lori Talley."

34. Matthew Mirapaul, "Pushing Hypertext in New Directions," *New York Times*, July 27, 2000.

35. James Joyce, *Ulysses* (New York: Vintage, 1990), 666–722. Pressman analyzes the relation between *Ulysses* and *The Jew's Daughter* in "*The Jew's Daughter*: Remediating, Remembering, and Rereading," in *Digital Modernism*, 205–264. Ciccoricco also has a fine detailed reading of the work, including its relation to *Ulysses*, in "Mythology Proceeding: Morrissey's *The Jew's Daughter*," in *Reading Network Fiction*.

36. Thomas Nagel, in *The View from Nowhere* (New York: Oxford University Press, 1989), popularized the phrase as representative of scientific objectivism, a position that was subsequently heavily criticized in science studies, for example, by Donna Haraway in "Situated Knowledge: The Science Question in Feminism as a Site of Discourse on the Privilege of Partial Perspective," *Feminist Studies* 14, no. 3 (1988): 575–599.

37. Daniel C. Dennett, *Consciousness Explained* (New York: Little, Brown, 1991).

38. Dennett comments that "as long as your *homunculi* [the neural processes that he likens to 'hordes of demons'] are more stupid and ignorant than the intelligent agent they compose, the nesting of homunculi within homunculi can be finite, bottoming out, eventually, with agents so unimpressive that they can be replaced by machines." Dennett, "Are We Explaining Consciousness Yet?" *Cognition* 79 (2001): 225.

39. Lutz Hamel, Judd Morrissey, and Lori Talley, "Automatic Narrative Evolution: A White Paper," www.errorengine.org/ane-white-paper.pdf.

40. Evolutionary coadaptation is also the point for a fantastic interactive book described in Neal Stephenson's *The Diamond Age: Or, a Young Lady's Illustrated Primer* (New York: Bantam, 1996), 84–86. The *Primer* has the ability to sense the environment and Nell's reaction, changing its pages and stories to fit her situation. It serves as her tutor, reengineering her neural responses in definitive ways as she matures. For example, in her first encounter with the *Primer*, Nell corrects her name, in response to which "a tiny disturbance propagated through the grid of letters on the facing page" (84), a description that could well be applied to *The Jew's Daughter* during a mouseover.

41. Intermediation is, of course, not the only theoretical framework available. Influential contributions include: from film studies, Lev Manovich's "five principles of New Media" in *The Language of New Media* (Cambridge, Mass.: MIT Press, 2002); from game studies, Espen Aarseth's functionalist cybertheory as "textology" in *Cybertext: Perspectives on Ergodic Literature* (Baltimore: Johns Hopkins University Press, 1997); from media theory, Friedrich A. Kittler's *Discourse Networks 1800/1900*, trans. Michael Matteer, with Chris Cullens (Stanford, Calif.: Stanford University Press, 1992) and *Gramophone, Film, Typewriter*, trans. Geoffrey Winthrop-Young and Michael Wutz (Stanford, Calif.: Stanford University Press, 1999); and from phenomenology/embodiment theory, Mark B. N. Hansen's *New Philosophy for New Media* (Cambridge, Mass.: MIT Press, 2006).

42. A strong example is provided by Markku Eskelinen, using Espen Aarseth's cybertext to rethink narratology, "Six Problems in Search of a Solution: The Challenge of Cybertext Theory and Ludology to Literary Theory," in *dichtung-digital* (2004), www.dichtung-digital.com/2004.3/Eskelinen/index.htm.

43. *Vectors: Journal of Culture and Technology in a Dynamic Vernacular*, http://vectors.iml.annenberg.edu/.

44. Bob Stein, Institute for the Future of the Book, www.annenberg.edu/projects/project.php?id=84.

6. NET.ART: DYSFUNCTIONALITY AND SELF-REFLEXIVITY
Marie-Laure Ryan

1. See Douglas Hofstadter, *I Am a Strange Loop* (New York: Basic Books, 2007).

2. See, e.g., Marc Hauser, Noam Chomsky, and Tecumseh Fitch, "The Faculty of Language: What It Is, Who Has It, and How Did It Evolve?" *Science* 298 (2002): 1569–1571.

3. Lewis Carroll, *Sylvie and Bruno: The Complete Illustrated Works of Lewis Carroll*, ed. Edward Guillaro (New York: Avenel Books, 1983), 726.

7. MOVING (THE) TEXT: FROM PRINT TO DIGITAL
Katalin Sándor

1. András Müllner, "A hipertextuális közlés anomáliái és a *Megbocsátás* hipertextualizálásának kérdése," *Literatura* (2003): 84.

2. David J. Bolter, "Ekphrasis, Virtual Reality and the Future of Writing," in *The Future of the Book*, ed. Geoffrey Nunberg, 253–272 (Berkeley: University of California Press, 1996).

3. J. Espen Aarseth, "Nem-linearitás és irodalomelmélet," *Helikon* (2004): 314.

4. Ibid., 325.

5. Péter Józsa, "Irodalom a digitális közegben," http://mek.oszk.hu/02300/02313/html (last accessed June 14, 2007).

6. Müllner, "A hipertextuális közlés anomáliái és a *Megbocsátás* hipertextualizálásának kérdése," 84.

7. Robert Simanowski, "Concrete Poetry in Digital Media: Its Predecessors, Its Presence and Its Future," *Dichtung Digital* 33, no. 3 (2004), www.dichtung-digital.org/2004/3-Simanowski.htm (last accessed April 17, 2007).

8. W. Friedrich Block, "Digital Poetics, or On the Evolution of Experimental Media Poetry," www.netzliteratur.net/block/poetics.html (last accessed January 3, 2008).

9. See Christian Moraru, "Topos/Typos/Tropos: Visual Strategies and the Mapping of Space in Charles Olson's Poetry," *Word & Image: A Journal of Verbal/Visual Enquiry* 14, no. 3 (1998): 257.

10. See, for example, Simanowski, "Concrete Poetry in Digital Media."

11. Shuen-shing Lee, "Explorations of Ergodic Literature: The Interlaced Poetics of Representation and Simulation," *Dichtung Digital* 21, no. 1, www.dichtung-digital.com/2002/05-26-Lee.htm (last accessed June 4, 2007).

12. Robert Simanowski, "Fighting/Dancing Words: Jim Andrews' Kinetic, Concrete Audiovisual Poetry," *Dichtung Digital* 21, no. 1 (2002), www.dichtung-digital.org/2002/01-10-Cramer.htm (last accessed May 8, 2007).

13. Friedrich Kittler, *Aufschreibesysteme 1800–1900* (Munich: Wilhelm Fink, 1995), 244.

14. András Müllner "A hipertext elmélete mint az interaktivitás technológiai ideológiája," in *A császár új ruhája: Esszék a könyv és a hipertext kapcsolatáról, valamint más médiumokról* (Budapest: Jószöveg Könyvek, 2007), 112.

15. Quoted in John Cayley, "Inner Workings: Code and Representations of Interiority in New Media Poetics," *Dichtung Digital* 29, no. 3 (2003), www.dichtung-digital.org/2003/3-cayley.htm (last accessed June 6, 2007).

16. Bolter, "Ekphrasis, Virtual Reality and the Future of Writing," 353.

17. Joachim Paech, "Artwork—Text—Medium. Steps en Route to Intermediality" (2000), www.uni-konstanz.de/FuF/Philo/LitWiss/Me-dienWiss/Texte/interm.html (last accessed December 15, 2004).

18. Simanowski, "Concrete Poetry in Digital Media."

8. TECHNOLOGY MADE LEGIBLE: SOFTWARE AS A FORM OF
WRITING IN SOFTWARE ENGINEERING
Federica Frabetti

1. Katherine Hayles, *My Mother Was a Computer: Digital Subjects and Literary Texts* (Chicago: University of Chicago Press), 48.

2. Paul DuGay et al., eds., *Doing Cultural Studies: The Story of the Sony Walkman* (London: Sage/Open University, 1997), 3.

3. Ibid., 10.

4. Adrien Mackenzie, "The Problem of Computer Code: Leviathan or Common Power?" (2003). Available at http://www.lancs.ac.uk/staff/mackenza/ papers/code-leviathan.pdf (last accessed on September 16, 2008).

5. Matthew Fuller, *Behind the Blip: Essays on the Culture of Software* (New York: Autonomedia, 2003), 18.

6. Elaine Scarry, *Resisting Representation* (Oxford: Oxford University Press, 1994).

7. Fuller, *Behind the Blip*, 34 n. 19.

8. See Frederick Brooks, "No Silver Bullet: Essence and Accidents of Software Engineering," *IEEE Computer* 20 (1987): 10–19; S. Watts Humphrey, *Managing the Software Process* (Harlow: Addison-Wesley, 1989).

9. Ian Sommerville, *Software Engineering* (Harlow, UK: Addison-Wesley, 1995), 4.

10. Software Engineering has been evolving through the decades in relation to the emergence of new programming technologies such as object orientation. The programmer's practices of writing have changed according to the advent of new design methodologies, such as Agile Programming or even free software and open source.

11. Peter Naur and Brian Randell, *Software Engineering: Report on a Conference Sponsored by the NATO Science Committee, Garmisch, Germany, 7th to 11th October 1968* (Brussels: NATO Scientific Affairs Division, 1969).

12. Jacques Derrida, "Structure, Sign, and Play in the Discourse of the Human Sciences," in Jacques Derrida, *Writing and Difference*, trans. Alan Bass (London: Routledge, 1980).

13. Jacques Derrida, "Letter to a Japanese Friend," in *Derrida and Différance*, ed. Robert Bernasconi and David Wood (Warwick: Parousia Press, 1985), 1–5. In "Structure, Sign, and Play in the Discourse of the Human Sciences," while reminding us that his concept of deconstruction was developed in dialogue with structuralist thought, Derrida speaks of "structure" rather than of conceptual systems or systems of thought. It is not possible to discuss this point in depth here, but I would like to point out how, in the context of that essay, "structure" hints at as complex a formation as, for instance, the ensemble of concepts underlying social sciences, or even the whole of Western philosophy.

14. I am making an assumption here—namely, that software is a conceptual system as much as it is a form of writing and a material object. In fact, the investigation of these multiple modes of existence of software is precisely what is at stake in my approach. In the context of the present chapter, and for the sake of clarity, I am concentrating on the effects of a deconstructive reading of a "structure" understood in quite an abstract sense.

15. According to Derrida, deconstruction is not a methodology, in the sense that it is not a set of immutable rules that can be applied to any object of analysis—because the very concepts of "rule," of "object," and of "subject" of analysis themselves belong to a conceptual system (broadly speaking, they belong to the Western tradition of thought), and therefore they are subject to deconstruction too. As a result, "deconstruction" is something that "happens" within a conceptual system, rather than a methodology. It can be said that any conceptual system is always in deconstruction, because it unavoidably reaches a point where it unties or disassembles its own presuppositions. On the other hand, since it is perfectly possible to remain oblivious to the permanent occurrence of deconstruction, there is a need for us to actively "perform" it, that is, to make its permanent occurrence visible. In this sense, deconstruction is also a productive, creative process.

16. Hayles, *My Mother*, 6.

17. Ibid., 15.

18. Jacques Derrida, *Of Grammatology*, trans. Gayatri Chakravorty Spivak (Baltimore: Johns Hopkins University Press, 1976); Fuller, *Behind the Blip*; Ellen Ullman, *Close to the Machine: Technophilia and Its Discontents* (San Francisco: City Lights Books, 1997); Ferdinand de Saussure, *Course in General Linguistics*, trans. Roy Harris (Peru, Ill.: Open Course, 1988).

19. Richard Beardsworth, *Derrida and the Political* (New York: Routledge, 1996) 7.

20. Ibid.

21. Ibid.

22. Ibid., 8.

23. Naur and Randell, *Software Engineering*, 21.

24. Ibid., 19.

25. Ibid., 31.

26. Gary Hall, *Culture in Bits: The Monstrous Future of Theory* (New York: Continuum, 2002), 111.

27. Jacques Derrida, *Archive Fever: A Freudian Impression*, trans. Eric Prenowitz (Chicago: University of Chicago Press, 1996).

28. Hall, *Culture in Bits*, 128.

29. Ibid., 115. For the scope of the present chapter, I accept Hall's term "cultural studies" as roughly equivalent to what I have named here "media and cultural studies," since this passage refers to a constitutive debate around the field's conceptual framework.

9. CINEMA AS A DIGEST OF LITERATURE: A CURE FOR ADAPTATION FEVER
Peter Verstraten

1. See also Angela Dalle Vacche, "Introduction: Unexplored Connections in a New Territory," in *The Visual Turn: Classical Film Theory and Art History*, ed. Angela Dalle Vacche (New Brunswick, N.J.: Rutgers University Press, 2003), 17. She relates Canudo's definition to Gotthold Lessing's famous essay "Laöcoon" (1766), on the borders between poetry and painting.

2. Tom Gunning, *D. W. Griffith and the Origins of American Narrative Film: The Early Years at Biograph* (Urbana: University of Illinois Press, 1994), 42.

3. Seymour Chatman, "What Novels Can Do That Films Can't (and Vice Versa)," *Critical Inquiry* 7 (1980): 130.

4. André Gaudreault, "Film, Narrative, Narration: The Cinema of the Lumière Brothers," in *Early Cinema: Space, Frame, Narrative*, ed. Thomas Elsaesser (London: BFI, 1990), 71.

5. Jan Simons, "Film en literatuur," *Tijdschrift voor Literatuurwetenschap* 2 (1997): 148.

6. See, for an elaboration of these arguments, Robert Stam, "Introduction: The Theory and Practice of Adaptation," in *Literature and Film: A Guide to the Theory and Practice of Film Adaptation*, ed. Robert Stam and Alessandra Raengo (Oxford: Blackwell, 2005), 3–8.

7. Donald is a totally fictive character, although he is mentioned in the credits as cowriter with his "brother" Charlie.

8. I derive the notion of adaptation fever from Désirée Jung, who in turn has alluded to Derrida's book title *Mal d'archive*, that is, "archive fever." The word "fever" is so very appropriate, since Orlean titled her original article in *The New Yorker* "Orchid Fever."

9. Cited in François Truffaut, *Hitchcock* (New York: Simon and Schuster, 1984), 72.

10. See Ginette Vincendeau, "Introduction," in *Film/Literature/Heritage: A Sight and Sound Reader*, ed. Ginette Vincendeau (London: BFI, 2001), xii.

11. See Truffaut, *Hitchcock*, 49.

12. André Bazin, *What Is Cinema?* (Berkeley: University of California Press, 1971), 70, 72.

13. Ibid., 69–74.

14. See Slavoj Žižek, *The Fright of Real Tears: Krzystof Kieslowski Between Theory and Post-theory* (London: BFI, 2001), 145–148.

10. CINEMATOGRAPHY AS A LITERARY CONCEPT IN THE (POST)MODERN AGE: PIRANDELLO TO PYNCHON
Lovorka Gruic and Kiene Brillenburg Wurth

1. For Eisenstein, montage epitomized the art of cinema. See for this Sergei M. Eisenstein, *Film Form: Essays in Film Theory*, ed. and trans. Jay Leyda (London: Dobson, 1951).

2. Ibid., 204–205; quoted in Laura Marcus, *The Tenth Muse: Writing about Cinema in the Modernist Period* (Oxford: Oxford University Press, 2007), 425. For more on Dickens and film—and on nineteenth-century literature projecting an epoch to come—see Graham Smith, *Dickens and the Dream of Cinema* (Manchester: Manchester University Press, 2003).

3. Alan Spiegel, *Fiction and the Camera Eye: Visual Consciousness in Film and the Modern Novel* (Charlottesville: University Press of Virginia, 1976).

4. Robert Stam, *Literature Through Film: Realism, Magic, and the Art of Adaptation* (Oxford: Blackwell, 2005), 148–154.

5. Eisenstein, *Film Form*, 12. For a more detailed analysis, see Alan Spiegel, "Flaubert to Joyce: Evolution of a Cinematographic Form," *Novel: A Forum on Fiction* 3 (1979): 229–243; and Scarlett Baron, "Flaubert, Joyce: Vision, Photography, Cinema," *Modern Fiction Studies* 54 (2008): 689–714. In the scene from *Madame Bovary*, montage boils down to a simulated simultaneity as the prefect's voice at the fair continues to sound as Rodolphe and Emma speak, and vice versa—and the contrast between the former's talk of duty, the force of the law, or devotion to the rural countryside on the one hand, and the imminent transgression of Emma and Rodolphe, as well as their "urban" romantic pursuit of happiness on the other, somehow ridicules both sides.

6. Spiegel, "Flaubert to Joyce," 231.

7. P. Adams Sitney, *Modernist Montage: The Obscurity of Vision in Cinema and Literature* (New York: Columbia University Press, 1990), 17–19; Irina Rajewski, *Intermediales Erzählen in der italienischen Literatur der Postmoderne: Von den Giovani Scrittori der 8oer zum Pulp der 90er Jahre* (Tübingen: Gunter Narr, 2003).

8. Marcus here also points to Winifred Holby, who already studied the inscription of the new medium of film in texts by Virginia Woolf, and cast her experimental technique as a specifically "cinematographic technique." See Marcus, *The Tenth Muse*, 129–130.

9. Julian Murphet and Lydia Rainford, eds., *Literature and Visual Technologies: Writing after Cinema* (New York: Macmillan, 2003).

10. David Trotter, "T. S. Eliot and Cinema," *Modernism/Modernity* 13, no. 2 (2006): 240.

11. Garrett Stewart, *Between Film and Screen: Modernism's Photo Synthesis* (Chicago: University of Chicago Press, 1999).

12. As Trotter indicates, in this instance Stewart "draws productively on Frederic Jameson's description of the "confluence," in a passage from E. M. Forster's *Howards End* (1910), "of movie technology on the one hand, and of a certain type of modernist or protomodernist language on the other," both of which seem to offer some space, some "third term," between the subject and the object of perception. For Jameson, Stewart observes, that third term is in effect the (literary/photographic) apparatus, the "disembodiment of perception by technique; automatism, in short." Trotter, "T. S. Eliot and Cinema," 240.

13. Garrett Stewart, "Cinecriture: Modernism's Flicker Effect," *New Literary History* 4 (1998): 727–768.

14. "Cinematographic" is, of course, a very broad term. As Steven Kellman has noted, it could mean anything from "Hollywood-plot-like" to "avant-gardist montage novel." Here: "cinematographic" is not used as a stable concept, but rather as emerging from the texts discussed. What these texts have in common is the *critical* foregrounding of a "cinematographic" perception, rather than its utopian embrace (as in the Italian futurists). Steven Kellman, "The Cinematic Novel: Tracking a Concept," *Modern Fiction Studies* 3 (1987): 467–475.

15. Henri Bergson, *Creative Evolution*, trans. A. Mitchell (New York: Henry Holt, 1911), 306.

16. As Bergson puts it in his *Introduction to Metaphysics*, the difference between intuition and intellect amounts to a difference between synthesis and

analysis, between imagining or virtually participating in an object and taking that object apart: "By Intuition is meant the kind of *intellectual sympathy* by which one places oneself within an object in order to coincide with what is unique in it and consequently inexpressible. Analysis is the operation which reduces the object to elements already known, that is, to elements common to it and other objects. To analyse, therefore, is to express a thing as a function of something other than itself. All analysis is thus a translation, a development into symbols, a representation taken from successive points of view from which we note as many resemblances as possible between the new object which we are studying and others which we believe we know already. In its eternally unsatisfied desire to embrace the object around which it is compelled to turn, analysis multiplies without end the number of its points of view in order to complete its always incomplete representation, and ceaselessly varies its symbols that it may perfect the always imperfect translation. It goes on therefore to infinity. But Intuition, if Intuition be possible, is a simple act. It is an act directly opposed to analysis, for it is a viewing in totality, as an absolute; it is a synthesis, not an analysis, not an intellectual act, for it is an immediate, emotional synthesis." Elsewhere, Bergson repeatedly states that he does not privilege intuition at the expense of intellect—but rather only claims a space for the former. Henri Bergson, *Introduction to Metaphysics*, trans. T. E. Hulme (London: Macmillan, 1913), 7.

17. This assumption is, of course, problematic. Yet it is an assumption that is dominant in earlier twentieth-century conceptions of film and (infinite) mechanic reproduction.

18. Gavriel Moses, "Gubbio in Gabbia: Pirandello's Cameraman and the Entrapments of Film Vision," *Modern Language Notes* 94 (1979): 36.

19. Luigi Pirandello, *Shoot! The Notebooks of Serafino Gubbio, Cinematograph Operator*, trans. C. K. Scott Moncrieff (Chicago: University of Chicago Press, 2005).

20. See Frank Nulf, "Luigi Pirandello and the Cinema," *Film Quarterly* 2 (1970–71): 40–48.

21. Pirandello, *Shoot!*, 7.

22. Ibid., 8–9.

23. In Arthur Schopenhauer's philosophy, the Will is a noumenal dimension that manifests itself as object, as phenomenon, in the bodies, gestures, and shapes of the world: the world, human beings, animals, vegetation, etc. are all objectifications of a blind, irrational, ungraspable Will—an collective, unconscious drive. Friedrich Nietzsche further develops this philosophy of the Will as life-Will, craving and feeding on life, in *Die Geburt der Tragödie*. See for this Arthur Schopenhauer, *Die Welt als Wille und Vorstellung* (Frankfurt: Suhrkamp, 1986); Friedrich Nietzsche, *Die Geburt der Tragödie aus dem Geiste der Musik* (Frankfurt: Insel, 1987).

24. Pirandello, *Shoot!*, 57, 59.

25. Ibid., 9.

26. See Gavriel Moses's extensive analyses of film-mimetic schemes in "Gubbio in Gabbia," 39–41.

27. Pirandello, *Shoot!*, 83.

28. Ibid., 68.

29. Following Katherine Hayles's analysis, posthuman subjectivities are here understood as (openly) mediated subjectivities—whether they be culturally or technologically "extended": subjectivities that are not "naturally" but "artificially" informed. For more on the posthuman, see Chapter 4. See also Katherine Hayles, *How We Became Posthuman: Virtual Bodies in Cybernetics, Literature, and Informatics* (Chicago: University of Chicago Press, 1999).

30. Alessandro Vettori, "Serafino Gubbio's Candid Camera," *MLN* 113 (1998): 79–107.

31. Pirandello, *Shoot!*, 7.

32. As Alessandro Vettori observes, "[the negative passivity] has eliminated all encumbering worldly burdens from his life, purifying his personality to the mode of mysticism, if only a secular version of mysticism." Ibid., 100.

33. These involve, as we have seen, close-ups, but also montage: Insofar as film captures Bergson's cinematographic mode of selecting or freezing and reassembling, this is rehearsed in, for instance, Gubbio's evocation of the modern city in chapters 1–2 of book 1—an evocation that typically goes hand in hand with allusions to film and cinematographic techniques in novels such as Alfred Döblin's *Berlin, Alexanderplatz* (1929) or John Dos Passos's *Manhattan Transfer* (1925) and the literary mimicry of "the external, that is to say, the mechanical framework of the life which keeps us clamorously and dizzily occupied and gives us no rest" (4)—or, as Gavriel Moses points out, the "tendency to build up a context through the accumulation of metonymic details"; that is, the "sectioned anatomy of facial and bodily features"; the "technique of placing a [virtual] camera on a moving object and photographing the resulting alteration in one's view of the world" (cf. the scene in the film studio laboratories), or the ways in which *Shoot!* approaches the status of a film script. Moses, "Gubbio in Gabbia," 40–42.

34. Moses, "Gubbio in Gabbia," 46.

35. Stanley Solomon, "Aristotle in Twilight: American Film Narrative in the 1980s," in *The Cinematic Text*, ed. R. Barton Palmer (New York: AMS, 1989), 76.

36. Robert Coover, *Gerald's Party* (New York: Grove Press, 1985); *La société du spectacle* (Paris: Gallimard, 1996). There is also a film adaptation of the book, made in 1973.

37. Jean Baudrillard, *Simulations*, trans. Paul Foss, Paul Patton, and Philip Beitchman (New York: Semiotext(e), 1983).

38. Charles Clerc, "Film in *Gravity's Rainbow*," in *Approaches to Gravity's Rainbow*, ed. Charles Clerc (Columbus: Ohio State University Press, 1983), 104.

39. Scott Simmon, "Beyond the Theater of War: Gravity's Rainbow as Film," in *Critical Essays on Thomas Pynchon*, ed. Richard Pearce (Boston: G. K. Hall, 1981), 127.

40. Thomas Pynchon, *Gravity's Rainbow* (New York: Penguin, 1991), 397.

41. Ibid., 398.

42. Ibid., 422.

43. Ibid., 388.

44. Robert Morss Lovett, "Literature and Its Rivals," *The Kenyon Review* 1 (1940): 97.

45. Tony Tanner, *Thomas Pynchon* (London: Methuen, 1982), 79.

46. Kathleen Fitzpatrick, *The Anxiety of Obsolescence: The American Novel in the Age of Television* (Nashville, Tenn.: Vanderbilt University Press, 2006).

47. Brian McHale, *Constructing Postmodernism* (New York: Routledge, 1992), 127.

48. Stanley Cavell, "The Fact of Television," in *Themes out of School* (San Francisco: North Point Press, 1984), 235–268. For a different perspective, see Samuel Weber, *Mass Mediauras: Form, Technics, Media*, ed. Alan Cholodenko (Stanford: Stanford University Press, 1996), and Jacques Derrida and Bernard Stiegler, *Echographies of Television* (Cambridge: Polity, 2002).

49. Raymond Williams, *Television, Technology, and Cultural Form* (London: Routledge, 2003).

50. John Ellis, *Seeing Things: Television in the Age of Uncertainty* (London: I. B. Tauris, 2000). See also Ellis's classic *Visible Fictions: Cinema, Television, Video* (London: Routledge, 1992).

51. Cecilia Tichi, "Television and Recent American Fiction," *American Literary History* 1 (Spring 1989): 121–125.

52. Ibid.

11. NOVELIZING TATI
Jan Baetens

1. In his essay "Epic and the Novel," Mikhail Bakhtin already launched the term "novelization" to refer to the ways in which non-novelistic genres such as drama become productively infected by novelistic forms (a process comparable to remediation, yet within text-based domains): enlivening old forms. Emphasizing the plasticity of the novel, and hence associating it with change and openness *as such*, an inherent incompleteness, Bakhtin argues that "the novelization of other genres does not imply their subjection to an alien generic canon; on the contrary, novelization implies their liberation from all that serves as a brake on their unique development, from all that would change them along with the novel into some sort of stylization of forms that have outlived themselves." Mikhail Bakhtin, "Epic and the Novel," in *The Dialogic Imagination*, ed. M. Holquist (Austin: University of Texas Press, 1981), 39. The novel is thus a presence, or rather a force, disseminating itself into other literary forms. In this essay, novelization rather applies to the "making textual" of fiction films.

2. Linda Hutcheon, *A Theory of Adaptation* (New York: Routledge, 2006), 38, 118–119.

3. Stanley Cavell, *In Pursuit of Happiness: Hollywood and the Comedy of Remarriage* (Cambridge, Mass.: Harvard University Press, 1981).

4. Deborah Cartmell and Imelda Whelehan, *Adaptations* (New York: Routledge, 2000).

5. Jan Baetens, "Novelization, a Contaminated Genre?" *Critical Inquiry* 32 (2005): 43–60; Jan Baetens "From Screen to Text: Novelization, the Hidden

Continent," in *The Cambridge Companion to Literature on Screen*, ed. Deborah Cartmell and Imelda Whelehan (Cambridge: Cambridge University Press, 2007), 226–238.

6. Brian McFarlane, *Novel to Film* (New York: Oxford University Press, 1996). In the terminology of the Groupe Mu, there are four forms of this "adaptation proper": suppression, adjunction, suppression-adjunction, and permutation. The best example of a discussion of these aspects is still François Truffaut's polemic against the so-called *qualité française* (Aurenche-Bost), which was founded on a particular interpretation of the adaptation of literary texts. See "Une certaine tendance du cinéma français," in *Le plaisir des yeux: Ecrits sur le cinéma* (Paris: Petite Bibliothèque des Cahiers du Cinéma, 2000), 293–314.

7. Jay Bolter and Richard Grusin, *Remediation: Understanding New Media* (Cambridge, Mass.: MIT Press, 1999).

8. Michel Foucault, "Des espaces autres (conférence au Cercle d'études architecturales, 14 mars 1967)," *Architecture, Mouvement, Continuité* 5 (1984): 46–49.

9. Lies Wesseling and Rob Zwijnenberg, eds., *Art In Time: On the Use and Abuse of Anachronisms in the History of Art* (London: Equinox, 2007).

10. Raymond Williams, *Television: Technology and Cultural Form* (New York: Routledge, 2003).

11. David Trotter, *Cinema and Modernism* (Cambridge: Cambridge University Press, 2007).

12. The same author would also make a novelization of *Mon oncle* (Paris: Lafont, 1958). According my knowledge, there have not been any other novelizations of films by Jacques Tati. In 2006, Lafont reprinted these two long-forgotten books.

13. Jeanne-Marie Clerc, *Littérature et cinéma* (Paris: Nathan, 1993).

14. Ibid., 97.

15. Jacques Kermabon, *Les vacances de M. Hulot de Jacques Tati* (Liège: Yellow Now, 1988).

16. David Bellos, Jacques Tati: His Life and Art *(London:* Harvill Press, 1999).

17. Antoine de Baecque, Jacques Tati: His Life and Art *(London:* Harvill Press, 2003).

18. Francois Truffaut, "D'un certaine tendance du cinema français" [1958], in *Le Plaisir des yeux: Ecrits sur le cinéma* (Paris: Petite Bibliothèque des Cahiers du cinéma, 2000) 293–314.

19. Francesca Leonardi, "La vie passionnée des *Cousins*: Les avatars d'un film Nouvelle Vague," in *Il racconto del film: La novellizzazione: Dal catalogo al trailer/Narrating the Film. Novelization: From the Catalogue to the Trailer*, ed. Alice Autelitano and Valentina Re (Udine: Forum, 2006), 179–195.

20. Jan Baetens, "Novelizing Jean-Luc Godard," in Autelitano and Re, *Il racconto del film*, 167–178.

21. Kermabon, *Les vacances de M. Hulot de Jacques Tati*, 24.

22. Clerc, *Littérature et cinema*, 97.

23. Ibid., 91.

24. Ibid., 101.

25. Jean Ricardou, *Une maladie chronique* (Paris: Les Impressions Nouvelles, 1989).

12. COPYCAT-AND-MOUSE: THE PRINTED SCREENPLAY AND THE LITERARY FIELD IN FRANCE
Matthijs Engelberts

1. Kamilla Elliot, *Rethinking the Novel/Film Debate* (Cambridge: Cambridge University Press, 2003), 83.

2. Elliott gives much space to some textual aspects of films, such as intertitles, but she does not discuss the screenplay extensively. It should be clear, however, that Elliott *explicitly* defends the function and importance of words in film, for instance when she states: "The film language analogy is marshaled with dazzlingly unjust brilliance not only against film words, but against any theory or criticism of film that would even consider these words worthy of study" (ibid., 85).

3. Kamilla Elliot, "Novels, Films, and the Word/Image Wars," in *A Companion to Literature and Film*, ed. Robert Stam and Alessandra Raengo (Oxford: Blackwell, 2004), 17.

4. See the first sentences of Gassner's preface in the first volume of his series of best screenplays: "There is now a literature of the screen—the screenplay. If this fact has not been widely recognized, it is only because screenplays have not been properly accorded the dignity of print." John Gassner, *Twenty Best Film Plays* (New York: Crown Publishers, 1966), vii.

5. Erwin Panofsky, *Three Essays on Style* (Cambridge, Mass.: MIT Press, 1995), 116; emphasis added.

6. "In a film, that which we hear remains, for good or worse, inextricably fused with that which we see; the sound, articulate or not, cannot express any more than is expressed, at the same time, by visible movement; and in a good film it does not even attempt to do so. To put it briefly, the play—or, as it is very properly called, the 'script'—of a moving picture is subject to what might be termed the *principle of coexpressibility*." Ibid., 100–101.

7. Béla Balázs, *Theory of the Film: Character and Growth of a New Art* (New York: Dover, 1977), 249.

8. Translation: "Will we see the birth, next to drama, of a 'literary' cinema in which the synopsis and the dialogues would stand the publication?" André Bazin, *Le cinéma de l'occupation et de la résistance (recueil de textes parus entre 1943 et 1945)* (Paris: UGE, 1975), 45.

9. Gassner, *Best Film Plays*, xxvii.

10. Larry McMurtry, "The Screenplay as a Non-Book: A Consideration," *American Film* 1, no. 10 (1976): 7.

11. Translation: "Screenplays do not but presuppose the film; they are without autonomy. These are dead pages." Michelangelo Antonioni, *Techniquement douce*, trans. Anna Buresi (Paris: Albatros, 1977), 9.

12. Jacqueline Wolfowicz, "Le scénario comme genre littéraire," *Neohelicon* 17 (1990): 283–289.

13. In her very well-researched book, Sternberg indeed does not mention Clerc's book or her previous ones—quite forgivably perhaps, given the number of contributions to this debate.

14. Claudia Sternberg, *Written for the Screen: The American Motion-Picture Screenplay as Text* (Tübingen: Stauffenburg, 1997), 232.

15. Translation: "The screenplay should not, in any case . . . be considered and studied as literature." Amélie Vermeesch, "Poétique du scenario," *Poétique* 138 (2004): 222.

16. Besides Panofsky and Balázs, another example would be Sternberg, who posits the "increased screenplay publication" in the second sentence of her introduction without substantiating this manifestly important claim.

17. I will limit myself to what is generally thought to be the only European national culture with an uninterrupted and extensive film production history—a view held by both French and foreign film historians and critics such as Jeanpierre Jeancolas, Michael Temple, and Michael Witt.

18. With some additions from other sources, such as the Bibliothèque Nationale de France.

19. I would like to thank the Bifi (particularly Sandra Laupa) and the Bibliothèque du Cinéma (particularly Jocelyne Le Darz) for their help with collecting the files, and Yvonne Jacob and Joyce Kraaijeveld for their help in treating the data.

20. Foreign texts, whether translated or not, have been excluded since they usually do not function in the literary field in the same way as texts that have been conceived in French.

21. Robert Morsberger and Katharine Morsberger, "Screenplays as Literature: Bibliography and Criticism," *Literature Film Quarterly* 3 (1975): 53.

22. This selection from the collections of the two libraries includes published screenplays of French feature films, with the exception of documentaries and television productions (if these have not had a theatrical release). "French" films have been defined as films that have been produced or coproduced by companies from France. The selection includes the (not very numerous) screenplays in French and published in France that have not been filmed. Reissues have been excluded except when they involve a change in publishing house or if the first publication predates 1945; volumes count as a single entry.

23. This date has been chosen because the decade that includes World War II (1939–1945) would obviously be impossible to integrate in the table, since publishing conditions were very different during the war. The only prewar decade would thus be the one that witnessed the advent of the spoken film (1925–1935), which for that reason cannot be put on a par with the postwar decades.

24. If authors have a specific editorial policy and willfully choose peripheral publishers for (part of) their work (as did Marcel Pagnol and Jean Cocteau), I have not excluded these. The second selection also includes the more than ten texts in the collection "scénars" published by Arte in cooperation with Hachette in the second half of the nineties, but it excludes the twenty issues of the same collection published after Hachette left the specialized consortium and was succeeded by Zéro heure (00h00), a publisher that specialized in digital texts and printing on demand.

25. This is a colloquial expression referring to three major literary publishers.

26. The results of the third column would not have changed fundamentally if Julliard, Fayard, and Albin Michel had been included among the renowned houses.

27. The first selection does indeed not include the issues of *L'Avant-scène cinéma* and *La petite bibliothèque des Cahiers du cinéma*. It is worth noting that adding the French scripts of these series to the figures would result in notably higher figures from the early 1960s onward.

28. Morsberger and Morsberger, "Screenplays as Literature," 46, 53.

29. W. J. T. Mitchell, "Showing Seeing: A Critique of Visual Culture," in *The Visual Culture Reader*, ed. Nicholas Mirzoeff (London: Routledge, 2002), 93.

13. THE NEW LITERACIES: TECHNOLOGY AND CULTURAL FORM
William Uricchio

1. Adrian Johns, *The Nature of the Book: Print and Knowledge in the Making* (Chicago: University of Chicago Press, 1998); Natalie Zemon Davis, *Society and Culture in Early Modern France: Eight Essays* (Stanford, Calif.: Stanford University Press, 1975); Elizabeth Eisenstein, *The Printing Revolution in Early Modern Europe* (Cambridge: Cambridge University Press, 1993).

2. See among others, Matthew Arnold, *Culture and Anarchy and Other Writings* (Cambridge: Cambridge University Press, 1993); Michael Denning, *Mechanic Accents: Dime Novels and Working-Class Culture in America* (New York: Verso, 1998); John Springhall, *Youth, Popular Culture and Moral Panics: Penny Gaffs to Gangsta-Rap, 1830–1996* (New York: St. Martin's Press, 1998).

3. Raymond Williams, *Television: Technology and Cultural Form* (London: Collins, 1974).

4. William Uricchio, "The Algorithmic Turn: Photosynth, Augmented Reality and the State of the Image," *Visual Studies* 26 (2011): 25–35.

5. William Uricchio, "Cultural Citizenship in the Age of P2P Networks," in *European Culture and the Media*, ed. Ib Bondebjerg and Peter Golding (Chicago: University of Chicago Press, 2004), 139–164.

6. More recent studies note that 94 percent of all American teenagers—which it defines as twelve- to seventeen-year-olds—now use the Internet; 89 percent have Internet access in the home; and 66 percent have broadband Internet access in the home, suggesting that active posting rates have increased.

7. By contrast, peer-reviewed e-journals usually adhere to a very different logic and are not only freely available, but also encourage interaction with the readership.

8. It is equally evident that the culture industries are eager to put the genie back in the bottle, inasmuch as they purchase and attempt to capitalize on successful online communities and develop new policing tactics to trace their intellectual property.

9. Raymond Williams, *Problems in Materialism and Culture: Selected Essays* (London: Verso, 1980).

10. Jürgen Habermas, *The Structural Transformation of the Public Sphere* (Cambridge, Mass.: MIT Press, 1991).

11. MIT's MacArthur Foundation–supported Project New Media Literacies offers an example of a pedagogy that seeks to combine critical knowledge, hands-on skills, and ethics relevant to the new literacies. See Henry Jenkins et al., "Confronting the Challenges of Participatory Culture: Media Education for the 21st Century" (2011), www.newmedialiteracies.org/files/working/NMLWhitePaper.pdf.

14. VISIBILITY, BLOGGING, AND THE CONSTRUCTION OF
SUBJECTIVITY IN EDUCATIONAL SPACES
Asunción López-Varela Azcárate

1. http://rebooting.personaldemocracy.com/node/5476.

2. See Robert Darnton, "Google and the Future of Books," *New York Review of Books*, February 2009.

3. Gert Biesta, *Beyond Learning: Democratic Education for a Human Future* (Boulder, Colo.: Paradigm, 2006).

4. Mark Poster, *Information Please: Culture and Politics in the Age of Digital Machines* (Durham, N.C.: Duke University Press, 2006), 38.

5. Ibid., 52.

6. See Chapter 3. See also Alireza Doostar, "'The Vulgar Spirit of Blogging': On Language, Culture, and Power in Persian Weblogestan," *American Anthropologist* 4 (2004): 651–662; Mark Blumenthal, "What We Can Learn From the Blogosphere: Towards an Open Source Methodology," *Public Opinion Quarterly* 5 (2005): 36–41; Daniel W. Drezner and Henry Farrell, "Web of Influence," *Foreign Policy* 145 (November–December 2004): 32–40.

7. Asunción López-Varela, "The Relevance of Different Kinds of Supporting Materials" in *EOLSS: Social Sciences and Humanities. Encyclopedia of Life Support Systems*, ed. T. Franco Carvalhal, D. Romero, and Ackmar Dos Santos (Geneva: UNESCO, 2006).

8. See Néstor García Clanclini, *Consumers and Citizens: Globalization and Multicultural Conflicts* (Minneapolis: University of Minnesota Press, 2001); Pippa Norris, *Digital Divide: Civic Engagement, Information Poverty and the Internet Worldwide.* (Cambridge: Cambridge University Press, 2002); D. Boyd, "Viewing American Class Divisions through Facebook and MySpace," www.danah.org/papers/essays/ClassDivisions.htmlClassDivisions.html.

9. See Asunción López-Varela Azcárate, "Webness Revisited," in *A Pleasure of Life in Words: A Festschrift for Angela Downing*, ed. Marta Carretero et al. (Madrid: Universidad Complutense, 2006), 513–533.

10. Rebecca Blood, "Weblogs: A History and Perspective," www.rebeccablood.net/essays/weblog_history.html.

11. Pierre Bourdieu, *Practical Reason: On the Theory of Action* (Stanford: Stanford University Press, 1998), 81.

12. Henry Jenkins et al., "Confronting the Challenges of Participatory Culture: Media Education for the 21st Century," http://bit.ly/2bnWVo.

13. David Birchfield et al., "Embodied and Mediated Learning in SMALLab: A Student-Centered Mixed-Reality Environment," *ACM SIGGRAPH* 2009, http://bit.ly/GO6O7j.

14. Randall Packer and Ken Jordan, eds., *Multimedia: From Wagner to Virtual Reality* (New York: Norton, 2001).

15. Manuel Castells, *The Rise of the Network Society: The Information Age—Economy, Society and Culture* (Oxford: Blackwell, 1996), 1:412.

16. See Will Richardson, *Blogs, Wikis, Podcasts, and Other Powerful Tools for Classrooms* (Thousand Oaks, Calif.: Sage, 2006). See also Asunción López-Varela Azcaráte and Steven Tötösy de Zepetnek, "Comparative Cultural Studies, éducation, nouveaux médias et l'interculturalisme," trans. Anne Chalard-Fillaudeau, in *Le Complexe français: Quelle place pour les études et sciences de la culture en France?* ed. Anne Chalard-Fillaudeau (Vincennes: Presses Universitaires de Vincennes, 2009).

17. See R. C. Clark and R. E. Mayer, *E-Learning and the Science of Instruction: Proven Guidelines for Consumers and Designers of Multimedia Learning* (San Francisco: Pfeiffer, 2003).

18. See www.ucm.es/info/comparativeculturalstudies.org.

19. For dialogicity in education, see R. Alexander, *Towards Dialogic Teaching: Rethinking Classroom Talk* (Cambridge: Dialogos, 2004); G. Wells and Rebecca M. Arauz, "Dialogue in the Classroom," *Journal of the Learning Sciences* 3 (2006): 379–428.

20. Ian Watson, "When Thought-Mail Failed," in *The New English Library Book of Internet Stories*, ed. Maxim Jakubowski (London: Hodder & Stoughton, 2000), 279–294.

21. Jim Porter, "Why Technology Matters to Writing: A Cyberwriter's Tale," *Computers and Composition* 20 (2002): 375–394.

15. THE SINGULARITY OF NEW MEDIA
Gary Hall

1. The CSeARCH cultural studies open-access archive is available at www.culturemachine.net/csearch.

2. This is the definition offered by Peter Suber in his Open Access News blog: available at www.earlham.edu/~peters/fos/fosblog.html (last accessed June 24, 2007). For other definitions of open access, see the Budapest Open Access Initiative (2002), www.soros.org/openaccess; the Bethesda Statement on Open Access Publishing (2003), www.earlham.edu/~peters/fos/bethesda.htm#summary; and the Berlin Declaration on Open Access to Knowledge in the Sciences and Humanities (2003) http://oa.mpg.de/openaccess-berlin/berlin declaration.html. For more on open access generally, see Suber's "Open Access Overview," available at www.earlham.edu/~peters/fos/overview.htm.

3. Jeffery Sconce, "Tulip Theory," in *New Media: Theories and Practices of Digitextuality*, ed. Anna Everett and John Caldwell (New York: Routledge, 2003), 198.

4. Mark Poster, *What's the Matter with the Internet?* (Minneapolis: University of Minnesota Press, 2001), 140, 141.

5. N. Katherine Hayles, *Writing Machines* (Cambridge, Mass.: MIT Press, Hayles, 2002), 106.

6. Ibid., 33.

7. See in particular ibid., 29–33.

8. Mark Poster, *Information Please: Culture and Politics in the Age of Digital Machines* (Durham, N.C.: Duke University Press, 2006), 204.

9. The Project Oekonux website can be found at www.oekonux.org. See also Geert Lovink and Christoph Spehr, "Out-Cooperating the Empire?—Exchange with Christoph Spehr," posting to the nettime list July 9, 2006, available at www.networkcultures.org/geert/out-cooperating-the-empire-exchange-with-christoph-spehr (last accessed December 7, 2006).

10. Hilary Wainwright et al., eds., "Networked Politics: Rethinking Political Organisation in an Age of Movements and Networks," available at www.tni.org/reports/newpol/networkedpolitics.pdf (last accessed January 18, 2007).

11. Michael Hardt and Toni Negri, *Multitude: War and Democracy in the Age of Empire* (Harmondsworth: Penguin, 2004), 340.

12. For more, see Gary Hall, "Hyper-Cyprus: On Peace and Conflict in the Middle East," available in the CSeARCH archive at http://rime.tees.ac.uk/wiki/theUniversity3G/.

13. For example, one cannot simply transfer the situation regarding open access in the academy over to the decentered electronic distribution of films and argue that all films should be given away for free, too. That would raise a number of difficult policy-related questions, such as that concerned with how those involved in the making of films can earn the money to enable them to do so *and* make a living. Issues of this kind do not arise in the case of the majority of academics, since they tend to be employed to carry out research by their institutions. Which is not to say that the problem of developing a future funding policy for creative laborers cannot be resolved, no matter how precarious their work; just that it cannot necessarily be resolved in the same way in the case of film production and distribution as it can for the open-access publication of academic scholarship and research.

14. In 2005, Rupert Murdoch reportedly bought MySpace for $580 million and Yahoo! paid an estimated $35 million for Flickr, while in 2006 Google spent $1.65 billion taking over YouTube.

15. Dmytri Kleiner and Brian Wyrick, "Info-Enclosure 2.0," *Mute* 3, no. 4 (January 2007): 16.

16. Strictly speaking, Napster, Gnutella and Kazaa are (or were) peer-to-peer networks; eMule is a peer-to-peer file sharing application, working with the EDonkey network; FastTrack is a peer-to-peer protocol, used by the Kazaa (and other) file sharing programs; and BitTorrent is also a peer-to-peer file distribution protocol, as well as the name of a free software implementation of that protocol. Furthermore, Napster, in its original incarnation, was based on a central directory that listed the data that were being offered for exchange by other registered participants. It was not therefore a peer-to-peer network in the "pure" or proper sense of the term. "Pure" P2P file-sharing networks such as

Gnutella consist of a decentralized network of connected machines that are independent of either a centralized client server or a centralized directory. This allows the responsibility for any breaches of copyright to be transferred to the much harder to prosecute individual end user rather than lying with a central server.

17. John Willinsky, *The Access Principle: The Case for Open Access to Research and Scholarship* (Cambridge, Mass.: MIT Press, 2006).

18. See the website of the Open Citation Project http://opcit.eprints.org/oacitation-biblio.html (last accessed October 14, 2006).

19. "Permanently" has been placed in quotation marks here to indicate I am aware that digital media can quickly become obsolete, URLs can die, and so on. We should certainly not assume that the Internet will remain in its present form for the long or even midterm future. As the technology changes, it is quite possible that older forms will become outdated and increasingly inaccessible, just as it is now hard to watch a Betamax video or listen to an 8-track cassette.

20. Adrian Johns, *The Nature of the Book: Print and Knowledge in the Making* (Chicago: University of Chicago Press, 1998), 31–32.

21. For Levinas, we are always confronted by the alterity of the Other. This confrontation is both an accusation and a source of our ethical responsibility, which is why ethics is inevitable and foundational: why it is a first philosophy that precedes ontology. For Levinas, the latter is a philosophy of being in which the other is understood in terms of concepts and categories that belong to the same. Ontology here amounts to ascertaining the extent to which the Other can (or cannot) be recognized as the same, as being like me. Levinas, however, thinks of ethics somewhat differently. Indeed, for him, ethics is a *different* mode of thinking that comes before ontology (albeit not in a linear, temporal sense).

22. Jacques Derrida, *Spurs: Nietzsche's Styles* (Chicago: University of Chicago Press, 1997).

23. See Jacques Derrida, *Geneses, Genealogies, Genres and Genius: The Secrets of the Archive* (Edinburgh: Edinburgh University Press, 2006).

24. See Robert Young, "The Idea of a Chrestomatic University," in *Logomachia: The Conflict of the Faculties,* ed. Richard Rand (Lincoln: University of Nebraska Press, 1992), 97–126; Bill Readings, *The University in Ruins* (Cambridge, Mass.: Harvard University Press, 1996); and Diane Elam, "Why Read?" *Culture Machine* 2 (2006), http://culturemachine.tees.ac.uk/Backissues/j002/Articles/art_elam.htm.

25. Gary Hall, *Culture in Bits: The Monstrous Future of Theory* (New York: Continuum, 2002); Gary Hall, "Why You Can't Do Cultural Studies *and* Be a Derridean: Cultural Studies after Birmingham, the New Social Movements and the New Left," *Culture Machine* 6 (2004), http://culturemachine.tees.ac.uk/Cmach/Backissues/j006/Articles/hall.htm.

26. See Poster, *What's the Matter with the Internet?*, 205.

27. Derek Attridge, *The Singularity of Literature* (London: Routledge, 2005); Timothy Clark, *The Poetics of Singularity: The Counter-Culturalist Turn in Heidegger, Derrida, Blanchot and the Later Gadamer* (Edinburgh: Edinburgh University Press, 2005).

Aarseth, Espen. 1994. "Nonlinearity and Literary Theory." In *Hyper/Text/Theory*, edited by George P. Landow, 51–86. Baltimore: Johns Hopkins University Press.

———. 1997. *Cybertext: Perspectives on Ergodic Literature*. Baltimore: Johns Hopkins University Press.

Adamowicz, Elsa. 2005. *Surrealist Collage in Text and Image: Dissecting the Exquisite Corpse*. Cambridge: Cambridge University Press.

Antonioni, Michelangelo. 1977. *Techniquement douce*. Translated by Anna Buresi. Paris: Albatros.

Appadurai, Arjun. 1996. *Modernity at Large: Cultural Dimensions of Globalization*. Minneapolis: University of Minnesota Press.

Apter, Emily. 2006. *The Translation Zone: A New Comparative Literature*. Princeton, N.J.: Princeton University Press.

Arnold, Matthew. 1993. *Culture and Anarchy and Other Writings*. Cambridge: Cambridge University Press.

Attridge, Derek. 2005. *The Singularity of Literature*. London: Routledge.

Autelitano, Alice, and Valentina Re. 2006. *Il racconto del film: La novellizzazione—dal catalogo al trailer*. Udine: Forum.

Baecque, Antoine de. 2003. *La cinéphilie: Invention d'un regard, histoire d'une culture, 1944–1968*. Paris: Fayard.

Baetens, Jan. 2005. "Novelization, a Contaminated Genre?" *Critical Inquiry* 32: 43–60.

———. 2006. "Novelizing Jean-Luc Godard." In *Il racconto del film: La novel-lizzazione—dal catalogo al trailer*, edited by Alice Autelitano and Valentina Re, 167–178. Udine: Forum.

———. 2007. "From Screen to Text: Novelization, the Hidden Continent." In *The Cambridge Companion to Literature on Screen*, edited by Deborah Cartmell and Imelda Whelehan, 226–238. Cambridge: Cambridge University Press.

Baetens, Jan, and Jan van Looy. 2003. *Close Reading New Media: Analyzing Electronic Literature*. Leuven: Leuven University Press.

Bakhtin, Mikhail. 1982. *The Dialogic Imagination: Four Essays*. Edited by Michael Holquist. Translated by Caryl Emerson and Michael Holquist. Austin: University of Texas Press.

Balázs, Béla. 1970. *Theory of the Film: Character and Growth of a New Art*. New York: Dover.

Baron, Scarlett. 2008. "Flaubert, Joyce: Vision, Photography, Cinema." *Modern Fiction Studies* 54: 689–714.

Barthes, Roland. 1971. *Le bruissement de la langue*. Paris: Seuil.

———. 1979. "From Work to Text." In *Textual Strategies: Perspectives in Poststructural Criticism*, edited by Josué V. Harari, 73–81. Ithaca, N.Y.: Cornell University Press.

Baudrillard, Jean. 1983. *Simulations*. Translated by Paul Foss, Paul Patton, and Philip Beitchman. New York: Semiotext(e).

Bazin, André. 1971. *What Is Cinema?* Translated by Hugh Gray. Berkeley: University of California Press.

———. 1975. *Le cinéma de l'occupation et de la résistance (recueil de textes parus entre 1943 et 1945)*. Paris: UGE.

———. 2000. "Adaptation, or the Cinema as Digest." In *Film Adaptation*, edited by James Naremore, 19–27. London: Athlone Press.

Beardsworth, Richard. 1996. *Derrida and the Political*. New York: Routledge.

Bellos, David. 1999. *Jacques Tati: His Life and Art*. London: Harvill Press.

Benjamin, Walter. 1973. *Der Begriff der Kunstkritik in der deutschen Romantik*. Frankfurt am Main: Suhrkamp.

———. 1991. "Das Kunstwerk im Zeitalter seiner technischen Reproduzierbarkeit (Dritte Fassung)." In *Gesammelte Schriften*, edited by Rolf Tiedemann and Hermann Schweppenhäuser. Frankfurt am Main: Suhrkamp.

Bergson, Henri. 1911. *Creative Evolution*. Translated by A. Mitchell. New York: Henry Holt.

———. 1913. *Introduction to Metaphysics*. Translated by T. E. Hulme. London: Macmillan.

Bernasconi, Robert, and David Wood, eds. 1985. *Derrida and Différance*. Warwick: Parousia Press.

Birkerts, Sven. 1991. "Into the Electronic Millennium." *Boston Review*, October.

———. 1995. *The Gutenberg Elegies*. New York: Faber and Faber, 1995.

Block, Friedrich W., et al. 2004. *Ästhetik Digitaler Poesie / The Aesthetics of Digital Poetry*. Berlin: Hatje Cantz Books.

Blumenthal, Mark. 2005. "What We Can Learn from the Blogosphere: Towards an Open Source Methodology." *Public Opinion Quarterly* 5: 36–41.

Bolter, Jay David. 1991. *Writing Space: The Computer, Hypertext, and the History of Writing*. Mahwah, N.J.: Lawrence Erlbaum Associates.

———. 1996. "Ekphrasis, Virtual Reality, and the Future of Writing." In *The Future of the Book*, edited by Geoffrey Nunberg, 253–272. Berkeley: University of California Press.

Bolter, Jay, and Richard Grusin. 1999. *Remediation: Understanding New Media*. Cambridge, Mass.: MIT Press.

Borges, Jorge Luis. 1983. *Labyrinths*. Edited by Donald A. Yates and James E. Irby. New York: Modern Library.

Bourdieu, Pierre. 1998. *Practical Reason: On the Theory of Action*. Stanford, Calif.: Stanford University Press, 1998.

Boyd, D. 2007. "Viewing American Class Divisions Through Facebook and MySpace." www.danah.org/papers/essays/ClassDivisions.htmlClassDivisions.htm l (last visited January 2009).

Brooks, Frederick P. 1987. "No Silver Bullet: Essence and Accidents of Software Engineering." *IEEE Computer* 20, no. 4: 1069–1076.

Bush, Vannevar. 1945. "As We May Think." *Atlantic Monthly*, 101–108.

Butler, Judith. 1999. *Gender Trouble: Feminism and the Subversion of Identity*. New York: Routledge.

Buxton, John N., and Brian Randell, eds. 1970. *Software Engineering Techniques: Report on a Conference Sponsored by the NATO Science Committee, Rome, Italy, 27th to 31st October 1969*. Birmingham: NATO Science Committee.

Canudo, Ricciotto, 1988. "Reflections on the Seventh Art." In *French Film Theory and Criticism: A History/Anthology, 1907–1939. Volume I: 1907–1929*, edited by Richard Abel, 291–303. Princeton, N.J.: Princeton University Press.

Carrière, Jean-Claude. 1958. *Les vacances de M. Hulot*. Paris: Laffont.

———. 2007. *Les fantômes de Goya*. Paris: Plon.

Carroll, Lewis. 1983. *Sylvie and Bruno: The Complete Illustrated Works of Lewis Carroll.* Edited by Edward Guillaro. New York: Avenel Books.

Cartmell, Deborah, and Imelda Whelehan. 2000. *Adaptations.* New York: Routledge.

———, eds. 2007. *The Cambridge Companion to Literature on Screen.* Cambridge: Cambridge University Press.

Carvalhal, T. Franco, D. Romero, and Ackmar Dos Santos, eds. 2006. *EOLSS: Social Sciences and Humanities—Encyclopedia of Life Support Systems.* Geneva: UNESCO.

Castells, Manuel. 1996. *The Rise of the Network Society: The Information Age—Economy, Society and Culture, Vol. 1.* Oxford: Blackwell.

Cavell, Stanley. 1981. *In Pursuit of Happiness: Hollywood and the Comedy of Remarriage.* Cambridge, Mass.: Harvard University Press.

———. 1984. "The Fact of Television." In *Themes out of School,* 235–268. San Francisco: North Point Press.

Chatman, Seymour. 1980. "What Novels Can Do That Films Can't (and Vice Versa)." *Critical Inquiry* 7: 121–140.

Ciccoricco, David. 2007. *Reading Network Fiction.* Tuscaloosa: University of Alabama Press.

Clark, Ruth Colvin, and Richard E. Mayer. 2003. *E-Learning and the Science of Instruction: Proven Guidelines for Consumers and Designers of Multimedia Learning.* San Francisco: Pfeiffer.

Clark, Timothy. 2005. *The Poetics of Singularity: The Counter-Culturalist Turn in Heidegger, Derrida, Blanchot and the Later Gadamer.* Edinburgh: Edinburgh University Press.

Clarke, Bruce. 2008. *Posthuman Metamorphosis: Narrative and Systems.* New York: Fordham University Press.

Clerc, Charles. 1983. "Film in *Gravity's Rainbow.*" In *Approaches to Gravity's Rainbow,* edited by Charles Clerc, 103–152. Columbus: Ohio State University Press.

Clerc, Jeanne-Marie. 1993. *Littérature et cinema.* Paris: Nathan.

Cohen, Keith. 1979. *Film and Fiction: The Dynamics of Exchange.* New Haven: Yale University Press.

Cohen, Kris R. 2006. "A Welcome for Blogs." *Continuum: Journal for Media & Culture Studies* 20, no 2 (June): 161–173.

Conley, Tom. 2007. *Cartographic Cinema.* Minneapolis: University of Minnesota Press.

Coover, Robert. 2000. *Pricksongs and Descants: Fictions.* New York: Grove Press.

———. 2000. "Sherlock, Jr." In *Writers at the Movies*, edited by Jim Shepard, 68–70. New York: Harper.

Culler, Jonathan. 2007. "What Is Literature Now?" *New Literary History* 1: 229–237.

Dalle Vacche, Angela. 2003. "Introduction: Unexplored Connections in a New Territory." In *The Visual Turn: Classical Film Theory and Art History*, edited by Angela Dalle Vacche, 1–29. New Brunswick, N.J.: Rutgers University Press.

Danielewski, Mark. 2000. *House of Leaves*. New York: Doubleday.

Darnton, Robert. 2009. "Google & the Future of Books." *New York Review of Books* 56, no. 2 (February 12, 2009).

Davis, Natalie Zemon. 1975. *Society and Culture in Early Modern France: Eight Essays*. Stanford, Calif.: Stanford University Press.

Debord, Guy. 1996. *La société du spectacle*. Paris: Gallimard.

De Certeau, Michel. 1991. *The Practice of Everyday Life*. Translated by Steven Rendall. Berkeley: University of California Press.

Deleuze, Gilles, and Felix Guattari. 1980. *Mille Plateaux*. Paris: Minuit.

———. 1986. *Nomadology: The War Machine*. New York: Semiotext(e).

Dennett, Daniel C. 1991. *Consciousness Explained*. New York: Little, Brown.

———. 2001. "Are We Explaining Consciousness Yet?" *Cognition* 79: 225.

Denning, Michael. 1998. *Mechanic Accents: Dime Novels and Working-Class Culture in America*. New York: Verso.

Derrida, Jacques. 1976. *Of Grammatology*. Translated by Gayatri Chakravorty Spivak. Baltimore: Johns Hopkins University Press, 1976.

———. 1979. *Spurs: Nietzsche's Styles*. Chicago: University of Chicago Press.

———. 1980. *Writing and Difference*. Translated by Alan Bass. London: Routledge.

———. 1988. *Limited, Inc.* Translated by Samuel Weber. Evanston, Ill.: Northwestern University Press.

———. 1994. *Politiques de l'amitié*. Paris: Galilée, 1994.

———. 1995. *Archive Fever: A Freudian Impression*. Translated by Eric Prenowitz. Chicago: University of Chicago Press.

———. 1995. *Points . . . Interviews, 1974–1994*. Edited by Elisabeth Weber. Stanford, Calif.: Stanford University Press.

———. 1997. *Politics of Friendship*. Translated by George Collins. New York: Verso.

———. 2005. "Paper or Me, You Know . . . New Speculations on a Luxury of the Poor." In *Paper Machine*, 41–66. Translated by Rachel Bowlby. Stanford: Stanford University Press.

———. 2006. *Geneses, Genealogies, Genres and Genius: The Secrets of the Archive*. Edinburgh: Edinburgh University Press.

Derrida, Jacques, and Bernard Stiegler. 2002. *Echographies of Television*. Cambridge: Polity.

Doostar, Alireza. 2004. "'The Vulgar Spirit of Blogging': On Language, Culture, and Power in Persian Weblogestan." *American Anthropologist* 4: 651–662.

Douglas, Jane Yellowlees. 1994. "'How Do I Stop This Thing?': Closure and Indeterminacy in Interactive Narratives." In *Hyper/Text/Theory*, edited by George P. Landow, 159–188. Baltimore: Johns Hopkins University Press.

Downes, Stephen. 2007. "Places to Go: Facebook." *Innovate* 4, no. 1.

DuGay, Paul, Stuart Hall, Linda Janes, Hugh Mackay, and Keith Negus, eds. 1997. *Doing Cultural Studies: The Story of the Sony Walkman*. London: Sage/Open University.

Eisenstein, Elizabeth. 1993. *The Printing Revolution in Early Modern Europe*. Cambridge: Cambridge University Press.

Eisenstein, Sergei M. 1951. *Film Form: Essays in Film Theory*. Edited and translated by Jay Leyda. London: Dobson.

Elliott, Kamilla. 2003. *Rethinking the Novel/Film Debate*. Cambridge: Cambridge University Press.

Ellis, John. 1992. *Visible Fictions: Cinema, Television, Video*. London: Routledge.

———. 2000. *Seeing Things: Television in the Age of Uncertainty*. London: I. B. Tauris.

Emerson, Lori. 2006. "Numbered Space and Topographic Writing." *Leonardo Electronic Almanac* 14, nos. 5–6. http://leoalmanac.org/journal/Vol_14/lea_v14_no5-06/Lemerson.asp.

Enns, Anthony. 2001. "Don't Believe the Hype: Rereading Michael Joyce's *afternoon* and *Twelve Blue*." *Currents in Electronic Literacy*, www.cwrl.utexas.edu/currents/fall01/enns/enns.html.

Eskelinen, Marku. 2004. "Six Problems in Search of a Solution: The Challenge of Cybertext Theory and Ludology to Literary Theory." *Dichtung-digital*, www.dichtung-digital.com/2004.3/Eskelinen/index.htm.

Evenson, Brian. 2003. *Understanding Robert Coover*. Columbia: University of South Carolina Press.

Everett, Anna, and John Caldwell, eds. 2003. *New Media: Theories and Practices of Digitextuality*. New York: Routledge.

Fitzpatrick, Kathleen. 2006. *The Anxiety of Obsolescence: The American Novel in the Age of Television*. Nashville, Tenn.: Vanderbilt University Press.

Foucault, Michel. 1984. "Des espaces autres (conférence au Cercle d'études architecturales, 14 mars 1967)." *Architecture, Mouvement, Continuité* 5 (October): 46–49.

———. 1997. *Ethics: Subjectivity and Truth.* Edited by Paul Rabinow. London: Allen Lane.

———. 2005. *The Hermeneutics of the Subject: Lectures at the Collège de France, 1981–82.* Edited by Frederic Gros and Francois Ewald. Basingstoke: Palgrave Macmillan.

Foster, Thomas. 2005. *The Souls of Cyberfolk: Posthumanism as Vernacular Theory.* Minneapolis: University of Minnesota Press.

Freud, Sigmund. 1961. *Beyond the Pleasure Principle.* Translated by James Strachey. New York: Norton.

Friedberg, Anne. 2006. *The Virtual Window: From Alberti to Microsoft* Cambridge, Mass.: MIT Press.

Fuller, Matthew. 2003. *Behind the Blip: Essays on the Culture of Software.* New York: Autonomedia.

Funkhouser, Chris. 2007. *Prehistoric Digital Poetry: An Archeology of Forms.* Tuscaloosa: University of Alabama Press.

García Clanclini, Néstor. 2001. *Consumers and Citizens: Globalization and Multicultural Conflicts.* Translated by George Yúdice. Minneapolis: University of Minnesota Press.

Gassner, John. 1966. *Twenty Best Film Plays.* New York: Crown.

Gaudreault, André. 1990. "Film, Narrative, Narration: The Cinema of the Lumière Brothers." In *Early Cinema: Space, Frame, Narrative,* edited by Thomas Elsaesser, 68–75. London: BFI.

Géczi, János. 1996. *Képversek.* Veszprém, Hungary: Vár Ucca Tizenhét.

Gessler, Nicolas. "Evolving Artificial Cultural Things-That-Think and Work by Dynamical Hierarchical Synthesis." www.sscnet.ucla.edu/geog/gessler/cv-pubs/03naacsos.pdf.

Gibson, William. 1984. *Neuromancer.* New York: Ace Books.

Glazier, Loss Pequeño. 2001. *Digital Poetics: Hypertext, Visual-Kinetic Text, and Writing in Programmable Media.* Tuscaloosa: University of Alabama Press.

Golding, Alan. 2006. "Language Writing, Digital Poetics, and Transitional Materialities." In *New Media Poetics: Contexts, Technotexts, and Theories,* edited by Adelaide Morris and Thomas Swiss, 249–283. Cambridge, Mass.: MIT Press.

Graham, Elaine. 2002. *Representations of the Post/human: Monsters, Aliens, and Others in Popular Culture.* New Brunswick, N.J.: Rutgers University Press.

Greenberg, Clement. 1940. "Towards a Newer Laocoon." *Partisan Review* 7: 299–300.

Greene, Rachel. 2004. *Internet Art.* London: Thames & Hudson.

Gunning, Tom. 1994. *D. W. Griffith and the Origins of American Narrative Film: The Early Years at Biograph.* Urbana: University of Illinois Press.

Habermas, Jürgen. 1991. *The Structural Transformation of the Public Sphere.* Cambridge, Mass.: MIT Press.

Hall, Christian. 2006. "An Interview with Alan Levy." *net* 157 (December): 34–36.

Hall, Gary. 2002. *Culture in Bits: The Monstrous Future of Theory.* New York: Continuum.

———. 2004. "Why You Can't Do Cultural Studies *and* Be a Derridean: Cultural Studies after Birmingham, the New Social Movements and the New Left." *Culture Machine* 6, http://culturemachine.tees.ac.uk/Cmach/Backis sues/j006/Articles/hall.htm.

———. 2008. *Digitize This Book! The Politics of New Media, or Why We Need Open Access Now.* Minneapolis: University of Minnesota Press.

Hall, Steven. 2007. *The Raw Shark Texts.* Edinburgh: Canongate.

Hansen, Mark B. N. 2004. *New Philosophy for New Media.* Cambridge, Mass.: MIT Press.

Hansen, Miriam. 1981. "Introduction to Adorno: 'Transparencies on Film (1966).'" *New German Critique* 24–25: 186–198.

Haraway, Donna. 1988. "Situated Knowledge: The Science Question in Feminism as a Site of Discourse on the Privilege of Partial Perspective." *Feminist Studies* 14: 575–599.

———. 1991. *Simians, Cyborgs, and Women: The Reinvention of Nature.* New York: Routledge.

Hardt, Michael, and Toni Negri. 2004. *Multitude: War and Democracy in the Age of Empire.* Harmondsworth: Penguin.

Harris, Stephanie. 2009. *Mediating Modernity. German Literature and the "New" Media, 1895–1930.* University Park: Pennsylvania State University Press.

Hauser, Marc, Noam Chomsky, and Tecumseh Fitch. 2002. "The Faculty of Language: What It Is, Who Has It, and How Did It Evolve?" *Science* 298: 1569–1571.

Hayes, David. 2006. "'Take Those Old Records Off the Shelf': Youth and Music Consumption in the Postmodern Age." *Popular Music and Society* 29, no. 1: 51–69.

Hayles, Katherine. 1997. "The Posthuman Body: Inscription and Incorporation in *Galatea 2.2* and *Snow Crash*." *Configurations* 5, no. 2: 241–266.

———. 1999. *How We Became Posthuman: Virtual Bodies in Cybernetics, Literature, and Informatics*. Chicago: University of Chicago Press.

———. 2000. "Flickering Connectivities in Shelley Jackson's *Patchwork Girl*: The Importance of Media-Specific Analysis." www.iath.virginia.edu/pmc/text-only/issue.100/10.2hayles.txt (last visited January 2009).

———. 2000. "Visualizing the Posthuman." *Art Journal* (Fall).

———. 2002. "Saving the Subject: Remediation in *House of Leaves*." *American Literature* 4: 779–806.

———. 2002. *Writing Machines*. Cambridge, Mass.: MIT Press.

———. 2003. "Translating Media: Why We Should Rethink Textuality." *Yale Journal of Criticism: Interpretation in the Humanities* 2: 263–290.

———. 2004. "Print Is Flat, Code Is Deep: The Importance of Media-Specific Analysis." *Poetics Today* 1: 67–90.

———. 2005. *My Mother Was a Computer*. Chicago: University of Chicago Press.

———. 2008. *Electronic Literature: New Horizons for the Literary*. Notre Dame, Ind.: University of Notre Dame Press.

Heidegger, Martin. 2002. *Identity and Difference*. Chicago: University of Chicago Press.

Heim, Michael. 1999. *Electric Language: A Philosophical Study of Word Processing*. New Haven: Yale University Press.

Hitomi, Ishinabe. 1997. "Vinyl Turns the Tables on the Compact Disc." *Look Japan* (November): 32–33.

Hofstadter, Douglas. 1995. *Fluid Concepts and Creative Analogies: Computer Models of the Fundamental Mechanisms of Thought*. New York: Basic Books.

———. 2007. *I Am a Strange Loop*. New York: Basic Books.

Hölderlin, Friedrich. 1969. *Werke und Briefe*. Edited by F. Beissner and Jochen Schmidt. Frankfurt am Main: Insel.

———. 1990. "Urteil und Sein." *Friedrich Hölderlin: Werke, Briefe, Dokumente*. Munich: Winkler.

———. 2003. "Being Judgment Possibility." In *Classic and Romantic German Aesthetics*, edited by J. M. Bernstein, 191. Cambridge: Cambridge University Press.

Horkheimer, Max, and Theodor W. Adorno. 1993. "The Culture Industry: Enlightenment as Mass Deception." In *Dialectic of Enlightenment: Philosophical Fragments*, 120–166. New York: Continuum.

Hume, David. 2008. *An Enquiry Concerning Human Understanding*. Edited by Peter McMillan. Oxford: Oxford University Press.

Humphrey, Watts S. 1989. *Managing the Software Process*. Harlow: Addison-Wesley.

Hutcheon, Linda. 2006. *A Theory of Adaptation*. New York: Routledge.

Jackson, Shelley. 1995. *Patchwork Girl*. Watertown: Eastgate Systems.

Jakobson, Roman. 1960. "Closing Statement: Linguistics and Poetics." In *Style in Language*, edited by Thomas A. Sebeok, 350–377. Cambridge, Mass.: MIT Press.

Jeancolas, Jean-Pierre. 2005. *Histoire du cinéma français*. Paris: Colin.

Jenkins, Henry, et al. 2011. "Confronting the Challenges of Participatory Culture: Media Education for the 21st Century." www.newmedialiteracies.org/files/working/NMLWhitePaper.pdf.

Johns, Adrian. 1998. *The Nature of the Book: Print and Knowledge in the Making*. Chicago: University of Chicago Press.

Johnston, John. 1998. *Information Multiplicity: American Fiction in the Age of Media Saturation*. Baltimore: Johns Hopkins University Press.

Jung, Désirée. 2007. "Adaptation Fever: On *Solaris*." http://www.thefilm journal.com/issue9/adaptation.html.

Kant, Immanuel. 1990. *Kritik der reinen Vernunft*. Edited by Raymund Schmidt. Hamburg: Felix Meiner.

Kappanyos, András. 2003. "Irodalom a digitális közegben." *Literatura* 1: 59–79.

Katz, Mark. 2004. *Capturing Sound: How Technology Has Changed Music*. Berkeley: University of California Press.

Keller, Lynn. 2001. "Fields of Pattern-Bounded Unpredictability: Recent Palimptexts by Rosmarie Waldrop and Joan Retallack." *Contemporary Literature* 2 (Summer 2001): 376–412.

Kellman, Steven. 1987. "The Cinematic Novel: Tracking a Concept." *Modern Fiction Studies* 3: 467–475.

Kermabon, Jacques. 1988. *Les vacances de M. Hulot de Jacques Tati*. Liège: Yellow Now.

Kermode, Frank. 1968. *The Sense of an Ending*. New York: Oxford University Press.

Kirschenbaum, Matthew. 2008. *Mechanisms: New Media and the Forensic Imagination*. Cambridge, Mass.: MIT Press.

Kittler, Friedrich A. 1992. *Discourse Networks 1800/1900*. Translated by Michael Matteer, with Chris Cullens. Stanford, Calif.: Stanford University Press.

———. 1999. *Gramophone, Film, Typewriter*. Translated by Geoffrey Winthrop-Young and Michael Wutz. Stanford, Calif.: Stanford University Press.

Klein, Larry. 1994. "Audiophile Silliness: Absolute Sounds Off." *Electronics Now* (February): 80–81.

Kunzru, Hari. 2002. *The Impressionist.* New York: Dutton.

Kurzweil, Ray. 2005. *The Singularity Is Near: When Humans Transcend Biology.* New York: Penguin.

Landow, George P. 2006. *Hypertext 3.0: Critical Theory and New Media in an Era of Globalization.* Baltimore: Johns Hopkins University Press.

Lazzarato, Maurizio. n.d "From Biopower to Biopolitics." Translated by Ivan A. Ramirez. Available at www.geocities.com/immateriallabour/lazzarato-from-biopower-to-bio politics.html (last accessed May 31, 2007).

Lenhart, Amelia, and Mary Madden. 2005. "Teen Content Creators and Consumers." www.pewinternet.org/pdfs/PIP_Teens_Content_Creation.pdf (last visited January 2009).

Leonardi, Francesca. 2006. "La vie passionnée des Cousins: Les avatars d'un film Nouvelle Vague." In *Il racconto del film: La novellizzazione—dal catalogo al trailer,* edited by Alice Autelitano and Valentina Re, 179–195. Udine: Forum.

Leroi-Gourhan, André. 1993. *Gesture and Speech.* Cambridge, Mass.: MIT Press.

Levinas, Emmanuel. 1969. *Totality and Infinity: An Essay on Exteriority.* Translated by Alphonso Lingis. Pittsburgh: Duquesne University Press.

———. 1989. *The Levinas Reader.* Edited by Sean Hand. Oxford: Blackwell.

Levy, Pierre. 2001. *Cyberculture.* Translated by Robert Bononno. Minneapolis: University of Minnesota Press.

Leys, Ruth. 2000. *Trauma: A Genealogy.* Chicago: University of Chicago Press.

Liu, Alan. 2004. *The Laws of Cool: Knowledge Work and the Culture of Information.* Chicago: University of Chicago Press.

Locke, John. 1996. *Essay Concerning Human Understanding.* Edited by Kenneth P. Wrinkler. Indianapolis: Hackett.

López-Varela Azcárate, Asunción. 2006. "Webness Revisited." In *A Pleasure of Life in Words: A Festschrift for Angela Downing,* edited by Marta Carretero et al., 513–533. Madrid: Universidad Complutense.

López-Varela Azcaráte, Asunción, and Steven Tötösy de Zepetnek. 2009. "Comparative Cultural Studies, éducation, nouveaux médias et l'interculturalisme." In *Le Complexe français: Quelle place pour les études et sciences de la culture en France?,* edited by Anne Chalard-Fillaudeau, 73–93. Vincennes: Presses Universitaires de Vincennes.

Lovett, Robert Morss. 1940. "Literature and Its Rivals." *Kenyon Review* 1: 97–100.

Lovink, Geert. 2003. *Dark Fiber: Tracking Critical Internet Culture*. Cambridge, Mass.: MIT Press.

Mackenzie, Adrian. 2003. "The Problem of Computer Code: Leviathan or Common Power?" www.lancs.ac.uk/staff/mackenza/papers/code-leviathan.pdf.

Manguel, Alberto. 1996. *A History of Reading*. New York: Penguin Books.

Manovich, Lev. 2002. *The Language of New Media*. Cambridge, Mass.: MIT Press.

Marcus, Laura. 2007. *The Tenth Muse: Writing about Cinema in the Modernist Period*. Oxford: Oxford University Press.

Massumi, Brian. 2002. *Parables for the Virtual: Movement, Affect, Sensation*. Durham, N.C.: Duke University Press.

McCabe, Susan. 2005. *Cinematic Modernism: Modernist Poetry and Film*. Cambridge: Cambridge University Press.

McCarty, Clifford. 1971. *Published Screenplays: A Checklist*. Kent, Ohio: Kent State University Press.

McFarlane, Brian. 1996. *Novel to Film*. New York: Oxford University Press.

McGann, Jerome. 2004. *Radiant Textuality: Literature after the World Wide Web*. London: Palgrave.

McHale, Brian. 1992. *Constructing Postmodernism*. London: Routledge.

McLuhan, Marshall. 1964. *Understanding Media*. New York: McGraw-Hill.

McMurtry, Larry. 1976. "The Screenplay as a Non-Book: A Consideration." *American Film* 1, no. 10 (September): 7–15.

Mirzoeff, Nicholas, ed. *The Visual Culture Reader*. 2nd edition. London: Routledge.

Montgomery Bird, Robert. 2008. *Sheppard Lee, Written by Himself*. New York: NYRB Classics.

Moraru, Christian. 1998. "Topos/Typos/Tropos: Visual Strategies and the Mapping of Space in Charles Olson's Poetry." *Word & Image: A Journal of Verbal/Visual Enquiry* 14, no. 3: 253–266.

Moravec, Hans. 1990. *Mind Children: The Future of Robot and Human Intelligence*. Cambridge, Mass.: Harvard University Press.

Morgan, Richard. 2006. *Altered Carbon*. New York: Ballantine Books.

Morowitz, Harold J. 2002. *The Emergence of Everything: How the World Became Complex*. New York: Oxford University Press.

Morris, Adalaide, and Thomas Swiss, eds. 2006. *New Media Poetics: Contexts, Technotexts, and Theories*. Cambridge, Mass.: MIT Press.

Morris, Chris. 2002. "Audiophile Labels Put a New Spin on Vinyl." *Billboard* (August 17): 1–3.

Morsberger, Robert E., and Katharine M. Morsberger. 1975. "Screenplays as Literature: Bibliography and Criticism." *Literature Film Quarterly* 3, no. 1: 45–54.

Moses, Gavriel. 1979. "Gubbio in Gabbia: Pirandello's Cameraman and the Entrapments of Film Vision." *Modern Language Notes* 94: 36–60.

Mul, Jos de. 2002. *Een Cyberspace Odyssee*. Kampen: Klement.

Müllner, András. 2003. "A hipertextuális közlés anomáliái és a Megbocsátás hipertextualizálásának kérdése." *Literatura* 1: 80–97.

———. 2007. "A hipertext elmélete mint az interaktivitás technológiai ideológiája." In *A császár új ruhája: Esszék a könyv és a hipertext kapcsolatáról, valamint más médiumokról*, 87–117. Budapest: Jószöveg Könyvek.

Muri, Allison. 2004. "Virtually Human: The Electronic Page, the Archived Body, and Human Identity." In *The Future of the Page*, edited by Peter Stoicheff and Andrew Taylor, 231–254. Toronto: University of Toronto Press.

———. 2007. *The Enlightenment Cyborg: A History of Communications and Control in the Human Machine 1660–1830*. Toronto: University of Toronto Press.

Murphet, Julian, and Lydia Rainford, eds. 2003. *Literature and Visual Technologies: Writing after Cinema*. New York: Macmillan.

Murray, Janet H. 1995. "The Pedagogy of Cyberfiction: Teaching a Course on Reading and Writing Interactive Narrative." In *Contextual Media: Multimedia and Interpretation*, edited by Edward Barrett and Marie Redmond, 129–162. Cambridge, Mass.: MIT Press.

Nagel, Thomas. 1989. *The View from Nowhere*. New York: Oxford University Press.

Naur, Peter, and Brian Randell, eds. 1969. *Software Engineering: Report on a Conference Sponsored by the NATO Science Committee, Garmisch, Germany, 7th to 11th October 1968*. Brussels: NATO Scientific Affairs Division.

Nolan, Jonathan. 2001. "Memento Mori." *Esquire*, March.

Norris, Pippa. 2002. *Digital Divide: Civic Engagement, Information Poverty and the Internet Worldwide*. Cambridge: Cambridge University Press.

Nulf, Frank. 1970–71. "Luigi Pirandello and the Cinema." *Film Quarterly* 2: 40–48.

Ong, Aihwa. 1999. *Flexible Citizenship: The Cultural Logics of Transnationality*. Durham, N.C.: Duke University Press.

Orlean, Susan. 1998. *The Orchid Thief: A True Story of Beauty and Obsession*. New York: Ballantine Books.

Packer, Randall, and Ken Jordan, eds. 2001. *Multimedia: From Wagner to Virtual Reality*. New York: Norton.

Palahniuk, Chuck. 1996. *Fight Club*. New York: Henry Holt.

Palesis, Ioannis Antonios. 1979. "At the Crossroads of Cinema and Literature: A Study of the Scenario as a Genre." Ph.D. dissertation, University of Pennsylvania.

Palmer, Robert R. 1985. "Eisensteinian Montage and Joyce's Ulysses: The Analogy Reconsidered." *Mosaic* 18 (1985): 73–85.

———, ed. 2007. *Twentieth-Century American Fiction on Screen*. Cambridge: Cambridge University Press.

Panofsky, Erwin. 1995. *Three Essays on Style*. Cambridge, Mass.: MIT Press.

Pearce, Richard. 1983. *The Novel in Motion: An Approach to Modern Fiction*. Columbus: Ohio State University Press.

Perloff, Marjorie. 1991. *Radical Artifice*. Chicago: University of Chicago Press.

Peterson, Tim. 2006. "New Media Poetry and Poetics: From Concrete to Codework—Praxis in Networked and Programmable Media." *Leonardo Electronic Almanac* 14. http://leoalmanac.org/journal/Vol_14/lea_v14_no5-06/tpeterson.asp (last visited January 2009).

Pirandello, Luigi. 2005. *Shoot! The Notebooks of Serafino Gubbio, Cinematograph Operator*. Translated by C. K. Scott Moncrieff. Chicago: University of Chicago Press.

Plascencia, Salvador. 2005. *The People of Paper*. San Francisco: McSweeney's.

Porter, David, ed. 1997. *Internet Culture*. New York: Routledge.

Porter, Jim. 2002. "Why Technology Matters to Writing: A Cyberwriter's Tale." *Computers and Composition* 20: 375–394.

Poster, Mark. 1990. *The Mode of Information: Poststructuralism and Social Context*. Cambridge: Polity Press.

———. 2001. *What's the Matter with the Internet?* Minneapolis: University of Minnesota Press.

———. 2006. *Information Please: Culture and Politics in the Age of Digital Machines*. Durham, N.C.: Duke University Press.

Pressman, Jessica. 2007. "Digital Modernism: Making It New in New Media." Ph.D. dissertation, University of California, Los Angeles.

———. 2008. "The Strategy of Digital Modernism: Young Hae Chang Heavy Industry's *Dakota*." *Modern Fiction Studies* 2 (2008): 302–319.

Rajewski, Irina. *Intermediales Erzählen in der italienischen Literatur der Postmoderne: Von den Giovani Scrittori der 80er zum Pulp der 90er Jahre*. Tübingen: Gunter Narr, 2003.

Rand, Richard, ed. 2005. *Logomachia: The Conflict of the Faculties*. Lincoln: University of Nebraska Press.

Rawle, Graham. 2005. *Woman's World: A Graphic Novel*. London: Atlantic Books.

Rawson, Eric. 2006. "Perfect Listening: Audiophilia, Ambiguity, and the Reduction of the Arbitrary." *Journal of American Culture* 29, no. 2: 202–212.

Readings, Bill. 1996. *The University in Ruins*. Cambridge, Mass.: Harvard University Press.

Reas, Casey, and Ben Fry. 2007. *Processing: A Programming Handbook for Visual Designers and Artists*. Cambridge, Mass.: MIT Press.

Reed, Adam. 2005. "'My Blog Is Me': Texts and Persons in UK Online Journal Culture (and Anthropology)." *Ethnos* 70, no. 2 (June): 220–242.

Rettberg, Scott, ed. 2002. *State of the Arts: The Proceedings of the Electronic Literature Organization's 2002 State of the Arts Symposium*. Los Angeles: Electronic Literature Organization.

Ricardou, Jean. 1989. *Une maladie chronique*. Paris: Les Impressions Nouvelles.

Richardson, Will. 2006. *Blogs, Wikis, Podcasts, and Other Powerful Tools for Classrooms*. Thousand Oaks, Calif.: Sage.

Ryan, Marie-Laure. 2003. *Narrative as Virtual Reality: Immersion and Interactivity in Literature and Electronic Media*. Baltimore: Johns Hopkins University Press.

———. 2006. *Avatars of Story*. Minneapolis: University of Minnesota Press.

Saper, Craig. 2006. "Blogademia." *Reconstruction* 6, no. 4. http://reconstruction.eserver.org/064/saper.shtml.

Saussure, Ferdinand de. 1988. *Course in General Linguistics*. Translated by Roy Harris. Peru, Ill.: Open Course Publishing.

Sawyer, Robert. 2005. *Mind Scan*. New York: Tor Books.

Scarry, Elaine. 1994. *Resisting Representation*. Oxford: Oxford University Press.

Searle, John R. 1990. "Is the Brain's Mind a Computer Program?" *Scientific American*, 26–31.

Seyhan, Azade. 1992. *Representation and Its Discontents: The Critical Legacy of German Romanticism*. Berkeley: University of California Press.

Simmon, Scott. 1981. "Beyond the Theater of War: *Gravity's Rainbow* as Film." In *Critical Essays on Thomas Pynchon*, edited by Richard Pearce, 124–139. Boston: G. K. Hall.

Simons, Jan. 1997. "Film en literatuur." *Tijdschrift voor Literatuurwetenschap* 2: 148–162.

Sitney, P. Adams. 1990. *Modernist Montage: The Obscurity of Vision in Cinema and Literature*. New York: Columbia University Press.

Solomon, Stanley. 1989. "Aristotle in Twilight: American Film Narrative in the 1980s." In *The Cinematic Text*, edited by R. Barton Palmer, 63–80. New York: AMS.

Sommerville, Ian. 1995. *Software Engineering*. Harlow: Addison-Wesley.

Spiegel, Alan. 1976. *Fiction and the Camera Eye: Visual Consciousness in Film and the Modern Novel*. Charlottesville: University Press of Virginia, 1976.

———. 1979. "Flaubert to Joyce: Evolution of a Cinematographic Form." *Novel: A Forum on Fiction* 3: 229–243.

Springhall, John. 1998. *Youth, Popular Culture and Moral Panics: Penny Gaffs to Gangsta-Rap, 1830–1996*. New York: St. Martin's Press.

Stam, Robert. 2005. "Introduction: The Theory and Practice of Adaptation." In *Literature and Film: A Guide to the Theory and Practice of Film Adaptation*, edited by Robert Stam and Alessandra Raengo, 1–52. Oxford: Blackwell.

———. 2005. *Literature Through Film: Realism, Magic, and the Art of Adaptation*. Oxford: Blackwell.

Stefans, Brian Kim. 2003. *Fashionable Noise: On Digital Poetics*. Berkeley, Calif.: Atelos Press.

Stephenson, Neal. 1996. *The Diamond Age; or, a Young Lady's Illustrated Primer*. New York: Bantam.

Sterling, Bruce, ed. 1986. *Mirrorshades: The Cyberpunk Anthology*. New York: Arbor House.

Sternberg, Claudia. 1997. *Written for the Screen: The American Motion-Picture Screenplay as Text*. Tübingen: Stauffenburg.

Sterne, Jonathan. 2003. *The Audible Past: Cultural Origins of Sound Reproduction*. Durham, N.C.: Duke University Press.

Stewart, Garrett. 1998. "Cinecriture: Modernism's Flicker Effect." *New Literary History* 4 (1998): 727–768.

———. 1999. *Between Film and Screen: Modernism's Photo Synthesis*. Chicago: University of Chicago Press.

Stiegler, Bernard. 1998. *Technics and Time, 1: The Fault of Epimetheus*. Translated by Richard Beardsworth and George Collins. Stanford, Calif.: Stanford University Press.

———. 2003. "Technics of Decision: An Interview with Peter Hallward." Translated by Sean Gaston. *Angelaki* 8, no. 2: 151–168.

Symes, Colin. 2004. *Setting the Record Straight: A Material History of Classical Recording*. Middletown, Conn.: Wesleyan University Press.

Tabbi, Joseph. 2002. *Cognitive Fictions*. Minneapolis: University of Minnesota Press.

———. 2004. "The Processual Page: Materiality and Consciousness in Print and Hypertext." In *The Future of the Page*, edited by Peter Stoicheff and Andrew Taylor, 201–230. Toronto: University of Toronto Press.

Tanner, Tony. 1982. *Thomas Pynchon*. London: Methuen.

Temple, Michael, and Michael Witt. 2004. *The French Cinema Book*. London: British Film Institute.

Thomas, Scarlett. 2006. *The End of Mr. Y*. Edinburgh: Canongate.

Threndyle, Steven. 1998. "The Vinyl Word in Music." *Canadian Business* 13.

Tichi, Cecilia. 1989. "Television and Recent American Fiction." *American Literary History* 1 (Spring): 110–130.

Trotter, David. 2006. "T. S. Eliot and Cinema." *Modernism/Modernity* 2: 237–265.

———. 2007. *Cinema and Modernism*. Cambridge, Cambridge University Press.

Truffaut, François. 1984. *Hitchcock*. Translated by Helen G. Scott. New York: Simon and Schuster.

———. 2000. *Le plaisir des yeux: Ecrits sur le cinema*. Paris: Petite Bibliothèque des Cahiers du Cinéma.

Turkle, Sherry. 1997. *Life on the Screen: Identity in the Age of the Internet*. New York: Touchstone.

Tzara, Tristan. 2007. "Dada Manifesto of Feeble Love and Bitter Love." In *The Dada Painters and Poets*, edited by Robert Motherwell, 86–96. Cambridge, Mass.: Harvard University Press.

Ullman, Ellen. 1997. *Close to the Machine: Technophilia and Its Discontents*. San Francisco: City Lights Books.

Ulmer, Gregory. 1990. *Teletheory: Grammatology in the Age of Video*. New York: Routledge.

———. 2003. *Internet Invention: From Literacy to Electracy*. New York: Longman.

Uricchio, William. 2004. "Cultural Citizenship in the Age of P2P Networks." In *European Culture and the Media*, edited by Ib Bondebjerg and Peter Golding, 139–164. Chicago: University of Chicago Press, 2004.

———. 2011. "The Algorithmic Turn: Photosynth, Augmented Reality and the State of the Image." *Visual Studies* 26: 25–35.

Vermeesch, Amélie. 2004. "Poétique du scenario." *Poétique* 138: 213–234.

Vettori, Alessandro. 1998. "Serafino Gubbio's Candid Camera." *MLN* 113: 79–107.

Vincendeau, Ginette. 2001. "Introduction." In *Film/Literature/Heritage: A Sight and Sound Reader*, xi–xxv. Edited by Ginette Vincendeau. London: BFI.

Wardrip-Fruin, Noah. 2005. "Playable Media and Textual Instruments." www.brown.edu/Research/dichtung-digital/2005/1/Wardrip-Fruin.

Wardrip-Fruin, Noah, and Nick Montfort. 2003. *The New Media Reader*. Cambridge, Mass.: MIT Press.

Watson, Ian. 2000. "When Thought-Mail Failed." In *The New English Library Book of Internet Stories*, edited by Maxim Jakubowski, 279–294. London: Hodder & Stoughton.

Weber, Samuel. 2005. *Targets of Opportunity*. New York: Fordham University Press.

———. 2008. *Benjamin's –abilities*. Cambridge, Mass.: Harvard University Press.

Weizenbaum, Joseph. 1976. *Computer Power and Human Reason: From Judgment to Calculation*. New York: Freeman.

Wesseling, Lies, and Robert Zwijnenberg, eds. 2007. *Art in Time: On the Use and Abuse of Anachronisms in the History of Art*. London: Equinox.

Wiener, Norbert. 1948. *Cybernetics; or, Control and Communication in the Animal and the Machine*. Cambridge, Mass.: MIT Press.

Williams, Raymond. 1974. *Television: Technology and Cultural Form*. London: Collins.

———. 1980. *Problems in Materialism and Culture: Selected Essays*. London: Verso.

Willinsky, John. 2006. *The Access Principle: The Case for Open Access to Research and Scholarship*. Cambridge, Mass.: MIT Press.

Wills, David. 1995. *Prosthesis*. Stanford: Stanford University Press.

Winston, Douglas Garrett. 1973. *The Screenplay as Literature*. Rutherford, N.J.: Fairleigh Dickinson University Press.

Wolfowicz, Jacqueline. 1990. "Le scénario comme genre littéraire." *Neohelicon* 17, no. 2: 283–289.

Wolfram, Stefan. 2002. *A New Kind of Science*. New York: Wolfram Media.

Yadav, Sid. 2006. "Facebook: The Complete Biography." *Mashable Social Networking News*, August 25. http://mashable.com/2006/08/25/facebook-pro file (last visited January 2009).

Yi, Dongshin. 2010. *A Genealogy of Cyborgothic: Aesthetics and Ethics in the Age of Posthumanism*. Farnham: Ashgate.

Ziarek, Ewa Plonowska. 2001. *An Ethics of Dissensus: Postmodernity, Feminism, and the Politics of Radical Democracy*. Stanford, Calif.: Stanford University Press.

Žižek, Slavoj. 2001. *The Fright of Real Tears: Krzystof Kieslowski Between Theory and Post-theory*. London: BFI.

Anthony Curtis Adler is assistant professor in German and comparative literature at Underwood International College at Yonsei University in Seoul, South Korea. He has published articles on J. G. Fichte, Max Kommerell, and Robert Walser in *Angelaki, Continental Philosophy Review*, and *Eighteenth-Century Studies*.

Jan Baetens is professor at the University of Leuven (Belgium), where he mainly teaches word and image studies. He coedits the literary journals *Formules, Revue des Littératures à Contraintes*, and *FPC/Formes Poétiques Contemporaines*, as well as the peer-reviewed e-journal *Image & Narrative*. He is the author of *The Graphic Novel* (2001), *Writing and the Image Today* (2008), and other studies, as well as of eight books of poetry.

Kiene Brillenburg Wurth is associate professor of comparative literature at the University of Utrecht. Her current research focuses on intermediality, particularly on literature and new media. She is the author of *Musically Sublime* (Fordham, 2009), a textbook on literary studies, and numerous peer-reviewed articles on literature, music, aesthetics, and new media technologies. She was recently honored with the prestigious five-year VIDI research grant from the Dutch National Research Council.

Matthijs Engelberts is assistant professor of French literature and culture at the University of Amsterdam. He publishes on contemporary French literature, film, and theater.

Federica Frabetti is senior lecturer in communication, media, and culture at Oxford Brookes University. She has a diverse professional and academic background in critical theory and ICT. Her publications include *Leggere Halberstam* (*A Judith Halberstam Reader*) (2010) and a special issue of *E-journal* (2011) on the digital humanities.

Lovorka Gruic is research assistant at the English Department of the University of Rijeka, Croatia, where she teaches American literature, science fiction, postmodern literature, and the interpretation of the novel. She is coeditor of *Space and Time in Language and Literature* (2009) and is working on a book about Thomas Pynchon and his novel *Against the Day*.

Gary Hall is professor of media and performing arts in the School of Art and Design at Coventry University. He is the author of *Culture in Bits* (2002) and *Digitize This Book! The Politics of New Media, or Why We Need Open Access Now* (2008). He is also founding coeditor of the open-access journal *Culture Machine*, director of the cultural studies open-access archive CSeARCH, and coeditor of the Open Humanities Press.

N. Katherine Hayles is professor of literature and English at Duke University. Her book *How We Became Posthuman: Virtual Bodies in Cybernetics, Literature, and Informatics* (1999) won the Rene Wellek Prize for the best book in literary theory for 1998–99, and *Writing Machines* (2002) won the Suzanne Langer Award for Outstanding Scholarship. She is at work on a new study of digital technologies.

Asunción López-Varela Azcárate is professor of English at Complutense University Madrid. Her interests in research and publication include the semiotics of space and time in literary and cultural representation, multimodality and intermediality, interculturalism, (comparative) cultural studies, education, and the use of hypermedia technologies in teaching and scholarship.

Marie-Laure Ryan is an independent scholar based in Colorado. She is the author of: *Possible Worlds, Artificial Intelligence, and Narrative*

Theory (1992), which received the 1992 Prize for Independent Scholars from the Modern Language Association; *Narrative as Virtual Reality: Immersion and Interactivity in Literature and Electronic Media* (2001); and *Avatars of Story: Narrative Modes in Old and New Media* (2006).

Katalin Sándor is currently assistant lecturer at the Faculty of Letters of Babeş–Bolyai University, Cluj-Napoca, Romania. Her research areas and fields of interest include theories of intermediality, media theory, intermediality in literature, visual culture, (neo)avant-garde artistic practices, and visual poetry. She is a contributor to Lars Ellestrom's *Media Borders: Multimodality and Intermediality* (2010).

William Uricchio is Professor of Literature and Director of the Comparative Media Studies Program at the Massachusetts Institute of Technology and Professor of Comparative Media History at Utrecht University. His most recent books include *Media Cultures* (2006), on responses to media in post 9/11 Germany and the United States, and *We Europeans? Media, Representations, Identities* (2008).

Peter Verstraten is a lecturer in literary studies at the University of Leiden. His research focuses on narratology, psychoanalysis, and the relations between literature and other media, especially literature and film. He is author of *Film Narratology* (2009).

Samuel Weber is Paul de Man Chair at the European Graduate School EGS, the Avalon Professor of Humanities at Northwestern University, and one of the leading American thinkers across the disciplines of literary theory, philosophy, and psychoanalysis. His publications include *Mass Mediauras: Form, Technics, Media* (1996), *Theatricality as Medium* (Fordham, 2004), *Targets of Opportunity: On the Militarization of Thinking* (Fordham, 2005), *Acts of Reading* (2006), and *Benjamin's –abilities* (2008).

Joanna Zylinska is a cultural theorist writing on new technologies, ethics, cultural studies, and feminist theory. Her publications include *Bioethics in the Age of New Media* (2009), *The Ethics of Cultural Studies* (2002), and *On Spiders, Cyborgs and Being Scared: the Feminine and the Sublime* (2001).

INDEX

VERBAL ARTS: STUDIES IN POETICS
Lazar Fleishman and Haun Saussy, *series editors*

Jacob Edmond, *A Common Strangeness: Contemporary Poetry, Cross-Cultural Encounter, Comparative Literature*

Kiene Brillenburg Wurth (ed.), *Between Page and Screen: Remaking Literature Through Cinema and Cyberspace*